BOOM! TALKIN' ABOUT OUR GENERATION

By Joel Makower

A Tilden Press Book

CONTEMPORARY
BOOKS, INC.
CHICAGO

Library of Congress Cataloging in Publication Data

Makower, Joel, 1952-
Boom! : talkin' about our generation.

Includes index.
1. United States—Popular culture—History—20th century. 2. United States—Civilization—1945
3. Baby boom generation—United States. I. Title.
E169.12.M324 1985 973.92 85-16638
ISBN 0-8092-5203-1

Published by Contemporary Books, Inc.
180 North Michigan Avenue, Chicago, Illinois 60601
Manufactured in the United States of America
Library of Congress Catalog Card Number: 85-16638
International Standard Book Number: 0-8092-5203-1

Published simultaneously in Canada by Beaverbooks, Ltd.
195 Allstate Parkway, Valleywood Business Park
Markham, Ontario L3R 4T8 Canada

BOOM! THANKS

Thanks

A number of people contributed generously to this book and deserve recognition and thanks.

Alan Green, friend and colleague, provided endless resources and inspiration that helped make this book a reality. He was among several who provided technical expertise: Susan Arritt, Susan Chumsky, Chuck Freund, Ken Moss, Barry Parker, Carolyn Projansky, Randy Rieland, Lorraine Rose, and Eve Zibart. Among the researchers who helped dig up and check the many facts contained in these pages are Patty Borthwick, Jessica Cohen, Kathy Fountain, Betsy Nay, Nancy Segal, and Jenise Williamson.

Several others helped with the book's production: Molly Roberts worked tirelessly to produce the hundreds of photographs used in this book; Barbara Shapiro and crew at Grammarians Inc. applied their expertise to fine-tune the manuscript; art direction came from Schell Kaplan, Alice Kresse, Ed Schneider, along with the design and production services of Debbie Moorman, Sharon Rogers, Arthur Cadeaux, and Albert D. McJoynt at International Business Services. Special thanks to Steve Smith, Audrey Cowgill, Gaal Shepherd, and others at Chronicle Type & Design for efforts beyond the call of duty.

Many friends, relatives, and friends of friends and relatives provided recollections that appear in "Flashbacks" throughout this book: Joseph Alper, Eliot Applestein, Debbie Arritt, Mark Bello, Shelley Berman, Ronnie and Chalos Blakeney, Cathy Boggs, Bill Coulter, Michael and Johnesther Edwards, Susie Elkind, Kari Fischer, Billy Joe Fitts, Marian A. Galeano, Paul and Beth Gall, Ted Glickman, Champe and Jenny Green, Jill Groce, Peter Haas, Patricia Jones, Larry Kahaner, Sheila F. Katz, the Lyons family, Eric McClary, Eileen McGrath, Judy Patterson, Linda Projansky, Brian Rose, Gail Ross, Carolyn Roth, Marilynne Rudick, Kas Schwan, Phyllis Stanger, Robyn Stone, Marta Vogel, Susan Walton, Beni and Diana Warshawsky, and Jack Zibulski.

Thanks also to Patty Prendergast, American Film Institute; Patrick Montgomery, Archives Films; Nancy Dvorin, R.R. Bowker Company; Mark Miller, *Broadcasting* magazine; Jonathan Robbin and Denise O'Brien, Claritas, L.P.; Mary Ternes, D.C. Public Library; John Taylor, National Archives; Betty Rollins and Joe Caravella, National Council of Teachers of Mathematics; Rick Barnes, National Screen Service; Travis Whitlow, A.C. Nielson Company; Joanne Gampel and Kevin Zeese, NORML; Jesse Hamlin, Susan Griffin, Suzanne Custer, and Michael Hubbell, *San Francisco Chronicle*; and Diane Cardinale, Toy Manufacturers Association; And to several individuals: Dr. Ray Broekel, "Movie" Mike Clark, Susan Gordon, Abbie Hoffman, Bill Hogan, Joel Kaplan, Mr. and Mrs. Fay LeCompte, Peggy and Rowan LeCompte, Ted and Frances Makower, John May, Ronnie Newmyer, Warren Rogers, Joe Tinkelman, and Michael Weiss.

Finally, thanks to Nancy J. Crossman, Robb Pawlak, and others at Contemporary Books, and to literary agent Raphael Sagalyn—boomers all—without whose support and encouragement this book would be merely another "good idea" gone unfulfilled.

—J.M.
June 1985
Washington, D.C.

BOOM! CONTENTS

BOOM! CONTENTS

HO WE ARE • WHERE WE LIVE • HOW WE VOTE • WHAT WE THINK
AT, DRINK, AND DRIVE • HOW WE INVEST • BOOMER NAMES • WH
WHERE WE LIVE • HOW WE VOTE • WHAT WE THINK • WHAT WE E
ND DRIVE • HOW WE INVEST • BOOMER NAMES • WHO WE ARE •
IVE • HOW WE VOTE • WHAT WE THINK • WHAT WE EAT, DRINK,
HOW WE INVEST • BOOMER NAMES • WHO WE ARE • WHERE WE LIV
VOTE • WHAT WE THINK • WHAT WE EAT, DRINK, AND DRIVE • HOW
BOOMER NAMES • WHO WE ARE • WHERE WE LIVE • HOW WE VOTE
THINK • WHAT WE EAT, DRINK, AND DRIVE • HOW WE INVEST • BOOM
WHO WE ARE • WHERE WE LIVE • HOW WE VOTE • WHAT WE THIN
EAT, DRINK, AND DRIVE • HOW WE INVEST • BOOMER NAMES • WH
WHERE WE LIVE • HOW WE VOTE • WHAT WE THINK • WHAT WE E
ND DRIVE • HOW WE INVEST • BOOMER NAMES • WHO WE ARE •
IVE • HOW WE VOTE • WHAT WE THINK • WHAT WE EAT, DRINK,
HOW WE INVEST • BOOMER NAMES • WHO WE ARE • WHERE WE LIV
VOTE • WHAT WE THINK • WHAT WE EAT, DRINK, AND DRIVE • HOW
BOOMER NAMES • WHO WE ARE • WHERE WE LIVE • HOW WE VOT
THINK • WHAT WE EAT, DRINK, AND DRIVE • HOW WE INVEST • BO
WHO WE ARE • WHERE WE LIVE • HOW WE VOTE • WHAT WE THIN
EAT, DRINK, AND DRIVE • HOW WE INVEST • BOOMER NAMES • WH
WHERE WE LIVE • HOW WE VOTE • WHAT WE THINK • WHAT WE E
ND DRIVE • HOW WE INVEST • BOOMER NAMES • WHO WE ARE •
IVE • HOW WE VOTE • WHAT WE THINK • WHAT WE EAT, DRINK,
HOW WE INVEST • BOOMER NAMES • WHO WE ARE • WHERE WE LI
VOTE • WHAT WE THINK • WHAT WE EAT, DRINK, AND DRIVE • HOW
BOOMER NAMES • WHO WE ARE • WHERE WE LIVE • HOW WE VOT
THINK • WHAT WE EAT, DRINK, AND DRIVE • HOW WE INVEST • BOO

BOOM!
INTRO

Boomers

How it happened isn't really that important. The fact is, it happened: during nearly two decades following World War II, some 73 million babies were born in America, the largest population blip in our history. Dubbed the "baby boom generation," we would later be referred to by a variety of other epithets: "the TV generation," the "love generation," "the now generation," "the Vietnam generation," "the me generation," even "the Pepsi generation."

Whatever our name, America's baby boomers have made a mark these past four decades. Likened frequently to "a pig in a python"—in which an oversized object passes through a system, which must make constant adjustments to accommodate its bulk—we have helped to reshape our culture. As we've "passed through" the system, we've influenced changes in everything from housing to health, literature to law, religion to recreation. Of course, as is bound to happen when an oversized object passes through a body, we've also been known to produce dyspepsia.

Who exactly is the baby boom generation? Its members defy description, and with good reason: boomers represent a cross-section of American society. Media-manufactured images notwithstanding, we are not "young, upwardly mobile professionals," although there are "yuppies" among us. A very large portion of our generation can't afford to buy homes in the types of neighborhoods in which we were raised. (Indeed, many of us wouldn't buy such homes even if they were affordable, having developed proclivities for what have become known as "alternative lifestyles.") And despite mindboggling advances in the standards of living of most Americans and several decades of relative prosperity, many of us are worse off than our parents, at least financially.

Yet there is much to celebrate. By our sheer numbers, we wield awesome political and economic clout. We once strove to "smash the state"; now we strive to elect politicians to statehouses—and the White House. The baby boom-inspired revolutions are far more than political: as we've proceeded through life, we've triggered revolutions in child care, education, health care, the workplace, and family dynamics—and, as we gray, we will no doubt influence a radical improvement in the health, social, and economic well-being of older people. Reared during a period of economic growth, we've enjoyed a luxury of choice—in careers, in starting families, in living arrangements, in how and where we spend our leisure time. And with the help of technological advances that spurred the growth of mass media, we have participated in a veritable renaissance in the arts—music, film, radio, TV, literature, painting, theater, and on and on.

One thing is certain: ours is the most watched, analyzed, and discussed generation ever. In 1978, for example, the House Select Committee on Population held a week-long series of hearings on "The Consequences of Changing U.S. Population: Baby Boom and Bust," in which a parade of witnesses spoke about the generation's past, present, and future. Major think-tanks have placed baby boomers under sociopolitical microscopes, as has nearly every industry, from carpets to car parts. Together, they've produced a mountain of reports with titles such as "Maternity Clothes Shop Banks on Baby Boom" and "Drug Makers See Opportunity in Rise of Psychogeriatrics as Baby Boom Generation Ages." Everything from the cradle to the grave.

Where Have All the Boomers Gone?

Keeping tabs on members of a generation requires finding them, a task that has been taken on by Claritas, an Alexandria, Va., market-targeting firm that has crammed into its computers more than a billion bits of information about the lifestyles and buying habits of Americans. Claritas has developed an innovative system that statistically divides America's 36,000-plus zip codes into 40 neighborhood "clusters" with nicknames such as "Pools and Patios," "Norma Rae-ville," and "Young Suburbia." Each cluster is a portrait of a lifestyle, says Claritas, reflecting socioeconomic conditions and cultural attitudes shared by like-minded Americans. California and Georgia may

Where the Boomers Are

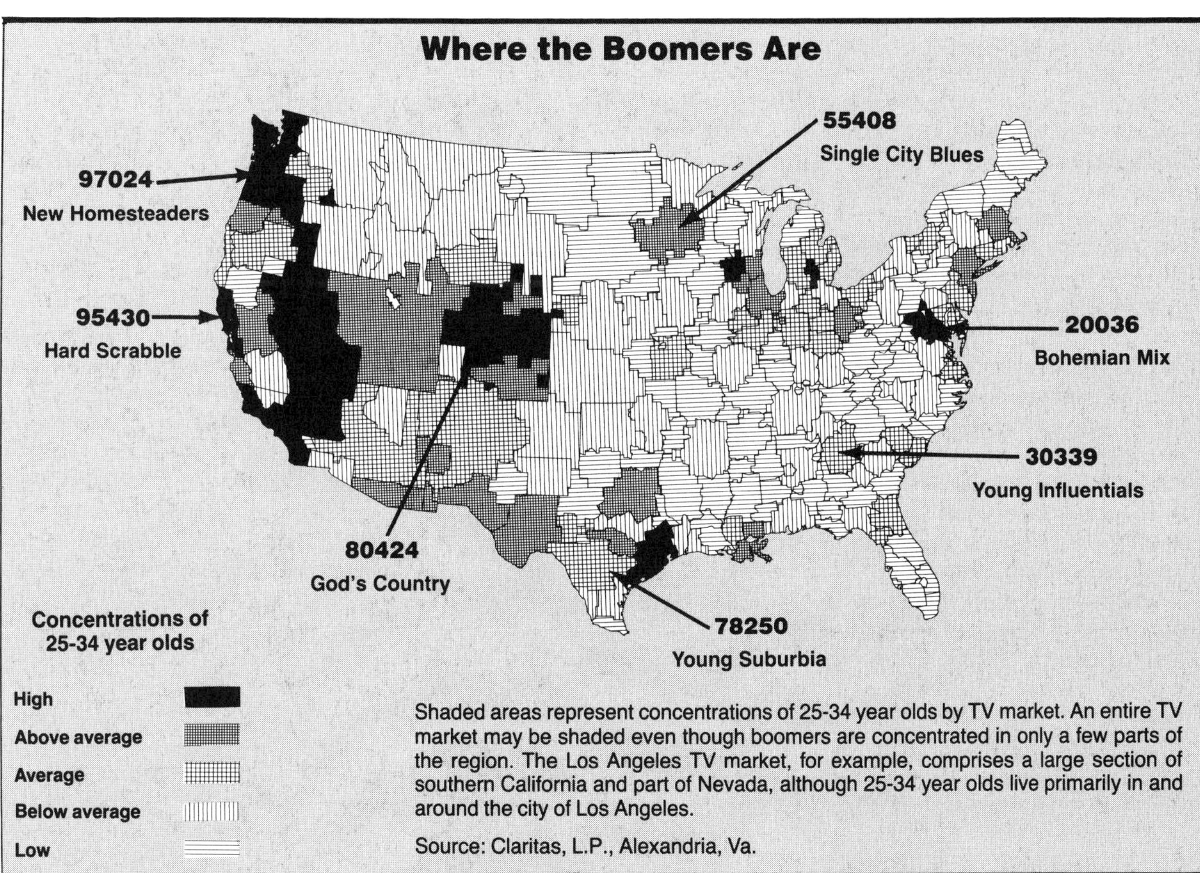

Shaded areas represent concentrations of 25-34 year olds by TV market. An entire TV market may be shaded even though boomers are concentrated in only a few parts of the region. The Los Angeles TV market, for example, comprises a large section of southern California and part of Nevada, although 25-34 year olds live primarily in and around the city of Los Angeles.

Source: Claritas, L.P., Alexandria, Va.

seem miles and light years apart, but Claritas' cluster system illustrates how residents of a cluster in, say, Marin can have much in common with their counterparts in Macon.

Claritas' data reveal the diverse places that baby boomers call "home." An analysis of those born between 1946 and 1955—the first decade of the baby boom and those most likely to have settled into careers and families—shows several trends in the types of neighborhoods in which boomers have chosen to live. Some examples:

■ **Zip Code 30339.** The Buckhead section of north Atlanta is a neighborhood Claritas calls "Young Influentials." This is Yuppieville, the kind of environment that makes marketing moguls and media mavens ooze with cliches. Here, the yuppie stereotype is based on reality: more than 80 percent of Buckhead's residents work in well-paying, white-collar jobs, according to *REZIDE*, a 10-volume Claritas publication showing profiles of all U.S. zip code areas; the 1984 median income, $27,395, is well above the national average of $21,886. More than 40 percent of Buckhead's residents were born between 1946 and 1955, twice the national average. Most live in relatively new apartments and condominiums near the restaurants and boutiques along Peachtree Road. Lenox Square, Atlanta's most fashionable shopping center, is located here, as is Georgia's governor's mansion and the "Disco Kroger's"—locals' nickname for a supermarket adjacent to a popular dance spot that's as much "meet market" as meat market. It is a relatively transient neighborhood: only a fifth of Buckhead's homes are owner-occupied, compared to about 65 percent nationally. One big reason is that Buckhead has a high percentage of singles—nearly 70 percent, compared with about 40 percent nationally—and less than 10 percent of its households contain a married couple with children. This may realistically be called the "smart set": 57 percent have at least a bachelor's degree, compared to only 16 percent nationally.

Although only 4 percent of those born between 1946 and 1955 live in "Young Influentials" types of neighborhoods, there are "Buckheads" throughout America, says Claritas—clusters of young, metropolitan sophisticates with exceptional high-tech, white-collar jobs; singles or childless couples with high incomes and lifestyles to match. Examples include zip codes 22209 in Rosslyn, Va. (across the Potomac River from Washington, D.C.); 33172 in Miami; 53719 in Madison, Wisc.; 75231 in Dallas; 90254 in Hermosa Beach, just south of Los Angeles; and 94114 in San Francisco.

■ **Zip Code 78250.** San Antonio's University Park neighborhood represents a type of neighborhood that Claritas calls "Young Suburbia." Although University Park isn't technically a suburb—it sits on the eastern edge of the city—it has several suburban characteristics, including large numbers of single-family tract homes located off Culebra Avenue and Bandera Road, the area's two main thoroughfares. University Park's homes contain largely young families—85 percent of its households contain married couples, and more than half house a married couple with children, almost twice the national average. A quarter of the population is under age 10, also twice the U.S. norm. These are young successful families, often stereotyped as the suburban family with 2.2 children, a color TV, a station wagon, and a front lawn. Three-quarters of the households have two wage earners—a very high percentage are in

white-collar jobs—and the 1984 median household income is a very healthy $33,294, making them strong consumers of most family products. Within a decade, many of these families will move to more upscale neighborhoods, with Claritas-given names like "Pools and Patios" or "Furs and Station Wagons." University Park's counterparts with large baby boomer populations include zip codes 75056 (outside Dallas), 60555 (Warrenville, Ill., outside Chicago), and 68130 (outside Omaha, Neb.).

■ **Zip Code 20036.** The Dupont Circle section of Washington, D.C., is a neighborhood cluster Claritas calls "Bohemian Mix." Less than a mile from the White House and on the northern edge of downtown, Dupont Circle contains a hodgepodge of high-income yuppies, low-income artists, college students, well-heeled middle-aged couples, and many elderly people living alone; the diversity is reflected in the neighborhood's racial mix. As is true for most of Washington, there are virtually no blue-collar workers here. Dupont Circle's 1984 median household income of $21,837 is just $50 below the national average. Baby boomers who live in the Dupont Circles of America tend to have more moderate incomes than their "Young Influential" and "Young Suburbia" brethren, although they may be as well educated (Dupont Circle boasts about the same number of college grads as Atlanta's Buckhead). Here, amid the busy streets, housing accommodations are older, smaller, and more affordable than in newer, less-congested, family-oriented neighborhoods; many boomers have remained around Dupont Circle after college, often saving their money towards a move to a "Young Influential" or "Young Suburbia" neighborhood.

Boomer-filled "Bohemian Mix" neighborhoods can be found in most urban areas. Many such neighborhoods were hippie havens during the 1960s: zip codes 10014 (New York's Greenwich Village), 02142 (Boston's Kendall Square), 60614 (Chicago's Lincoln Park), and 80218 (Denver's Capitol Hill) are several examples.

■ **Zip Code 80424.** The town of Breckenridge, Colo., in the Rocky Mountains (population: about 4,000) is "God's Country," according to Claritas. Breckenridge is one of several Colorado towns with high percentages (40 percent or higher) of predominantly single, moderate-income (1984 median household income: $26,431), well-educated 25-34-year-olds. They come to Breckenridge—and to Vail, Steamboat Village, Telluride, Nederland, Frisco, and Snowmass—to escape the city and to establish roots in an idyllic setting. Many "residents" of these towns maintain second homes here, with primary residences—apartments, typically—in larger metropolitan areas; they view their country homes as places to settle down or retire. But there are many year-round residents, too, and about half are renters.

"God's Country" is by no means limited to Colorado. According to Claritas' data, large percentages of baby boomers can be found in the "God's Country" towns of Plainsboro, N.J., near Princeton; Glen Echo, Md., on the Potomac River outside Washington, D.C.; Boulder Creek and La Honda, Calif., in the Santa Cruz Mountains south of San Francisco; Vernon Hills, Ill., just north of Chicago; and Studley, Va., near where the Chesapeake Bay meets the Atlantic Ocean.

■ **Zip Code 97024.** The small town of Fairview, Ore., (population: 1,600) sits on the Columbia River just a few miles east of Portland's city limits. Situated on the foothills of the Cascade Mountains not far from Mt. Hood, it is a pretty setting, although not the idyllic "God's Country." Claritas has dubbed Fairview "New Homesteaders," representing the small towns that are among the chief recipients of baby boomers' urban exodus. Fairview, with more than a third of its residents born between 1946 and 1955, is popular partly because of its low taxes—in mid-1985, property taxes were about a fifth of those of nearby Gresham. (But Fairview offers few city services—there is but one policeman, for example.) It's an affordable place for a young person working in Portland to buy a first home. This is a young family town: residents' median age is about 27, with 75 percent of them married. Sixty percent of Fairview's households contain at least one child, a figure twice the national average. Fairview's residents are several rungs down the socioeconomic ladder from those in "God's Country"; 1984 median household income was $21,250, about the national average. The town has no college graduates and three out of four workers are employed in sales, clerical jobs, or are crafts workers.

"New Homesteaders" is one of the country's largest and fastest-growing clusters, particularly in the West, says Claritas—it comprises nearly 7 percent of those born between 1946 and 1955. Other examples include Silverado, Calif., in Orange County south of Los Angeles; Moscow, Vt., halfway between Burlington and Montpelier; Stateline, Calif., on the Nevada

What Boomers Buy

FAST FOOD		*DRINKS*	
Company	**Index***	**Product**	**Index***
Jack-in-the-Box	147	Bottled natural spring water	123
Taco Bell	134	Imported beer	120
Shakey's	126	Domestic white table wine	118
Arby's	117	Domestic rose table wine	116
Denny's	114	Imported white table wine	115
Sizzler Steak House	110	Budweiser	114
Church's Fried Chicken	109	Domestic red table wine	113
Wendy's	105	Imported rose table wine	112
Bob's Big Boy	104	Imported red table wine	112
Dunkin' Donuts	104	Ale	111
A & W	103	Draft beer	110
Burger King	102	Sangria/pop/party wines	110
Burger Chef	102	Seven-up	109
McDonald's	102	Malt liquor	109
Red Lobster	102	Regular domestic beer	108
Arthur Treacher	98	Miller Lite	107
Kentucky Fried Chicken	98	Canned/bottled fruit juice	106
Popeye's	96	Diet/low-cal sodas	103
Bonanza	92	Coca-Cola	100
Long John Silver	92	Pepsi-Cola	100
Dairy Queen	86	Powdered soft drinks	99
Hardee's	71		

*Index numbers compare the rate of consumption for persons age 25-34 to the U.S. average for persons 18 and over. An index of "200," for example, represents consumption of twice the national average; an index of "50" indicates consumption of half the national average.

Source: Claritas, L.P., Alexandria, Va.

border near Lake Tahoe; Louisville, Colo., near Boulder; and North Liberty, Ia., north of Iowa City.

What Boomers Do

LIFESTYLE

Activity	Index*
Belong to health club	125
Play racquetball	121
Buy classical records/tapes	119
Took an adult education course last year	116
Attended a physical fitness program last year	116
Bought rock records/tapes	116
Went to 4+ movies last 90 days	114
Attended live theater or concert last year	114
Bought 6+ books last year	113
Went bowling	110
Contribute to public TV	109
Have a personal computer	108
Belong to a union	108
Collected stamps last year	107
Host cocktail party 1+ times/month	105
Went sailing	105
Spent $10+ at last Tupperware party	104
Bought country records/tapes	103
Visited a theme park	103
Smoke nonfilter cigarettes	102
Went fresh-water fishing	101
Belong to a fraternal order	101
Own video cassette recorder	100
Did outdoor gardening last year	97
Smoke small cigars/cigarillos	94
Belong to a veterans club	92
Went hunting	87
Use chewing tobacco	80

*Index numbers compare the rate of participation in an activity for persons age 25-34 to the U.S. average for persons 18 and over. An index of "200," for example, represents participation in an activity at twice the national average; an index of "50" indicates participation of half the national average.

Source: Claritas, L.P., Alexandria, Va.

■ **Zip Code 55408.** The Calhoun Isles section of Minneapolis is an example of "Single City Blues," says Claritas. Here are dense, urban, downscale singles areas, found in most major cities; about 2 percent of the U.S. population live in such neighborhoods. With its melange of races, classes, and transients, Calhoun Isles and like neighborhoods may be aptly dubbed a poor man's "Bohemian Mix." Calhoun Isles, located on the east side of Lake Calhoun, is an "emerging neighborhood," in the parlance of city planners. There are poor minorities and blue-collar workers as well as young, urban professionals, who have bought and fixed up old, often vacant homes. The 1984 median income in Calhoun Isles was only $15,237, about 30 percent below the national average. A new indoor mall carved out of several buildings' original facades has become a magnet for fancy boutiques—and for those with the money to shop there. Like the eclectic mix of people, the area's homes offer a wide variety: plain single-family houses stand next to six-unit Spanish-style apartments, which exist side by side with restored Victorians. This neighborhood is truly eclectic: at night, yuppies dine at Figlio's cafe while punk rockers and low-income locals hang out nearby at McDonald's.

Calhoun Isles may be to singles what Fairview is to familes: an affordable place to live in or near a big city. Other examples of "Single City Blues" neighborhoods populated with large numbers of boomers include zip codes 10006 in lower Manhattan, 14607 in Rochester, N.Y., 98134 in Seattle, and 48226 in Detroit.

■ **Zip Code 95430.** Just off the northern California coast, about 50 miles north of San Francisco, is a community called Duncan Mills, a cluster Claritas calls "Hard Scrabble." The term comes from an old phrase meaning to scratch a hard living from hard soil, and it describes America's poorest rural areas—Appalachia, the Ozarks, Mexican border country, and Dakota Bad Lands,

Name That Boomer

Most Popular First Names, 1950

Boys	Girls
1. John	Mary
2. Robert	Susan
3. James	Deborah
4. Michael	Linda
5. David	Patricia
6. Steven	Barbara
7. William	Nancy
8. Richard	Catherine
9. Thomas	Karen
10. Mark	Carol(e)
11. Charles	Ann(e)
12. Gary	Kathleen
13. Paul	Elizabeth
14. Jeffrey	Janet
15. Joseph	Margaret
16. Donald	Cynthia
17. Ronald	Pamela
18. Daniel	Dian(n)e
19. Kenneth	Sandra
20. George	Jane
21. Alan	Judith
22. Dennis	Gail
23. Douglas	Christine
24. Gregory	Sharon
25. Edward	Donna

Based on university students, mainly middle-class whites, born in 1950. Figures include alternate spellings of popular names (e.g., Steven and Stephen, Debra and Deborah).

Source: *First Names First*, by Leslie Alan Dunkling.

for example. But despite the gloom, something is going on in such communities: young people are moving in. Many of these are "back-to-the-land" types, often remnants of 1960s-style communes. Duncan Mills (population: 500), for example, is only miles from the popular Russian River resort area, although its land is prairie-like and not very fertile. Half of Duncan Mills' residents were born between 1946 and 1955—one of the highest percentages in the country—and virtually everyone has moved there since 1970. But this is no well-heeled yuppie haven: the 1984 median household income in Duncan Mills' is a paltry $8,125. (There are some oddities in Duncan Mills, according to U.S. Census data. Statistics indicate that 26.3 percent of Duncan Mills' residents are married, and *all* the rest are divorced; there are no single, never-married citizens of Duncan Mills. Moreover, although the ratio of men to women in Duncan Mills is better than three to one, the work force is 100 percent female, according to Census Bureau data.)

"Hard Scrabble" communities like Duncan Mills tend to result from "empty nesters"—homes in which kids have grown up and moved out, leaving their parents in large, relatively empty residences. As the parents move out or die, their homes are being taken over by younger people who may find such areas to have the only affordable housing. It is a pioneering lifestyle, not often a pleasant one. Other "Hard Scrabble" communities with large percentages of young people include Vada, Ky.; Colburn, Ida.; Green Sulfur Springs, W.Va.; Brownstown, Wash.; and Monhegan, Me.

The types of neighborhoods represented by these seven clusters represent only a slice of the baby-boomer pie—about a fifth of those born during the decade beginning 1946 live in one of the types of areas described above. There are also boomers in neighborhoods Claritas calls "New Beginnings" (highly mobile, employed, divorced, and renters, many moving south or west seeking new opportunities and lifestyles), "Middle America" (mid-sized, middle-class suburbs and towns, with average incomes), and "Levittown, U.S.A." (tract homes in new suburbs for young white-collar and well-paid blue-collar workers), among other clusters. The point is that boomers are everywhere.

What Boomers Do

MEDIA

Activity	Index*
Listen to track and field on radio	135
Listen to soft rock radio	128
Listen to all-news radio	118
Watch tennis on TV	114
Listen to basketball on radio	114
Watch soccer on TV	112
Listen to baseball on radio	108
Watch roller derby on TV	107
Listen to beautiful music on radio	105
Watch baseball on TV	105
Have cable TV	103
Listen to religious radio	99
Watch prime-time TV films	98
Watch prime-time half-hour programs on TV	96
Listen to golden oldies on radio	96
Watch prime-time sit coms on TV	94
Watch early evening TV news	94
Watch wrestling on TV	90
Watch weekday soaps on TV	87
Watch weekday quiz shows on TV	83

What Boomers Drive

CARS

Model	Index*
Mitsubishi Tredia	128
Volkswagen Scirocco	121
Mazda 626	121
Honda Civic	120
Honda Prelude	118
Plymouth Sapporo/Conquest	116
Toyota Celica/Supra	116
Toyota Tercel/Corolla	114
Fiat Strada	114
Plymouth Colt	112
All imported cars	112
Datsun Pulsar	111
Renault Le Car	111
Volkswagen Rabbit	109
Pontiac Firebird	107
Chevrolet Camaro	107
Ford Mustang	106
Buick Skyhawk	105
Mercury Capri	104
Cadillac Cimarron	101
Oldsmobile Omega	100
Ford Escort	100
Buick Riviera	99
Dodge Aries	97
All domestic cars	96
Chevrolet Celebrity	95
Ford Tempo/Fairmont	94
Oldsmobile Delta 88	90
Mercedes Benz 300D	89
Lincoln Mark VI/VII	88
Cadillac Fleetwood	87
Ferrari	86
Buick Electra	82
Dodge Diplomat	79
Jaguar	75
Rolls Royce	70

*Index numbers compare the rate of consumption of 1983 model cars for persons age 25-34 to the U.S. average for persons 18 and over. An index of "200," for example, represents consumption of twice the national average; an index of "50" indicates consumption of half the national average.

Source: Claritas, L.P., Alexandria, Va.

Thinking For Ourselves

We don't think as a group, either, although there are some trends. Alexander W. Astin, a professor in the University of California at Los Angeles' School of Education, has been tracking baby-boomer attitudes since 1966, each year sending a survey to some 300,000 college freshmen around the country. The results track a select sample—college students tend to be from somewhat higher socioeconomic backgrounds than the population at large—but his data shed light on the changing personal values of a generation. Among the trends:

What Boomers Buy

TRAVEL

Activity	Index*
Traveled to Mexico	134
Traveled by railroad	134
Traveled to Hawaii	126
Traveled by rented car	125
Traveled to Britain/Ireland	118
Any foreign trip within last 3 years	117
Domestic air travel last year	116
Took any cruise last 3 years	116
Car trip with overnight camping equipment last year	114
Traveled to Alaska/Canada	114
Have a passport	113
Domestic trip by bus last year	110
Traveled for business last year	108
Traveled to Eastern Europe/Middle East last year	106

How Boomers Invest

FINANCES

Activity	Index*
Used bank credit card last mo.	115
Have a brokerage account	113
Made 3+ stock transactions last year	112
Have vacation/investment prop.	112
Have American Express card	112
Have $100,000+ life insurance policy	112
Have IRA or Keough account	110
Carry term life insurance	106
Acquired a personal loan last year	106
Have money market fund	102
Carry whole life insurance	98
Own $25,000+ in securities	97
Carry Blue Cross/Blue Shield	91

*Index numbers compare the rate of consumption for persons age 25-34 to the U.S. average for persons 18 and over. An index of "200," for example, represents consumption of twice the national average; an index of "50" indicates consumption of half the national average.

Source: Claritas, L.P., Alexandria, Va.

■ Although only half as many freshmen described themselves as "liberal" in 1984 as in 1969 (45 percent vs. 22 percent), the number of "conservatives" was down, too (24 percent vs. 21 percent). The real growth was in those describing themselves as "middle-of-the-road" (31 percent vs. 57 percent).

■ Money is of greater importance than ever before. Astin asked respondents to choose from a list of statements "the importance to you personally of each of the following." The item showing the strongest upward trend is "being very well-off financially." Just over 40 percent chose that statement in 1967; by 1984, the number had climbed to about 70 percent. At the same time, those selecting "developing a meaningful philosophy of life" dropped in half, from more than 80 percent to about 40 percent. All of which gives credence to one wag's notion that "money is the long hair of the '80s."

■ Today's students (66.7 percent) are much more likely than students in the early 1970s (49.9 percent) to say that a major reason for attending college is "to be able to make more money." By contrast, values showing the largest declines relate to matters of altruism and social concern: helping others, promoting racial understanding, cleaning up the environment, participating in community action programs, and keeping up with political affairs.

■ Today's students believe more strongly that marijuana should be legalized (26 percent in 1983; 19 percent in 1969), but far less than the 53 percent who supported legalization in 1977. Students have felt gradually less strongly that the death penalty be abolished (54 percent in 1969; 33 percent in 1977; 29 percent in 1983). And support has dropped for those believing that abortion should be legalized (76 percent in 1969; 55 percent in 1983); consistent with that, there is less support for the idea that "parents should be discouraged from having large families" (69 percent in 1969; 36 percent in 1983).

How do baby boomers feel about the future? The answer has a lot to do with when in the "boom" one was born. Older boomers, for example—those born between 1946 and 1955—have a rosier perspective. Boomers in that "first wave" generally are prospering more than those born since the mid-1950s. Those who graduated from college or who otherwise entered the workforce since 1975 have had the misfortunes of beginning careers in a stagnant economy, a problem compounded by the sheer number of boomers competing for jobs. Our parents probably earned more at age 30 (adjusted for inflation) than most of have or will at that age, according to a study by the Urban Institute, despite our being hyped in the media as the generation that can "have it all." Ironically, the living standards many of us enjoyed as children seem wildly out of reach today.

Where No Boomer Has Gone Before

Optimists to the end, however, we see mostly bright futures. Nearly a third of us are "very satisfied" with the way things are going personally, according to a survey of baby boomers conducted by the American Council of Life Insurance. ACLI found that another 55 percent are "somewhat satisfied," and fewer than one in five are "not at all satisfied." Moreover, 70 percent of us think that things will get better over the next few years; only 7 percent think things will get worse.

Ultimately, of course, no one knows exactly what the future will bring. There are too many variables, too many unknowns. But as the pages that follow clearly illustrate, we share a rich and colorful heritage, filled with political prodding, musical wizardry, and a sexual revolution that has shaken the foundations of family life. In ways subtle and not-so-subtle, we've made our mark, and we will no doubt continue to do so.

What follows is an illustrated, anecdotal history of the baby boom generation covering the years 1955 through 1975, two rich decades during which most boomers were growing up and influencing—and being influenced by—the events of the day. The four chapters—music, media, culture, and politics—represent admittedly arbitrary divisions, but combined encompass the vast spectrum of activities and events most of us encountered. Some of the "events" could have spanned several divisions; while the space shots easily could be included under "media" or "politics," for example, they are contained largely in the "culture" chapter. But such ambiguities merely illustrate the complex patchwork of our beings and the rich heritage baby boomers share.

Together, these four chapters paint a portrait of a generation, a picture of who we are based on where we've been. It isn't always a pretty picture, to be sure, but it is a colorful one. And despite the uncertainty about our future, our collective history reveals at least one undeniable truth: if the past is any indication, there will be precious few dull moments as long as we're around.

How Boomers Vote

Year	Liberal/ Far Left	Middle-of-the-Road	Conservative/ Far Right
1969	32.6%	44.4%	22.9%
1970	44.6	31.3	24.1
1971	38.1	46.8	15.2
1972	35.2	48.3	16.6
1973	33.6	53.5	13.0
1974	30.2	55.1	14.7
1975	30.0	53.8	15.2
1976	27.8	56.0	16.2
1977	27.0	56.6	16.4
1978	25.4	57.8	16.9
1979	24.5	57.9	17.5
1980	21.7	60.0	18.3
1981	19.7	59.6	20.7
1982	20.7	59.8	19.4
1983	21.1	60.3	18.7
1984	22.1	57.4	20.5

Responses are from approximately 300,000 incoming freshmen at a nationally representative sample of about 500 colleges and universities. Students were asked, "How would you characterize your political views?" Data are not representative of the entire population, because more college freshmen tend to be white and middle class than the population at large.

Source: Higher Education Research Institute, University of California at Los Angeles.

LMAN BROTHERS • ALTAMONT • THE BEACH BOYS • THE BEATLE
RRY • THE BRITISH INVASION • BUBBLEGUM • CONCERTS FOR BANG
UNTRY JOE • JIM CROCE • MILES DAVIS • THE DEAD • THE DOORS
VIS • ROBERTA FLACK • PINK FLOYD • FOLK MUSIC • GIRL GROU
AHAM • GREASE • GROUPIES • WOODY GUTHRIE • *HAIR* • HENDR
OLIDAY • BUDDY HOLLY • THE JACKSON 5 • JANIS JOPLIN • ELTON
HN AND YOKO • BETTE MIDLER • JONI MITCHELL • MONTEREY POP
PAUL IS DEAD • PAYOLA • ROCK FESTS • SAN FRANCISCO SCENE •
ARFUNKEL • LYNYRD SKYNYRD • SPRINGSTEEN • ROD STEWART • T
JAMES TAYLOR • THE WHO • STEVIE WONDER • WOODSTOCK • FRA
D ZEPPELIN • ALLMAN BROTHERS • ALTAMONT • THE BEACH BOY
EATLES • CHUCK BERRY • THE BRITISH INVASION • BUBBLEGUM •
R BANGLA DESH • COUNTRY JOE • JIM CROCE • MILES DAVIS • T
E DOORS • DYLAN • ELVIS • ROBERTA FLACK • PINK FLOYD • FO
RL GROUPS • BILL GRAHAM • *GREASE* • GROUPIES • WOODY GUTH
HENDRIX • BILLIE HOLIDAY • BUDDY HOLLY • THE JACKSON 5 • JAN
TON JOHN • JOHN AND YOKO • BETTE MIDLER • JONI MITCHELL •
P • MOTOWN • PAUL IS DEAD • PAYOLA • ROCK FESTS • SAN FRA
LMAN BROTHERS • ALTAMONT • THE BEACH BOYS • THE BEATLE
RRY • THE BRITISH INVASION • BUBBLEGUM • CONCERTS FOR BAN
UNTRY JOE • JIM CROCE • MILES DAVIS • THE DEAD • THE DOOR
VIS • ROBERTA FLACK • PINK FLOYD • FOLK MUSIC • GIRL GROU
AHAM • GREASE • GROUPIES • WOODY GUTHRIE • *HAIR* • HEND
OLIDAY • BUDDY HOLLY • THE JACKSON 5 • JANIS JOPLIN • ELTO
HN AND YOKO • BETTE MIDLER • JONI MITCHELL • MONTEREY PO
PAUL IS DEAD • PAYOLA • ROCK FESTS • SAN FRANCISCO SCENE •
ARFUNKEL • LYNYRD SKYNYRD • SPRINGSTEEN • ROD STEWART • T
JAMES TAYLOR • THE WHO • STEVIE WONDER • WOODSTOCK • FR

BOOM!
MUSIC

Rescue Me

MAY 13, 1955. Elvis Presley, 20, who has recorded several singles for Sun Records, performs in Jacksonville, Fla., where he is physically attacked by a wild audience; several girls try to tear off his clothes.

D. Crockett, Superstar

MAY 28, 1955. *Billboard* reports that "The Ballad of Davy Crockett" is the most popular song in America, having sold some 18 million copies from 23 different recordings in the U.S. alone. The song has been recorded in a dozen other languages, including 20 different versions in French.

Fess as Davy: Coonskin craze.

Comets' Tale

JUNE 29, 1955. Bill Haley and the Comets' "Rock Around the Clock" becomes the first rock 'n' roll song to reach number one on the American pop charts. Among other things, Haley will help make rock music acceptable to white audiences, which have so far associated rock 'n' roll with the "race music" played by blacks.

Parker Pens Presley

NOVEMBER 20, 1955. Elvis Presley makes Col. Tom Parker his manager. Parker, a flamboyant promoter—whose previous experience includes the "Great Parker Pony Circus" and "Tom Parker and His Dancing Turkeys"—is a veteran of carnivals, medicine shows, and various other entertainment enterprises. He isn't really a colonel; while he served in the U.S. military, the title was bestowed by the governor of Louisiana. In a few days, Parker will sign a Presley recording contract with RCA, giving Presley an unprecedented $5,000 in back royalties and Sun Records $35,000 for previously recorded masters. Parker will benefit handsomely from Presley's future success. Instead of the traditional 20 percent manager's fee, Parker will take up to half of Presley's income, sometimes more. In 1973, for example, Parker will sell RCA the rights to Presley's entire backlist of recordings in a deal in which Parker will gross $1.75 million more than Presley.

Liberace's Legacy

JANUARY 27, 1956. "Heartbreak Hotel," Elvis Presley's first recording on RCA, is released. By late April it will reach number one. Presley records will hold the number-one spot for 25 weeks during 1956; "Heartbreak" will be followed by "I Want You, I Need You, I Love You," "Don't Be Cruel," "My Baby Left Me," "Hound Dog," "Love Me Tender," and "Any Way You Want Me." By midyear he reportedly will have earned more than $6 million in royalties. His overwhelming popularity notwithstanding, Presley will be subject to criticism from a variety of fronts, including several DJs. In July *Billboard* will call him "the most controversial entertainer since Liberace." In September, following Presley's performance of "Love Me Tender" on "The Ed Sullivan Show," record buyers will strip stores of the record within days.

Klan's Ban

MARCH 31, 1956. Asa Carter of the North Alabama White Citizen's Council claims that rock 'n' roll is a plot by black people to subvert white teenagers. He names the National Association for the Advancement of Colored People as the primary force behind this conspiracy.

Bitch Along With Mitch

APRIL 15, 1956. Mitch Miller, music director of Columbia Records, appears on CBS television with two psychiatrists to discuss the potentially negative effects of rock 'n' roll on teenagers. This is the first of Miller's several TV and radio programs knocking rock 'n' roll, including a Westinghouse radio interview during which he will be supported by Sammy Davis, Jr.

Rock 'n' Reel

SEPTEMBER 25, 1956. Twentieth Century-Fox announces production of *Do Re Me*, a rock 'n' roll film starring Little Richard and Fats Domino. It is the first of a tidal wave of rock 'n' roll films from major studios hoping to capitalize on the surging rock "fad."

"The New Left sprang, a predestined pissed-off child, from Elvis' gyrating pelvis."
Jerry Rubin

Kurt Russell as Elvis: The clone also rises.

In coming months, several other titles will be announced, including a film by Elvis Presley that will never be made; a film produced by DJ Alan Freed called "Don't Knock the Rock," featuring Chuck Berry and Frankie Lymon and the Teenagers; and "Jamboree," starring Jerry Lee Lewis, Berry, Frankie Avalon, Connie Francis, and others.

Sun Sets On Record

DECEMBER 4, 1956. "The Million Dollar Quartet"—an improvisational session featuring Sun Records artists Johnny Cash, Carl Perkins, Jerry Lee Lewis, and Elvis Presley—is recorded at Sun studios in Memphis, although the fruits of their labors won't be released until 1981.

Pvt. Presley: Physically fit.

Soldier Boy

JANUARY 8, 1957. Elvis Presley passes the Army's preinduction examination in Memphis. It is his 22nd birthday. In little more than a year he will be inducted into the Army as recruit number 53310761 for a two-year stint in what is primarily a public relations tour.

The Adventures of Ricky

APRIL 24, 1957. Seventeen-year-old Ricky Nelson, son of bandleader Ozzie Nelson and his singer-wife Harriet, releases his first single, "Teenager's Romance." Ricky already is well known to teenagers through his role in "The Adventures of Ozzie and Harriet" TV show, which debuted when Ricky was only eight. The record will be an instant hit, selling more than 50,000 copies in the first week and earn-

Flashback

Top Singles—1955

Ain't That a Shame	Fats Domino
Baby, Let's Play House	Elvis Presley
Ballad of Davy Crockett	Bill Hayes
Do, Baby, Do	Ernie K-Doe
Earth Angel	Penguins
The Great Pretender	Platters
I Forgot to Remember to Forget Her	Elvis Presley
Maybelline	Chuck Berry
Milkcow Blues Boogie	Elvis Presley
My Babe	Little Walter
Only You	Platters
Pledging My Love	Johnny Ace
Rock Around the Clock	Bill Haley and the Comets
See You Later, Alligator	Bill Haley and the Comets
Shake, Rattle, and Roll	Bill Haley and the Comets
Sincerely	McGuire Sisters
Sixteen Tons	Tennessee Ernie Ford
Speedo	Cadillacs
Tutti Frutti	Little Richard
Tweedle Dee	LaVern Baker
Unchained Melody	Roy Hamilton

Top Albums—1955

Brubeck Time	Dave Brubeck
Les and Mary	Les Paul and Mary Ford
Lonesome Echo	Jackie Gleason
Love Me or Leave Me	Doris Day
Miss Show Business	Judy Garland
Music for Tonight	Steve Allen
Original Talking Union	Pete Seeger
Red Hot and Cool	Dave Brubeck
So Smooth	Perry Como
Starring Sammy Davis, Jr.	Sammy Davis, Jr.

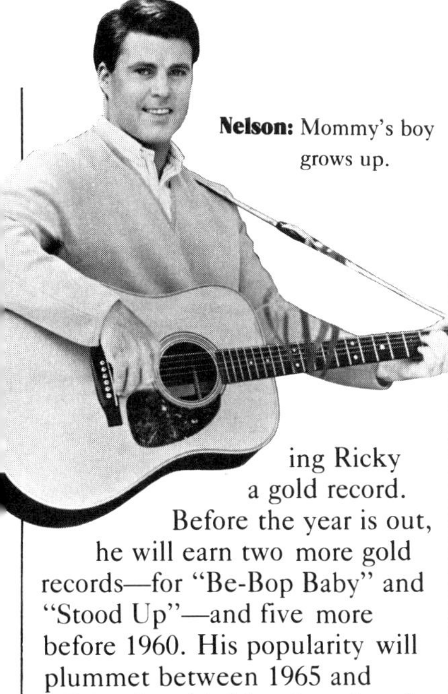

Nelson: Mommy's boy grows up.

ing Ricky a gold record. Before the year is out, he will earn two more gold records—for "Be-Bop Baby" and "Stood Up"—and five more before 1960. His popularity will plummet between 1965 and 1972, when his bitterly pointed "Garden Party" single will go gold.

That'll Be the Day

MAY 27, 1957. Twenty-year-old Charles Hardin "Buddy" Holly and his band, the Crickets, release "That'll Be the Day," their only record to reach number one. The band first recorded in 1955 on Decca, but was dropped from that label, then "discovered" by Coral Records, which has recorded "That'll Be the Day." Holly's music later will represent some of the most innovative rock sounds of the era—a synthesis of a variety of styles, including his own distinctive voice and a yodel reminiscent of legendary country star Hank Williams—a musical legacy he will leave behind when he is killed at age 22 in an airplane crash. The Holly catalog eventually will be sold to Paul McCartney.

Flashback

Top Singles—1956

Be Bop a Lula	Gene Vincent
Blueberry Hill	Fats Domino
Blue Suede Shoes	Carl Perkins
Don't Be Cruel	Elvis Presley
Hallelujah I Love Her So	Ray Charles
Heart and Soul	Clef-Tones
Heartbreak Hotel	Elvis Presley
Hound Dog	Elvis Presley
Jim Dandy	Lavern Baker
Let the Good Times Roll	Shirley and Lee
Long Tall Sally	Little Richard
Love Is Strange	Mickey and Sylvia
Love Me Tender	Elvis Presley
Magic Touch	Platters
No Money Down	Chuck Berry
Please, Please, Please	James Brown
Rip It Up	Little Richard
Roll Over Beethoven	Chuck Berry
Slippin' and Slidin'	Little Richard
That's All Right Mama	Elvis Presley
Too Much Monkey Business	Chuck Berry
Wayward Wind	Gogi Grant
Why Do Fools Fall in Love?	Frankie Lymon and the Teenagers

Top Albums—1956

Belafonte	Harry Belafonte
Bubbles in the Wine	Lawrence Welk
Calypso	Harry Belafonte
Elvis	Elvis Presley
Elvis Presley	Elvis Presley
Four Freshmen and Five Trombones	Four Freshmen
Holiday in Rome	Michel Legrande
Howdy	Pat Boone
Julie Is Her Name	Julie London
The King and I	soundtrack
The Misty Miss Christy	June Christy
Music to Change Her Mind	Jackie Gleason
My Fair Lady	soundtrack
Night Winds	Jackie Gleason
Oklahoma	soundtrack
The Platters	Platters
Sounds for Swingin' Lovers	Frank Sinatra
This Is Fats Domino	Fats Domino
This Is Sinatra	Frank Sinatra

Flashback

Top Singles—1957

All Shook Up	Elvis Presley
At the Hop	Danny and the Juniors
Banana Boat Song	Harry Belafonte
Be Bop Baby	Ricky Nelson
Blue Monday	Fats Domino
Bye Bye Love	Everly Brothers
Come Go With Me	Del Vikings
Diana	Paul Anka
Great Balls of Fire	Jerry Lee Lewis
I'm Walkin'	Fats Domino
Jailhouse Rock	Elvis Presley
Jenny Jenny	Little Richard
Love Letters in the Sand	Pat Boone
Over the Mountain	Johnny and Joe
Party Doll	Buddy Knox
Peggy Sue	Buddy Holly and the Crickets
Searchin'	Coasters
Silhouettes	Rays
Tammy	Debbie Reynolds
Teenager's Romance	Ricky Nelson
That'll Be the Day	Buddy Holly and the Crickets
Too Much	Elvis Presley
Wake Up Little Susie	Everly Brothers
Whole Lotta Shakin'	Jerry Lee Lewis
You Send Me	Sam Cooke

Top Albums—1957

An Evening With Harry Belafonte	Harry Belafonte
April Love	Pat Boone
Around the World in 80 Days	soundtrack
Belafonte Sings of the Caribbean	Harry Belafonte
Close to You	Frank Sinatra
Day by Day	Doris Day
Dukes of Dixieland Vol. 3	Dukes of Dixieland
Ellington at Newport	Duke Ellington
Elvis' Christmas Album	Elvis Presley
Four Freshmen and Five Trumpets	Four Freshmen
Hymns	Tennessee Ernie Ford
The Great Ray Charles	Ray Charles
Just One of Those Things	Nat "King" Cole
Love Is the Thing	Nat "King" Cole
Lovin' You	Elvis Presley
Pat's Great Hits	Pat Boone
We Get Letters	Perry Como

Kissin' Cousins

JUNE 12, 1957. Jerry Lee Lewis' second release, "Whole Lotta Shakin' Goin' On," a song he recorded in only one take, makes the pop charts. The song will have wide appeal, hitting number one on the country-and-western and rhythm-and-blues charts and number three on the pop chart. Lewis will be criticized for his piano playing, a hard, pounding style; one critic will say that Lewis "raped" the piano. Despite such criticism, he will be popular on the concert circuit until next year, when he marries his 14-year-old cousin. The revelation will cause Lewis' 37-date British tour to be cancelled after only three performances, the beginning of the end of his career.

Lewis: Piano raper.

Let Me Introduce Myself

JULY 6, 1957. A drunk John Lennon meets a sober Paul McCartney. It is the St. Peter's Parish Church picnic, in the Liverpool suburb of Wooton, at which Lennon's band, the Quarrymen, has performed. The 14-year-old McCartney will dazzle the 16-year-old Lennon and friends with his guitar wizardry, which includes, among other things, deftly tuning a guitar, a feat the others have yet to achieve. Lennon will soon invite McCartney to join the Quarrymen and the two will become good friends and musical collaborators, writing more than 100 songs within three years.

Anka Hits

AUGUST 31, 1957. "Diana," the first single by Ottawa-born Paul Anka, who also wrote the tune, reaches number one.

I'm a Believer

JANUARY 28, 1958. Little Richard announces he has gotten religion after an airplane in which he was flying caught fire and he promised God that he'd give up "the devil's work" and devote himself to gospel if he lived. He enrolls in Oakwood College, a school for blacks run by the Seventh Day Adventist Church in Alabama, but will be back on the rock concert circuit by the early 1960s.

Flashback

Top Singles—1958

All I Have to Do Is Dream	Everly Brothers
Breathless	Jerry Lee Lewis
Chantilly Lace	Moonglows
Do You Wanna Dance?	Bobby Freeman
Don't	Elvis Presley
Hard-Headed Woman	Elvis Presley
I Wonder Why	Dion and the Belmonts
It's Only Make Believe	Conway Twitty
Johnny B. Goode	Chuck Berry
Poor Little Fool	Ricky Nelson
Purple People Eater	Sheb Wooley
Rockin' Robin	Bobby Day
Shout	Isley Brothers
Splish Splash	Bobby Darin
Sugartime	McGuire Sisters
Summertime Blues	Eddy Cochran
Tears On My Pillow	Little Anthony and the Imperials
Tequila	Champs
The Chipmunk Song	David Seville and the Chipmunks
To Know Him Is to Love Him	Teddy Bears
Tom Dooley	Kingston Trio
Volare	Domenico Modugno
When	Kalin Twins
Who's Sorry Now?	Connie Francis
Yakety Yak	Coasters
You Are My Destiny	Paul Anka

Top Albums—1958

Chet Atkins at Home	Chet Atkins
Christmas Sing Along With Mitch	Mitch Miller
Come Fly With Me	Frank Sinatra
The Fabulous Johnny Cash	Johnny Cash
Gigi	soundtrack
Johnny's Greatest Hits	Johnny Mathis
King Creole	Elvis Presley
The Kingston Trio	Kingston Trio
The Music Man	soundtrack
Only the Lonely	Ricky Nelson
Pete Seeger With Sonny Terry	Pete Seeger
Ricky	Ricky Nelson
Ricky Nelson	Ricky Nelson
St. Louis Blues	Nat "King" Cole
Sam Cooke Sings	Sam Cooke
Stardust	Pat Boone

Iran's Ban

FEBRUARY 14, 1958. Walter Cronkite reports on the "CBS Evening News" that the Iranian government has banned rock 'n' roll, stating that it is counter to the beliefs of Islam.

I Write the Songs

APRIL 30, 1958. Carole King's first single, "The Right Girl," is released. King, who grew up in Brooklyn and attended Queens College with Neil Diamond and Paul Simon, has joined forces with her songwriter husband, Gerry Goffin. When former date Neil Sedaka heard her songs, he introduced her to his publisher, Don Kirshner, who paid King a weekly stipend to produce songs. King's own recordings won't receive much attention until the early 1970s. Meanwhile, she'll pen several hit songs, including "Will You Love Me Tomorrow" (Shirelles), "Take Good Care of My Baby" (Bobby Vee), "Up on the Roof" (Drifters), "He's a Rebel" (Crystals), "Loco-Motion" (Little Eva), "One Fine Day" (Chiffons), and "Go Away, Little Girl" (Steve Lawrence).

Don't Play That Song

JULY 7, 1958. *Contacts*, a Catholic youth magazine, initiates a contest aimed at creating "wholesome lyrics" to popular music. An accompanying article takes to task many popular songs, including Elvis Presley's "Wear Your Ring Around My Neck," because it advocates going steady.

Making the Charts

AUGUST 8, 1958. *Billboard* introduces "The Hot 100" singles chart, which will become the most influential measure of national sales in the industry.

Phil's Millions

AUGUST 12, 1958. "To Know Him Is to Love Him" is released on the Dore label by the Teddy Bears. The song was arranged and composed by Phil Spector, 18; its title was inspired by the epitaph on his father's tombstone. In November the song will be number one for three weeks, but will be knocked off by "The Chipmunk Song," a phenomenally popular novelty record. Although "To Know Him" will sell more than 1.2 million copies, Spector's group will receive only a small fraction of its royalties; Dore's owner will claim the contract is invalid because the three Teddy Bears signed as minors without parental consent. Spector will go on to become one of rock's seminal producers, showing an uncanny knack for catching adolescent ears with his songs, most celebrating postpubescent passion: "Be My Baby," "Then He Kissed Me," and "Wait 'Til My Bobby Gets Home," among others. In 1961,

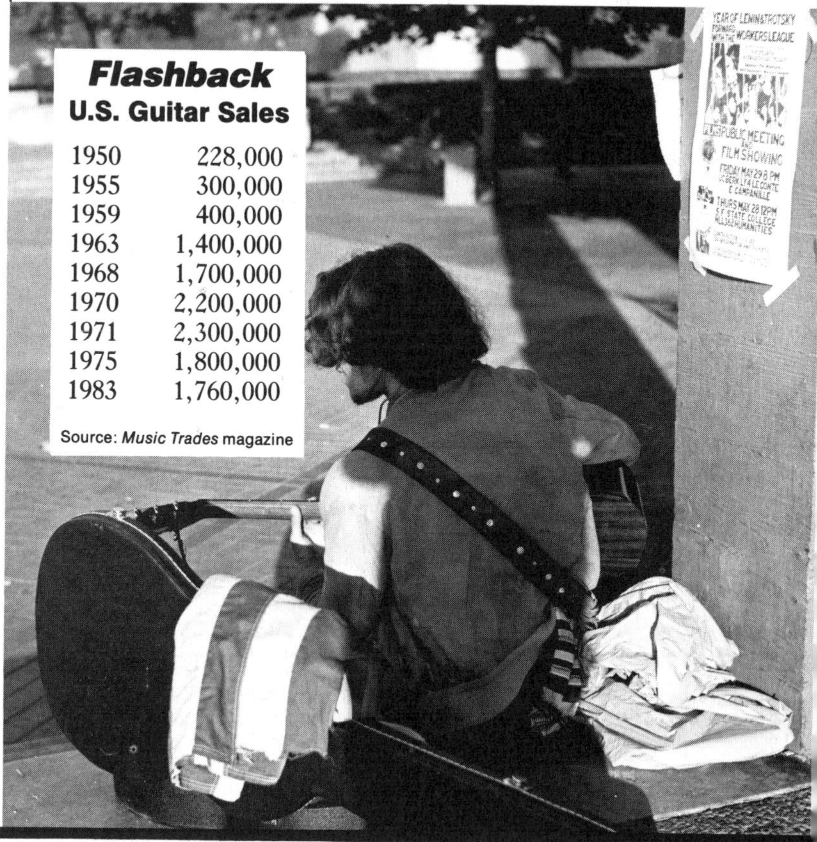

Flashback
U.S. Guitar Sales

Year	Sales
1950	228,000
1955	300,000
1959	400,000
1963	1,400,000
1968	1,700,000
1970	2,200,000
1971	2,300,000
1975	1,800,000
1983	1,760,000

Source: *Music Trades* magazine

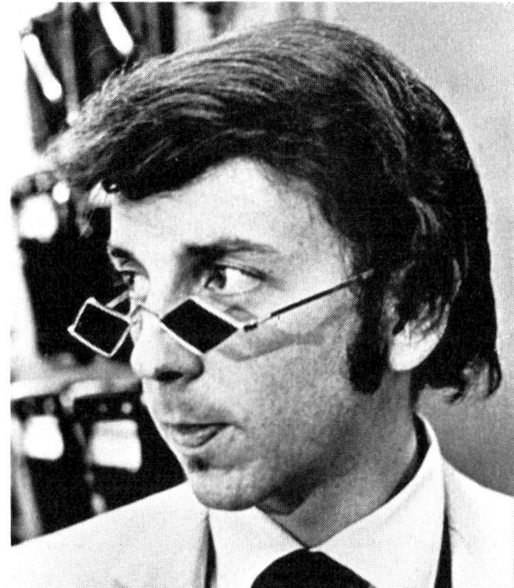

Spector: Girls just wanna make music.

he and Lester Sill will form the Philles (for "Phil" and "Les") label, making Spector the youngest record label executive ever and a millionaire at age 21. Over the next 15 years, Spector will be responsible for creating such "girl group" sounds as the Crystals and the Ronettes (he will marry lead singer Veronica "Ronnie" Bennett); form Mother Bertha Productions, a sheet music publisher (his mother, Bertha, will act as bookkeeper); introduce Sonny to Cher; launch the careers of the Righteous Brothers; play guitar on a Rolling Stones album; and produce records by Lenny Bruce, Dion, the Beatles, George Harrison, John Lennon, and Yoko Ono.

Have Nun, Will Travel

August 24, 1958. "Nel Blu Dipinto Di Blu," by Domenico Modugno, commonly known as "Volare," becomes the first foreign-language single to reach number one and will stay at

Flashback

Top Singles—1959

Baby Talk	Jan and Dean
A Big Hunk of Love	Elvis Presley
The Battle of New Orleans	Johnny Horton
Charlie Brown	Coasters
Come Softly to Me	Fleetwoods
Donna	Richie Valens
I Only Have Eyes for You	Flamingos
It Doesn't Matter Anymore	Buddy Holly and the Crickets
Lonely Boy	Paul Anka
Love Potion No. 9	Clovers
Mack the Knife	Bobby Darin
Mary Lou	Ronnie Hawkins
Oh! Carol	Neil Sedaka
Personality	Lloyd Price
Poison Ivy	Coasters
Remember When?	Platters
Sea Cruise	Frankie Ford
Shout	Isley Brothers
Since I Don't Have You	Skyliners
16 Candles	Crests
Smoke Gets In Your Eyes	Platters
Sweeter Than You	Ricky Nelson
There Goes My Baby	Drifters
Venus	Frankie Avalon
What'd I Say?	Ray Charles
You're So Fine	Falcons

Top Albums—1959

A Date With Elvis	Elvis Presley
Belafonte at Carnegie Hall	Harry Belafonte
Blue Hawaii	Billy Vaughn
The Buddy Holly Story	Buddy Holly
Come Dance With Me	Frank Sinatra
Fabulous Fabian	Fabian
The Fabulous Little Richard	Little Richard
Here We Go Again	Kingston Trio
Hold That Tiger	Fabian
Let's All Sing With the Chipmunks	The Chipmunks
Peter Gunn	Henry Mancini
Swingin' on a Rainbow	Frankie Avalon

the top for five weeks. Kyu Sakamoto will hold the top slot for three weeks in the summer of 1963 with "Sukiyaki"; a few months later "Dominique," by the Singing Nun, will hit number one, where it will remain through December. (The nun, Soeur Sourire, a.k.a. Jeanine Deckers, will perform on "The Ed Sullivan Show," have a crisis of faith brought upon by her celebrity status, and leave the convent in 1966; she will commit suicide in 1985, due largely to depression over financial problems.)

And George Makes Three

JANUARY 14, 1959. Paul McCartney introduces John Lennon to George Harrison, McCartney's pimply faced childhood friend, who soon will sit in with McCartney and Lennon's group, now performing as Johnny and the Moondogs, at a dank basement club known appropriately as "The Morgue." Harrison isn't a particularly impressive player, but his mother will help feed the band, and he will be invited to become a permanent member.

The Day the Music Died

FEBRUARY 2, 1959. Buddy Holly makes his last stage appearance, with Ritchie Valens at a club in Clear Lake, Ia. The following day the tour plane in which they are traveling will crash, killing Holly, Valens, and J.P. Richardson, who, under the name the "Big Bopper," recorded "Chantilly Lace," among other songs; only Crickett bassist Waylon Jennings, grounded with a cold, will survive. In 1972 this day will be immortalized in Don McLean's song, "American Pie," as "the day the music died."

Drifters Redux

MARCH 24, 1959. With the release of "There Goes My Baby," a song created for them by writers/producers Jerry Leiber and Mike Stoller, a second generation of the Drifters hits the top of the U.S. and European charts. The original Drifters, formed in 1953 behind former Dominoes' lead vocalist Clyde McPhatter, had seven "top-10" rhythm-and-blues hits before McPhatter joined the Army in 1955. The band continued to tour and record for the next few years and was featured in several major Dick Clark Caravan and Alan Freed tours. By 1958, however, despite the addition of Five Clowns' vocalist Bobby Hendricks, the group had lost its audience and decided to disband. Earlier this year, the Five Clowns, headed by Ben E. King, were persuaded to fulfill the Drifters' contract obligations; and "There Goes My Baby" becomes the first of three gold records the new Drifters will earn this year. Next year, after the major success of "This Magic Moment" and "Save the Last Dance for Me," King will leave for a solo career, although the Drifters will continue their string of hits with "Some Kind of Wonderful," "On Broadway," "Up on the Roof," and "Under the Boardwalk."

Drifters: Breakin' up is hard to do.

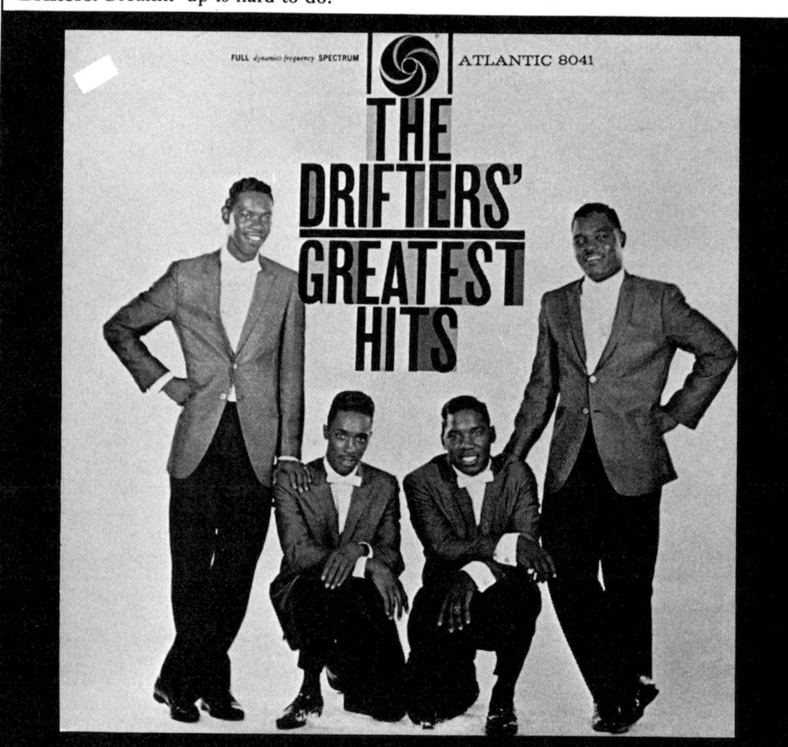

Winning Chipmunks

MAY 4, 1959. The first annual Grammy Awards are presented by the National Academy of Recording Arts and Sciences. Winners have been selected by more than 3,000 voting members of the Academy, each a creative contributor to the recording industry. Among this year's winners are the Kingston Trio for "Tom Dooley," Domenico Modugno's "Volare," Perry Como's "Catch a Falling Star," Henry Mancini's "Peter Gunn," and the Champs, for "Tequila." Also honored are Ella Fitzgerald, Count Basie, the original cast recording of "The Music Man," and Ross Bagdasarian for "The Chipmunk Song," which wins three awards, the most this year.

Tape It or Leave It

JUNE 1, 1959. *Billboard* reports that taping of music off the radio is growing rapidly among American teenagers, but doesn't associate this trend with the decreased number of million-seller albums in recent years.

My Little Runaway

JUNE 5, 1959. Robert Zimmerman, 18, graduates from Hibbing High School in Hibbing, Minn. Having previously run away from home at ages 10, 12, 13, 15, 15½, and 17, he will soon head down U.S. Highway 61 to Minneapolis, where he will enroll at the University of Minnesota arts school on a scholarship.

Flashback

57 Varieties of Dance Steps

The Alligator
The Barefoot
The Bear Hug
The Bird
The Boogaloo
The Bop
The Boston Monkey
The Bristol Stomp
The Bump
The Bus Stop
The Calypso
The Chicken
The Circle
The Continental Walk
The Crawl
The Duck
The Fish
The Fly
The Freddie
The Frug
The Funky Chicken
The Grind
The Hand Jive
The Hitchhiker
The Horse
The Hully Gully
The Jerk
The Junkanoo
The Latin Hustle
The Limbo
The Locomotion
The Madison
The Maverick
The Mashed Potato
The Monkey
The Mouse
The Philly Dog
The Pogo
The Pony
The Popeye
The Queenstown
The Shag
The Shake
The Shimmy
The Shuffle
The Skate
The Slop
The Strand
The Stroll
The Swim
The Temptation Walk
The Tuna
The Twine
The Twist
The Waddle
The Walk
The Watusi

Baez, Dylan: Music with a message.

Baez' Best

JULY 11, 1959. Joan Baez, 18, makes her debut at the first Newport Folk Festival, where she sings "the Virgin Mary had a little baby" and is well received by the audience. The daughter of a physicist and a drama professor, she began playing guitar at age 12. After her graduation from high school in Palo Alto, Calif., her family moved to Boston, where she was introduced to the Coffee Grinder, a local folk music coffeehouse. As she began singing in such Boston coffeehouses as the Golden Vanity, the Ballad Room, and Club '47, she acquired as followers Theodore Bikel and Harry Belafonte, the latter of whom invited her to sing with his group. While performing in Chicago in 1959, she was invited to play at the upcoming Newport festival. Although not listed on the program, her clear, vibrant, strong voice will bring the crowd to its feet. By 1961 she will produce a record a year for several years. Increasingly, she will become one of the most visible members of the vanguard for social justice and change in America: in 1963 she will refuse to sing on ABC-TV's "Hootenanny" in protest of the show's blacklisting of folksinger Pete Seeger; the following year she will begin withholding part of her federal income taxes to protest defense spending; a year later she will co-found the Institute for the Study of Non-Violence in Carmel, Calif.

Goodnight, Lady Day

JULY 17, 1959. Legendary vocalist Billie Holiday dies at age 44 of a drug overdose. Known as a blues singer, her unique singing style transcended any one musical genre. Some likened her voice to a brass instrument, pouring out small, cool tones much the way Louis Armstrong did with his trumpet. Her ability to shape a melody endowed her songs with an intense emotionality that became her signature. Born in Baltimore in 1915, she began earning a living at age six, scrubbing doorsteps and bathrooms in her neighborhood. When her mother moved to New York to work as a maid, Billie lived with her grandparents. At age 13 she too moved to New York and found herself working in a brothel in Harlem. When she refused to service a client who happened to be a political power broker, she ended up in jail for four months. Upon her release, she turned to her principal source of comfort—music—as a means for living. Hired by one Harlem dive after another, she worked her way up the club hierarchy, graduating to the more prestigious clubs frequented by top musicians and producers. One listener was John Hammond, a jazz critic who was immediately taken by her sound. Another who heard her was Benny Goodman, who invited her to record with him in 1933. Later, she landed her own contract with Decca and toured as vocalist with the bands of Count Basie and Artie Shaw. Although she never made much money from her recordings, she was paid well for her performances to support her growing addiction to drugs. By the late 1940s, she had spent time in a sanatorium and again in prison. She continued to perform despite constant emotional pain. Last

> *"I don't want to be the world's oldest living folk singer."*
> **Joan Baez**

month, she was arrested again for heroin but was spared a prison sentence by her quiet death in a hospital bed. In 1972 her story will be dramatized in the movie *Lady Sings the Blues* starring Diana Ross as Holiday.

Darin Does Vegas

OCTOBER 9, 1959. Bobby Darin opens at the Sands Hotel in Las Vegas at age 22, the youngest performer ever to headline there. Darin first drew attention in 1956 when he was introduced to the world by the Dorsey brothers on their weekly CBS-TV program "Stage Show" as "the 19-year-old singing sensation." He already has several hits to his name, the first being "Splish Splash," which he wrote with Jean Murray at the suggestion of his mother's friend. Later this year he will win a Grammy for "Mack the Knife," which will be named "Record of the Year." Darin will die in 1973 at age 37 during his second open-heart surgery.

Flashback
Dance Spots

- BBC, Chicago
- Cardinal Bar, Madison, Wisc.
- The Cave, Washington, D.C.
- Cinnamon Cinder, Denver
- Emerald City, Cherry Hill, N.J.
- Faces, Chicago
- Fire Alarm, Appleton, Wisc.
- The Gangplank, Washington, D.C.
- Gerards, Baltimore
- K-K-K-Katy's, Boston
- Lucifer's, Boston
- Mad Hatter, Milwaukee
- MGM Grande, Chicago
- Mothers, Milwaukee
- Mr. Ricky's, Chicago
- Peppermint Lounge, New York
- The Pier, Washington, D.C.
- Rogue's Gallery, Virginia Beach, Va.
- Teddy's, Milwaukee
- Teendezvous, New Shrewsbury, N.J.
- Tramps, Washington, D.C.
- Wagners, Philadelphia

Next Stop, Greenwich Village

JANUARY 18, 1960. Robert Zimmerman drops out of art school to focus on his guitar playing and singing. Using the last name "Dylan," derived from poet Dylan Thomas, he will perform at local clubs like the Scholar for $2 to $3 a night; he'll quit when he demands and is refused a raise to $5. Within a year, he will head to New York City with little more than his guitar and the clothes on his back. In 1970, despite his short tenure in college, he will receive an honorary degree from Princeton.

All That Glitters

FEBRUARY 17, 1960. Elvis Presley receives his first gold album, for "Elvis," which will be followed by 37 other gold and four platinum albums.

Cooke's Tour

MARCH 14, 1960. Sam Cooke begins his first tour of the Caribbean with a concert in Montego Bay, Jamaica. Cooke, whose previous songs made the rhythm-and-blues charts, including a blockbuster hit, "You Send Me," will set attendance records during his two-week West Indies tour. Among those he will influence are several Jamaican singers, including Bob Marley and Jimmy Smith. Later this year he will sign with RCA Victor, for which he will record several hits, including "Another Saturday Night," "Chain Gang," and "Twistin' the Night Away," before he is shot to death in 1964 at age 29 by a female motel operator who claimed Cooke was about to attack her.

His Master's Voices

APRIL 4, 1960. RCA Victor becomes the first company to release all 45 rpm singles in both mono and stereo.

On Borrowed Time

APRIL 17, 1960. Eddie Cochran, whose "Summertime Blues," released in 1958, is a rock 'n' roll classic, dies of multiple head wounds after his chauffeur-driven limousine crashes into a lamppost. Cochran had been scheduled to accompany Buddy Holly on his fatal concert tour and had told friends since Holly's death that he was living on borrowed time. Gene Vincent, of "Be-Bop-a-Lula" fame, was with Cochran in the limo; although he will survive the crash, an old Army leg wound will be aggravated. In constant pain, Vincent will turn to alcohol, from which he will die in 1967.

Pocketful of Miracles

MAY 16, 1960. According to *Billboard*, Detroit songwriter and record producer Berry Gordy, Jr. is about to start his own record label. Son of a Georgia-born plasterer, Gordy grew up in the Detroit slums, dropped out of high school, and pursued his interest in music and boxing. A professional featherweight, he won 10 of 14 bouts, then grew discouraged because he "never fought anybody worthwhile." After a stint in the Army he opened a record shop but went broke. Now 30, a $90-a-week chrome trimmer at a local Ford Motor Company assembly plant, Gordy has spent his spare time writing songs, some of which have been used by local singers. In recent months, friends have convinced Gordy to start his own company to record several promising local groups, including the Miracles, headed by William "Smokey" Robinson. With $700, borrowed mostly from his family's credit union, he will start Gordy Records. Its first release, by the Miracles, will be a Gordy tune, "Way Over There," which will sell a remarkable 60,000 copies. The company will do well enough to spawn two labels, Tamla and Motown. It will be the Tamla label that produces the first hit, "Shop Around," another Gordy tune performed by the Miracles. By the end of next year, Gordy will boast his first gold record,

"Please Mr. Postman," recorded by the Marvelettes, followed by records from Mary Wells, Marvin Gaye, Martha and the Vandellas, Little Stevie Wonder, the Temptations, and the Supremes. In 1967, Gordy-produced records will reach sales of $30 million. As well as virtually creating the "Detroit sound" and launching the careers of a score of seminal performers, Gordy will break ground for blacks in the record business, an industry almost exclusively white up to this point; and will demonstrate that hits can be produced outside New York and Los Angeles, the two meccas of American music.

Miracles: Motown music moguls.

Flashback

Top Singles—1960

A Big Hunk of Love	Elvis Presley
Alley Oop	Hollywood Argyles
Are You Lonesome Tonight?	Elvis Presley
Baby (You Got What It Takes)	Brook Benton and Dinah Washington
Bye, Bye Baby	Mary Wells
Cathy's Clown	Everly Brothers
Chain Gang	Sam Cooke
Georgia On My Mind	Ray Charles
Handy Man	Jimmy Jones
I'm Sorry	Brenda Lee
It's Now or Never	Elvis Presley
Itsy Bitsy Teenie Weenie Yellow Polkadot Bikini	Lee Pockriss and Paul J. Vance
Let the Little Girl Dance	Bobby "Blue" Bland
Mr. Custer	Larry Verne
New Orleans	Gary "U.S." Bond
Only the Lonely	Roy Orbison
Puppy Love	Paul Anka
Running Bear	Johnny Preston
Save the Last Dance for Me	Drifters
Shop Around	Miracles
Stuck On You	Elvis Presley
Sweet Sixteen	B.B. King
Teen Angel	Mark Dinning
Tell Laura I Love Her	Ray Peterson
Theme From *A Summer Place*	Percy Faith
The Twist	Chubby Checker
Walk, Don't Run	Ventures
Why	Frankie Avalon
You Got What It Takes	Marv Johnson
You Talk Too Much	Joe Jones

Top Albums—1960

Genius of Ray Charles	Ray Charles
G.I. Blues	Elvis Presley
Gotta Move Your Baby	Lightnin' Hopkins
Joan Baez	Joan Baez
More Chuck Berry	Chuck Berry
Nice 'n' Easy	Frank Sinatra
String Along	Kingston Trio
Theme From *A Summer Place*	Billy Vaughn
Walk Don't Run	Ventures

Venture Capital

JULY 24, 1960. "Walk Don't Run," released on a private label by lead guitarist Don Wilson's mother, becomes a regional hit on the West Coast; picked up and distributed by Liberty Records, it will mark the first chart appearance of the Ventures and the beginning of a craze for instrumental rock that will keep the Ventures in business for more than two decades. Their sound, a blend of insistent, Kahuna-crazy drumming and somber reverb guitar, will make such hits as "Telstar" and "Ghost Riders in the Sky" into compulsory courses for a whole generation of aspiring rock musicians. The Ventures' sound will be apparent in early Beach Boys and Jan and Dean surfing songs. The Ventures also will be the first rock group to record and make hits of TV and movie themes, including "Batman" and their most widely recognized signature, "Hawaii Five-O."

Ray Times Four

NOVEMBER 21, 1960. Four songs by Ray Charles are currently on the charts: "Georgia on My Mind," which will win him a Grammy award, "Hard Hearted Hannah," "Come Rain or Come Shine," and "Ruby." Charles, 31, has been making records for nearly a decade and is considered one of the most versatile singers in the business, crossing over from rhythm and blues to rock, pop, and country. His recent rise, however, is attributed in part to his having changed labels, from Atlantic to ABC-Paramount, which has permitted him the flexibility he demands. In 1962 ABC-Paramount will create a new subsidiary label for Charles, Tangerine, under Charles' artistic control. Eventually, though, he will form his own label, appropriately named Crossover.

Hello, Stranger

DECEMBER 25, 1960. Detroit native Mary Wells, at 17 already a seven-year veteran of local church and music events, celebrates Christmas by watching her own composition, "Bye Bye Baby," reach the rhythm-and-blues top 10. Wells' first hit is one of Motown's first as well; Wells was "discovered" at a walk-in audition for aspiring artists. She will become Berry Gordy's first teen queen, supplying Motown with 11 pop hits in the next five years, many of them—including "My Guy," a top-10 hit in England as well as the U.S.—tailored for her by writer/producer Smokey Robinson. Wells also will be the first in a series of female vocalists to be paired with Marvin Gaye. Although her record sales will slow after she leaves Motown, Wells will continue to be a successful nightclub and revue performer.

Smokey and the Band Hits

FEBRUARY 12, 1961. "Shop Around," written by Smokey Robinson, becomes Motown's first million-seller, kicking off what will be a 15-year string of chartbusters for the Miracles. Although the group, whose members began singing together as soon as they entered high school, have already released a couple of earlier hits on the Chess label, it is the soul brotherhood of the 18-year-old Robinson and producer Berry Gordy that has launched Motown. As songwriter, producer, vice president, and falsetto star, Robinson will be greatly responsible for the sound of Motown, as well as its look—the Miracles are early proponents of the coordinated dress and choreography that will become a Motown hallmark. After more than 10 years Robinson will leave the Miracles, ostensibly to devote more time to his executive duties with the label, although his first solo album will follow quickly.

Robinson: Miracle worker.

Leader of the Pack

MARCH 10, 1961. Jeff Barry signs an exclusive songwriting contract with Trinity Music, ushering in rock's own Tin Pan Alley era. Along with Ellie Greenwich, whom he will marry next year; the other husband-and-wife teams of Carole King and Gerry Goffin and Barry Man and Cynthia Weil; Neil Sedaka and Howard Greenfield, among others, Barry will develop a pop hit production line that will make Brooklyn a musical mecca. Among the Barry-Greenwich creations will be: "Da Doo Ron Ron" (Crystals), "Chapel of Love" (Dixie Cups), "Leader of the Pack" (Shangri-Las), "Chery Chery" (Neil Diamond, who will eventually join the songwriting troops), and "Do Wah Diddy" (Manfred Mann).

Moondog Serenade

MARCH 21, 1961. Johnny and the Moondogs perform at the Cavern Club, a dank basement club in downtown Liverpool. The group soon will become the house band, playing at lunchtime and some evenings for 25 shillings a day. The group has changed its name to the Silver Beatles, a name derived partly from admiration for Buddy Holly's group, the Crickets. (The spelling of the insect was changed slightly to form the word "beat"; the word "silver" was tagged on in an attempt to add class but will soon be dropped.) The group includes John Lennon, Paul

The History of the Twist

It began with a rock song, "The Twist," by Hank Ballard, written in 1958 and released a year later by Hank Ballard and the Midnighters. The song went largely unnoticed until 1961, when Chubby Checker recorded the song and it soon became a runaway bestseller. Checker, a 20-year-old singer and dancer from Philadelphia, was born Ernest Evans. He was an admirer of Antoine "Fats" Domino, a rhythm 'n' blues singer and songwriter, whose first hit was "The Fat Man," a song Domino, who weighed 250 pounds, had written about himself. Checker's name, in fact, was a take-off on Domino's, whom Checker resembled physically.

Prior to his musical career, Checker had been a chicken plucker who was always entertaining friends with his singing. His songwriter/friend Kal Mann became convinced that Checker had professional potential. Mann wrote "The Class," which Checker recorded. Its success led to other releases, one of which was "The Twist."

Checker performed "The Twist" on "The Ed Sullivan Show" on June 14, 1961, adding a solo dance as he sang. The performance has been credited with starting a nationwide, then worldwide, craze for the new dance. Describing his new dance, Checker explained: "There are no basic steps. You move chest, hips, and arms from side to side and balance on the balls of the feet."

Craze status notwithstanding, the Twist came under fierce attack in some circles. In early 1962, for example, Bishop Burke of the Buffalo, N.Y., Catholic Diocese banned the Twist from being danced, sung about, or listened to in any Catholic school, parish, or youth organization. Later that year, the Twist was banned from community center dances in Tampa, Fla., and several other cities. Writing in *New York* magazine, Beverly Nichols observed that "The essence of the Twist, the curious perverted heart of it, is that you dance it alone."

Ultimately, more than 300 songs were inspired by the Twist, from Checker's own "Let's Twist Again" (which won a 1961 Grammy as the year's best recording) to Sam Cooke's "Twistin' the Night Away" and the Beatles' "Twist and Shout."

Checker: "There are no basic steps."

Revere, Raiders: Ersatz English.

McCartney, George Harrison, and an assortment of drummers, most notably Pete Best.

Blue Hawaii

MARCH 25, 1961. Elvis Presley performs a concert at Pearl Harbor, a benefit for the U.S.S. Arizona memorial fund. It will be his last live performance for eight years.

Like Long Hair

APRIL 2, 1961. Paul Revere and the Raiders, whose Revolutionary-Edwardian uniforms and clubbed hair will lend them the look of a British Invasion group, slide in on the ground floor of the rock revolution with a Northwest regional hit called "Like Long Hair," followed by a version of "Louie, Louie." In 1965 the Raiders' first national hit, "Steppin' Out," will catch the ear of Dick Clark, preparing to launch "Where the Action Is" for ABC-TV. As regulars on the show, the band will become teen idols, especially vocalist Mark Lindsay, who will dominate teen fan mags like *16*. The band's major hits, including "Kicks," "Hungry," and "Good Thing," will stretch into the early 1970s.

Vinyl Tribute

APRIL 11, 1961. Bob Dylan, 19, newly arrived in New York, makes his stage debut, opening for John Lee Hooker at Gerde's Folk City in Greenwich Village—a venue that appears to bring him luck. In two weeks Dylan will make his recording debut playing harmonica behind Harry Belafonte on "Midnight Special," earning him $50. In September Dylan will return to Gerde's as the opening act for the Greenbriar Boys; this time his performance will garner his first press notice—in the *New York Times*, no less. The next day, he will play harmonica on a Caroline Hester album being produced by John Hammond, who will be so impressed he will sign Dylan to a Columbia Records contract on the spot. His first album will be recorded in October—all in one day—at a cost of $400.

Ten Years After

MAY 31, 1961. Marking the end of Chuck Berry's first decade in the music business, a theme park named in his honor opens in Wentzville, Mo., near St. Louis, where he grew up (he was born in San Jose, Calif.). Berry actually studied to be a cosmetician, a trade he practiced for about six months. He formed a combo in 1952 and wrote "Ida

"My songs don't have any meaning. They're just words."
Bob Dylan

Red" for the Chess brothers, owners of a small record company. Later, they changed the song's title to "Maybellene," which caught the ears of Alan Freed and other mid-1950s disk jockeys. In the years since, he has written a score of classics, including "Johnny B. Goode," "Roll Over Beethoven," and "Sweet Little Sixteen," a song that will appear in a revised form in two years as the Beach Boys' "Surfin' U.S.A."

Berry: A score of classics.

Flashback

Top Singles—1961

Big Bad John	Jimmy Dean
Blue Moon	Marcels
Bristol Stomp	Dovells
Cryin'	Roy Orbison
Every Beat of My Heart	Gladys Knight and the Pips
Happy Birthday Sweet Sixteen	Neil Sedaka
Hit the Road Jack	Ray Charles
I Like It Like That	Chris Kenner
In the Still of the Night	Five Satins
It's Gonna Work Out Fine	Ike and Tina Turner
(I Wanna) Love My Life Away	Gene Pitney
The Lion Sleeps Tonight	Tokens
Mama Said	Shirelles
Mother-in-Law	Ernie K-Doe
One Hundred Pounds of Clay	Gene McDaniels
Please, Mr. Postman	Marvelettes
Pony Time	Chubby Checker
Quarter to Three	Gary "U.S." Bonds
Rain Drops	Dee Clark
Runaround Sue	Dion
Runaway	Del Shannon
Running Scared	Roy Orbison
Shop Around	Miracles
Spanish Harlem	Ben E. King
Stand By Me	Ben E. King
Take Good Care of My Baby	Bobby Vee
Those Oldies But Goodies	Little Caesar and the Romans
Tossin' and Turnin'	Bobby Lewis
Who Put the Bomp?	Barry Mann
Will You Still Love Me Tomorrow?	Shirelles

Top Albums—1961

Blue Hawaii	Elvis Presley
The Bobby Darin Story	Bobby Darin
Bob Dylan	Bob Dylan
Bye Bye Baby	Mary Wells
Calcutta	Lawrence Welk
Camelot	soundtrack
Judy at Carnegie Hall	Judy Garland
Somethin' for Everybody	Elvis Presley
Wonderland by Night	Bert Kaempfert

Supremes: Dream Girls' debut.

In the Name of Love

JULY 17, 1961. The Supremes, previously known as the Primettes (the Primes will become the Temptations), release their first single on Motown Records. Although Diana Ross, Florence Ballard, and Mary Wilson had been singing together around Detroit since elementary school, Motown founder Berry Gordy told them to finish high school before signing a contract; even then he allowed them to start only as a backup group. For the next three years, Gordy will put the three through a polishing—overseeing their dress, makeup, hairstyles, and even diction training—that will become almost a formal part of the "Motown finishing school." Gordy will release a few carefully chosen singles while the fledgling Supremes work day jobs and rehearse at night, performing on weekends. By the summer of 1964, "Where Did Our Love Go?" will sell two million copies nationwide. "Baby Love" (originally released in 1961) will top the singles charts and the group will not drop out of the top 10 until the end of 1969, when Ross will leave to start a solo career. In 1965-66 the Supremes will be the first American group to have five successive songs hit number one. Ballard, who will be replaced by Cindy Birdsong in 1967 because the stress is affecting her health, will die, a welfare recipient, in 1976.

Piano Man

OCTOBER 23, 1961. Pianist Dave Brubeck's "Take Five" single reaches the number-25 spot on the pop charts, the first jazz single to break the top 40.

We Can Work It Out

OCTOBER 28, 1961. The first of several customers enters Liverpool's North End Music Store, searching for "My Bonnie," a record made in Germany by a group called the Beatles. Discovering that the group performs daily at the Cavern Club, some 200 yards away, music shop manager Brian Epstein will go listen. Impressed, he will begin a long campaign to get close to the group, particularly to John Lennon, for whom Epstein develops a deep sexual attraction. Although the Beatles (and some of their parents) are initially suspicious of the "Jew boy," the suave Epstein will seduce the band into letting him be its manager, even though he is woefully unprepared for such a role. Their management agreement will be modeled after a mail-order contract Epstein has purchased for the occasion.

New Wave

DECEMBER 8, 1961. At the suggestion of his brother Dennis, the only one of the three Wilson brothers ever to have set foot on a surfboard, Brian Wilson writes "Surfin'," which has been released first on a local California label before making the national charts. Nearly frozen with stage fright, the band will be booked for its first live appearance on New Year's Eve at the Municipal Audi-

Beach Boys: Surfing, cruising, making out.

torium in Long Beach; despite a repertoire of only three songs, it will be a hit. "Carl and the Passions" will rechristen themselves the Beach Boys and become the most famous proponents of surf rock—a melodic, often intricately harmonized mythology of surfing, cruising, and making out.

Beatles Blow It

JANUARY 1, 1962. Brian Epstein arranges a recording audition for the Beatles at the London studio of Decca Records. The group will be turned down for a recording contract.

Village People

JANUARY 29, 1962. Just when performers such as Harry Belafonte and Odetta have given the "folk music" movement a sense of social consciousness, Peter Yarrow, Paul Stookey, and Mary Travers sign with Warner Bros., becoming a stylized liaison between the Greenwich Village folk scene and the emerging civil rights movement. With their increasingly complex harmonies and arrangements, Peter, Paul, and Mary will give a commercially acceptable gloss to the writings of Pete Seeger, Gordon Lightfoot, and Bob Dylan—most memorably with Dylan's "Blowin' in the Wind," which in 1963 will become an anthem of the March on Washington. Their political activism will backfire among certain audiences; despite their carefully

Flashback

You Knew Them When

Star	*Original Band*
Eric Clapton	The Yardbirds
Dash Croft	The Champs
David Crosby	The Byrds
John Denver	Chad Mitchell Trio
Cass Elliot	The Mugwumps
Jimi Hendrix	Jimmy James and the Blue Flames
Waylon Jennings	Buddy Holly and the Crickets
Billy Joel	The Hassles
Ben E. King	The Drifters
Al Kooper	The Royal Teens
Patti LaBelle	The Blue Belles
Curtis Mayfield	The Impressions
Van Morrison	Them
Graham Nash	The Hollies
Kenny Rogers	The First Edition
Linda Ronstadt	The Stone Poneys
Jim Seals	The Champs
Rod Stewart	Jeff Beck Group
Stephen Stills	Buffalo Springfield
Jackie Wilson	The Dominoes
Stevie Winwood	Spencer Davis Group
Jesse Colin Young	The Youngbloods
Neil Young	Buffalo Springfield

Peter, Paul, Mary: Far-out folkies.

packaged clean image, they will be accused of promoting marijuana with a children's song called "Puff the Magic Dragon."

It's All Right, Ma

MAY 27, 1962. The release of *The Freewheelin' Bob Dylan* marks the first of Dylan's several musical epiphanies: from his interpretation of classic blues and his Woody Guthrie-style talkin' blues, Dylan emerges with several of what will be the most enduring ballads of the decade, including "Blowin' in the Wind," "Don't Think Twice, It's All Right," and "Girl from the North County." With the release next year of *The Times They Are a-Changin'*, Dylan will be well on his way to ensuring his cult figure status.

Mick's Mix

JULY 12, 1962. Mick Jagger and Keith Richard appear with Ian Stewart, Dick Taylor, and future Kinks drummer Mick Avory at the Marquee Club in London. Richard will later remember these days as a time when musicians tended to favor one of two styles: Presley or Holly. Jagger and Richard introduce Jones to the traditional blues they love, and along with Charlie Watts and Bill Wyman, form a group named after a Muddy Waters' song, "Rolling Stone."

Last of the Best

AUGUST 12, 1962. The Beatles audition again, this time at the Abbey Road studios of Parlophone, an obscure comedy and novelty record label owned by EMI. Parlophone producer George Martin will like the group, but not drummer Pete Best. Within days, Best will be fired by manager Brian Epstein and replaced by Richard "Ringo" Starkey, Jr., drummer for Rory Storm and the Hurricanes. Best's sacking will lead to an EMI recording contract, albeit at the ridiculously low royalty rate of a penny per single sold. Best's firing will outrage many fans, who will briefly picket the Cavern Club. Best will become a baker, eventually marrying the biscuit-counter girl at Woolworth's.

Ringo: Better than Best.

Valli Boys

AUGUST 25, 1962. The Four Seasons' "Sherry" hits the charts. In the 1950s the band was known first as the Varietones, then as the Four Lovers, both headed by Frankie Castelluccio, who later changed his last name to Valli. One night after performing at the Four Seasons Cocktail Lounge in a Newark, N.J., bowling alley, they found inspiration for their current name. Centered around Valli's near-screeching falsetto, their first entry moved up the charts quickly, as will a second, "Big Girls Don't Cry," and a third, "Walk Like a Man."

Brian's Song

SEPTEMBER 12, 1962. The Beatles' first EMI recording session is held, resulting in a single, "Love Me Do," backed by "P.S. I Love You." When released in October, the record will receive almost no publicity or support from EMI. Only after a Brian Epstein-orchestrated campaign—with parents, friends, and fans urging radio stations to play the record and Epstein himself ordering 10,000 copies for his stores—will the tunes receive air play, surprising everyone by climbing the charts. A second single, "Please Please Me," will reach number one, selling a half-million copies.

One Fine Day

FEBRUARY 23, 1963. The Chiffons, four recent high school graduates from upper Manhattan and the Bronx, have their first chartmaker with "He's So Fine," which will soon become a millionseller. Although the Chiffons will have several other hits, including "One Fine Day" and "Sweet-Talkin' Guy," they will drop off the charts after the mid-1960s. "He's So Fine" will re-emerge in 1976 when George Harrison is convicted of "subconscious plagiarism" of it in his 1971 number-one single, "My Sweet Lord;" in 1981 Harrison will be ordered to pay $587,000 damages.

Flashback

Top Singles—1962

Baby It's You	Shirelles
Big Girls Don't Cry	Four Seasons
Breaking Up Is Hard to Do	Neil Sedaka
Bring It On Home to Me	Sam Cooke
Can't Help Falling in Love	Elvis Presley
Don't Play That Song	Ben E. King
Dream Baby	Roy Orbison
Duke of Earl	Gene Chandler
He's a Rebel	Crystals
I Can't Stop Loving You	Ray Charles
Johnny Angel	Shelley Fabares
Let's Twist Again	Chubby Checker
Loco-Motion	Little Eva
Monster Mash	Bobby "Boris" Pickett
On Broadway	Drifters
Palisades Park	Freddy Cannon
Party Lights	Claudine Clark
Peppermint Twist	Joey Dee and the Starliters
Return to Sender	Elvis Presley
Roses Are Red	Bobby Vinton
She Cried	Jay and the Americans
Sheila	Tommy Roe
Sherry	Four Seasons
Soldier Boy	Shirelles
Surfin'	Beach Boys
Surfin' Safari	Beach Boys
Telstar	Tornadoes
The Twist	Chubby Checker
Twist and Shout	Isley Brothers
Twistin' the Night Away	Sam Cooke
Up On the Roof	Drifters
What's Your Name?	Don and Juan
You Beat Me to the Punch	Mary Wells

Top Albums—1962

Best of Sam Cooke	Sam Cooke
Breakfast at Tiffany's	Henry Mancini
The Freewheelin' Bob Dylan	Bob Dylan
Girls! Girls! Girls!	Elvis Presley
Ian and Sylvia	Ian and Sylvia
In Concert, Part One	Joan Baez
Only Love Can Break a Heart	Gene Pitney
Peter, Paul and Mary	Peter, Paul, and Mary
Ramblin' Rose	Nat "King" Cole
Stormy Monday	Lou Rawls
Two Lovers	Mary Wells
West Side Story	soundtrack

For Pete's Sake

APRIL 6, 1963. "Hootenanny" premieres on ABC, despite protests of blacklisting of certain musicians, including Pete Seeger, a practice that will end this fall when Seeger is allowed to appear. The show will travel each week to a different college campus, where it will be taped before a live audience. "Hootenanny's" producers will stay away from pure "folkies," opting instead for more commercial acts, like the Chad Mitchell Trio (one of whose members is John Denver), the Limeliters, and the Smothers Brothers.

Seeger: TV taboo.

Wonder Boy

MAY 21, 1963. Little Stevie Wonder records *The Twelve-Year-Old Genius* (although he is now 13) on Berry Gordy's Tamla label. Wonder, blind from birth, was born Steveland Judkins and grew up in Saginaw, Mich. His mother, who separated from her husband while Wonder was an infant, brought her children to Detroit to pursue work. Wonder began playing piano at age four and soon created tunes on a four-hole harmonica. A fan of the rhythm and blues he heard on the radio, he pursued his musical interests with passion. Ronnie White, one of the Miracles, brought Wonder to the Motown studios, fostering what became Wonder's near obsession of hanging out at the studio, playing any instrument he could get his hands on. His ability to play so many instruments and write songs at such a tender age—he wrote "Lonely Boy" when he was 10—led to studio personnel calling him "the little wonder boy." When Motown signed him to his first contract, it dubbed him Little Stevie Wonder (the "Little" will disappear as Wonder grows up). Like most of Gordy's acts, Wonder will take off from his first album, which includes a cut called "Fingertips," the first of many Wonder gold records.

Wonder: Blind ambition.

Out In Left Field

JULY 6, 1963. Chubby Checker and Dee Dee Sharp perform before a Saturday night New York Mets baseball game at New York's Polo Grounds, as Mets management attempts to lure more young people to the game.

We Shall Overcome

AUGUST 28, 1963. Bob Dylan, Odetta, Joan Baez, Mahalia Jackson, and Peter, Paul, and Mary are among the musicians who perform at a massive demonstration on the steps of the Lincoln Memorial in Washington, D.C., as nearly a quarter-million demonstrators rally for civil rights during the March on Washington.

Canned Music

AUGUST 30, 1963. *Time* magazine reports that thanks to Muzak, "the total musicization of

"The electric guitar is an abomination. Who ever has heard of an electric violin? Or, for that matter, an electric singer?"

Andres Segovia

America is by now almost complete." More than 60 million Americans hear the canned music each day, says *Time*—it even plays during top-secret conferences at the Pentagon to confound eavesdroppers. The 29-year-old company has a scientifically developed format designed to increase productivity in offices and factories and boost the moods of shoppers in department stores and the growing number of shopping malls sprouting in suburbs. Says *Time*: "Ladies listening to Muzak through earphones placed in beauty-shop hair dryers have the consolation of knowing that their husbands are hearing the same thing down at the sanitation plant."

Chic, Rattle, Roll

NOVEMBER 5, 1963. The Beatles give a command performance before Princess Margaret and Queen Elizabeth at the Prince of Wales Theatre. On stage, John Lennon requests that "the people in the cheaper seats clap your hands, the rest of you just rattle your jewelry."

Flashback

Top Singles—1963

Another Saturday Night	Sam Cooke
Baby Workout	Jackie Wilson
Be My Baby	Ronettes
Blowin' in the Wind	Peter, Paul, and Mary
Blue Velvet	Bobby Vinton
Da Doo Ron Ron	Crystals
Dominique	Singing Nun
Easier Said Than Done	Essex
Fingertips—Pt. 2	Little Stevie Wonder
Heat Wave	Martha and the Vandellas
He's So Fine	Chiffons
Hey, Paula	Paul and Paula
I Will Follow Him	Little Peggy March
If You Wanna Be Happy	Jimmy Soul
It's My Party	Lesley Gore
Just One Look	Doris Troy
Love Me Do	Beatles
Mickey's Monkey	Miracles
Mockingbird	Inez and Charlie Foxx
My Boyfriend's Back	The Angels
Our Day Will Come	Ruby and the Romantics
Please Please Me	Beatles
Pride and Joy	Marvin Gaye
Release Me	Little Esther Phillips
Rhythm of the Rain	Cascades
Ruby Baby	Drifters
Sally Go Round the Roses	Jaynettes
Sugar Shack	Jimmy Gilmer and the Fireballs
Surfer Girl	Beach Boys
Surfin' U.S.A.	Beach Boys
Two Lovers	Mary Wells
Walk Like a Man	Four Seasons
Walk Right In	Roof Top Singers
You've Really Got a Hold On Me	Miracles

Top Albums—1963

Call On Me	Bobby "Blue" Bland
Freewheelin' Bob Dylan	Bob Dylan
In the Wind	Peter, Paul, and Mary
Jim Kweskin and the Jug Band	Jim Kweskin
Judy Collins #3	Judy Collins
Little Deuce Coup	Beach Boys
The 12-Year-Old Genius	Stevie Wonder
Peter, Paul, and Mary in the Wind	Peter, Paul, and Mary
Surfin' U.S.A.	Beach Boys
The Singing Nun	The Singing Nun
We Shall Overcome	Pete Seeger

All the Kingsmen

FEBRUARY 3, 1964. "Louie, Louie" by the Kingsmen is declared to be "pornographic" by Indiana governor Matthew Welsh, who asks Indiana radio stations to stop playing the tune. The governor's request will intensify the debate over whether the song does contain sexual references, a question clouded by the fact that no one will be able to say for certain exactly what the Kingsmen's lyrics are. That small problem notwithstanding, the Whatcom, Wash. county council will pass a resolution in 1985 recommending that "Louie, Louie"—by the Washington-based Kingsmen—be proclaimed the official Washington state song, a recommendation that won't garner much attention outside the county.

The Big Shoe

FEBRUARY 7, 1964. The Beatles arrive in the U.S. to appear on the top-rated "Ed Sullivan Show." Their single on Capitol Records (EMI's American affiliate), "I Want to Hold Your Hand," has just sold 3.5 million copies in a few weeks and their first album, *Meet the Beatles*, has become the fastest-selling album in American history. The Beatles' U.S. arrival will be a major news event, with radio stations providing moment-by-moment bulletins. Capitol Records has cleverly prerecorded interview answers with the band for use by local DJs, creating the effect of an exclusive hometown interview. Their first night in America, George Harrison will come down with the flu, creating more breathless news

Harrison: Feverish debut.

Flashback
Top Singles—1964

A Hard Day's Night	Beatles
A World Without Love	Peter and Gordon
Always Something There to Remind Me	Sandie Shaw
Baby I Need Your Loving	Four Tops
Baby Love	Supremes
Can't Buy Me Love	Beatles
Chapel of Love	Dixie Cups
Do Wah Diddy Diddy	Manfred Mann
Downtown	Petula Clark
Glad All Over	Dave Clark Five
Hi Heel Sneakers	Tommy Tucker
House of the Rising Sun	Animals
How Sweet It Is (to Be Loved By You)	Marvin Gaye
I Feel Fine	Beatles
I Get Around	Beach Boys
I Want to Hold Your Hand	Beatles
Leader of the Pack	Shangri-Las
Little Marie	Chuck Berry
Little Red Rooster	Rolling Stones
Louie Louie	Kingsmen
My Guy	Mary Wells
Nadine	Chuck Berry
No Particular Place to Go	Chuck Berry
Oh, Pretty Woman	Roy Orbison
Rag Doll	Four Seasons
Reach Out For Me	Dionne Warwick
Ringo	Lorne Greene
Running Out of Fools	Aretha Franklin
She Loves You	Beatles
She's Not There	Zombies
Under the Boardwalk	Drifters
Walk On By	Dionne Warwick
Where Did Our Love Go?	Supremes
You Really Got Me	Kinks

coverage. Despite his fever, he will perform on the show for more than 70 million viewers.

British Invaders

FEBRUARY 15, 1964. On the heels of the Beatles' U.S. visit, *Billboard* heralds the "British invasion," stating that England "hasn't been as influential to American affairs since 1775." Indeed, British groups will be anxious to capture a piece of the Beatles' success in the lucrative American market. In coming months, American teenagers will see a steady stream of British musicians, including the Dave Clark Five, Gerry and the Pacemakers, Freddie and the Dreamers, the Yardbirds, the Hollies, Dusty Springfield, the Animals, the Who, the Rolling Stones, the Kinks, and Herman's Hermits.

Ticky Tacky

FEBRUARY 28, 1964. "Little Boxes," a song by 63-year-old Malvina Reynolds, makes *Billboard's* "hot 100" list. The song, which describes "little boxes made of ticky tacky," was inspired by monotonous rows of cheap tract homes in Daly City, Calif., a suburb of San Francisco. The song will become an anthem for a generation fighting the trend to grow up and adopt the conformist suburban lifestyle.

Feat of Clay

MARCH 3, 1964. On the heels of Cassius Clay's defeat of Sonny Liston, Clay's six-month-old album, "I Am the Greatest," becomes a hot seller. Clay will tell the press, "I'm prettier than Chubby Checker."

> *"Groups of guitars are on the way out."*
>
> **Decca record company executive to the Beatles**

Hello, Satchmo

MAY 9, 1964. Louis Armstrong's rendition of "Hello, Dolly!" becomes the first song in months to knock the Beatles off the top of the bestseller charts. Armstrong's is only one version of the tune, which has been performed in recent months by everyone from Paul Anka to Benny Goodman to Andre Kostelanetz.

This Could Be the Last Time

JUNE 1, 1964. The Rolling Stones arrive in New York to begin their first U.S. tour, which will include opening sets by Bobby Goldsboro, Bobby Vee, and the Chiffons; and an appearance on the TV show "Hollywood Palace," hosted by Dean Martin. Concert promoters are nervous about the tour, fearing that the mugging and riots that took place at some Stones' performances in Europe will dog them on their American visit. The fears will turn out to be ill-founded; there will be

Flashback
Top Albums—1964

A Hard Day's Night	Beatles
Ain't Nothin' You Can Do	Bobby "Blue" Bland
Ain't That Good News	Sam Cooke
All Summer Long	Beach Boys
All the News That's Fit to Sing	Phil Ochs
The Beach Boys Concert	Beach Boys
The Beatles' Second Album	Beatles
Beatles '65	Beatles
Chuck Berry's Greatest Hits	Chuck Berry
Golden Hits of Jerry Lee Lewis	Jerry Lee Lewis
Hello, Dolly	Louis Armstrong
It Hurts to Be in Love	Gene Pitney
It's My Way	Buffy Sainte-Marie
The Judy Collins Concert	Judy Collins
Meet the Beatles	Beatles
Meet the Temptations	Temptations
People	Barbra Streisand
The Rolling Stones	Rolling Stones
The Times They Are a-Changin'	Bob Dylan
Unforgettable	Aretha Franklin
You Really Got Me	Kinks

no major problems on this trip, although violence will infect future Rolling Stones U.S. performances. Meanwhile, screaming teenage girls will riot later this month at a Beatles concert in Cleveland.

Help!

AUGUST 7, 1964. *Time* magazine pans the Beatles' new film, *A Hard Day's Night*, advising readers to "avoid this film at all costs."

A Hard Day's Night

Concert fans:
Voices of approval.

John, Paul, George, Ringo, and Simon

AUGUST 24, 1964. *The Chipmunks Sing the Beatles Hits*, an album by Alvin, Theodore, and Simon (courtesy of Ross Bagdasarian, a.k.a. David Seville), is released in the U.S. It reportedly will sell up to 25,000 copies a day for several weeks.

Going to Pot

AUGUST 28, 1964. During the group's second U.S. tour, Bob Dylan turns the Beatles on to marijuana for the first time, in their room at the Delmonico Hotel in New York. The four Beatles, who for years had hyped themselves up on amphetamines before performances, were at first reluctant to get high, equating dope smokers with heroin junkies. The event is pivotal for the group's members: they will soon begin composing while stoned.

All Together Now

SEPTEMBER 20, 1964. In their last concert of the tour, the Beatles perform at a cerebral palsy benefit in Brooklyn, sharing the bill with Steve Lawrence and Eydie Gorme.

Nice, Neat Boys

NOVEMBER 1, 1964. In their first U.S. tour, the Dave Clark Five perform their hit "Glad All Over" on "The Ed Sullivan

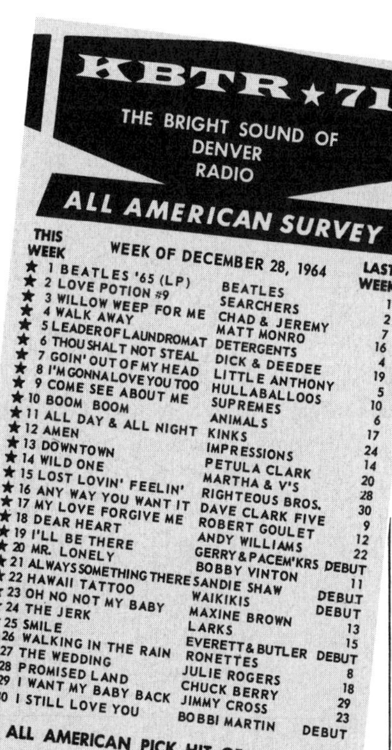

KBTR ★ 71
THE BRIGHT SOUND OF DENVER RADIO
ALL AMERICAN SURVEY
WEEK OF DECEMBER 28, 1964

THIS WEEK			LAST WEEK
★ 1	BEATLES '65 (LP)	BEATLES	1
★ 2	LOVE POTION #9	SEARCHERS	2
★ 3	WILLOW WEEP FOR ME	CHAD & JEREMY	7
★ 4	WALK AWAY	MATT MONRO	16
★ 5	LEADER OF LAUNDROMAT	DETERGENTS	4
★ 6	THOU SHALT NOT STEAL	DICK & DEEDEE	19
★ 7	GOIN' OUT OF MY HEAD	LITTLE ANTHONY	5
★ 8	I'M GONNA LOVE YOU TOO	HULLABALLOOS	10
★ 9	COME SEE ABOUT ME	SUPREMES	6
★ 10	BOOM BOOM	ANIMALS	17
★ 11	ALL DAY & ALL NIGHT	KINKS	24
★ 12	AMEN	IMPRESSIONS	14
★ 13	DOWNTOWN	PETULA CLARK	20
★ 14	WILD ONE	MARTHA & V'S	28
★ 15	LOST LOVIN' FEELIN'	RIGHTEOUS BROS.	30
★ 16	ANY WAY YOU WANT IT	DAVE CLARK FIVE	9
★ 17	MY LOVE FORGIVE ME	ROBERT GOULET	12
★ 18	DEAR HEART	ANDY WILLIAMS	22
★ 19	I'LL BE THERE	GERRY & PACEM'KRS	DEBUT
★ 20	MR. LONELY	BOBBY VINTON	11
★ 21	ALWAYS SOMETHING THERE	SANDIE SHAW	DEBUT
★ 22	HAWAII TATTOO	WAIKIKIS	DEBUT
★ 23	OH NO NOT MY BABY	MAXINE BROWN	13
★ 24	THE JERK	LARKS	15
★ 25	SMILE	EVERETT & BUTLER	DEBUT
★ 26	WALKING IN THE RAIN	RONETTES	8
★ 27	THE WEDDING	JULIE ROGERS	18
★ 28	PROMISED LAND	CHUCK BERRY	29
★ 29	I WANT MY BABY BACK	JIMMY CROSS	23
★ 30	I STILL LOVE YOU	BOBBI MARTIN	DEBUT

ALL AMERICAN PICK HIT OF THE WEEK
TERRY TWINKLE

Show." The song had made news in England last year by becoming the first to knock the Beatles out of the top spot on British record charts. Sullivan calls the group "nice, neat boys." In the next year, the group will receive three gold records for "Catch Us If You Can," "I Like It Like That," and "Over and Over."

Dance the Night Away

JANUARY 12, 1965. "Hullabaloo" debuts on NBC-TV in response to ABC's successful show, "Shindig!" On the opening show, host Jack Jones introduces Gerry and the Pacemakers, the New Christy Minstrels, and comedian Woody Allen.

Rivers a-Go-Go

JANUARY 15, 1965. Elmer Valentine opens the Whiskey a-Go-Go in Los Angeles. Valentine already owned an L.A. night spot called PJ, but while vacationing in Paris, he visited the original Whiskey a-Go-Go in that city, a "discotheque" where customers dance to recorded rock music. For opening night of his new L.A. club, Valentine hires Johnny Rivers, a relative unknown, to perform. Rivers' performance, which is recorded, will launch the top-10 hit "Memphis" and launch him as the first rock star to emerge from a discotheque. The album, meanwhile, will help create a boom in discotheques, with close to 5,000 venues opening within a year, 20 in Manhattan alone.

Rivers: Go-Go boy.

BOOM! MUSIC

Flashback

Top Singles—1965

As Tears Go By	Rolling Stones
California Girls	Beach Boys
Can't Help Myself	Four Tops
Day Tripper	Beatles
Do You Believe In Magic?	Lovin' Spoonful
Eight Days a Week	Beatles
Eve of Destruction	Barry McGuire
For Your Love	Yardbirds
Get Off My Cloud	Rolling Stones
Help Me, Rhonda	Beach Boys
Here Comes the Night	Them
(I Can't Get No) Satisfaction	Rolling Stones
I Can't Help Myself	Four Tops
I Got You (I Feel Good)	James Brown
I Got You Babe	Sonny and Cher
I Hear a Symphony	Supremes
I Know a Place	Petula Clark
The In Crowd	Dobie Gray
In the Midnight Hour	Wilson Pickett
I've Been Loving You Too Long	Otis Redding
King of the Road	Roger Miller
The Last Time	Rolling Stones
Lightning Strikes	Lou Christie
Like a Rolling Stone	Bob Dylan
Mr. Tambourine Man	Byrds
Mrs. Brown, You've Got a Lovely Daughter	Herman's Hermits
My Generation	Who
My Girl	Temptations
The Name Game	Shirley Ellis
1-2-3	Len Barry
Over and Over	Dave Clark Five
Papa's Got a Brand New Bag	James Brown
Rescue Me	Fontella Bass
Ride Your Pony	Lee Dorsey
She's About a Mover	Sir Douglas Quintet
Shotgun	Jr. Walker and the All Stars
Stop! In the Name of Love	Supremes
Ticket to Ride	Beatles
The Times They Are A-Changin'	Bob Dylan
Tired of Waiting for You	Kinks
The Tracks of My Tears	Smokey Robinson and the Miracles
Turn! Turn! Turn!	Byrds
Uptight (Everything's Alright)	Stevie Wonder
Wooly Bully	Sam the Sham
Yesterday	Beatles
You've Lost That Lovin' Feelin'	Righteous Brothers

Clark: Child star grows up.

Britain's Pet

MARCH 1, 1965. "Downtown" by Petula Clark, which hit the U.S. charts late in 1964, goes gold. Clark, a former child star on the BBC and in British films, will also receive a Grammy for "Downtown" as the best single of the year. Later this month, another Clark tune, "I Know a Place," will hit the charts—and win another Grammy.

Stones Pissed

MARCH 18, 1965. The Rolling Stones, furthering their bad-boy image, are arrested in London for urinating on the wall of a gas station after being refused permission to use the men's room. They will be charged with "insulting behavior" and fined £5 each.

Dylan Sells Out

MAY 9, 1965. Bob Dylan performs in a sold-out concert at London's Royal Albert Hall. In the audience are the Beatles and Donovan.

Flashback
a-Go-Go

A-Go-Go, Aspen, Colo.
Blu-Note a-Go-Go, Whitesboro, N.Y.
Bucket a-Go-Go, Park City, Utah
Champagne a-Go-Go, Madison, Wisc.
Friskey a-Go-Go, San Antonio, Tex.
Whiskey a-Go-Go, Los Angles

"We were a bunch of loonies, taking drugs and trying to be honest."
George Harrison

No Satisfaction

JUNE 1, 1965. "(I Can't Get No) Satisfaction" by the Rolling Stones hits the charts, despite being banned by several U.S. radio stations because of its suggestive lyrics. The song, which will be credited with creating the "fuzz tone" guitar sound mimicked by many groups, will hit number one in a matter of weeks and will become a rock 'n' roll classic.

Jagger: Suggestive single.

Hard Day's Knight

JUNE 15, 1965. The Beatles receive the Member of the British Empire award from Queen Elizabeth, causing a major controversy in Britain. Several previous MBE recipients will turn in their awards, including an army officer who says he doesn't want to share the honor with "vulgar nincompoops." Just before the ceremony, the band will sneak off to a bathroom in Buckingham Palace to smoke one of several joints John Lennon has carried in his boots.

I Got You, Babe

JULY 10, 1965. Sonny and Cher release their first single, "I Got You Babe," which will also be their only bona fide number-one

Sonny, Cher: Exaggerated hippies.

Flashback
Top Albums—1965

Album	Artist
Beatles VI	Beatles
Bluesbreakers	John Mayall
Bringing It All Back Home	Bob Dylan
Confessin' the Blues	B.B. King
Eve of Destruction	Barry McGuire
Farewell, Angelina	Joan Baez
Goldfinger	soundtrack
Having a Rave-Up With the Yardbirds	Yardbirds
Help!	Beatles
Highway 61 Revisited	Bob Dylan
I Ain't a'Marchin' Anymore	Phil Ochs
Mr. Tambourine Man	Byrds
Out of Our Heads	Rolling Stones
Pain in My Heart	Otis Redding
Paul Butterfield Blues Band	Butterfield Blues Band
Rolling Stones No. 2	Rolling Stones
Rubber Soul	Beatles
Them	Them
12 x 5	Rolling Stones
Wednesday Morning, 3 AM	Simon and Garfunkel
Whipped Cream and Other Delights	Herb Alpert and the Tijuana Brass

record, although Cher will have several as a solo artist in the 1970s. Cher La Piere had begun singing backup at New York recording sessions in her midteens; by the time she was 17, she was backing the Ronettes for producer Phil Spector, where she met Sonny Bono, a long-time Spector friend and sometime songwriter who had supplied material for the Crystals and Righteous Brothers, among others. Now married, they will release a second single, "Baby Don't Go," while developing a shrewd public image: their exaggerated hippie look—bellbottoms, eye-shadowing bangs—will get them a lot of publicity, including TV guest spots on such shows as "The Man From U.N.C.L.E." Eventually, they will polish their shrewish wife/submissive husband act into a major Las Vegas draw.

"We were the youngest moneyed people, and we were just bigger kids about it."

Mama Cass Elliot

Taking Off

JULY 13, 1965. The Jefferson Airplane performs for the first time, at the Matrix Club in San Francisco. The group, formed around two San Francisco performers, Marty Balin and Paul Kanter, already includes Jorma Kaukonen and Jack Casady; on this engagement, they will meet drummer Spencer Dryden. After release of their first album, in October 1966 the group's lead singer, Signe Anderson, will quit and be replaced by Grace Slick, previously with another San Francisco band, the Great Society.

The Times, They Are a-Changin'

JULY 19, 1965. Bob Dylan is booed at the Newport Folk Festival by folk song purists after performing with an electric guitar for the first time. Dylan, who has just released his first electric album, *Bringing It All Back Home,* explains his transformation to folk-rock: "I got bored with my old songs." Despite the audience's rejection, another Dylan electric album, *Highway 61 Revisited,* released next month, will become a Dylan classic.

Life in the Fast Lane

AUGUST 15, 1965. The Beatles perform for 56,000 at Shea Stadium, playing 12 songs in 30 minutes. They are introduced by Ed Sullivan.

Day Trippers

AUGUST 24, 1965. While secluded at a Beverly Hills retreat, the Beatles are visited by Peter Fonda, actress Eleanor Bron, and members of the Byrds. According to Fonda, "...we dropped acid and began tripping for what would prove to be all night and most of the next day; all

The Name Game

Before the Fab Four Were . . .

1956: The Rebels (George)
1956: The Quarrymen (John, Paul; later George)
1957: Ed Clayton Skiffle Group (Ringo)
1958: The Nurks (John, Paul)
1958: Johnny and the Moondogs (John, Paul, George)
1959: Rory Storm and the Hurricanes (Ringo)
1960: Long John and the Silver Beatles (John, Paul, George)
1960: The Beat Brothers (John, Paul, George)
1960: The Silver Beatles (John, Paul, George)
1960: The Beatles (John, Paul, George; later Ringo)

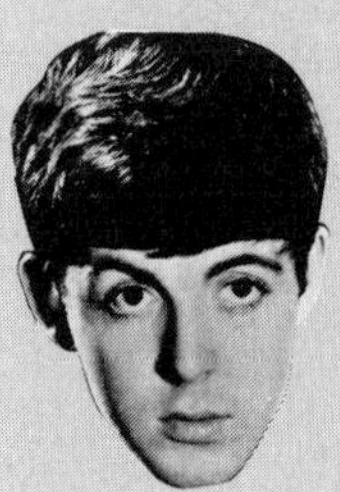

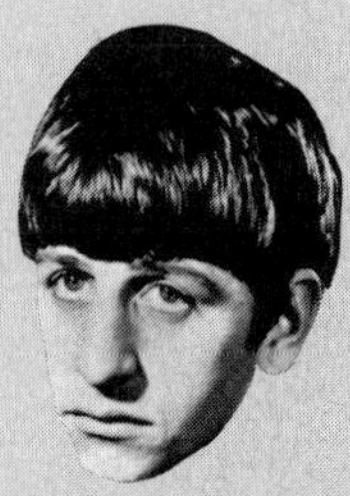

of us...eventually ended up inside a huge, empty sunken tub in the bathroom, babbling our minds away."

Meet the Beatles

AUGUST 27, 1965. The Beatles meet Elvis Presley at his Bel Air mansion. The four spend much of the time in awe, staring silently at their long-time idol. Presley will later deny that the meeting ever took place.

Dog Days

OCTOBER 16, 1965. Chet Helms, a budding rock entrepreneur, and the Family Dog, a hippie group interested in promoting psychedelic rock, produce the first "dance concert" at San Francisco's Longshoremen's Hall, featuring the Jefferson Airplane and the Great Society. The show's success will spur more Family Dog productions, most at the Avalon Ballroom, where they will remain until 1968, when they will lose their operating license largely because of neighbors' complaints about the loud, late-night events. The Family Dog productions will move to a variety of other venues. Later, Helms will become manager of Big Brother and the Holding Company.

Jefferson Airplane: All in the Family Dog.

Graham's First Bill

NOVEMBER 10, 1965. Bill Graham, formerly a New York cab driver with a degree in business administration, produces his first rock concert; a benefit for the San Francisco Mime Troupe. He has chosen an old auditorium on Fillmore Street, in the heart of San Francisco's ghetto, which he rented for $60. The success of that first effort—featuring the Jefferson Airplane, the Grateful Dead, and the Charlatans—will spur him to lease the Fillmore full-time to produce rock concerts featuring the cream of the San Francisco rock scene, and eventually every major rock group except the Beatles. The original Fillmore will eventually give way to a bigger "Fillmore West," followed in 1968 by a New York version, "Fillmore East." Both rock palaces will close in 1971, with the Fillmore West being razed to create a Howard Johnson's; another San Francisco site, Winterland Auditorium, will continue to feature Graham productions until 1978. Despite his vital role in nurturing the national music scene, Graham, born Wolfgang Grajonca, will be criticized during the late 1960s, as his heavy capi-

Graham: Everyone but the Beatles.

Flashback
21 Kinds of Rock

- Acid Rock
- Blues Rock
- Bubblegum Rock
- Country Rock
- Cowboy Rock
- Disco Rock
- Folk Rock
- Funk Rock
- Fusion Rock
- Hard Rock
- Hillbilly Rock
- Jazz Rock
- Pet Rock
- Psychadelic Rock
- Punk Rock
- Rock 'n' Roll
- Rockabilly
- Skiffle Rock
- Soft Rock
- Space Rock
- Surf Rock

talistic instinct clashes with an era emphasizing free food, free love, and free everything. When a group of New York revolutionaries called the Motherfuckers tries to "liberate" the Fillmore East in 1968, charging that Graham has "sucked the blood of the community...," Graham will send them away, saying, "Nobody wanted to liberate this place a year ago when it was a rat-infested dump."

Guthrie: Literary litterbug.

The Son Also Rises

NOVEMBER 25, 1965. Folksinger Arlo Guthrie, spending Thanksgiving Day with friends in Stockbridge, Mass., is arrested for dumping a truckload of garbage "off the side of a side road," as he will later explain it. At the Newport Folk Festival in 1967, Guthrie will tell the tale of his arrest and its consequences in a 20-minute monologue, part of a song called "Alice's Restaurant," a tract against war, police, the draft, and authority in general. That song will raise Guthrie's stature from folksinger to folk hero and will inspire a 1969 movie of the same name in which Guthrie will appear.

Sweet and Wholesome

DECEMBER 12, 1965. The Young Rascals release "Good Lovin'," which will become their second hit (the first is "I Ain't Gonna Eat Out My Heart Anymore") and their first of three to reach number one. The band is one of several groups, including the Association and the Carpenters, to buck the heavy guitar-and-drums trend in favor of sweet, wholesome vocals. Later, they will shorten their name to the Rascals, reflecting their rising ages.

Rascals: Clean-teen rockers.

Spirit of America

JANUARY 1, 1966. The Beach Boy's 23rd hit song, "Barbara Ann," makes the charts. More than a decade later, in the wake of the American hostage crisis in Iran, fans will alter the lyrics of the chorus to "Bomb Iran."

Monkee Business

JANUARY 14, 1966. David Bowie debuts his new group, David Bowie and the Lower Third. Until recently, Bowie had performed under his given name, David

Flashback

Do You Know Me?

Real Name	*Stage Name*	*Real Name*	*Stage Name*
Martin Aday	Meat Loaf	David Jones	David Bowie
Roberta Joan Anderson	Joni Mitchell	Eddie Jones	Guitar Slim
Dennis Blandford	Peter Townshend	Herbert Khaury	Tiny Tim
Eva Narcissus Boyd	Little Eva	Billy Levise	Mitch Ryder
Russell Bridges	Lou Russell	John Lydon	Johnny Rotten
Martin Jere Buchwald	Marty Balin	Pauline Mathews	Kiki Dee
Chester Burrett	Howlin' Wolf	Declan McManus	Elvis Costello
Walden Robert Cassotto	Bobby Darin	Perry Miller	Jesse Colin Young
Francis Castelluccio	Frankie Valli	Steveland Judkins Morris	Stevie Wonder
Ronald Crosby	Jerry Jeff Walker	Mary O'Brien	Dusty Springfield
Henry John Deutschendorf, Jr.	John Denver	George O'Dowd	Boy George
Reg Dwight	Elton John	James Jewell Osterburg	Iggy Pop
Ernest Evans	Chubby Checker	Richard Penniman	Little Richard
Louis Firbank	Lou Reed	Chester Powers	Dino Valenti
Constance Franconero	Connie Francis	Wynette Pugh	Tammy Wynette
George Frayne	Commander Cody	John Ramistella	Johnny Rivers
Vincent Furnier	Alice Cooper	Mac Rebennack	Dr. John
Stephen Demetri Georgiou	Cat Stevens	Robert Ridarelli	Bobby Rydell
Stuart Goddard	Adam Ant	Melanie Safka	Melanie
Wolfgang Grajonca	Bill Graham	Richard Starkey	Ringo Starr
Anthony Gourdine	Little Anthony	Sylvester Stewart	Sly Stone
Yvette Marie Holland	Chaka Khan	Richard Valenzuela	Richie Valens
Baldemar Huerta	Freddie Fender	Don Van Vliet	Captain Beefheart
George Ivan	Van Morrison	Charles Westover	Del Shannon
Thomas Gregory Jackson	Tommy James	Henry Fredericks Williams	Taj Mahal
Marion Walter Jacobs	Little Walter	Robert Zimmerman	Bob Dylan
James Johnson	Rick James		

Jones, but changed it to avoid confusion with Davy Jones of the Monkees.

Daddy's Little Girl

JANUARY 22, 1966. Nancy Sinatra, daughter of famous father Frank, enters the charts with "These Boots Are Made for Walkin'." For a brief period, the 25-year-old streaked blonde with the pouty lips will be one of America's favorite sex symbols, touring Vietnam in 1967, where troops will name her their number-one pinup girl. Later that year she will have another chartmaker: "Somethin' Stupid," a duet with her dad. "Boots" will inspire an American tire maker to advertise a model called the Wide Boot, complete with ads featuring Sinatra's tune.

Sinatra: Blonde ambition.

Flashback

Top Singles—1966

Along Comes Mary	Association
The Ballad of the Green Berets	Barry Sadler
Bus Stop	Hollies
Cherish	Association
Daydream	Lovin' Spoonful
Don't Mess With Bill	Marvelettes
Eight Miles High	Byrds
Eleanor Rigby	Beatles
Get Ready	Temptations
Gloria	Them
Good Lovin'	Young Rascals
Good Vibrations	Beach Boys
Have You Seen Your Mother, Baby	Rolling Stones
Hey Joe	Jimi Hendrix Experience
Hold On, I'm Coming	Sam and Dave
I Am a Rock	Simon and Garfunkel
I Had Too Much to Dream Last Night	Electric Prunes
I'm a Believer	Monkees
Knock On Wood	Eddie Floyd
Last Train to Clarksville	Monkees
Let's Go Get Stoned	Ray Charles
Lightnin' Strikes	Lou Christie
Mellow Yellow	Donovan
Monday Monday	Mamas and the Papas
19th Nervous Breakdown	Rolling Stones
96 Tears	? and Mysterians
Nowhere Man	Beatles
Paperback Writer	Beatles
Poor Side of Town	Johnny Rivers
Rain	Beatles
Rainy Day Woman #12 and #35	Bob Dylan
Reach Out, I'll Be There	Four Tops
Sounds of Silence	Simon and Garfunkel
Summer in the City	Lovin' Spoonful
Summertime	Billy Stewart
The Sun Ain't Gonna Shine Anymore	Walker Brothers
Sunny Afternoon	Kinks
Sunshine Superman	Donovan
Try a Little Tenderness	Otis Redding
Uptight	Stevie Wonder
Walk Away Renee	Left Banke
We Can Work It Out	Beatles
When a Man Loves a Woman	Percy Sledge
Wild Thing	Troggs
Yellow Submarine	Beatles
You Keep Me Hanging On	Supremes
(You're My) Soul and Inspiration	Righteous Brothers

Macho Music

FEBRUARY 5, 1966. "The Ballad of the Green Berets" by Sgt. Barry Sadler hits the charts. Much to the surprise of many, it skyrockets to number one and goes gold during a time of increasing protest against American involvement in Vietnam. Sadler's subsequent album containing this and other prowar songs also will go gold.

I Fought the Law

MARCH 24, 1966. The nation's first "bootlegging" law is passed in New York state. The law intends to stop the unauthorized recording of concerts, which are later released on record, but it will do little to stem the tide of bootleg albums by major artists, including Bob Dylan and the Beatles. In six years, the federal government will pass Public Law 92-140, the Anti-Bootlegging Law, providing enforcement nationally.

Dead Man's Curve

APRIL 12, 1966. Two years after his top-10 hit "Dead Man's Curve," Jan Berry, of Jan and Dean fame, is seriously hurt when his Corvette smashes into a parked vehicle in Los Angeles. He will be totally paralyzed for awhile, and will suffer brain damage. The duo will attempt a comeback in the early 1970s, but without much success.

Boss' Loss

MAY 22, 1966. Bruce Springsteen, 16, records his first album with his band, the Castilles. The album will never be released.

Meat the Beatles

JUNE 15, 1966. The Beatles' *Yesterday and Today* is released in the U.S. with a controversial "butcher cover," depicting the band members in white smocks, with decapitated dolls and fresh red meat strewn everywhere. The horrifying cover will generate so many complaints to record stores that 750,000 copies will be recalled and a quarter-million-dollar ad campaign will be cancelled. *Yesterday and Today* will have the distinction of being the only Beatles album to lose money, but the original cover will become a collector's item, bringing up to $400 at auctions.

"Top Forty radio . . . is dead, and its rotting corpse is stinking up the airwaves."

Tom Donahue, San Francisco DJ

Cream Surfaces

JULY 12, 1966. The rock group Cream is founded by bassist Jack Bruce and drummer Ginger Baker, both formerly with the

Jan and Dean: Smash hit.

Flashback

Top Albums—1966

Aftermath	Rolling Stones
Blonde on Blonde	Bob Dylan
Buffalo Springfield	Buffalo Springfield
East-West	Butterfield Blues Band
The Fugs	The Fugs
High Tide and Green Grass	Rolling Stones
I Hear a Symphony	Supremes
If You Can Believe Your Eyes and Ears	Mamas and the Papas
Jefferson Airplane Takes Off	Jefferson Airplane
Lightfoot	Gordon Lightfoot
Lou Rawls Live	Lou Rawls
Meet the Supremes	Supremes
The Monkees	Monkees
Parsley, Sage, Rosemary, and Thyme	Simon and Garfunkel
Pet Sounds	Beach Boys
Phil Ochs in Concert	Phil Ochs
Relax Your Mind	Jim Kweskin
Revolver	Beatles
The Seeds	Seeds
Sounds of Silence	Simon and Garfunkel
Spinout	Elvis Presley
Summer Days	Beach Boys
Summertime	Billy Stewart
Supremes A'Go-Go	Supremes
Take a Little Walk With Me	Tom Rush
Turn! Turn! Turn!	Byrds
Sweet Talkin' Guy	Chiffons
Sunshine Superman	Donovan
Uptight	Stevie Wonder
The Who Sings My Generation	Who
Yesterday and Today	Beatles
The Young Rascals	Young Rascals

Cream: Rising to the top.

Graham Bond Organization, and guitarist Eric Clapton, most recently with the Yardbirds. Clapton quit the Yardbirds after disagreements over artistic control of their songs and was replaced by guitarist Jeff Beck. Cream will quickly become one of the seminal bands of the decade, producing such hits as "Sunshine of Your Love" and "White Room." In early 1969 Baker and Clapton will join with singer/keyboardist Stevie Winwood, formerly of the group Traffic, to form Blind Faith.

Eve of Destruction

JULY 29, 1966. Bob Dylan is nearly killed when he crashes his Triumph motorcycle in upstate New York, suffering broken vertebrae, a concussion, and several deep cuts. Rumors abound about his condition, including premature reports of his death. He will remain isolated for 18 months, recording with the Band in the basement of his house. When *Nashville Skyline* appears in 1969, critics will say Dylan has lost both his voice and his energy.

Things We Said Today—I

AUGUST 1, 1966. *Datebook*, an American teen magazine, prints a British interview with John Lennon in which he muses on the futility of organized religion, stating, "We are more popular than Jesus now." The resulting furor—including a statement from the Vatican—will lead to Beatles records being banned at many radio stations, particularly in the U.S. Bible Belt, where records and Beatles memorabilia will be burned at church rallies. (Longview, Tex. station KLUE will sponsor one such record burning; the next day, its broadcast tower will be struck by lightning, knocking the station off the air.) In South Carolina, the Ku Klux Klan will nail Beatles records to burning crosses. Later, Lennon will muse: "If I had said television was more popular than Jesus, I might have gotten away with it."

Hello Goodbye

AUGUST 29, 1966. The Beatles perform their last live concert, at San Francisco's Candlestick Park.

Beatles: We write the psalms.

Made for TV

SEPTEMBER 12, 1966. "The Monkees" debuts on NBC-TV, a show depicting a group of rock musicians who, according to some, look like the Beatles run through a Xerox machine. Indeed, the group had been assembled by a Hollywood producer hoping to capitalize on the success of the Beatles' film *A Hard Day's Night*. Last fall, nearly 500 performers auditioned for the four principal parts, with Davy Jones, Mike Nesmith, Peter Tork, and Mickey Dolenz—each of whom bore some resemblance to one of the Beatles—winning the starring roles. The biggest obstacle to overcome was musical competence. Although Tork and Nesmith had some musical experience, the other two were professional actors; Dolenz, at 10, had been the child star of TV's "Circus Boy." The show will follow the quartet's weekly escapades, ranging from the ridiculous to the merely silly. It will last for two years, its final episode airing in August 1968, although it will later be rerun on Saturday mornings on CBS.

Monkees: From the ridiculous to the merely silly.

Patti's Page

OCTOBER 17, 1966. George Harrison, with wife Patti, travels to Bombay, India, to vacation. While there, he will take sitar lessons from Ravi Shankar, India's most famed traditional musician. Shankar's music already

Flashback

Rock Clubs

Agora, Cleveland
Alice's Revisited, Chicago
The Bayou, Washington, D.C.
Bitter End, New York
Black Dome, Cincinnati
Blue Parrott, Cambridge
Blue Unicorn, San Francisco
Boston's Tea Party, Boston
Bottom Line, New York
CBGB's, New York
Cellar Door, Washington, D.C.
Club 47, Boston
Club Venus, Baltimore
Coffee and Confusion, San Francisco
Crazy Horse, Washington, D.C.
Daily Planet, Milwaukee
Dirty Sam's, Ft. Collins, Colo.
The Fox, Brooklyn
Gerde's Folk City, New York
Horseshoe, Leesburg, Va.
Keystone Korner, San Francisco
King's Beach Bowl, Lake Tahoe
La Pichet, Denver
Ludlow Garage, Cincinnati
The Main Point, Bryn Mawr, Pa.
The Matrix, San Francisco
No Exit, Chicago
Quiet Knight, Chicago
Ratso's, Chicago
Robbies, Berkeley
Rock Pile, Toronto
The Roxy, Los Angeles
Second City, Chicago
Steppenwolf, Berkeley
The Stone Pony, Asbury Park, N.J.
The Troubadour, Los Angeles

has been introduced to Americans through the jazz innovations of Dave Brubeck, John Coltrane, and Bud Shank, but Harrison's visit will spur a much-copied trend toward Indian instruments in rock music. Patti Boyd Harrison will later inspire Eric Clapton's lost-love ballad "Layla"; she and Clapton will marry in 1979, with Harrison, Paul McCartney, Ringo Starr, and Mick Jagger entertaining, as well as Clapton.

An American in Paris

OCTOBER 18, 1966. The Jimi Hendrix Experience performs for the first time, in Paris. A native of Seattle, Hendrix until recently had been singing and playing blues guitar in New York coffeehouses until being "discovered" by Chas Chandler, one-time bassist with the Animals. Chandler convinced Hendrix that his style would be more readily accepted in Europe than America and persuaded him to move to England, where he met future band members Noel Redding and Mitch Mitchell. After his Parisian debut, Hendrix will return to England to receive rave reviews—critics will agree that he is, indeed, an "experience"; one U.S. critic will dub him "the wild man of rock"—before taking America by storm early next year with his hit single "Hey Joe."

Hendrix: Experience counts.

Things We Said Today—II

OCTOBER 24, 1966. In an interview, Boston's Archbishop Cardinal Cushing acknowledges that the Beatles are, indeed, better known throughout the world than Jesus.

Birth of the Blues

OCTOBER 29, 1966. Beale Street in Memphis, long acknowledged as the home of the blues, is declared a national landmark.

I've Just Seen a Face

NOVEMBER 9, 1966. At the invitation of a friend, John Lennon attends "Unfinished Paintings and Objects by Yoko Ono," an exhibit by a penniless Japanese artist recently moved to London.

Cat's First

JANUARY 24, 1966. "Cats and Dogs," the first album by Cat Stevens, is released in England. Although this album will never appear in America, Stevens' following in Europe will pave the way for his enormous popularity in the early 1970s.

Stevens: U.K., not U.S.

A Month in the Life

JANUARY 19, 1967. Recording begins on "A Day in the Life," part of the upcoming album, *Sergeant Pepper's Lonely Hearts Club Band*. The song will take more than three weeks to finish; the entire album will take only four months. "A Day in the Life" includes a 42-piece orchestra dressed in black tie, which plays 24 bars of music, climaxed by the song's final note, lasting an unprecedented 45 seconds. The song will become the landmark cut on a landmark album; its lyrics will be dissected, studied, and discussed for years.

"Hope I die before I get old."

Peter Townshend

Who Debut

MARCH 25, 1967. The Who debuts in the U.S. as a low-billed act in a New York rock revue. The group, first recorded

The Birth of FM Rock

At 8 PM on April 7, 1967, when "Big Daddy" Tom Donahue turned on the mike at KMPX-FM in San Francisco, radio history was in the making. Donahue, only weeks earlier a DJ on San Francisco's AM bubblegum-rock station KYA, had convinced KMPX's owner to give him the 8 PM-to-midnight slot on what was otherwise a foundering foreign-language station. The idea was to present something radically different: music for people who had outgrown top-40 bubblegum but who were not yet ready for Muzak.

The first few weeks of Donahue's new show were touch and go. Advertisers were as scarce as the records in the KMPX library. But as word spread through San Francisco's hippie network about The Music, records and advertisers came—first walking, then running. The station became a community effort, with help from the likes of The Committee, a progressive improvisational theater group, and Ralph Gleason, music critic of the *San Francisco Chronicle*, later a founder of *Rolling Stone*. An emerging success, KMPX turned full-time to "underground" radio, as it had come to be called. KPPC in Los Angeles, recently purchased by KMPX's owner from the Pasadena Presbyterian Church, leaped on the rock bandwagon.

Despite apparent success, however, trouble came to underground radio. KMPX's owner bumped heads frequently with Donahue and his coterie of announcers, engineers, long-haired ad reps, and more than a few hangers-on. In March 1968 KMPX staffers announced—on the air—that they would go on strike. When they walked out after flipping off the station's transmitter at 3 AM, they were greeted by throngs waiting outside, including Creedence Clearwater Revival, Blue Cheer, and the Grateful Dead, who produced a spontaneous late-night rock-in—complete with light show—for the strikers. KMPX went back on the air a few hours later, but without Donahue's crew, who called themselves the Amalgamated American Federation of International FM Workers of the World, Ltd., North Beach Local No. 1. Within weeks, the AAFIFMWW strikers took to the airwaves again, this time at KSAN, a classical music station owned by Metromedia. It was an odd marriage—the free-love crowd working for a large corporate employer—but the music somehow united all into a working amalgam later described as "hip capitalism." KMPX and KSAN became on-air rivals.

It was a stormy first few years. Management-worker problems raged at both stations, caused in part by many announcers' unwillingness to do commercials for businesses with which they did not agree philosophically. And then there were problems with the Federal Communications Commission, resulting largely from the free-wheeling, uncensored format, replete with lively interviews with political and sexual radicals.

But throughout it all there was The Music—and The Music endured.

Flashback
Top Singles—1967

All You Need Is Love	Beatles
Baby I Love You	Aretha Franklin
Brown-Eyed Girl	Van Morrison
Daydream Believer	Monkees
Cold Sweat	James Brown
Different Drum	Linda Ronstadt
For What It's Worth	Buffalo Springfield
Funky Broadway	Wilson Pickett
Gimme Some Lovin'	Spencer Davis Group
Groovin'	Young Rascals
Happy Jack	Who
Happy Together	Turtles
Hello Goodbye	Beatles
I Can See for Miles	Who
I Heard It Through the Grapevine	Gladys Knight and the Pips
I Never Loved a Man	Aretha Franklin
I Second That Emotion	Smokey Robinson and the Miracles
I Was Made to Love Her	Stevie Wonder
I'm a Man	Spencer Davis Group
Kind of a Drag	Buckinghams
Let's Spend the Night Together	Rolling Stones
The Letter	Box Tops
Light My Fire	Doors
Love Is Here and Now You're Gone	Supremes
Massachusetts	Bee Gees
Never My Love	Association
Ode to Billie Joe	Bobbie Gentry
Penny Lane	Beatles
Purple Haze	Jimi Hendrix
Respect	Aretha Franklin
Ruby Tuesday	Rolling Stones
San Francisco (Be Sure to Wear Flowers in Your Hair)	Scott McKenzie
Silence Is Golden	Tremeloes
Society's Child	Janis Ian
Soul Finger	Bar-Kays
Soul Man	Sam and Dave
Strawberry Fields Forever	Beatles
This Diamond Ring	Gary Lewis and the Playboys
To Sir With Love	Lulu
Up, Up and Away	Fifth Dimension
A Whiter Shade of Pale	Procol Harum
Windy	Association

in 1963 as the Hi-Numbers, had only last year become the pet group of the British mod set. The quartet will capture the imagination of Americans with its freakish style, epitomized by guitarist Peter Townshend's Cyrano de Bergerac nose and his coat cut from a Union Jack. The group has specialized in near-maniacal performances that include smashing guitars, kicking drums, blowing up amplifiers, throwing microphones, detonating smoke bombs, and creating sometimes excrutiating feedback. Such shenanigans aside, the Who's music will shine, including "My Generation," which will become an anthem for British and American youth, "I Can See for Miles," and "Pinball Wizard," part of the ground-breaking "rock-opera" *Tommy*. Later this year the group will begin their first full-fledged U.S. tour—as the opening act for Herman's Hermits.

Who: Up in smoke.

Down in Monterey

APRIL 11, 1967. Los Angeles concert promoter Alan Pariser and booking agent Ben Shapiro sign an agreement to jointly produce the Monterey International Pop Festival, to be held June 16-18 at the Monterey County Fairgrounds. In coming weeks, the two, along with veteran rock publicist Derek Taylor, will quickly put together what will be the largest assemblage of rock and soul stars ever. Money for the project will come partly from loans from songwriter Paul Simon, "Papa" John Phillips, record producer Lou Adler, singer Johnny Rivers, and others. Although many top musicians will decline to perform—including the Beatles, the Rolling Stones, Chuck Berry, Bob Dylan, Cream, and the Beach Boys—the talent that does appear will be considerable: Simon and Garfunkel, the Steve Miller Band, Buffalo Springfield, the Who, the Grateful Dead, the Mamas and the Papas, Otis Redding, Laura Nyro, the Jefferson Airplane, the Byrds, Booker T and the MGs, Moby Grape, Canned Heat, the Association, Country Joe and the Fish, the Paul Butterfield Blues Band, Ravi Shankar, and Jimi Hendrix in his American debut. All told, more than 50,000 euphoric fans will attend the three-day, five-concert festival, blocking all roads in and out of Monterey for days.

Grateful Dead: Monterey rockers.

Doors Open

JUNE 3, 1967. "Light My Fire," the first release by the Doors, a Los Angeles-based group, debuts. They will quickly become one of rock's "bad boy" groups, largely as a result of the antics of leader Jim Morrison, a tall, anorectic drug addict known to wear tight black leather pants and perform sadistic sexual acts on stage. His controversial performancs will pit Morrison and the Doors against local police in several cities, including New Haven and Miami. Their smash first single will be backed by several more hits, including "Hello, I Love You," "People Are Strange," and "Love Me Two Times."

AC/DC

JULY 1, 1967. Amplified instruments make a big splash at the annual convention of the National Association of Music Merchants in Chicago, as instrument makerstry to cash in on the success of electric guitars and organs in rock bands. Featured at the convention are everything from electric violins to electric tubas. One manufacturer, Vox, offers 64 different electronic instruments and gadgets. Another firm aims to capitalize on the Indian music trend sweeping American rockers with its electric sitar. Reporting on the convention, *Time* magazine predicts a boom in sales of earplugs for grownups.

Not Your Steppin' Stone

JULY 17, 1967. The Jimi Hendrix Experience opens for the Monkees at Forest Hills stadium in New York; the group is booed by the Monkees' less-adventuresome audiences, however, and will be dropped from the tour before it ends.

Monument to the DAR

AUGUST 13, 1967. Joan Baez is denied permission to perform at DAR Constitution Hall in Washington, D.C., by the hall's proprietor, the Daughters of the American Revolution, which objects to Baez' antiwar protests. But Baez is prepared. Anticipating DAR's denial, she has quietly arranged with the U.S. Interior Department for a "folk-singing peace-in" at the nearby Washington Monument. On stage, she will dedicate her first number to the DAR.

East Meets West

AUGUST 24, 1967. George Harrison, John Lennon, and Paul McCartney hear a talk by the Maharishi Mahesh Yogi at the Park Lane Hilton. The Maharishi preaches that transcendental meditation, practiced twice a day, will lead to spiritual enlightenment, a "high" achievable without drugs. He will later invite the three Beatles to his suite and ask them to attend a 10-day seminar he is giving. There, the three will hold a press conference and announce, much to the world's amazement, that they are giving up drugs. They will later return to their pre-enlightened, drug-induced habits, however.

Been Down So Long

AUGUST 27, 1967. Beatles' manager Brian Epstein is found dead from an overdose of bromide, the climax to years of depression and confusion over matters both personal and professional. It is his second suicide attempt. The Beatles will soon form Apple Corp. (the name is a pun created by Paul) to manage their affairs. Its subsidiaries will include Apple Boutique, Apple Electronics, Apple Films, Apple Publicity, Apple Retail, Apple Wholesale—and Apple Records. Among its other artists will be

Flashback
Top Albums—1967

A Whiter Shade of Pale	Procul Harum
Album 1700	Peter, Paul, and Mary
Alice's Restaurant	Arlo Guthrie
Are You Experienced?	Jimi Hendrix
Bee Gees	Bee Gees
Best of the Lovin' Spoonful	Lovin' Spoonful
Buffalo Springfield Again	Buffalo Springfield
Days of Future Passed	Moody Blues
Disraeli Gears	Cream
The Doors	Doors
Electric Music for the Mind and Body	Country Joe and the Fish
Feel Like I'm Fixin' to Die	Country Joe and the Fish
Forever Changes	Love
Four Tops Greatest Hits	Four Tops
Freak Out	Mothers of Invention
Fresh Cream	Cream
Goodbye and Hello	Tim Buckley
Grateful Dead	Grateful Dead
Happy Jack	Who
I Never Loved a Man	Aretha Franklin
In My Life	Judy Collins
Loaded	Velvet Underground
Magical Mystery Tour	Beatles
Moby Grape	Moby Grape
Pleasures of the Harbor	Phil Ochs
Sgt. Pepper's Lonely Hearts Club Band	Beatles
Stand Back	Charlie Musslewhite
Strange Days	Doors
Surrealistic Pillow	Jefferson Airplane
Their Satanic Majesties Request	Rolling Stones
Vanilla Fudge	Vanilla Fudge
The Velvet Underground and Nico	Velvet Underground
The Who Sells Out	Who
Younger Than Yesterday	Byrds

Flashback
S.F. Rock Scene, 1967

- Big Brother and the Holding Company
- The Charlatans
- The Chocolate Watch Band
- Country Joe and the Fish
- The Grateful Dead
- The Great Society
- The Heavenly Blues Band
- The Jefferson Airplane
- The Loading Zone
- Moby Grape
- Notes from the Underground
- Quicksilver Messenger Service
- The Sons of Champlain

Mary Hopkin, Badfinger, Billy Preston, and the then-unknown James Taylor.

Bound for Glory

SEPTEMBER 3, 1967. Renowned folksinger Woody Guthrie dies at age 52. The singer and songwriter had made major contributions to American popular music since the 1930s, when he wrote

Guthrie: So long.

"So Long, It's Been Good to Know Yuh" after watching a dust storm on the Texas Panhandle; the song was part of his best-selling 1951 album, *Dust Bowl Ballads*. Guthrie was both criticized and lionized for his left-leaning politics. His tune "Union Maid" is a classic labor movement song about women. Other Guthrie tunes include "Blowing Down This Old Dusty Road," about the trials of migratory workers, the antifascist "Round, Round Hitler's Grave," and the American folk standard "This Land Is Your Land." His work influenced numerous musicians whose roots are in folk music, including Bob Dylan and Joan Baez. Many—including Dylan, Judy Collins, Pete Seeger, Richie Havens, Odetta, and Woody's son Arlo Guthrie—will come together in early 1968 for a memorial concert at Carnegie Hall. The story of Guthrie's life will be made into a movie starring David Carradine, titled *Bound for Glory*, based on a semiautobiographical 1943 book of the same title.

Things We Said Today—III

SEPTEMBER 30, 1967. Frank Zappa, in an interview, acknowledges that the Beatles are, indeed, better known throughout the world than Jesus.

Flashback
Major Rock Fests

- ☐ Magic Mountain Music Festival (June 10-11, 1967), Marin County, Calif.
- ☐ Monterey Pop Festival (June 16-18, 1967), Monterey, Calif.
- ☐ Newport Pop Festival (August 4-5, 1968), Costa Mesa, Calif.
- ☐ Sky River Rock Festival (August 31-September 2, 1968), Sultan, Wash.
- ☐ Miami Pop Festival (December 28-30, 1968), Hallandale, Fla.
- ☐ Newport '69 (June 20-22, 1969), Northridge, Calif.
- ☐ Denver Pop Festival (June 27-28, 1969), Denver, Colo.
- ☐ Atlanta Pop Festival (July 4-5, 1969), Atlanta, Ga.
- ☐ Seattle Pop Festival (July 25-27, 1969), Woodenville, Wash.
- ☐ Atlantic City Pop Festival (August 1-3, 1969), Atlantic City, N.J.
- ☐ Woodstock (August 15-17, 1969), Woodstock, N.Y.
- ☐ Sky River Rock Festival (August 30-September 1, 1969), Tenino, Wash.
- ☐ Texas Pop Festival (August 30-September 1, 1969), Lewisville, Tex.
- ☐ New Orleans Pop Festival (August 31-September 1, 1969), Prairieville, La.
- ☐ Altamont (December 6, 1969), Livermore, Calif.
- ☐ Powder Ridge Rock Festival (July 30-August 1, 1970), Middlefield, Conn.
- ☐ Atlanta Pop Festival (July 3-5, 1970), Byron, Ga.
- ☐ New York Pop Concert (July 17-19, 1970), Randall's Island, N.Y.
- ☐ Mt. Pocono Festival (July 8, 1972), Long Pond, Pa.
- ☐ Watkins Glen Summer Jam (July 28, 1973), Watkins Glen, N.Y.
- ☐ California Jam (April 6, 1974), Ontario, Calif.

Let the Sunshine In

OCTOBER 29, 1967. *Hair*, subtitled "An American Tribal Love-Rock Musical," opens at the Public Theater in New York. The production brings together a wide range of voices of rebellion against war, racism, the draft, and middle-class values in general. Among other things, it is one of the first plays to introduce total nudity to the legitimate theater. The nudity comes at the end of the first act, but there are uninhibited discussions of sex—the beauty of bodies, interracial relationships, and sexual perversions—throughout. It will play the Public Theater for only eight weeks before moving uptown to a former discotheque. Later it will undergo a massive overhaul—omitting whatever plot it once had, some critics will say—before it opens on Broadway at the Biltmore Theater in April 1968 for 1,729 performances, then traveling for years throughout the U.S. and in eight countries. It will spawn four top-10 singles: the Cowsills' "Hair"; Oliver's "Good Morning, Starshine"; Three Dog Night's "Easy to be Hard"; and the Fifth Dimension's "Aquarius/Let the Sunshine In," which will become an anthem of the peace movement. Other rock musicals—including *Grease* and *Godspell*—will follow, but none will be as successful.

Mr. Otis Regrets

DECEMBER 10, 1967. As his star is rising, R&B great Otis Redding, along with several

Redding: On the edge of stardom.

members of the Bar-Kays, is killed in a plane crash; his body, lost in the icy waters of a Wisconsin lake, will never be recovered. Redding, who had already achieved stardom in Europe, was wildly received at the 1967 Monterey Pop Festival, and Atlantic Records executives were predicting that his next single would cement his success in the U.S. They were right: recorded 2½ weeks before his death, "(Sittin' on the) Dock of the Bay" will reach the number-one spot in March.

Here Comes the Knight

DECEMBER 16, 1967. Fourteen years after seven-year-old Gladys Knight won the "Ted Mack Amateur Hour" grand prize, she and her three cousins, known as the Pips, break into the top 10 with a version of Marvin Gaye's "I Heard It Through the Grapevine."

Be True to Your School

FEBRUARY 12, 1968. The Jimi Hendrix Experience performs at Garfield High in Seattle, the high school from which he dropped out.

Come Together

FEBRUARY 19, 1968. All four Beatles meet in Rishikesh, India, to begin a meditation course with the Maharishi. All will drop out of the course before completion (Ringo Starr will claim it is because his stomach can't take the spicy food), although George Harrison will soon use letterhead stationery bearing the name "Spiritual Regeneration Movement Foundation of India Under the Divine Guidance of His Holiness Maharishi Mahesh Yogi of Uttar Kaski."

Blues à la King

APRIL 4, 1968. In memory of Martin Luther King, Jr., who was shot earlier in the day, Jimi Hendrix, B.B. King, and others play an evening of blues in a New York club, collecting money for King's Southern Christian Leadership Conference.

Zappa: Revenge.

Baby, You're a Rich Man

JULY 12, 1968. After several defections, including superstars Jeff Beck and Eric Clapton, the Yardbirds break up. Jimmy Page tries to form a new group called the New Yardbirds, but later changes the name to Led Zeppelin. The group's first album, which includes the hit "Good Times, Bad Times," will cost less than $4,000 to produce but will gross more than $7 million and spur the group to a massive money-making run in which it will gross an estimated $30 million a year during the early 1970s.

Frankly Speaking—I

APRIL 12, 1968. Frank Zappa, invited to perform at the annual National Academy of Recording Arts and Sciences dinner in New York, tells the audience of record producers, "All year long you people have manufactured this crap, now for one night you're going to have to listen to it."

Double Fantasy

MAY 19, 1968. Having written some 20 songs during their stay in India, the Beatles begin recording them at the Abbey Road studios. Present throughout the recording sessions is Yoko Ono, who is being seen increasingly in John Lennon's presence, much to the dismay of his wife Cynthia. Lennon insists his relationship with Ono is strictly intellectual, but her presence will cause public speculation and uneasiness among band members, who feel threatened by Ono's eccentricities. In July Lennon will publicly end speculation by proclaiming his love for Ono and begin divorce proceedings. Months later, public and press outrage will culminate in the announcement that Ono, still unmarried, is pregnant with Lennon's child (she will miscarry within six weeks), followed days later by the couple's arrest on drug charges after a raid on Ringo Starr's London apartment.

Ono: Portrait of the artist.

BOOM! MUSIC

Hey, Joe

AUGUST 24, 1968. At the Democratic National Convention in Chicago, several bands perform for thousands of Yippie demonstrators. One such band, Country Joe and the Fish, will later be assaulted by angry Vietnam veterans.

Down On Me

SEPTEMBER 28, 1968. Janis Joplin, 25, announces that she will leave Big Brother and the Holding Company to pursue a solo career. Joplin will form her own rock band, which will debut at the Fillmore East in February 1969, before touring nationally, then in Europe, then returning home for a triumphant sold-out concert at Madison Square Garden in December. The $20,000 to $30,000 she will command per performance—well above the $4 a night she got when beginning with Big Brother—will enable Joplin to indulge her myriad vices—alcohol, drugs, sex with both men and women—which will, in turn, contribute to her demise. She will record two albums and one hit single, "Me and Bobby McGee." The second album, *Pearl*, will be recorded just weeks before she is found dead on October 10, 1960, at age 27, of a heroin overdose.

Flashback
Top Singles—1968

Abraham, Martin, and John	Dion Dimucci
A Beautiful Morning	Rascals
Bend Me, Shape Me	American Breed
Born to Be Wild	Steppenwolf
Chain of Fools	Aretha Franklin
Dance to the Music	Sly and the Family Stone
Fire	Crazy World of Arthur Brown
For Once in My Life	Stevie Wonder
Hello, I Love You	Doors
Hey Jude	Beatles
Hurdy Gurdy Man	Donovan
I Got the Feelin'	James Brown
I Heard it Through the Grapevine	Marvin Gaye
I Wish It Would Rain	Temptations
In-a-Gadda-Da-Vida	Iron Butterfly
I've Got to Get a Message to You	Bee Gees
Judy in Disguise (With Glasses)	John Fred and His Playboy Band
Jumpin' Jack Flash	Rolling Stones
Lady Madonna	Beatles
Light My Fire	Jose Feliciano
Love Child	Supremes
Midnight Confession	Grass Roots
Mrs. Robinson	Simon and Garfunkel
Piece of My Heart	Janis Joplin
Revolution	Beatles
Say It Loud (I'm Black and I'm Proud)	James Brown
Scarborough Fair	Simon and Garfunkel
(Sittin' On) The Dock of the Bay	Otis Redding
Spoonful	Cream
Stoned Soul Picnic	Fifth Dimension
Sunshine of Your Love	Cream
Sympathy for the Devil	Rolling Stones
Tighten Up	Archie Bell and the Drells
The Time Has Come Today	Chambers Brothers
White Room	Cream
With a Little Help From My Friends	Joe Cocker
Young Girl	Gary Puckett and the Union Gap

"I don't drink anything on the rocks. Cold is bad for my throat."

Janis Joplin

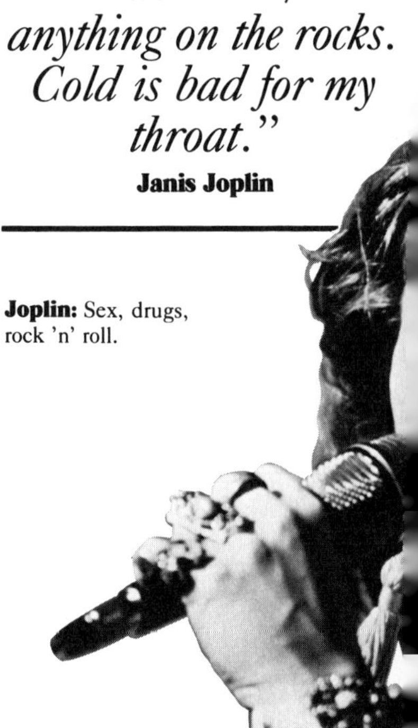

Joplin: Sex, drugs, rock 'n' roll.

BOOM! MUSIC

Feliciano: Red, white, and booed.

Jose, Can You See

OCTOBER 17, 1968. Jose Feliciano releases his bluesy version of "The Star-Spangled Banner," which he first performed earlier this month before a not-very-appreciative crowd at the World Series.

Flashback
Top Albums—1968

A Gift From a Flower to a Garden	Donovan
A Man and His Soul	Ray Charles
Astral Weeks	Van Morrison
Beggars Banquet	Rolling Stones
Bookends	Simon and Garfunkel
Cheap Thrills	Big Brother and the Holding Co.
Child Is Father to the Man	Blood, Sweat, and Tears
Children of the Future	Steve Miller
The Circle Game	Tom Rush
Creedence Clearwater Revival	Creedence Clearwater Revival
Dance to the Music	Sly and the Family Stone
Electric Ladyland	Jimi Hendrix
For Once in My Life	Stevie Wonder
Greatest Hits	Hollies
Green Onions	Booker T. and the MGs
Gris-Gris	Dr. John
Hurdy Gurdy Man	Donovan
In-a-Gadda-Da-Vida	Iron Butterfly
Johnny Cash at Folsom Prison	Johnny Cash
Lady Soul	Aretha Franklin
Lucille	B.B. King
Mr. Fantasy	Traffic
Mixed Bag	Richie Havens
Music From Big Pink	Band
Randy Newman	Randy Newman
The Resurrection of Pigboy Crabshaw	Butterfield Blues Band
Sailor	Steve Miller
Shine On Brightly	Procul Harum
Steppenwolf	Steppenwolf
Sweetheart of the Rodeo	Byrds
The Time Has Come	Chambers Brothers
Traffic	Traffic
Truth	Jeff Beck
Vincebus Eruptum	Blue Cheer
Waiting for the Sun	Doors
Wheels of Fire	Cream
White Album	Beatles
Wildflowers	Judy Collins

Pop Goes Miami

DECEMBER 28, 1968. The Miami Pop Festival, the first major rock festival outside California, opens. Held at Gulfstream, a large horseracing track in the town of Hallandale, the festival attracts nearly 100,000 fans for what is also the first true profit-making festival; previous ones had either not made money or had donated profits to charity. Through the innovative use of two stages at opposite ends of the track, each alternating performers, the three-day festival features a wide range of rock, folk, jazz, and country music: Joni Mitchell, Marvin Gaye, the Box Tops, Lester Flatt and Earl Scruggs, Jose Feliciano, Three Dog Night, Procul Harum, Fleetwood Mac, the Turtles, Iron Butterfly, Canned Heat, Buffy Sainte-Marie, Country Joe and the Fish, Richie Havens, Charles Lloyd, the Grateful Dead, Chuck Berry, and many more.

Flashback
Top Singles—1969

Aquarius/Let the Sunshine In	Fifth Dimension
Bad Moon Rising	Creedence Clearwater Revival
The Ballad of John and Yoko	Beatles
The Boxer	Simon and Garfunkel
Come Together	Beatles
Crimson and Clover	Tommy James and the Shondells
Cripple Creek	Band
Easy to Be Hard	Three Dog Night
Eli's Coming	Three Dog Night
Everybody's Talkin'	Harry Nilsson
Everyday People	Sly and the Family Stone
Games People Play	Joe South
Get Back	Beatles
Get Together	Youngbloods
Give Peace a Chance	Plastic Ono Band
Good Morning Starshine	Oliver
Green River	Creedence Clearwater Revival
He Ain't Heavy	Hollies
Honky Tonk Woman	Rolling Stones
I Can't Get Next to You	Temptations
In the Ghetto	Elvis Presley
In the Year 2525	Zager and Evans
It's Your Thing	Isley Brothers
Lay Lady Lay	Bob Dylan
Leaving On a Jet Plane	Peter, Paul, and Mary
Ob-La Di, Ob-La-Da	Beatles
Oh, Happy Day	Edwin Hawkins Singers
Oh, What a Night	Dells
One	Three Dog Night
Okie From Muskogee	Merle Haggard
Pinball Wizard	Who
Proud Mary	Creedence Clearwater Revival
Someday We'll Be Together	Diana Ross and the Supremes
Something	Beatles
These Eyes	Guess Who
Too Busy Thinking About My Baby	Marvin Gaye
Touch Me	Doors
The Thrill Is Gone	B.B. King
Whole Lotta Love	Led Zeppelin
Yester-Me, Yester-You, Yesterday	Stevie Wonder
You Made Me So Very Happy	Blood, Sweat, and Tears

Piece Symbol

FEBRUARY 28, 1969. *Time* magazine reports that the "groupie"—"a girl who goes to bed with members of rock-and-roll bands"—is the latest rock phenomenon. Frank Zappa informs *Time's* reporter that "Every trade has its groupies. Some chicks dig truck drivers. Some go for men in uniform—the early camp followers. Ours go for rock musicians." Anna, "a pretty, 25-year-old San Franciscan," explains further: "A girl is a groupie only if she has numerous relationships. A groupie will maybe sleep with three people all in one night from one group—from the equipment man to whoever is most important."

Double Exposure

MARCH 1, 1969. The Doors' Jim Morrison is arrested at

a Miami performance, charged with exposing himself and masturbating while on stage. He will be charged with lewd and lascivious behavior (in Florida, a felony with a maximum three-year jail sentence), profanity, and drunkenness, cancelling all further Doors concerts for months. In August 1970, the day before his sentencing, he will be arrested again in Miami after passing out drunk on the porch of an elderly woman's house. Later he will be acquitted of lewd behavior but found guilty of indecent exposure. His sentence of eight months' hard labor will be under appeal in 1971, when Morrison dies of a drug overdose in Paris.

Morrison: Lewd and lascivious.

Flashback
Top Albums—1969

A Salty Dog	Procul Harum
Abbey Road	Beatles
Alone Together	Dave Mason
Aoxomoxoa	Grateful Dead
Aretha's Gold	Aretha Franklin
At San Quentin	Johnny Cash
The Band	Band
Bayou Country	Creedence Clearwater Revival
Beach Boys '69	Beach Boys
Blind Faith	Blind Faith
Blood, Sweat, and Tears	Blood, Sweat, and Tears
Chicago Transit Authority	Chicago
Crosby, Stills, and Nash	Crosby, Stills, and Nash
Diana Ross and the Supremes Join the Temptations	Supremes and Temptations
Everybody Knows This Is Nowhere	Neil Young
First Take	Roberta Flack
Giant Step	Taj Mahal
Goodbye	Cream
Green River	Creedence Clearwater Revival
Hair	original cast
Hot Buttered Soul	Isaac Hayes
Joe Cocker	Joe Cocker
Johnny Cash at San Quentin	Johnny Cash
Led Zepplin II	Led Zepplin
Let It Bleed	Rolling Stones
Loosen Up Naturally	Sons of Champlain
Nashville Skyline	Bob Dylan
On the Threshold of a Dream	Moody Blues
Peter, Paul, and Mommy	Peter, Paul, and Mary
Pickin' Up the Pieces	Poco
Retrospective	Buffalo Springfield
River Deep, Mountain High	Ike and Tina Turner
Santana	Santana
The Second	Steppenwolf
Spooky Two	Spooky Tooth
Three Dog Night	Three Dog Night
Tommy	Who
Two Virgins	John Lennon and Yoko Ono
Volunteers	Jefferson Airplane
Willy and the Poor Boys	Creedence Clearwater Revival
We're Only In It For the Money	Mothers of Invention
Yellow Submarine	Beatles

I Married Paul

MARCH 12, 1969. Paul McCartney and American photographer Linda Eastman walk into the Marylebone Registrar's Office in London, accompanied by his brother, singer Mike McGear, to be married, thus beating his long-time partner John Lennon to the altar by a week.

Undercover Operation

MARCH 20, 1969. John Lennon and Yoko Ono marry in Gibraltar, then fly to Holland to begin a "bed-in" for peace at the Amsterdam Hilton. Media from the world over will flock to their bedside to record the event, the first of several bed-ins the two will stage. At a bed-in in Montreal, Timothy Leary, Tommy Smothers, Mick Jagger, and others will join Lennon and Ono for a bed-in sing-in, during which Lennon's new song, "Give Peace a Chance," will be recorded. It will become an international anthem for peace demonstrators.

Lady of the Canyon

APRIL 4, 1969. Joni Mitchell, for years a successful songwriter, comes of age as her album *Clouds* reaches bestseller status. Born in Saskatchewan, Canada, Mitchell had taken up music seriously just five years ago when, at age 19, she began playing the ukulele as an art student at Calgary, then drifted into folk music. In

Flashback

Top DJs

Bob Barry	WOKY, Milwaukee
Ron Britain	WSAI, Cincinnati
Cousin Brucie	WABC, New York
Juicy Brucey	WBZ, Boston
Jack Carney	WIL, St. Louis
Tom Clay	WJBK, Detroit
Cerphe Colwell	WHFS, Washington, D.C.
Frankie "The Love Man" Crocker	WADO, New York
Fat Daddy	WWIN, Baltimore
Dandy Dan Daniels	WABC-AM, New York
Don Dillard	WDON, Washington, D.C.
Doctor Daddy	KDKO, Denver
"Big Daddy" Tom Donahue	KMPX, (also KSAN), San Francisco
Alan "Moondog" Freed	WWJ, Cleveland (also WINS, Los Angeles, WQAM, Miami)
Arnie "Woo Woo" Ginsburg	WMEX, Boston
Jocko Henderson	WADO, New York
Wolfman Jack	XERB, Mexico (later, 200+ stations nationwide)
Waylon Jennings	KLLL, Lubbock, Tex.
Dr. Jive	WWRL, New York
Murray the K	WINS, New York (also WMCA, New York)
"Casey at the Mike" Kasem	KEWB (later KNEW), Oakland, Calif.
Herb Kent "the Cool Gent"	WBON, Chicago
Russ "Weird Beard" Knight	KLIF, Dallas
Larry Lujack	WLS, Chicago
Uncle Mike McKuen	KHOW, Denver
Cousin Bruce Morrow	WABC, New York
Scott Muni	WMCA, New York
Tony Pygg	WPLJ, New York
Bill Randle	WERE, Cleveland
Dusty Rhodes	WSAI, Cincinnati
Barry Richards ("the boss with the hot sauce")	WHMC, Washington, D.C.
Rockin' Robbie D	WCHB, Detroit
Danny Schecter	WBCN, Boston
Robin Seymour	WKMH, Detroit
Jack Spector ("the News Dissector")	WMCA, New York
Allison Steele	WNEW, New York
Real Don Steele	KHJ, Los Angeles
Brother Sebastian Stone	WOR-FM, New York
Dusty Street	KSAN, San Francisco
"Symphony Sid" Torin	WABC, New York
Peter Tripp	WMGM, New York
Bob Wrightman	WZMF/WTOS, Milwaukee
Michael Xanadu	WEBN-FM, Cincinnati

Toronto she worked as a salesgirl to earn the $14 she needed to join the musicians union, enabling her to perform in city cafes. Her tender ballad "Both Sides Now" has been recorded successfully by Frank Sinatra, Bing Crosby, and Judy Collins, but her own performing remained in the background until her appearance at the Miami Pop Festival in December, which helped create a swelling army of admirers. In the next few years, Mitchell will record several top-selling albums, including *Ladies of the Canyon*, *Blue*, and *Court and Spark*, her first of three gold records.

Mitchell: From salesgirl to superstar.

Newport News

JUNE 20, 1969. Newport '69, a rock festival featuring Jimi Hendrix, Taj Mahal, Steppenwolf, Creedence Clearwater Revival, Joe Cocker, the Chambers

Brothers, and many others, opens in Northridge, Calif. It is the first of what will be a summer full of festivals, with nearly a dozen major events held throughout the U.S.

Aftermath

JULY 7, 1969. Brian Jones is found dead in his swimming pool only 24 days after quitting the Rolling Stones. Jones, whose heavy womanizing and drug use had led to tensions within the group, will be replaced by 20-year-old Mick Taylor—who had previously replaced Eric Clapton in John Mayall's Bluesbreakers—until 1974, when he will leave and be replaced by Ron Wood, formerly with Jeff Beck and Small Faces.

Elvis is Back

JULY 31, 1969. Elvis Presley, trying to make a comeback, debuts at the Las Vegas International Hotel for a four-week run, for which he reportedly is paid $1 million. It will be the first of several Las Vegas appearances for Presley.

Elvis: Winning big at Vegas.

Yasgur's Farm

AUGUST 15, 1969. The Woodstock Music and Art Fair, subtitled "An Aquarian Exposition," opens on an alfalfa field in Bethel in the mountains of upstate New York. The project is the brainchild of four young men: John Roberts, heir to the Polident fortune, who has put up $2.5 million; his good friend Joel Rosenman, who wants to use his father's money to finance a career in entertainment; Michael Lang, an ex-head shop owner; and his friend Artie Kornfeld, a part-time producer and lyricist for a top-40 band, the Cowsills. The four originally hoped to attract 50,000 people to a concert that would be a big money-making event, but the project has mushroomed beyond anyone's expectations. Blocked by a court order from their proposed festival site near Woodstock, they pay $50,000 to farmer Max Yasgur to lease his 1,000 acres of farmland, pasture, and woodland on a lake in Bethel, 30 miles away. Yasgur already has taken an interest in young people: last year he leased his property to the Boy Scouts for their National Jamboree. As word of the concert spreads, attendance projections have been hiked to 200,000, but the day before the festival, even those projections were raised. By the end of this first day, a monstrous traffic jam will clog roads for 15 miles in all directions around Bethel, forcing performing rock groups to be flown by helicopter to the stage area. Food will be another problem: By the end of this first day, a half-million hot dogs and hamburgers will be gone and well water will become contaminated or will stop flowing altogether. Still another problem will be weather. It will rain most of the weekend, turning the grounds into acres of mud; the rain will also wash away the dirt covering electrical cables as well as some of the cables' insulation. But such problems will be handled without serious mishap. In the end, more than 400,000 people will show up, most without

Flashback
Woodstock Payroll

Max Yasgur	$50,000
Jimi Hendrix	18,000
Blood, Sweat, and Tears	15,000
Joan Baez	10,000
Creedence Clearwater Revival	10,000
The Band	7,500
Janis Joplin	7,500
The Jefferson Airplane	7,500
Sly and the Family Stone	7,500
Canned Heat	6,500
The Who	6,250
Richie Havens	6,000
Arlo Guthrie	5,000
Crosby, Stills, Nash, and Young	5,000
Ravi Shankar	4,500
Johnny Winter	3,750
Ten Years After	3,250
Country Joe and the Fish	2,500
The Grateful Dead	2,250
The Incredible String Band	2,250
Mountain	2,000
Tim Hardin	2,000
Joe Cocker	1,375
Sweetwater	1,250
John Sebastian	1,000
Melanie	750
Sha Na Na	700

Woodstock: "Death of the American dinosaur."

tickets, forcing the promoters to declare the event open and free. For three days, 24 bands will play, including Jimi Hendrix, Janis Joplin, the Who, the Jefferson Airplane, Arlo Guthrie, Joan Baez, Richie Havens, Joe Cocker, the Grateful Dead, Santana, Sly and the Family Stone, Canned Heat, Ravi Shankar, and Crosby, Stills, Nash, and Young, the group's first public appearance as a foursome. Tickets, for those who bought them, are $7 per day, $18 for all three. The successful festival will be heralded as the calling card of a generation—the Woodstock Generation, it will be called—although the press will be slow to recognize the significance of nearly a half-million young people coming together peacefully for three days of music. Although poet Allen Ginsberg will call Woodstock "a major planetary event" and radical Abbie Hoffman will declare that it signaled "the death of the American dinosaur," the *New York Times* will liken the festival to a march of lemmings to the sea and the conservative *National Review* will complain that the event demonstrated "mass infantilism." Early next year, Max Yasgur will be sued for $35,000 damages by neighboring farmers and the concert's promoters will announce that they lost more than $1 million, which they will recoup in sales of the record and film made of the event.

Frankly Speaking—II

AUGUST 20, 1969. The Mothers of Invention disband after leader Frank Zappa declares that he is "tired of playing for people who clap for all the wrong reasons."

Bubblegum

SEPTEMBER 20, 1969. "Sugar, Sugar" by the Archies becomes the first "bubblegum" single to hit the number-one spot, although other bubblegum groups, including the Ohio Express and the 1910 Fruitgum Company, have edged into the top 10 during the past year. Bubblegum is a light, simple-minded style aimed at the subteen market which, though demonstrably willing to spend money for records, fanzines, and concert tickets, is perceived as being uninterested in the antiwar, prodrug sentiments that underlie "serious" rock releases; however, sex, slightly sanitized, is a viable topic. Bubblegum was primarily the brainchild of Buddah Records whiz Neil Bogart, who in 1974 will show that he remembered his lessons by creating an irresistibly photogenic, exaggerated glitter image for the marginally talented Kiss, whom he will sign to his own Casablanca Records.

I Buried Paul

SEPTEMBER 23, 1969. Rumors that "Paul is dead" begin with an article in *Northern Star*, the newspaper of Illinois University. The rumors will take off three weeks later when Detroit DJ Russ Gibb will claim to have received reliable word of Paul McCartney's death, alleged to have taken place November 9, 1966, as described in the Beatles tunes, "I Am the Walrus" and "A Day in the Life." (According to Gibb, McCartney "blew his mind out in a car" because he "didn't notice that the light had changed.") Hysterical fans, pointing to clues on the covers of *Sgt. Pepper* and *Abbey Road*, will theorize that a lookalike named Billy Spear has been impersonating the dead Beatle. As rumors spread, McCartney poses for the cover of *Life* magazine to provide living proof. He will later say, "If I was dead, I'm sure I'd be the last to know."

National Anthem

NOVEMBER 14, 1969. "Give Peace a Chance" by John Lennon and Yoko Ono's Plastic Ono Band is adopted as the unofficial anthem of the antiwar movement at peace demonstrations throughout the country. The gatherings, topped by more than a quarter-million demonstrators on the Mall in Washington, D.C., are part of a two-day National Moratorium.

Flashback
Top Singles—1970

ABC	Jackson 5
Ain't No Mountain High Enough	Diana Ross
All Right Now	Free
American Woman	Guess Who
A Ball of Confusion	Temptations
Border Song	Elton John
Bridge Over Troubled Waters	Simon and Garfunkel
Candida	Tony Orlando
Close to You	Carpenters
Fire and Rain	James Taylor
I Want You Back	Jackson 5
Instant Karma	Plastic Ono Band
Knock Three Times	Tony Orlando
Let It Be	Beatles
The Letter	Joe Cocker
The Long and Winding Road	Beatles
Love On a Two-Way Street	Moments
Love the One You're With	Stephen Stills
The Love You Save	Jackson 5
Make Me Smile	Chicago
Mama Told Me (Not to Come)	Three Dog Night
No Time	Guess Who
Ohio	Neil Young
Raindrops Keep Falling On My Head	B.J. Thomas
Reach Out and Touch Somebody's Hand	Diana Ross
Signed Sealed Delivered I'm Yours	Stevie Wonder
Someday We'll Be Together	Supremes
Spirit in the Sky	Norman Greenbaum
Stoned Love	Supremes
Tears of a Clown	Smokey Robinson and the Miracles
Thank You	Sly and the Family Stone
The Tears of a Clown	Miracles
25 or 6 to 4	Chicago
Woodstock	Crosby, Stills, Nash, and Young
Your Song	Elton John

Ball and Chain

NOVEMBER 15, 1969. Janis Joplin is arrested in Tampa, Fla., on charges of using "vulgar and indecent language." The incident follows local police efforts to restrain a surging, frenzied audience at her concert. When the police resorted to a bullhorn, Joplin shouted, "There won't be any trouble if you just leave!" The police didn't and Joplin let loose a string of blistering obscenities, resulting in her arrest. Free on bail, she will proclaim that "I don't mind getting arrested because I've turned a lot of kids on."

Rolling Stones: Angels of death.

Helter Skelter

DECEMBER 6, 1969. The Rolling Stones play host to 300,000 fans at a free "thank you" concert at Altamont Speedway in Livermore, Calif. The idea had been tried last July at a free concert in London's Hyde Park for 250,000 fans. It was natural to want to replicate the event in the U.S. during a festival-crazy 1969. Actually, Ken Kesey and his Merry Pranksters, along with the California-based Hell's Angels, suggested the idea to the Stones in late 1968. Despite the long leadtime, the actual performance has been planned hastily, largely because of a last-minute change in location only two days ago. Among other things, there hadn't been sufficient time to arrange for adequate security from local police, so the task has fallen to the Hell's Angels, who are hired for $500 worth of beer. The Angels turn out to cause more problems than they solve, beating several spectators and fatally stabbing one. Even the bands—which, in addition to the Stones include Santana, the Jefferson Airplane, and Crosby, Stills, Nash, and Young—must cut their performances short because of the unruly crowds; trying to stop the violence, the Airplane's lead singer Marty Balin is kicked uncon-

Flashback
Top Albums—1970

A Question of Balance	Moody Blues
Abraxas	Santana
After the Gold Rush	Neil Young
All Things Must Pass	George Harrison
American Beauty	Grateful Dead
Band of Gypsies	Jimi Hendrix
Bridge Over Troubled Water	Simon and Garfunkel
Chapter Two	Roberta Flack
Cosmo's Factory	Creedence Clearwater Revival
Deja Vu	Crosby, Stills, Nash, and Young
Elton John	Elton John
Emerson, Lake, and Palmer	Emerson, Lake, and Palmer
Get Your Ya-Ya's Out!	Rolling Stones
Gonna Take a Miracle	Laura Nyro
Hey Jude	Beatles
If You Could Read My Mind	Gordon Lightfoot
In My Life	Judy Collins
In the Court of the Crimson King	King Crimson
J. Geils Band	J. Geils Band
Jesus Christ Superstar	original cast
John Barleycorn Must Die	Traffic
John Sebastian	John Sebastian
Ladies of the Canyon	Joni Mitchell
Layla and Other Assorted Songs	Derek and the Dominoes
Led Zeppelin III	Led Zeppelin
Let It Be	Beatles
Live at Monterey	Jimi Hendrix
Mad Dogs and Englishmen	Joe Cocker
McCartney	Paul McCartney
Moondance	Van Morrison
Morrison Hotel	Doors
On Tour	Delaney and Bonnie and Friends
Pendulum	Creedence Clearwater Revival
Ry Cooder	Ry Cooder
Supersession	Mike Bloomfield, Al Kooper, Steve Stills
Sweet Baby James	James Taylor
Trout Mask Replica	Capt. Beefheart and His Magic Band
Wonderful World, Beautiful People	Jimmy Cliff
Woodstock	various artists
Workingman's Dead	Grateful Dead

scious. Only four months after Woodstock, Altamont will put a period to the so-called Summer of Love. The following day, Mick Jagger will say, "If Jesus had been there, he would have been crucified."

Local Boys Make Good

JANUARY 10, 1970. Five brothers aged 12 to 19, hometown boys introduced by Gary, Ind., mayor Richard Hatcher to visiting star Diana Ross, become teen idols when their first single, "I Want You Back," hits number one. The Jackson 5 will have three top-10 albums before the end of the year. Their stage act, which includes flashy, fringy, post-Hendrix outfits and coordinated choreography, will at first echo but soon surpass that of the Osmonds; the white five-brother band, having spent some years on the Disneyland and Andy Williams circuits, will take the hint and release its own first teen-idol album early next year.

Jackson 5: Supreme intervention.

Moog Music

JANUARY 24, 1970. The "Mini-Moog" synthesizer is introduced by its creator, Robert Moog, 34, an amateur musician with a Ph.D. in engineering physics from Cornell. It is a smaller version of his previously introduced contraption that looks like the control panel of a jet airliner with an organ keyboard grafted on it. The original version has produced, among other things, the bing-bong theme that for years preceded all CBS-TV color shows and produced a bestselling album, *Switched-On Bach*, by composer Walter Carlos in 1966. The new Mini-Moog has been designed for concert stages and sells for $2,000, a far cry from the $100,000 price tag of some original models. The American Federation of Musicians will soon consider a ban on the Mini-Moog, fearing that such "automation" could put its members out of business.

The Sounds of War

JANUARY 28, 1970. The Vietnam Moratorium Committee sponsors a benefit concert at Madison Square Garden featuring such performers as Jimi Hendrix; Blood, Sweat, and Tears; Peter, Paul, and Mary; Judy Collins; Richie Havens; Dave Brubeck; Harry Belafonte; and the cast of the musical *Hair*. The event will raise nearly $150,000.

Blue Cheer

MARCH 19, 1970. After leading the Worcester, Mass., audience in his anthemic "Fish Cheer"—"Give me an F...Give me a U...Give me a C...Give me a K"—Country Joe McDonald is fined $500 for obscenity.

Girls Just Wanna Have Fun

MAY 16, 1970. The Jefferson Airplane's Marty Balin is arrested in his hotel room in Bloomington, Minn., after being discovered with several girls aged 12 to 17. He will be sentenced to a year's hard labor but will only pay a $100 fine.

Fab Four's Finale

MAY 20, 1970. The film *Let It Be* premieres at the London Palladium, but none of the Beatles shows up, reflecting increasing animosity among the four. Example: John Lennon, Paul McCartney, and Ringo Starr have feuded recently over whose solo album will be released when. Soon, several Beatles will consider suing the others to dissolve their partnership and divide their considerable assets. On New Year's Eve, McCartney will take that step, serving papers on the other three. A brief trial will be followed by a lengthy appeal, during which the assets of Apple Corp. will bc put into receivership, the final step in the group's demise.

Elvis Presley, Secret Agent

In 1970, on a flight from Los Angeles, Elvis Presley bumped into California's Sen. George Murphy. He confessed to Murphy that, although he had many honors, including a special badge from Richard Nixon making him an honorary agent of the Bureau of Narcotics and Dangerous Drugs, he had always longed to meet FBI director J. Edgar Hoover. On his behalf, Murphy called the FBI.

The bureau was hesitant. In Presley's favor were his honorable service in the U.S. Army in Germany, his lack of a police record, and the fact that the Junior Chamber of Commerce had singled out Elvis that year as one of America's "Ten Outstanding Young Men."

However, in the FBI files were also a notation that Presley "is presently involved in a paternity suit" and this: "During the latter part of the 1950s and early 1960s, his gyrations while performing were the subject of considerable criticism by the public and comment in the press."

The conclusion of Hoover's underlings: "Presley's sincerity and good intentions notwithstanding, he is certainly not the type of individual whom the director would wish to meet. It is noted at the present time he is wearing his hair down to his shoulders and indulges in the wearing of all sorts of exotic dress." Agents who had seen careers ruined by unsquared pocket handkerchiefs and sweaty palms were not about to risk theirs on a singer who dressed as if it were Mardi Gras.

Presley was offered a special tour of FBI headquarters, but no visit with Hoover, who was officially "out of town for the holidays." On the tour, conducted New Year's Eve, 1970 the agents got a surprise.

An FBI summary reads: "Despite his rather bizarre personal appearance, Presley seemed a sincere, serious-minded individual who expressed concern over some of the problems confronting our country, particularly those involving young people."

The report said Presley blamed the Beatles for "many of the problems we are having with young people by their filthy, unkempt appearances and suggestive music." And he said Jane Fonda and the Smothers Brothers would "have a lot to answer for in the hereafter for the way they have poisoned young minds by disparaging statements and unsavory activities." Presley apologized for his long hair and unusual dress, explaining that they were "tools of the trade."

The director and his top staffers were pleased especially with this part of the report:

Presley advised that he . . . from time to time is approached by individuals and groups in and outside of the entertainment business whose motives and goals he is convinced are not in the best interests of this country and who seek to have him lend his name to their questionable activities. In this regard, he volunteered to make such information available to the Bureau on a confidential basis whenever it came to his attention. He further indicated that he wanted the director to know that should the Bureau ever have any need of his services in any way, that he would be delighted to be of assistance.

The final irony is that Elvis' good intentions and special narcotics-agent badge he liked to flash didn't save him from dying in 1977 of a drug overdose.

It Ain't Me, Babe

JUNE 9, 1970. High school dropout Bob Dylan is awarded an honorary Ph.D. in music at Princeton University's graduation ceremonies.

Southern Man

JULY 5, 1970. Georgia Governor Lester Maddox announces that he will seek a law to ban rock festivals in his state. The announcement follows the end of the three-day Atlanta Pop Festival, during which a rash of drug problems prompted area doctors to ask government authorities to declare the festival a disaster area. At this festival, Jimi Hendrix performed his legendary version of "The Star-Spangled Banner" on the Fourth of July. Maddox's proposed bill will get nowhere.

I Don't Live Today

AUGUST 26, 1970. Jimi Hendrix makes his last public appearance, at the Isle of Wight Pop Festival in England. Joining him are Joni Mitchell, Joan Baez, Bob Dylan, and others, performing for the 250,000 fans. During the five-day festival, the area will become so crowded that one man will jump onto the stage during a Joni Mitchell performance to declare, "This is just a hippie concentration camp!" Within a month Hendrix will be dead, the victim, according to the death certificate, of "inhalation of vomit due to barbiturate intoxication."

All Things Must Pass

OCTOBER 9, 1970. John Lennon, the oldest Beatle, turns 30.

I Right the Songs—I

OCTOBER 24, 1970. In a speech to a White House conference of radio broadcasters, President Nixon appeals for rock lyrics to be screened and for those urging drug use to be banned.

I Right the Songs—II

NOVEMBER 7, 1970. MGM president Mike Curb, 25, begins a campaign against drugs by dropping 18 acts from his roster in a

Francis: Curbed.

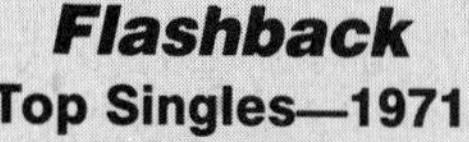

Ain't No Sunshine	Bill Withers
Brown Sugar	Rolling Stones
Domino	Van Morrison
18	Alice Cooper
How Can You Mend a Broken Heart?	Bee Gees
Imagine	John Lennon
If You Could Read My Mind	Gordon Lightfoot
Isn't It a Pity?	George Harrison
It's Too Late	Carole King
Joy to the World	Three Dog Night
Lonely Days	Bee Gees
Maggie May	Rod Stewart
Me and Bobby McGee	Janis Joplin
My Sweet Lord	George Harrison
One Bad Apple	Osmonds
One Toke Over the Line	Brewer and Shipley
Peace Train	Cat Stevens
Proud Mary	Ike and Tina Turner
Riders on the Storm	Doors
Spanish Harlem	Aretha Franklin
Uncle Albert	Paul McCartney
What's Going On?	Marvin Gaye

move to discredit musicians who "exploit and promote hard drugs through music." Among the acts dropped is Connie Francis, but not Eric Burdon, although he soon will leave the label. Says Curb: "Hard drug groups come into your office, wipe out your secretary, waste the time of your promotion people, abuse the people in your organization, show no concern in the recording studio, abuse the equipment, and then to top things off, they break up." Soon, President Nixon will commend Curb for his "forthright stand," but some industry skeptics will claim that Curb was more motivated by economic rather than moral considerations. Later Curb's motivations will prove to be political: in 1973 he will leave MGM, then run successfully for lieutenant governor of California.

Sweet Baby James

MARCH 10, 1971. Madison Square Garden bursts with the throngs who've come to hear James Taylor, 23, proclaimed by many as the first pop music superstar of the 1970s. His recent album *Sweet Baby James* has already gone platinum, boosted by one of its cuts, "Fire and Rain." Taylor's success comes from his unique blend of sounds, which combines soft rock with country and western, folk, and blues. Born in Boston to a wealthy family, he won a hootenanny contest at age 15—a week's work in a coffeehouse. He dropped out of Milton Academy, an exclusive boarding school near Boston, to join a rock band, the Fabulous Corsayers. Back in Milton for his senior year, he suffered severe emotional problems, attempted suicide, and committed himself to a mental institution. He emerged healthy and with a friend formed a rock group, the Flying Machine. The group moved to New York, where Taylor knocked around and indulged in heavy drugs, including heroin. In 1968, desperate for salvation, he sent a demo tape to Peter Asher (formerly of Peter and Gordon), the new director of Apple Records, recently founded by the Beatles. Asher signed him to a three-year contract. The first album didn't do well, but Taylor's career began to flourish in 1970. A recording contract with Warner Bros. resulted in *Sweet Baby James*

Flashback
Top Albums—1971

Allman Brothers Band at Fillmore East	Allman Brothers Band
American Pie	Don McLean
Anticipation	Carly Simon
Aqualung	Jethro Tull
Best of the Guess Who	Guess Who
Blue	Joni Mitchell
Boz Scaggs	Boz Scaggs
Earth, Wind, and Fire	Earth, Wind, and Fire
Every Picture Tells a Story	Rod Stewart
Four Way Street	Crosby, Stills, Nash, and Young
Future Games	Fleetwood Mac
Gasoline Alley	Rod Stewart
Here Comes the Sun	Nina Simone
Joy of Cooking	Joy of Cooking
Live at the Fillmore West	King Curtis
Lost in the Ozone	Commander Cody and His Lost Planet Airmen
Love It to Death	Alice Cooper
Meaty, Beaty, Big, and Bouncy	Who
Mudlark	Leo Kottke
Mud Slide Slim and the Blue Horizon	James Taylor
New Riders of the Purple Sage	New Riders of the Purple Sage
Nilsson Schmilsson	Harry Nilsson
Pearl	Janis Joplin
Rita Coolidge	Rita Coolidge
Sticky Fingers	Rolling Stones
Tapestry	Carole King
Tea for the Tillerman	Cat Stevens
There's a Riot Goin' On	Sly and the Family Stone
Tumbleweed Connection	Elton John
Tupulo Honey	Van Morrison
What's Going On	Marvin Gaye
Who's Next	Who
The Yes Album	Yes

Taylor: Desperate for salvation.

and will produce several other successful albums, including *Mudslide Slim*, *One Man Dog*, *Gorilla*, and *JT*. In 1972 he will marry singer/songwriter Carly Simon.

Don't Look Back

May 24, 1971. Bob Dylan, temporarily observing his religious roots, celebrates his 30th birthday at the Wailing Wall in Jerusalsm.

Dylan: Born again.

Acid Test

MAY 30, 1971. After a concert by the Grateful Dead at San Francisco's Winterland Auditorium, more than 30 fans are hospitalized after unknowingly drinking apple juice spiked with LSD. The band will be accused of spiking the drink, but insufficient evidence will be found to press charges.

King: Never too late, baby.

Just Desserts

JUNE 7, 1971. Carole King's *Tapestry* goes gold. The album, which contains her number-one hit "It's Too Late," finally brings star status to King, who has been writing hit songs for other performers since 1962. *Tapestry* will become one of the bestselling albums of all time, remaining on the charts for more than three years.

When the Music's Over

JULY 31, 1971. Jim Morrison is reported dead in Paris, variously of a heart attack and a heroin overdose. This, the third drug death of a major rock star in less than a year (after Jimi Hendrix and Janis Joplin), will provoke some fans to charge that all three are either alive in hiding (a theme that will inspire several novels and movies in coming years) or have been assassinated by antirock forces.

Help Us If You Can

AUGUST 1, 1971. The Concerts for Bangla Desh, produced by George Harrison for starving people in that Asian country, are held in New York, featuring Ringo Starr, Billy Preston, Eric Clapton, and Ravi Shankar. Days earlier, Harrison had released a single, "Bangla Desh," in which he urged listeners to "help us save some lives." The song will close the concert.

Brothers Gibb

AUGUST 7, 1971. The Bee Gees achieve their first number-one hit with the single "How Can You Mend a Broken Heart?" The group, who many claim sound like the early Beatles, includes three brothers, Andy, Barry, and Maurice Gibb; the band's name comes from the initials for "brothers Gibb." Britons who grew up in Australia, the brothers first

Bee Gees: From drought to disco.

reached the charts in 1967 with "New York Mining Disaster 1941," but haven't been heard from much since. Following this success, they will lapse into another artistic drought, emerging in 1974 as a disco-rock band. They will produce six number-one songs, culminating with the soundtrack for *Saturday Night Fever* in 1978, which will dominate the airwaves for months and set new industry sales records.

Sax and Violence

AUGUST 14, 1971. King Curtis (Curtis Ousley) is stabbed to death in a Manhattan alley, apparently by a jealous lover. Curtis, best known as a saxophonist, although he also sang and played guitar, was one of the premier session men of the 1960s, backing such artists as the Coasters, Connie Francis, Sam Cooke, and Nat "King" Cole. A few years ago, as his Atco albums began to attract a wider audience, Curtis became a popular concert and rock festival draw; his *Live at Fillmore West* album will remain on the national charts for several months after his death.

A King and a Duke

SEPTEMBER 8, 1971. Elvis Presley receives the Bing Crosby Award, given to members of the recording industry who "have made creative contributions of outstanding artistic or scientific significance...." Previous honorees Duke Ellington, Irving Berlin, and Frank Sinatra.

Rod the Mod

OCTOBER 1, 1971. Rod Stewart's single "Maggie Mae" and album *Every Picture Tells a Story* both hit number one, establishing "Rod the Mod" as a star in his own right after years of performing with others. Stewart, 26, sang on the streets throughout Europe until the mid-1960s, first hooking up with the Five Dimensions, one of Chuck Berry's backup bands, and with guitarist Jeff Beck on his classic 1968 album *Truth*. A 1969 solo release, *The Rod Stewart Album*, was a temporary departure from Beck and, although not commercially successful, was a proving ground for Stewart's most recent effort. Latching onto a talented backup group, Small Faces, later shortened to "Faces," Stewart will produce two more albums—including the much-acclaimed *A Nod Is as Good As a Wink*—before slipping into relative obscurity in England in 1976. There he will become the object of London punkers' wrath as the personification of disgusting wealth and "celebrity," a charge Stewart has fueled by first living with actress Britt Eklund, then marrying George Hamilton's ex-wife Alana. Stewart will be back, however, in the early 1980s.

Stewart: The wrath of Mods.

Better Known Than Beatles

OCTOBER 20, 1971. *Jesus Christ, Superstar*, a staged version of the Tim Rice/Andrew Lloyd Webber rock-opera (originally released on Decca in 1969), debuts at New York's Mark Hellinger Theatre; it will run for 720 performances before closing in the summer of 1973. Ben Vereen stars as Judas, Jeff Fenholt as Jesus, and Yvonne Elliman as Mary Magdalene. Elliman's recording of "I Don't Know How to Love Him" will become her first single.

Blood on the Tracks

OCTOBER 29, 1971. Duane Allman, 24, is killed in a motorcycle accident near Macon, Ga. With his brother Gregg, Allman founded the Allman Brothers Band in the late 1960s, part of a phenomenon that will later be known as "Southern rock." In 1969 the band became the first act recorded by Capricorn Records, an independent label created by Phil Walden, formerly Otis Redding's manager. Its third album, *At Fillmore East*, propelled the group to national popularity, spurred by the innovative counterpoint guitar duets of Duane Allman and Dickey Betts. Despite Allman's death, the band will continue to tour successfully, although public attention will begin to focus more on the group's legal problems and on Gregg Allman's marriage to Cher Bono. In just over a year, another Allman Brothers member, bassist Berry Oakley, will die in an identical motorcycle accident just three blocks from the site of Allman's crash.

Allmans: Death in Dixie.

Flashback
Top Singles—1972

American Pie	Don McLean
Alone Again (Naturally)	Gilbert O'Sullivan
Backstabbers	O'Jays
Doctor My Eyes	Jackson Browne
Don't Mess With Jim	Jim Croce
Family Affair	Sly and the Family Stone
The First Time Ever I Saw Your Face	Roberta Flack
Heart of Gold	Neil Young
Honky Cat	Elton John
A Horse With No Name	America
I Am Woman	Helen Reddy
I Can See Clearly Now	Johnny Nash
If Loving You Is Wrong	Luther Ingram
I'll Take You There	Staple Singers
Layla	Derek and the Dominoes
Let's Stay Together	Al Green
Morning Has Broken	Cat Stevens
Mother and Child Reunion	Paul Simon
My Ding-a-Ling	Chuck Berry
Nights in White Satin	Moody Blues
Papa Was a Rolling Stone	Temptations
Rocket Man	Elton John
Summer Breeze	Seals and Crofts
Take It Easy	Eagles
Without You	Harry Nilsson

After All These Years

FEBRUARY 5, 1972. Paul Simon releases "Mother and Child Reunion," his first record without Art Garfunkel. Having grown up three blocks from each other in Queens, N.Y., they have been linked since the mid-1950s, when, as sixth-graders, they used to listen to Alan Freed's radio program together. A demonstration record of "Hey, Schoolgirl"—lyrics by Garfunkel, melody by Simon—won them an appearance on Dick Clark's radio program, where they performed under the names "Tom and Jerry." By 1960 they had nearly given up on music, both pursuing other professions, until Simon was moved by the murder of a black college friend who had gone to Mississippi to participate in civil rights demonstrations. The event inspired Simon to write "He Was My Brother," which led to a contract with Columbia Records. The duo produced *Wednesday Morning, 3 a.m.* in 1964, a relative failure, although when reissued in 1969 it went gold. One of the album's cuts, "Sounds of Silence," did receive air play, leading Columbia to remix the spare arrangement and market it as a single. The song captured the listening public at a time when folk and rock music were increasingly merging. By their third album, *Parsley, Sage, Rosemary and Thyme*, the two musicians had matured considerably, creating a sound that was both musically and lyrically sophisticated. That album produced several Simon and Garfunkel classics, including "The 59th Street Bridge Song (Feelin' Groovy)," "Scarborough Fair/Canticle," and the haunting "7 O'Clock News/Silent Night," all written by Simon. The duo parted in 1969, in part because Garfunkel was pursuing an acting career that resulted in roles in *Catch 22* (1970) and *Carnal Knowledge* (1971). But there were other reasons. Said Simon at the time: "You can't go for a long period of time as a partner, not anybody." Simon will produce two more acclaimed albums in the ear-

Simon and Garfunkel: Old friends.

Flashback

Top Albums—1972

A Good Feelin' to Know	Poco
Ballad Book	Joan Baez
Boomer's Story	Ry Cooder
Concert for Bangladesh	George Harrison
Crusaders I	Crusaders
The Divine Miss M	Bette Midler
Don't Shoot Me, I'm Only the Piano Player	Elton John
Eat a Peach	Allman Brothers Band
Give It Up	Bonnie Raitt
Gumbo	Dr. John
The Harder They Come	Jimmy Cliff
History of Eric Clapton	Eric Clapton
Home Free	Dan Fogelberg
Hot Licks, Cold Steel and Trucker's Favorites	Commander Cody and His Lost Planet Airmen
Hot Rocks	Rolling Stones
Jackson Browne	Jackson Browne
John Prine	John Prine
Last Days and Time	Earth, Wind, and Fire
Last of the Red Hot Burritos	Flying Burrito Brothers
Live with the E.S.C.	Procol Harum
Living in the Past	Jethro Tull
Lou Reed	Lou Reed
The Man Who Sold the World	David Bowie
My Time	Boz Scaggs
No Secrets	Carly Simon
Paul Simon	Paul Simon
Rockpile	Dave Edmunds
Sail Away	Randy Newman
Sittin' In	Loggins and Messina
Stairway to Heaven	Led Zeppelin
Talking Book	Stevie Wonder
Winds of Change	Peter Frampton
The World Is a Ghetto	War
You Don't Mess Around With Jim	Jim Croce
Young, Gifted, and Black	Aretha Franklin

ly 1970s, *There Goes Rhymin' Simon* and *Still Crazy After All These Years*, which will win two Grammy awards. Simon and Garfunkel will reunite briefly in October 1975 on NBC's "Saturday Night Live," and again in 1982 for a concert in New York's Central Park.

Gimme Shelter

FEBRUARY 29, 1972. John Lennon begins a four-year fight to remain in the U.S. following the expiration of his immigration visa. Lennon has been denied a renewal because of his 1968 conviction for marijuana possession, although Lennon believes it's in retaliation for his antiwar protests, particularly at the 1972 Republican convention in Miami. Despite an immigration law granting special status to "outstanding artists whose presence would be of cultural advantage to the U.S.," federal officials press their case against Lennon. In July 1974, the Justice Department will order him to leave the country within two months, although Lennon will appeal, sue Nixon administration officials John Mitchell and Richard Kleindienst, then in 1975 win the right to stay. In its decision, the U.S. Court of Appeals will call Lennon's four-year battle "a testimony to his faith in this American dream."

Politicos

MARCH 9, 1972. Carole King, James Taylor, and Barbra Streisand are among those performing at a benefit for presidential candidate George McGovern in Los Angeles. The concert will begin a tradition of rock musicians' efforts for political candidates. Over the next few months, other performers—including Warren Beatty, Judy Collins, Mama Cass Elliot, Michelle Phillips, Goldie Hawn, Simon and Garfunkel, Peter, Paul, and Mary, Mike Nichols, Elaine May, and Jack Nicholson—will work on McGovern's behalf. The marriage of politics and performers will blossom in the 1976 campaign, with Capricorn Records president Phil Walden putting his entire roster—including the Allman Brothers and the Marshall Tucker Band—behind former Georgia governor Jimmy Carter. In 1979 the Eagles, Linda Ronstadt, Chicago, and Helen Reddy will be among the artists who stump for California governor Jerry Brown—at that time Ronstadt's boyfriend.

Flashback
Only the Good Die Young

Duane Allman, 24	10/29/71
Mike Bloomfield, 36	2/15/81
Marc Bolan, 29	9/17/77
Tim Buckley, 28	6/29/75
Karen Carpenter, 32	2/4/83
Harry Chapin, 38	7/16/81
Sam Cooke, 29	12/11/64
Jim Croce, 30	9/20/73
Bobby Darin, 37	12/20/73
Sandy Denny, 30	4/21/78
Cass Elliot, 30	7/29/74
Bill Haley, 55	2/9/81
Tim Hardin, 39	12/29/80
Donnie Hathaway, 33	1/31/79
Jimi Hendrix, 37	9/18/70
Buddy Holly, 20	2/3/59
Brian Jones, 27	7/3/69
Janis Joplin, 27	10/4/70
John Lennon, 40	12/8/80
Frankie Lymon, 25	4/29/75
Bob Marley, 36	5/11/81
Ron "Pigpen" McKernan, 27	38/73
Keith Moon, 31	9/7/78
Jim Morrison, 27	7/3/71
Phil Ochs, 35	4/9/76
Gram Parsons, 26	9/19/73
Elvis Presley, 42	8/16/77
Otis Redding, 26	12/10/67
Tammy Terrell, 33	3/16/70
Sid Vicious, 21	2/2/79

Young America

MARCH 18, 1972. Neil Young's "Heart of Gold" single hits number one and is immediately replaced by "A Horse With No Name," the debut single by three American "military brats" living in England but proclaiming their loyalties with the name America. Because of the vocal resemblance, it will be widely believed that America is really Neil Young working under an alias.

Que Sera, Sera

APRIL 1, 1972. The Mar y Sol (Sea and Sun) Festival opens in Vega Baja on the north coast of Puerto Rico. Featuring such bands as Emerson, Lake, and Palmer, the Allman Brothers, B.B. King, and the J. Geils Band, it is held on what was once a huge dairy farm separated from the sea by a stretch of sun-soaked, sandy white beach, an idyllic setting. The promoters, including Alex Cooley, who two years ago produced the Atlanta Pop Festival, have arranged package deals, enabling attendees to fly from New

York round-trip for $152, including admission to the festival. Buses will wait at San Juan's airport to transport people 35 miles to the festival site. But despite such attention to detail, the festival will turn into a disaster. One problem will be that Puerto Rico's secretary of health has tried to stop the festival, fearing a plague of drug abuse, but has been overruled at the last minute by San Juan's Superior Court. Once the festival begins, however, the real problems will emerge: a lack of fresh water, outrageously priced food, severe sunburn, women harassed by local men, and—perhaps the ultimate insult—a shortage of flights home.

The First Time

APRIL 19, 1972. Roberta Flack, 33, a former public school music teacher in Washington, D.C., gets her first gold record for "The First Time Ever I Saw Your Face," which will spend six weeks as the number-one single and win a Grammy award. Born in North Carolina but raised in the Washington suburbs, Flack started piano lessons at age nine. As a student at Howard University, she organized choral groups, accompanied several opera singers, directed church choirs, and coached vocal students. In the fall of 1967 she performed at Mr. Henry's, a Capitol Hill nightclub, which led to a record contract with Atlantic. Her first album, *First Take*, started Flack's string of gold records. Several later songs, including another Grammy winner, "Where Is Love," will be recorded with Donny Hathaway.

Fifties Redux

JUNE 7, 1972. With 1950s nostalgia catching on, the musical *Grease*, a satirical look at that decade, opens on Broadway. The characters, lower-middle-class teenagers at a Midwestern high school, take a look back at the fads, fetishes, and neuroses of the '50s. Among the songs for which it will be remembered are "Beauty School Dropout" and "Look at Me, I'm Sandra Dee." *Grease* will set records as the longest-running Broadway play, lasting nearly eight years and 3,388 performances. A subsequent 1978 movie version starring John Travolta and Olivia Newton-John will spawn four top-10 songs, including the title, written by Barry Gibb and recorded by Frankie Valli.

Born to Run

JUNE 12, 1972. Bruce Springsteen signs a contract with

Flack: Capital success.

Springsteen: Promoting the Boss.

Columbia Records producer John Hammond, the music pioneer who discovered Billie Holiday, Bessie Smith, and Count Basie, among other legends. The 22-year-old Springsteen has been seized with a passion for rock 'n' roll since age 13 and through college played in several local bands around his native Ashbury Park, N.J. Hailed as the new Bob Dylan, he will release a Columbia album, *Greetings from Asbury Park, N.J.*, that will be a disappointment, but a subsequent effort, *The Wild, the Innocent, and the E Street Shuffle*, will help garner FM air play. By 1975, when *Born to Run* is released, excitement over Springsteen will result in simultaneous cover stories in both *Time* and *Newsweek*, ensuring Springsteen—"The Boss," as he is now known—top billing for another 10 years.

Out of Our Heads

JULY 17, 1972. The Rolling Stones continue to nurture

their "bad-boy" images. On this date, the band's equipment truck is bombed in Montreal, ruining its sound system (radio stations will receive dozens of calls claiming responsibility). Over the next year, the band also will be arrested in Rhode Island for assaulting a news photographer; Mick Jagger will be refused a visa to Japan because of a previous drug arrest, forcing the band to cancel an Asian tour; and Jagger will be named in an unsuccessful paternity suit in London by a woman claiming he fathered her two-year-old daughter. On the better behavior side of the ledger, the Stones will organize a benefit concert for victims of a disastrous December 1972 earthquake in Nicaragua—home of Jagger's wife Bianca—which will raise $300,000 for that country, a sum to which Jagger will personally add $150,000.

Miles of Fusion

SEPTEMBER 9, 1972. Trumpeter Miles Davis premieres a new nine-piece band at New York's Lincoln Center. Davis, a Juilliard-trained jazz musician who once lived with legendary saxophonist Charlie Parker in New York, has been performing since the mid-1940s with such jazz greats as Gerry Mulligan, Lee Konitz, John Lewis, Max Roach, and Gil Evans. A much-acclaimed musician, Davis has turned increasingly to "jazz-rock," a fusion sound that combines Davis' traditional Bop sound with the electronic age of rock. His 1969 double album *Bitches Brew,* recorded with little rehearsal and without formal

"Message songs, as everybody knows, are a drag."
Bob Dylan

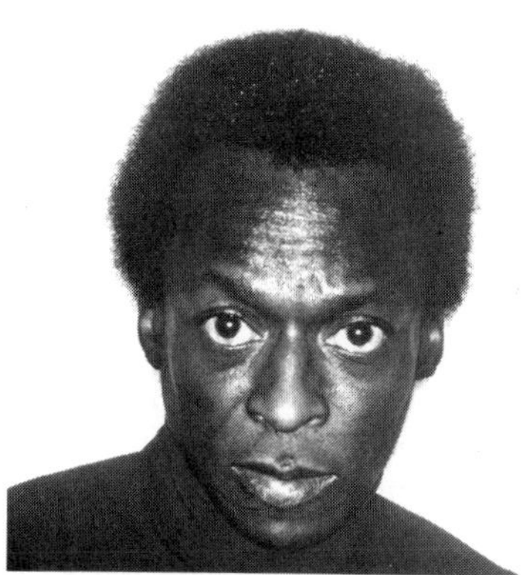

Davis: Horn of plenty.

charts, will practically create fusion on the spot. The musicians on the album will include such future apostles of fusion as Joe Zawinul and Wayne Shorter, founders of Weather Report; Chick Corea, father of the group Return to Forever; and John McLaughlin, of the Mahivishnu Orchestra. *Bitches Brew*, although originally marketed as a jazz album, will steadily gain ground and be certified gold in May 1976.

Dirty Ditty

OCTOBER 21, 1972. After 17 years as one of the pioneer singer/songwriters of rock 'n' roll, Chuck Berry finally gets a number-one hit, "My Ding-a-Ling," a not-very-subtle attempt to lace a grade-school ditty with sexual references. Berry, now 46, is known as one of the hardest-working pop musicians around and one of the most enduring—he has been playing professionally now for 20 years. In 1975 he will be named to the Rock Hall of Fame.

Rocket Man

OCTOBER 30, 1972. Elton John gives a command performance before Queen Elizabeth, the first rock musician to do so since the Beatles made their appearance nearly a decade ago. John, 25, one of pop music's most eccentric musicians in years—some call him the Liberace of rock—started playing in London in 1964 in a band called Bluesology. Three years later, he teamed up with lyricist Bernie Taupin to produce songs for albums, the second of which, *Elton John*, appeared in 1969. But it was John's public appearances that brought him attention, particularly one at the Troubadour in Los Angeles in Au-

John: Rock's Liberace.

gust 1970, which one record producer later called "one of the most spectacular openings for an unknown artist I've ever seen." The *Los Angeles Times* called him "staggeringly original." *Elton John* went gold in 1971, as did his next album, *Tumbleweed Connection*. John's performances, which will become increasingly outrageous, will continue to be his principal draw, as he jumps up and down around his piano, dressed in some glittery object from his vast wardrobe, reportedly worth more than a quarter-million dollars. (Indeed, his collection of rose-colored and electrified glasses alone will be reported to be worth $40,000.) He will become one of the top money-making musicians of the 1970s. By 1976 he will have sold 42 million albums and 18 million singles, earning him royalties of more than $8 million.

Reddy or Not

DECEMBER 9, 1972. "I Am Woman," sung and co-written by Australian Helen Reddy, briefly tops the charts. The song, which will become a kind of theme for the feminist movement, launches Reddy on what will develop more as a nightclub than a rock career.

Peace Has Come

JANUARY 23, 1973. Neil Young interrupts his New York concert to announce that "peace has come," the result of a message handed to him that a cease-fire has taken effect in Vietnam.

Flashback
Rock Palaces

Aragon Ballroom, Chicago
Auditorium Theater, Chicago
Avalon, San Francisco
Boston Tea Party, Boston
California Hall, San Francisco
Capital Theater, Passaic, N.J.
Cheetah, Los Angeles
Cow Palace, San Francisco
Electric Circus, New York
Electric Factory, Philadelphia
Fillmore East, New York
Fillmore West, San Franicsco
Grande Ballroom, Detroit
Kinetic Circus, Chicago
Longshoreman's Hall, San Francisco
Winterland, San Francisco

Grateful Death

MARCH 8, 1973. Ronald "Pigpen" McKernan, 27, organist for the Grateful Dead, dies of cirrhosis of the liver, the result of years of heavy drinking. In 1964 he was one of the original three musicians, including Bob Weir and Jerry Garcia, to form the Warlocks, which later became the Dead.

Long-Playing

MARCH 17, 1973. Pink Floyd's *Dark Side of the Moon* hits *Billboard's* chart at number 95. A decade later, it will remain on the charts, setting records for the longest run as a bestseller. (It will drop off the charts for two brief periods during the mid 1970s.) The album is Pink Floyd's 10th and last on Capitol Records; none of the others ever made the charts. Praised for its top-quality engineering and innovative use of synthesizers, acoustic instruments, and taped effects, the album will sell more than eight million copies; an audiophile version, originally priced at $50, will sell to collectors for up to $1,000 each.

The Divine Miss M

APRIL 15, 1973. The first album from Bette Midler, *The Divine Miss M*, goes gold, as Midler becomes one of the hottest acts of the year. With her interpretations of songs by everyone from Bob Dylan to Hoagy Carmichael to Johnny Mercer, Midler has earned a reputation as the best white song stylist since Barbra

Midler: Calculated bad taste.

Streisand. Like Judy Garland, she will develop a strong homosexual following, which will be transferred to her proteges Barry Manilow and Melissa Manchester. At year's end, however, Midler will go into temporary retirement, resurfacing again in April 1975 on Broadway in *Bette Midler's Clams on the Half Shell Revue*, a collection of her songs and verbal asides in a fully staged and choreographed production that the *New York Times*' Clive Barnes will call "an explosion of energy and minutely calculated bad taste."

I Shoulda Known Better

MAY 23, 1973. Clive Davis, president of Columbia Records, and his assistant David Wynshaw are fired by CBS for allegedly misappropriating company funds for personal use—including a pricey bar mitzvah for Davis' son—although rumors will allege that the firing resulted from the company's reputed payola practices. Davis will later emerge as head of Arista records and produce a self-congratulatory autobiography.

Days of Future Passed

JUNE 28, 1973. "Oldies shows" begin featuring bands of the mid-1960s, including several British groups such as Herman's Hermits and Gerry and the Pacemakers, which appear on a bill at Madison Square Garden.

Summer Jam

JULY 28, 1973. The largest rock festival of all time, organized by Bill Graham, takes place in Watkins Glen, N.Y. More than 600,000 people—about one out of every 350 Americans—squeeze into the Watkins Glen Grand Prix Raceway for what is billed as a "Summer Jam"; some 80,000 arrived two days ago. Despite the large numbers, little of note goes on at this festival. The performing groups—the Grateful Dead, the Allman Brothers, and the Band—each play long sets (the Dead play for five hours), but the performances will not be looked back upon as noteworthy. The day produces few problems, despite the by-now routine festival "crises" of inadequate toilets, food, and water, and traffic jams extending for miles in every direction.

Aftermash

AUGUST 25, 1973. For the third time since 1962, "Monster Mash," a novelty song by Bobby ("Boris") Pickett, hits the charts.

Flashback
Top Singles—1973

Angie	Rolling Stones
Crocodile Rock	Elton John
Daniel	Elton John
Do It Again	Steely Dan
Drift Away	Dobie Gray
D'Yer Mak'er	Led Zeppelin
Killing Me Softly With His Song	Roberta Flack
Kodachrome	Paul Simon
Let's Get It On	Marvin Gaye
Living in the Past	Jethro Tull
Love Train	O'Jays
Me and Mrs. Jones	Billy Paul
Midnight Train to Georgia	Gladys Knight and the Pips
My Love	Wings
Ramblin' Man	Allman Brothers Band
Right Place Wrong Time	Dr. John
Rocky Mountain High	John Denver
Smoke on the Water	Deep Purple
Space Oddity	David Bowie
Stuck in the Middle With You	Stealer's Wheel
Superstition	Stevie Wonder
Your Mama Don't Dance	Loggins and Messina
You're So Vain	Carly Simon

Time in a Bottle

SEPTEMBER 20, 1973. Only two months after "Bad, Bad Leroy Brown" gives Jim Croce his first number-one song, Croce is killed, along with long-time sidekick Maury Muehleisen, when their privately chartered plane crashes on takeoff in Louisiana. Croce, a Philadelphia native who took up guitar at age 18, had developed an irregular picking style to compensate for having broken a finger with a sledge hammer during one of his many stints as a day laborer. Although he had struggled for years to break into the business, driving trucks and finally having to pawn his guitar collection after an early album flopped, his debut album for ABC Records, *You Don't Mess Around With Jim*, provided him with two top-20 hits—the title song and "Operator." His recently released second album will remain on the charts posthumously; the appropriately titled "Time in a Bottle" will reach number one in three months.

Croce: Hard landing.

Dylan Sells Out Again

DECEMBER 2, 1973. In one day, 658,000 tickets for an upcoming Bob Dylan tour, his first tour since 1965, sell out. Post offices in several cities are jammed for blocks as people line up to mail ticket orders. On tour Dylan and his backup group, the Band, will cause both congestion on local streets and controversy among fans, who protest the high $10 concert ticket prices. While in Atlanta, Dylan will be invited to a party at the mansion of Georgia governor Jimmy Carter.

Flashback
Top Albums—1973

A Nice Pair	**Pink Floyd**
A White Sport Coat and a Pink Crustacean	**Jimmy Buffett**
Aladdin Sane	**David Bowie**
Band on the Run	**Paul McCartney and Wings**
Best of Procul Harum	**Procul Harum**
Brain Salad Surgery	**Emerson, Lake, and Palmer**
Brothers and Sisters	**Allman Brothers Band**
Countdown to Ecstasy	**Steely Dan**
Dark Side of the Moon	**Pink Floyd**
Desperado	**Eagles**
Dixie Chicken	**Little Feat**
Double Gold	**Neil Diamond**
Extension of a Man	**Donny Hathaway**
For Everyman	**Jackson Browne**
Frampton's Camel	**Peter Frampton**
Goodbye Yellow Brick Road	**Elton John**
Greetings From Asbury Park, N.J.	**Bruce Springsteen**
Highway	**Free**
Innervisions	**Stevie Wonder**
Laid Back	**Gregg Allman**
Last of the Brooklyn Cowboys	**Arlo Guthrie**
Let's Get It On	**Marvin Gaye**
Life and Times	**Jim Croce**
Maria Muldaur	**Maria Muldaur**
Masterpiece	**Temptations**
Pat Garrett and Billy the Kid	**Bob Dylan**
Piano Man	**Billy Joel**
Pointer Sisters	**Pointer Sisters**
Ray Charles Live	**Ray Charles**
Sold American	**Kinky Friedman**
Sweet Revenge	**John Prine**
Takin' My Time	**Bonnie Raitt**
There Goes Rhymin' Simon	**Paul Simon**
Toulouse Street	**Doobie Brothers**
True Stories and Other Dreams	**Judy Collins**

Yes, No Ads

FEBRUARY 18, 1974. The band Yes plays to a sold-out Madison Square Garden, a feat remarkable for the fact that the group did no advertising for the event.

The Comeback

MARCH 2, 1974. Stevie Wonder is this year's big Grammy winner, claiming five awards for his album *Innervisions* and two singles, "You Are the Sunshine of My Life" and "Superstition." Wonder had been nominated for six awards, a Grammy record. Later this month, Wonder, who suffered a near-fatal car accident last August, will receive a hero's welcome at a triumphant concert at Madison Square Garden. The Grammys are only the first of this year's honors. In coming months Wonder will be named by record buyers as top male vocalist in a poll conducted by ABC; named soul artist of the year by the National Association of Recording Merchandisers; and given the American Music Award for "Superstition" as the top soul single. Next year, Wonder will sign a new contract with Motown, giving him the highest guarantee in the history of the recording industry: $13 million for the next seven years.

New Ole Opry

MARCH 16, 1974. The Grand Ole Opry moves out of its home in the old Ryman Auditorium off Nashville's lower Broadway strip and moves to new digs at Opryland, USA, an "American music" theme park that cost $28 million.

Early Rock

APRIL 6, 1974. Cal Jam, a rock festival held at the Ontario Motor Speedway in Ontario, Calif., is one of the smoothest-running rock fests ever. Performing are Rare Earth, the Eagles, Seals and Crofts, Deep Purple, Emerson, Lake, and Palmer, Black Sabbath, and Earth, Wind, and Fire. The festival will be looked back on less for its music—it is uneventful, reflecting rock's current state of lethargy—than for the precision with which the event takes place: 200,000 people are expected, which is exactly how many attend. Even more impressive, Rare Earth, the show's opening act, takes the stage 15 minutes *ahead* of schedule. This success will lead to a Cal Jam II in 1978.

Music and Mayhem

APRIL 27, 1974. Music takes the back seat to mayhem as a four-hour riot ensues at the Cherry Blossom Music Festival in Richmond, Va., featuring the Steve Miller Band and Boz Scaggs. The mishap is one of several such events at upcoming concerts. At a Jackson 5 concert in Washington, D.C., next month, dozens of people will be injured by thrown bottles (sadly, the event is a "Human Kindness Day" celebration); a young girl will die and more than 1,000 will be treated for injuries at an upcoming David Cassidy concert in London; and nearly 100 people will be arrested in Atlanta at a Robin Trower-Edgar Winter concert.

Flashback
Top Singles—1974

Band on the Run	Wings
Blue Collar Worker	Bachman-Turner Overdrive
Can't Get Enough	Bad Company
Cat's in the Cradle	Harry Chapin
Don't Let the Sun Go Down On Me	Elton John
Feel Like Makin' Love	Roberta Flack
I Shot the Sheriff	Eric Clapton
I've Got the Music in Me	Kiki Dee
The Joker	Steve Miller
Lover Please	Billy Swann
Lucy in the Sky With Diamonds	Elton John
Midnight at the Oasis	Maria Muldaur
Rock the Boat	Hues Corporation
Rock Your Baby	George McRae
The Show Must Go On	Leo Sayer
Sweet Home Alabama	Lynyrd Skynard
Takin' Care of Business	Bachman-Turner Overdrive
Tell Me Something Good	Rufus
Tin Man	America

Stone: Return engagement.

Sly Move

JUNE 5, 1974. Sly Stone marries Kathy Silva at a gala wedding on stage at a Madison Square Garden concert. Silva will file for divorce in less than six months.

MJQ, Adieu

JUNE 30, 1974. The Modern Jazz Quartet, which since 1952 has led the trend toward small jazz combos, plays the first of a series of "farewell concerts," this one in San Francisco. The group—which includes John Lewis on piano, Milt Jackson on vibraphone, Percy Heath on bass, and Connie Kay on drums—has been credited with bringing a new dignity to jazz, not only in the clean, almost classical sound it created, but also in its sophisticated suit-and-tie stage presence. In November a "farewell" concert at New York's Lincoln Center will produce a highly acclaimed album, appropriately titled *The Last Concert.*

Mama, Don't Go

JULY 7, 1974. Cass Elliot, formerly of the Mamas and the Papas, dies in the same London flat where Who drummer Keith Moon will die in 1978. Her death at first will be reported as resulting from choking on a ham sandwich, but a coroner's report will conclude that the 220-pound singer died from a heart attack brought on by obesity.

Family Man

AUGUST 24, 1974. Paul Anka's comeback single, "(You're) Having My Baby," hits number one. Feminists object to the word "my"—they say it should be titled "(You're) Having *Our* Baby," and Anka concedes, changing the lyrics in live performances.

Grease Lady

OCTOBER 9, 1974. Olivia Newton-John, 26, earns a gold record for her single "I Honestly Love You," one of five gold records she will receive this year. The English-born, Australian-raised singer, daughter of a Nobel laureate physicist, began her career as a folksinger in a coffeeshop

Flashback

Top Albums—1974

African Herbsman	Bob Marley and the Wailers
Alice Cooper's Greatest Hits	Alice Cooper
Anthology	Four Tops
AWB	Average White Band
Back to Oakland	Tower of Power
Before the Flood	Bob Dylan
Court and Spark	Joni Mitchell
Eldorado	Electric Light Orchestra
Good Old Boys	Randy Newman
Heart Like a Wheel	Linda Ronstadt
Heroes Are Hard to Find	Fleetwood Mac
History of the Bonzos	Bonzo Dog Band
Houses of the Holy	Led Zeppelin
Janis	Janis Joplin
Machine Gun	Commodores
On Stage	Loggins and Messina
On the Border	Eagles
Paradise and Lunch	Ry Cooder
Phoebe Snow	Phoebe Snow
Second Helping	Lynyrd Skynyrd
Wrap Around Joy	Carole King

owned by her brother-in-law. Winning first prize in a talent show later enabled her to come to London. At age 19, having joined a mediocre singing group, she launched a solo career, cutting her first record in 1971. Her first successful American hit came with a country-and-western tune, "Let Me Be There," which won Newton-John a 1973 Grammy as the top country vocalist. Her biggest hit, however, will come in 1978, with her co-starring role (with John Travolta) in the movie *Grease*.

Ronstadt: Long, long time to stardom.

Mr. Harrison Goes to Washington

DECEMBER 13, 1974. George Harrison goes to the White House to meet President Ford at the invitation of Ford's son Jack. The President gives Harrison a *WIN* ("Whip Inflation Now") button. Rumors will abound about cocaine being snorted in White House bathrooms.

Green's Golds

JANUARY 22, 1975. Soul singer Al Green wins the second of two gold records this month, the 15th and 16th of his career, for "Sha-La-La (Make Me Happy)." Green, who grew up in Forrest City, Ark., began singing in a gospel group at age nine with his four brothers. He headed a soul band in high school and made his first recording in 1967 at age 21 as Al Green and the Creations. Green has written most of his own songs, generally dealing with the theme of love.

Heart Like a Wheel

FEBRUARY 15, 1975. After nearly a decade of cult status on the club circuit, Linda Ronstadt has her first number-one single with "You're No Good," which also marks the beginning of her association with producer Peter Asher, formerly of Peter and Gordon. Ronstadt will rocket to superstardom; a few years later, *Billboard* chart analyst Joel Whitburn will describe her flatly as "the leading female rock singer of the past decade." Ronstadt has had several regional hits, most notably the 1968 release "Different Drum"

Flashback
Top Singles—1975

Bad Blood	Neil Sedaka
The Best of My Love	Eagles
Boogie On Reggae Woman	Stevie Wonder
Doctor's Orders	Carol Douglas
Get Down Tonight	KC and the Sunshine Band
Jive Talkin'	Bee Gees
Lady Marmalade	Patti LaBelle
Loving You	Minnie Riperton
Never Can Say Goodbye	Jackson 5
Not in Love	10cc
That's the Way I Like It	K.C. and the Sunshine Band
Whatever Gets You Through the Night	John Lennon
When Will I Be Loved?	Linda Ronstadt
You Are So Beautiful	Joe Cocker

with the Stone Poneys and "Long, Long Time," which epitomized her original country-rock style.

Graham SNACKs

MARCH 23, 1975. Music impressario Bill Graham resurfaces to produce a benefit concert at Kezar Stadium in San Francisco to raise money for SNACK—"Students Need Athletics, Culture, and Kicks"—to provide money for extracurricular activities in the city's funds-starved public schools. Performing are the Grateful Dead, the Jefferson Starship (a recast version of the Jefferson Airplane), Neil Young, Joan Baez, and Bob Dylan.

Looking Out for #1

MARCH 29, 1975. Led Zeppelin has six albums on the charts simultaneously, a feat even the Beatles never accomplished. At the top is its most recent release, *Physical Graffiti*. The Who will dominate the charts next month, with all three versions of its rock-opera *Tommy*—including one recorded by the London Symphony Orchestra—on the charts simultaneously.

Not Fade Away

MAY 1, 1975. The Rolling Stones announce their forthcoming North American tour by performing on the back of a flatbed truck driving down Fifth Avenue in New York City. The tour will get off to a shaky start: during the first performance next month at Madison Square Garden, the Stones' amplifiers will pick up TV and radio signals throughout the performance.

Southern Curse

JUNE 27, 1975. Lynyrd Skynyrd's third album, *Nuthin' Fancy*, goes gold. The Jacksonville-based band has gained a reputation as a hard-boogieing band through its incessant touring rather than through radio exposure; its highest-ranking single, "Sweet Home, Alabama," a redneck rabble-rouser, only reached number eight. Unregenerate as it was, "Sweet Home, Alabama" displayed some basic humor: "I hope Neil Young will remember/'Southern Man' don't need him around," wrote lead singer Johnny Van Zandt, responding to Young's famous pro-civil rights song. Van Zandt, whose two brothers are also lead singers with Florida bands, will die in a plane crash, along with his sister and several others, in October 1977. The "Southern Curse," considered to have begun with Duane Allman's death in 1971, will claim Tommy Caldwell of Marshall Tucker in 1980.

Flashback
Top Albums—1975

Atlantic Crossing	Rod Stewart
Back in the Alley	B.B. King
Blood on the Tracks	Bob Dylan
Born to Run	Bruce Springsteen
Chicago IX	Chicago
First Minute of a New Day	Gil Scott-Heron
Gorilla	James Taylor
Gratitude	Earth, Wind, and Fire
High On You	Sly and the Family Stone
The Hissing of Summer Lawns	Joni Mitchell
Inseparable	Natalie Cole
John Fogerty	John Fogerty
Mahogany	Diana Ross
Main Course	Bee Gees
One of These Nights	Eagles
Physical Graffiti	Led Zeppelin
Pick of the Litter	Spinners
Pieces of the Sky	Emmylou Harris
Prisoner in Disguise	Linda Ronstadt
Red Headed Stranger	Willie Nelson
Searchin' for a Rainbow	Marshall Tucker Band
Stampede	Doobie Brothers
Still Crazy After All These Years	Paul Simon
Tonight's the Night	Neil Young
Will o' the Wisp	Leon Russell

MERICAN BANDSTAND" • *BERKELEY BARB* • BOGIE • JAMES BON
ULLWINKLE SHOW" • "CAPTAIN KANGAROO" • CENSORSHIP • CH
OOKS • COLOR TV • JAMES DEAN • DENNIS THE MENACE • DICK AN
IP • *DR. STRANGELOVE* • *THE FEMININE MYSTIQUE* • FILM CLASS
LINTSTONES" • FM ROCK • GAME SHOW SCANDALS • ALLEN GINSB
ITCHCOCK • "THE HONEYMOONERS" • KID VID • "LAUGH-IN" • LIZ
UCY AND DESI • *MAD MAGAZINE* • "M*A*S*H" • "THE MICKEY MOU
ARILYN MONROE • "THE MAN FROM U.N.C.L.E." • *MS.* • *PLAYBOY* •
ORNOGRAPHY • *ROLLING STONE* • "ROMPER ROOM" • *SILENT SP
MOTHERS BROTHERS • SOUPY SALES • ED SULLIVAN • *TROPIC OF
DO! • UNCLE WALTER • UNDERGROUND PRESS • *VILLAGE VOICE* • JO
HE WHOLE EARTH CATALOG • WOODWARD AND BERNSTEIN • ZAP
AMERICAN BANDSTAND" • *BERKELEY BARB* • BOGIE • JAMES BON
ULLWINKLE SHOW" • "CAPTAIN KANGAROO" • CENSORSHIP • CH
OOKS • COLOR TV • JAMES DEAN • DENNIS THE MENACE • DICK AN
IP • *DR. STRANGELOVE* • *THE FEMININE MYSTIQUE* • FILM CLASS
LINTSTONES" • FM ROCK • GAME SHOW SCANDALS • ALLEN GINSB
ITCHCOCK • "THE HONEYMOONERS" • KID VID • "LAUGH-IN" • LIZ
UCY AND DESI • *MAD MAGAZINE* • "M*A*S*H" • "THE MICKEY MOU
AMERICAN BANDSTAND" • *BERKELEY BARB* • BOGIE • JAMES BON
ULLWINKLE SHOW" • "CAPTAIN KANGAROO" • CENSORSHIP • CH
OOKS • COLOR TV • JAMES DEAN • DENNIS THE MENACE • DICK AN
IP • *DR. STRANGELOVE* • *THE FEMININE MYSTIQUE* • FILM CLASS
LINTSTONES" • FM ROCK • GAME SHOW SCANDALS • ALLEN GINSB
ITCHCOCK • "THE HONEYMOONERS" • KID VID • "LAUGH-IN" • LI
UCY AND DESI • *MAD MAGAZINE* • "M*A*S*H" • "THE MICKEY MOU
ARILYN MONROE • "THE MAN FROM U.N.C.L.E." • *MS.* • *PLAYBO*
ORNOGRAPHY • *ROLLING STONE* • "ROMPER ROOM" • *SILENT S*
MOTHERS BROTHERS • SOUPY SALES • ED SULLIVAN • *TROPIC O*
DO! • UNCLE WALTER • UNDERGROUND PRESS • *VILLAGE VOICE* •

BOOM!
MEDIA

Meet the Press

JANUARY 19, 1955. President Eisenhower opens presidential press conferences to TV cameras for the first time. Three years earlier, Eisenhower's aides had tried to bar cameras from the President's first major campaign press conference; CBS insisted, however, that it would send its cameramen, and to head off bad publicity the ban was lifted. In February ABC will begin TV coverage of Eisenhower's weekly news conferences.

The Miracle Worker

JANUARY 19, 1955. "The Millionaire" debuts. For the next five years, Michael Anthony will heed the weekly instructions of his never-seen boss, John Beresford Tipton, and deliver $1 million, tax free, to some unsuspecting beneficiary. The giveaway is pure fiction, of course, but millions of Americans will prosper vicariously from the experience.

Jailhouse Rock

MARCH 20, 1955. Richard Brooks' *Blackboard Jungle* opens, based on Evan Hunter's novel exploiting the front-page problems of city juvenile delinquency. Brooks has chosen Bill Haley's "Rock Around the Clock" as its theme song to evoke the new world of dangerous youth. It will be the first of many uses of rock 'n' roll in film. Next year, director Sam Katzman will use Haley's song as the title for the first rock exploitation movie, *Rock Around the Clock*.

9-30-55

SEPTEMBER 30, 1955. James Dean, driving his Porsche from the set of the film *Giant* to participate in an auto race in Salinas, Calif., is killed in an accident. His death will trigger one of the most bizarre cults in Hollywood history, perhaps unequalled since the hysteria that surrounded the death of Rudolph Valentino. In his brief career, Dean has come to embody alienated postwar youth. Teens throughout the country have emulated his hair style, expressions, speech patterns, and dispossessed, uninvolved attitude. Dean created a finely honed image of a man who loved to speed, was intentionally sloppy, and rejected weak and corrupt adults. Upon news of the accident, many people will refuse to believe he really is dead; in the next few weeks, the number of letters sent to him at his studio and fan club will actually increase. One popular rumor will be that the disfigured body in Dean's car was that of a hitchhiker, and that Dean is alive in an asylum somewhere. Dean's smashed car will tour the country, with admission charged, before being cut into pieces and sold to his fans. Dean's major roles were in *Rebel Without a Cause* (1955), *East of Eden* (1955), and *Giant* (to be released in 1956), but it was *Rebel* that will become a seminal alienated-youth film. Directed by Nicholas Ray, *Rebel* used the title of a then-popular psychology book, but its theme was drawn from Philip Wylie's book, *Generation of Vipers*, an attack on the feminization of American culture. In the film Jim Backus played Dean's weak dad, with Sal Mineo as the effeminate Plato and Natalie Wood in her first adult role. Sadly, all three youth stars will die violent deaths. The date of Dean's death will become the title of a 1977 film, *9-30-55*.

Dean: *Rebel* rouser.

Sullivan Signs On

SEPTEMBER 18, 1955. "Toast of the Town," which has been a Sunday night staple on CBS for seven years, becomes "The Ed Sullivan Show." For the next 16 years, the biggest names in music and show business will join Sullivan and his regulars, including the June Taylor Dancers; Topo Gigo, the Italian mouse; and Senor Wences and his talking box. Stars like Bob Hope and the Beatles will make their American TV debuts on Sullivan's stage; others, like Elvis Presley, will see their careers take off after appearing on the show.

A Sharper Image

SEPTEMBER 28, 1955. Sports fans get a better look at Dodger blue and Yankee pinstripes, as NBC telecasts the first World Series game in color. The Bronx Bombers beat the Bums 6 to 5 at Yankee Stadium, but Brooklyn will fight back to win its first world championship.

And Away We Go

OCTOBER 1, 1955. The first of 39 half-hour episodes of "The Honeymooners" airs. Although the Kramden and Norton families—Jackie Gleason and Audrey Meadows, and Art Carney and Joyce Randolph, respectively—will not become prime-time hits, the show will be a perennial favorite in reruns, often appearing several times a week on different stations in the same city. In 1985 Gleason will announce that he has copies of early shows from which "The Honeymooners" evolved, and a deal will be signed to release about 75 "new" episodes.

Honeymooners: Many happy returns.

Clarabell Makes Good

OCTOBER 3, 1955. "Captain Kangaroo" debuts on CBS, with 28-year-old Robert Keeshan as host. Keeshan, who previously played Clarabell the clown on NBC's "Howdy Doody" (he left the show in a pay dispute), will attract legions of preschoolers to the Treasure House, where he will be joined by such characters as Mr. Greenjeans, Grandfather Clock, and Silly Billy. "Captain Kangaroo" will be retired in September 1968, 10 years after winning an award for being "the only one which puts the welfare of the children ahead of the sponsor."

Keeshan: Kangaroo kudos.

Annette & Co.

OCTOBER 3, 1955. The hour-long "Mickey Mouse Club," with Jimmie Dodd as host, debuts on ABC and will quickly become a late-afternoon favorite. The Walt Disney-produced show will feature everything from cartoons and live performers to short films and Jiminy Cricket lectures. The real stars, however, will be the Mouseketeers—including Annette Funicello, Cubby O'Brien, Karen Pendleton, and Darlene Gillespie and two of Mickey Rooney's sons, Tim and Mickey, Jr.—who often will be seen in such ongoing serials as "The Adventures of Spin and Marty," "The Hardy Boys," and "Corky and White Shadow," featuring, among others, Buddy Ebsen. Occasional guests will be named "honorary Mousketeers" ("Here's your hat, and here's your ears."); in 1957, one such guest will be a young Jerry Brown, 15

Annette, Hardy Boys: Mouseketeer to movie star.

years away from becoming governor of the Spaceship California. The success of the "Mickey Mouse Club" will be unprecedented; fan mail will pour in at the rate of 7,500 letters a month. Annette will attract the most attention, receiving 6,000 letters a month herself at her height of popularity. She will go on to make several records, including *Hawaiianette* and *Annette Sings Anka*, then move to beach party movies and peanut butter commercials, retaining her Mouseketeer wholesomeness throughout. "The Mickey Mouse Club" will sign off in September 1959.

And the Beat Goes On

OCTOBER 13, 1955. Beat poet Allen Ginsberg, 29, gives his first public reading of "Howl," at the Six Gallery in San Francisco. The reading is part of the city's mushrooming "beat" scene—*San Francisco Chronicle* columnist Herb Caen has dubbed participants "beatniks," a take-off on the Soviet Sputnik—which has attracted a wide range of poets and other writers, including Richard Brautigan, Jack Kerouac, Lawrence Ferlinghetti, Michael McClure, Gary Snyder, and, soon, Bob Dylan. Much of the action centers around Ferlinghetti's City Lights Bookstore, opened three years ago. But readings will take place all over town, at beat bars and coffeehouses such as the Co-Existence Bagel Shop, the Hungry I, the Anxious Asp, Kush's Cloud House, Panjandrum, the Cellar, and the Place.

"What, me worry?"
Alfred E. Neuman

A New Voice

OCTOBER, 26, 1955. The *Village Voice* begins publication. The 12-page, 5-cent weekly has been started by Daniel Wolf and Edward Fancher, who raised $15,000. The two will sell the paper in 15 years for $3 million after building an alternative newspaper model that will be copied in most major cities in the country. One *Voice* innovation that will gain widespread popularity during the next three decades is the "personals" classified ads, which will become a meeting place for singles—and marrieds—in cities large and small.

Mr. Wilson's Revenge

OCTOBER 9, 1955. With sales of *More Dennis the Menace*, cartoonist Hank Ketchem's second book, reportedly at 2,000 copies a week, Henry Holt & Company, the book's publisher, is disturbed that the book hasn't made the *New York Times* bestseller list. So today's edition of the *Times* has an ad from the publisher with a cartoon of Dennis asking, "Whatcha gotta do to get on the *Times'* bestseller chart—know somebody?"

TV Dennis: Victim of the *Times*.

Flashback

Local Kid Vid

Bozo's Circus	Chicago
Captain Bob Show	Boston
Captain Mal Show	Mobile, Ala.
Captain Satellite Show	San Francisco
Chief Halftown	Philadelphia
Colonel Caboose	Green Bay, Wisc.
Cowboy Colt	Detroit
Fred Kirby, the Singing Cowboy	Charlotte, N.C.
Hoppity Skippity	Washington, D.C.
Jingles Show	Fort Wayne, Ind.
Mac the Mailman	Milwaukee
Magic Toy Shop	Syracuse, N.Y.
Major Quinn	Albany, N.Y.
Mayor Art Show	San Francisco
Miss Pat's Playroom	Fresno, Calif.
Mr. Jupiter	Cleveland
Old Rebel and Pecos Pete Show	Salem, N.C.
Pick Temple	Washington, D.C.
Ranger Hal	Washington, D.C.
Ranger Joe	Philadelphia
Rex Trailer's Ranch House	Philadelphia
Ridin' the Trail	Philadelphia
Saddle Pal Club	New York
Salty Brine's Shack	Providence, R.I.
Tales of the West	Schenectady, N.Y.
Tinker's Workshop	NewYork
Uncle Gus Show	Manchester, N.H.
Uncle Howdy's Junior Flint Jamboree	Lansing, Mich.
Uncle Hugo and Popeye	Milwaukee
Uncle Lumpy's Cabin	New York
Wonderama	New York

Red Hearing

NOVEMBER 15, 1955. This is NBC-TV's original air date for "Nightmare in Red," a Cold War view of the Communist revolution. The show's sponsor, Pontiac, and the Soviet delegation in Washington have expressed concern about the show's strong anti-Communist ending at a time when American business is looking to increase trade with the Russians. General Motors decided to drop its sponsorship of "Nightmare in Red," but Armstrong Cork will step in. The show, part of the NBC series "Project 20," will air on December 27 and receive high ratings.

Of Mice and Kids

DECEMBER 10, 1955. "Mighty Mouse Playhouse," the first animated cartoon on Saturday morning network TV, debuts on CBS. Although the opera-singing Mighty Mouse will become a hit with kids, parents won't be so enthusiastic. In 1959 the National Congress of Parents and Teachers will charge that the show should only be "recommended for mice."

Mixed Media

DECEMBER 26, 1955. RKO sells 740 feature films to C&C Television Corp., followed three days later by Columbia Pictures' sale of 104 features to TV. Previously, Hollywood studio execs have tried to fight off TV with a series of bizarre technical innovations, such as 3-D, Smell-O-Vision, and Cinerama, none of which has caught on. They also have tried to keep their stars off the tube. Now they've decided it's O.K. to sell their pre-1948 films to television. (Films made after 1948 fall under a separate agreement with the Screen Actors Guild requiring higher pay rates to actors.) This is the first accommodation the film industry has made to its fledgling rival. However, the competition of TV has encouraged Hollywood to become less cautious about using color, which has been extremely expensive to produce because of Technicolor's virtual monopoly on color cinematography. After World War II, Eastmancolor, a less-expensive technique, became available and will gain an increasing market share.

Queen Gems

JANUARY 3, 1956. "Queen for a Day" premieres on NBC. For more than a decade women will sit on host Jack Bailey's throne and—with the help of the studio audience, which will coronate each show's winner with an applausemeter—watch their troubles evaporate. The public, meanwhile, will make "Queen for a Day" one of America's most popular daytime shows.

Bailey: Queen maker.

Duke Skywalker

MAY 26, 1956. *The Searchers* is released, a monumental John Ford-directed western featuring John Wayne in what will be one of the best performances of his career. Wayne himself is so taken by Ethan, the character he plays, that he will name one of his sons after him. Throughout the film Wayne repeats the phrase, "That'll be the day!" which reportedly will inspire Buddy Holly to write a song of that title. Among a handful of 1950s westerns to increase in stature as the years pass, *The Searchers* theme—about Wayne's search for a little girl (Natalie Wood) who has been taken by Indians—will be adopted by many films, including *Star Wars* (1977), which some critics will claim pays shot-by-shot homage to the Wayne original.

Wayne in The Searchers: Buddy Holly's inspiration?

Soap's On

APRIL 2, 1956. After more than two successful decades on radio, the first daily 30-minute soap operas debut on CBS television. "As the World Turns" and "The Edge of Night" will soon garner big ratings and soaps will proliferate; 25 years later, the networks will devote 55 hours a week to the shows. Although some "daytime dramas," as they will be called, come and go, others will thrive. Three decades later, for example, "As the World Turns" will still be in the CBS schedule.

Film Flashbacks
Juvenile Delinquents

- Blackboard Jungle
- Eighteen and Anxious
- Explosive Generation
- Girls Town
- High School Confidential
- Hot Rod Gang
- Platinum High School
- Rebel Without A Cause
- Reform School Girl
- Rock All Night
- Wild for Kicks

Blackboard Jungle

Play It Again

APRIL 14, 1956. At a TV trade association meeting in Chicago, Ampex Corporation demonstrates its new TV tape recorder for use by television stations to store broadcast material on videotape. The machine will be the hit of the show, generating more than $4 million in orders.

"What's My Line?": Goodson and Todman have got a secret.

Huntley Meets Brinkley

AUGUST 13, 1956. The Democratic National Convention opens in Chicago, and joining Bill Henry on NBC are two new co-anchors, Chet Huntley and David Brinkley. Six months later, Huntley, in New York, and Brinkley, in Washington, will take over the network's nightly news show. Their nightly sign-off of "Goodnight, Chet" and "Goodnight, David" will become a broadcasting trademark.

Huntley, Brinkley: A toil of two cities.

Higher! Freeze!

NOVEMBER 26, 1956. "The Price Is Right," with host Bill Cullen, makes its debut on afternoon TV. Next September, the show will also move into an evening prime-time slot, where it will run, first on NBC, then on ABC, for seven years. Like many game shows, "The Price Is Right" carries this line: "A Mark Goodson/Bill Todman production," referring to the show's two prolific producers, who also will be responsible for such game show classics as "Beat the Clock," "I've Got a Secret," and "What's My Line?" Next month, another Goodson/Todman production, "To Tell the Truth," will air with Bud Collyer as emcee. Among the regulars who will try to flush impostors from panels of contestants will be Polly Bergen, Kitty Carlisle, Orson Bean, and Peggy Cass. In May 1967 "Will the real . . . please stand up?" will be heard for the last time.

Book Flashback
Bestsellers—1955-60

Advise and Consent	Alan Drury
The Apprenticeship of Duddy Kravitz	Mordecai Richler
The Art of Loving	Erich Fromm
Atlas Shrugged	Ayn Rand
Dandelion Wine	Ray Bradbury
Diamonds Are Forever	Ian Fleming
Dr. No	Ian Fleming
Dr. Zhivago	Boris Pasternak
The Elements of Style	William Strunk Jr. and E.B. White
Exodus	Leon Uris
The Floating Opera	John Barth
From Russia With Love	Ian Fleming
Goldfinger	Ian Fleming
Goodbye, Columbus	Philip Roth
Growing Up Absurd	Paul Goodman
Howl	Allen Ginsberg
Lady Chatterley's Lover	D.H. Lawrence
Lolita	Vladimir Nabokov
Lord of the Rings	J.R.R. Tolkein
The Magician of Lublin	Isaac Bachevis Singer
The Martian Chronicles	Ray Bradbury
The Naked Lunch	William Burroughs
On the Road	Jack Kerouac
The Organization Man	William H. Whyte, Jr.
Parkinson's Law	C. Northcote Parkinson
Peyton Place	Grace Metalious
Profiles in Courage	John F. Kennedy
Run, Rabbit, Run	John Updike
The Sotweed Factor	John Barth
The Status Seekers	Vance Packard
Steppenwolf	Herman Hesse
The Ugly American	Eugene Berdick and William Lederer
The White Negro	Norman Mailer

Cardinal Sins

DECEMBER 16, 1956. Under the auspices of the "Legion of Decency," the Catholic Church's film-rating organization, Cardinal Francis Spellman attacks the film *Baby Doll* from the pulpit of St. Patrick's Cathedral in New York, warning Catholics to stay away "under pain of sin." Although *Time* magazine has called *Baby Doll* "the dirtiest American-made motion picture that has ever been legally exhibited," *Baby Doll* has the approval of the Production Code Administration, which monitors Hollywood's morals and affixes its seal on "approved" films. Directed by Elia Kazan, *Baby Doll* is a Tennessee Williams story set in the South about a child-bride, her not-too-bright husband, and his crooked partner who wants to exploit both of them. Spellman's remarks will set off a national furor, with many Protestant clergy speaking publicly in favor of the film. Catholics will be barred from attending and picket lines will appear and bomb threats made. Some bishops and archbishops will even impose six-month boycotts against theaters showing *Baby Doll.* This will be the Legion of Decency's last real effort to influence general movie-going. Although it will object to other films, it will never again attain its former importance. In 1958 it will change its classification system, separating movie-going audiences into better-defined age groups. In the 1960s the once-powerful Legion will fade from sight.

Bell Du Jour

DECEMBER 28, 1956. "Ding Dong School" shuts down after a four-year run, and Dr.

Miss Frances: Dead ringer.

Frances Horwich—better known to millions of viewers as "Miss Frances"—will move on. It is largely the victim of advertiser whim: as network kiddie shows have proliferated, several sponsors have dropped "Ding Dong School" in search of a better bang for their advertising buck. NBC, meanwhile, has decided that the show can't run as a money-losing public service. Dr. Horwich, formerly head of Roosevelt College of Education in New York, aimed her show at the two-to-five-year-old set. TV cameras were lowered to give a kid's-eye-view of the daily proceedings, which ranged from stories to crafts to show-and-tell. With teaching credits from 11 universities, Dr. Horwich will be smart enough to retain the rights to "Ding Dong School," and in 1959 it will move to Los Angeles and enjoy a new, albeit short, life.

The Big Sleep

JANUARY 14, 1957. Humphrey Bogart dies at age 58. Although he maintained above-the-title star status to the end, many of his 1950s films, such as *We're No Angels*, have been undistinguished. In the 1960s, however, they will be rediscovered by movie-going audiences in "Bogie" film revivals, books, and posters. In his major films—including *High Sierra, Casablanca, Treasure of Sierra Madre, Key Largo, The Maltese Falcon, African Queen, To Have and Have Not*, and *The Big Sleep*—Bogart has played the tough guy, imposing his genuine go-to-hell style on whichever character he portrayed. Bogart's appeal has been in his worldly-wise self-sufficiency, a quintessential American tough guy who has a strong sense of justice and is willing to put himself on the line to defend it. Bogart became legendary for his stormy marriages, some reportedly filled with physical violence. Lauren (Betty) Bacall is his last wife; they met on the set of *To*

Bogie: Quintessential tough guy.

Flashback
Kid Vid

Abbott and Costello Show
Adventures of Kit Carson
Adventures of Rin Tin Tin
Andy's Gang
Annie Oakley
Betty Crocker Star Matinee
Bozo the Clown
Buck Rogers
Buster Crabbe Show
Captain Kangaroo
Captain Midnight
Captain Video and His Video Rangers
Dennis the Menace
Ding Dong School
Flipper
Fury
G.E. College Bowl
Hardy Boys
Hopalong Cassidy
Howdy Doody
It's Academic
Johnny Jupiter
Kukla, Fran and Ollie
Lassie
Leave It to Beaver
Little Rascals

Willard Scott as Bozo: Clown prince.

Lone Ranger
Mister Rogers Neighborhood
My Friend Flicka
National Velvet
Oky Doky Ranch
Our Gang
Pinky Lee Show
Rootie Kazootie
Roy Rogers Show
Sesame Street
Shari Lewis Show
Sky King
Small Fry Club
Soupy Sales Show
Space Patrol
Tom Corbett, Space Cadet
Uncle Al Show
Watch Mr. Wizard
Wild Bill Hickok
Winky Dink and You
Youth Wants to Know

Have and Have Not, where they shared some famous suggestive dialogue.

Clean Bill of Health

MARCH 25, 1957. U.S. Customs agents seize a press run of Allen Ginsberg's *Howl and Other Poems*, which had been printed in England for Lawrence Ferlinghetti's City Lights Books publishing company. The small book of poetry has gained a following through public readings by Ginsberg and has received critical acclaim in the literary world, but has been deemed obscene by federal, state, and local officials. Soon Ferlinghetti, who also owns City Lights Bookstore, will be arrested and charged with selling obscene literature. Following a lengthy trial Ferlinghetti will be acquitted and Judge Clayton Horn will make a historic ruling: material will not be deemed obscene if it has even the slightest redeeming social value. The ruling will set precedent for a variety of obscenity cases in the next decade, involving publications ranging from Henry Miller's *Tropic of Cancer* to *Zap* comics.

Ginsberg: Poetic justice.

What's in a Name?

MARCH 27, 1957. Robert Rich wins an Oscar for his screenplay of *The Brave One*. In fact, there is no Robert Rich; it is one of the pseudonyms employed by Dalton Trumbo, who has been unable to work under his own name since the anti-Communist crusade launched in Hollywood in the early 1950s. The Motion Picture Academy of America has a rule disqualifying "Fifth Amendment witnesses"—those who invoked their constitutional rights—from receiving Oscars. Trumbo will keep his silence but will orchestrate a campaign to create the impression that many recent major films have actually been written in secret by blacklisted writers. (*The Front*, a 1976 Woody Allen film, will be about this phenomenon.) His campaign will pay off in two years, when *The Defiant Ones* script receives an Oscar nomination. This film was cowritten by "Nathan E. Douglas," an alias of the blacklisted Nedrick Young. Young will disclose the truth and the Academy will be pressured to rescind its rule. Trumbo will soon announce the truth about "Robert Rich," and in 1960 director Otto Preminger will announce that *Exodus* also was written by Trumbo, and that he'll receive screen credit. Jumping on the bandwagon, Kirk Douglas will agree to give Trumbo screen credit for *Spartacus*. Hollywood's own cold war will be over.

Medium Hot

APRIL 28, 1957. After a successful late-night run on New York television, "Mike Wallace Interviews" moves to the ABC network. "Hot interviewing" is the term applied to Wallace's technique of pressing guests for candid statements. Interviewees will continue to feel the heat when Wallace moves to "60 Minutes," which will premiere on CBS in September 1968.

Wallace: Candid camera.

Oldest Living Teenager

AUGUST 5, 1957. "American Bandstand" makes its national TV debut. The show had started five years ago as "Bandstand," a local music show, hosted by Philadelphia DJ Bob Horn. Dick Clark, the son of a cosmetics salesman, who had bumped around radio stations before getting an on-air job at Philadelphia's WFIL, took over as host in 1956 after Horn was charged in a statutory rape case. ABC will give the live rock 'n' roll show an evening

Clark: Only his age changes.

tryout in October which will last only until December 30; eventually, "Bandstand" will move to a Saturday afternoon slot. The early reviews will be mixed—*Billboard*, in a review, will write that "If this is the wholesome answer to the 'detractors' of rock 'n' roll, bring on the rotating pelvises." But by early next year, the show will be the top-ranked daytime TV show and "American Bandstand" and Clark will become two of rock 'n' roll's most enduring institutions. Although the show's style and music will change, Clark will manage to look much the same for three decades—he will become known as "America's oldest living teenager"—and he will build an empire of TV, radio, music, film, and concert productions and amass a personal fortune worth more than $100 million.

A Star is Born

OCTOBER 5, 1957. The day after the Sputnik satellite is launched, producer/director Roger Corman, 31, tells Steve Broidy, head of the small Allied Artists film studio, to start promoting a new movie, *War of the Satellites*. Corman, however, has no cast, money, script—nothing except the resolve to exploit Sputnik, but he promises the film will be in theaters in eight weeks. Broidy agrees and Corman keeps his word. *War of the Satellites* will open eight weeks later, a climax of sorts for Corman, who already has made several other exploitation films and will make many, many more. Indeed, his name will become virtually synonymous with 1950s and 1960s youth exploitation. As a producer/director for American-International Films, he will make monster movies, horror movies, hot rod movies, end-of-the-world movies, rock movies, gangster movies, biker movies, westerns, and jail movies—such titles as *Swamp Women*, *It Conquered the World*, *The Undead*, *Attack of the Crab Monsters*, *Rock All Night*, *Viking Women and the Sea Serpent*, *Teenage Caveman*, *Bucket of Blood*, *Wasp Woman*, *House of Usher*, *Little Shop of Horrors*, *Young Racers*, *The Trip*, *Bloody Mama*, and *Gas-s-s-s*. Many will be produced on unbelievably low budgets, some completed in two or three days. Best known will be a string of Edgar Allan Poe movies, all starring Vincent Price and made in the early 1960s, some shot in England using standing sets abandoned by completed big-budget films. Corman will give breaks to a great many now-established Hollywood names, including Price, Francis Ford Coppola, Jack Nicholson, Peter Fonda, Peter Bogdanovich, and Martin Scorsese.

House of Usher: Low budget, high camp.

And God Created Women: Sex-kitten debut.

Foreign Matters

OCTOBER 21, 1957. *And God Created Woman*, a French film, opens. It will soon be taken to court for obscenity in Pennsylvania, Texas, Rhode Island, and many other locations. The film tells the story of a sensual young woman who marries one brother but loves the other, starring an as-yet-unknown Brigitte Bardot and directed by her husband Roger Vadim. *And God Created Woman* will draw an immense audience and establish Bardot's sex-kitten image. More important, it will help generate an audience for foreign films that are more daring, adventurous, creative, and sexually explicit, such as Frederico Fellini's *La Dolce Vita* (1959), which will cause a similar public uproar. By the early 1960s most large American cities will have theaters specializing in foreign films, especially those of Italy's "neorealist" generation (Fellini, Michelangelo Antonioni, Luchino Visconti), France's "new wave" directors (Jean-Luc Godard, Francois Truffaut, Eric Rohmer), Britain's "free cinema" (Lindsay Anderson, Karel Reisz, Tony Richardson), and films from Sweden and India, among other countries. Such films will have a strong effect on a later generation of American directors, who will find foreign films more stimulating and challenging than the Hollywood model.

Scouting Report

JANUARY 13, 1958. *Publishers Weekly* reports that sales of *Handbook for Boys*, the official manual for Boy Scouts, have picked up, now reaching about 500,000 a year, reflecting the growing interest in scouting. In the 45 years since it was first published, the book has sold some 15.5 million copies.

Realistically Speaking

MAY 27, 1958. The first issue of *The Realist* is published, bearing the legend "free-thought criticism and satire." The legend will remain for eight years, during which *The Realist* will establish itself as a brilliant absurdist humor magazine that accurately zeroes in on the madness of the times. The magazine was founded by Paul Krassner, who formerly worked for *MAD* magazine. Krassner, who later will be credited with coining the term "yippie" for members of the Youth International Party, will attract a varied cross-secion of contributors to *The Realist*, including Lenny Bruce, Ken Kesey, Woody Allen, Mort Sahl, Joseph Heller, Alan Watts, and Terry

Flashback
Boomer Magazines

Avant Garde
Boys Life
Calling All Girls
Circus
Cracked
Highlights
Humpty Dumpty
Ingenue
Junior Scholastic
MAD
National Lampoon
New Times
Ramparts
Ranger Rick
Rolling Stone
17
Sick
16
Teen
The Realist
Tiger Beat
Weekly Reader
Zoo

Southern. Among best-remembered satiric pieces will be "The Parts Left Out of the Kennedy Book" and a "Disneyland Orgy" poster.

Up Against the Gun

SEPTEMBER 24, 1958. The Stone family is introduced to network TV in the guise of "The Donna Reed Show." Included in the cast is Shelley Fabares, who will soon make the pop charts with her song "Johnny Angel." Breaking onto the list of most-watched shows will prove difficult, however, because the nation seems hooked on Wild West fare; of the top-10 shows on the Nielsen National Index, seven are shoot-'em-ups, including "Gunsmoke," "Wagon Train," "Have Gun, Will Travel," "Rifleman," "Maverick," "Wells Fargo," and "Wyatt Earp."

Stone family: Tough competition.

The Ginchiest

OCTOBER 10, 1958. "77 Sunset Strip" debuts, with Efrem Zimbalist, Jr. as private eye Stuart Bailey and Ed Byrnes as Gerald Lloyd "Kookie" Kookson III. The show will give us the song "Kookie, Kookie, Lend Me Your Comb" and the expression "You're the ginchiest." (Translation: You're swell.)

Kookie: Have comb, will travel.

"There's only one secret to television and that's to make the audience come away saying, 'I like that guy.'"

Dick Clark

No Comment

NOVEMBER 23, 1958. Ronald Reagan makes one of his last TV appearances as an actor as he performs with his wife Nancy in a "General Electric Theater" production of "A Turkey for the President."

Good Morning, America

APRIL 19, 1959. Cuban Premier Fidel Castro, in the U.S. at the invitation of the American Society of Newspaper Editors, is interviewed on NBC's "Meet the Press." Two months earlier, on CBS' "Person to Person," Edward R. Murrow had conducted a live interview with Castro, who appeared to be wearing pajamas.

The First Wave

APRIL 22, 1959. *Gidget*, starring Sandra Dee and James Darin, opens, based on a story written by Frederick Kohner, a

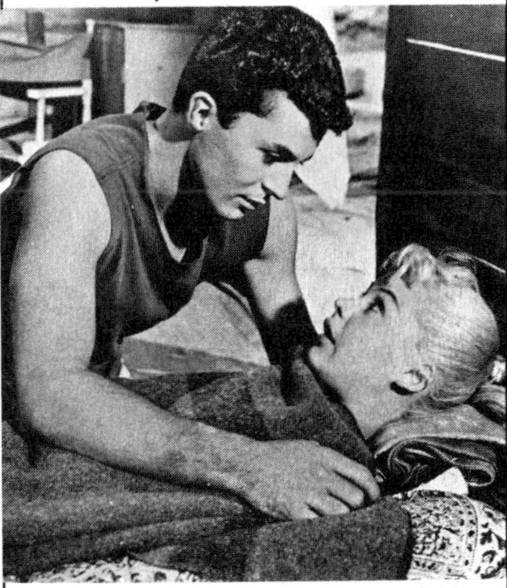

Darin, Dee: Trend setters.

refugee writer from Hitler's Germany who has settled in a large community of Germans in Los Angeles. Two years ago, after his young daughter had assimilated and he felt she had grown up a stranger to him, he wrote a novel about the southern California environment to which she belonged, titling the main character and the book, Gidget. The enormously successful film not only will be followed by four more Gidget movies and a Gidget TV series, but will smooth the sand for a tidal wave of teen beach movies starring Annette Funicello, Frankie Avalon, and others.

Going in Style

SEPTEMBER 23, 1959. Forty-one years after it was published privately by an English professor at Cornell as a text for his students, *The Elements of Style* becomes a national bestseller. A new edition of professor William Strunk, Jr.'s 70-page book on the principles of clear writing has been published, re-edited by one of Strunk's most illustrious students, essayist/poet/humorist E.B. White. Two years ago, a college friend sent White one of the few surviving copies of Strunk's original book. White wrote an article for the *New Yorker* on Strunk, which was read by an editor at Macmillan, who convinced White to revise the book. Over the next 12 years, Macmillan will sell more than two million copies of the little book, most for use in college courses.

Film Flashbacks
Clean Teens

- April Love
- Beach Blanket Bingo
- Beach Party
- Bernadine
- Bikini Beach
- Endless Summer
- Gidget
- How to Stuff a Wild Bikini
- Muscle Beach Party
- Ride the Wild Surf
- Surf Party
- Tammy
- When the Boys Meet the Girls
- Where the Boys Are
- Wild on the Beach

April Love

Arts and Minds

OCTOBER 9, 1959. After a successful 19-year run on radio, the musical variety show "The Bell Telephone Hour" moves to NBC-TV. For the next seven and a half years, the show will highlight the best in classical, jazz, and popular music. Performers will include Benny Goodman and Bing Crosby; Rudolph Nureyev and Joan Sutherland will make their American debuts on the show.

The Eye Has It

OCTOBER 27, 1959. Edward R. Murrow helps launch "CBS Reports" with a one-hour documentary, "Biography of a Missile." The series employs many staff members of Murrow's "See It Now," which was last telecast in July 1958; included on the staff is Fred Friendly, Murrow's former partner, who will later become president of CBS News. "CBS Reports" will run for more than a decade, setting new standards for news reporting and analysis.

How the West Was #1

SEPTEMBER 12, 1959. The Cartwright clan ambles into

Cartwrights: A bonanza for NBC.

American living rooms as "Bonanza," the first western regularly broadcast in color, airs on NBC. Ben, Little Joe, Hoss, and Adam spend two years in a low-rated Saturday night time slot; when they move to Sunday night, however, the Virginia City gang will become the second-most-watched show, and in 1964 "Bonanza" will begin a three-year reign as America's favorite TV show.

Name That Scam

DECEMBER 8, 1959. Scandals involving TV quiz shows claim CBS president Louis G. Cowan, who is forced to resign. Cowan was originally producer of the incredibly successful "The $64,000 Question," which last year spurred a raft of fierce competition from other me-too game shows, including "Top Dollar," "Name That Tune," "Tic Tac Dough," and "The Price Is Right." With the competition, however, came some shady tactics: desirable contestants, it turned out, were given answers in advance to keep them on the show. The practice became apparent when one contestant happened upon a notebook containing answers belonging to a

Serious Ness

OCTOBER 15, 1959. "The Untouchables" premieres on ABC and will quickly blast its way into the top 10. Robert Stack's performance as agent Eliot Ness will win him an Emmy, but by September 1963 the battles with the Mafia will end and the show will become history.

Ness & Co.: Award-winning agents.

woman who had been the previous day's winner. After the first show, "Dotto," came under suspicion, others soon followed. Two months ago, several producers and contestants were hauled before a congressional investigative committee. The scandal will lead to the removal of most quiz shows from the air, to return later in new, sanitized versions.

Game shows: The price is fixed.

Good Sports

JANUARY 3, 1960. Shades of things to come: CBS airs its first "Sunday Sports Spectacular," giving sports fans an afternoon of everything from rodeo and rowing to skiing and stock car racing. Its success will cause ABC to serve up "Wide World of Sports" in April 1961, with Jim McKay hosting and Roone Arledge at the helm.

Kid Lit

JANUARY 14, 1960. The National Library Week committee announces that new children's books published in 1959 totaled nearly 1,500, 100 more than 1958, largely as a result of the fast-growing number of beginning readers. Another reason, says the group, is the growing popularity of "book fairs," held mostly in large cities—week-long events with book displays and entertainment for both children and adults. "Most are sponsored by local PTA groups as a means of introducing children to good literature and at the same time raising funds," the group reports. In early 1963, *Publishers Weekly* will report that the number of children's books published in 1962 grew to 2,584.

Under the Table, Over the Air

FEBRUARY 8, 1960. On the heels of the TV game show scandals, Congress begins hearings on a series of "payola" scandals in the music industry. The hearings result from the admission by DJ Tom Clay, of WJBK in Detroit, that he accepted payola—cash and other gifts—in exchange for record air play. Already the Federal Trade Commission has filed complaints against a number of record manufacturers and distributors, based partly on "American Bandstand" host Dick Clark's investment in three companies whose records he featured. (Example: Clark played "Sixteen Candles" by the Crests with Johnny Maestro only four times in 10 weeks; after investing in the song's publishing company, the tune was heard on his program 27 times in 13 weeks.) Several months ago, when Congress got into the act, investigators determined that 207 DJs in 42 cities received more than $250,000 dollars in payola. When Clark himself testifies before the House subcommittee, he will reveal that a $125 investment in Jamie Records, a Philadelphia label that included Duane Eddy among its acts, netted him a profit of nearly $12,000. As the hearings progress, members of Congress will extract confessions from several DJs, some of whom accepted thousands of dollars in cash and gifts; one Boston station manager will admit receiving a $10,000 car. The subcommittee will probe deep into record industry practices. At one point, Massachusetts congressman Thomas "Tip" O'Neill will ask the Federal Communications Commission to investigate all stations whose employees are involved with payola, eventually pushing through antipayola amendments to the Federal Communications Act. But not before the biggest fish of all is netted: Alan Freed, one of the pioneer DJs of rock 'n' roll, will plead guilty to receiving $30,650 from music companies, but will be given a suspended sentence. For the next few years, Freed will bounce from station to station as he faces an Internal Revenue Service investigation and additional charges, many of which will be pending when he dies in January 1965 at age 43.

Lucy's Plot

MAY 4, 1960. Lucille Ball divorces Desi Arnaz. The first lady of TV comedy, married for 19 years, will claim that "she

Fun With Dick and Jane

f u cn rd ths, u cn go 2 colij

The debate over how best to teach reading to children is as old as the printed page, but it reached new intensity as Baby Boomers flooded elementary schools. The debate flared in 1955, with publication of Rudolf Flesch's *Why Johnny Can't Read*, the first book on the subject for a popular audience. Flesch's book took the nation by storm, remaining on bestseller lists for nearly eight months and running as a serial in dozens of newspapers. Ironically, the public's acceptance was not matched by education professionals: they almost unanimously rejected it.

Flesch challenged the prevailing "look-say" method of reading, in which children were taught to build a vocabulary of memorized words, repeated over and over in texts—a method well known to the millions taught to "See Spot run. Run, Spot, run. Run, run, run." The mainstay introductory text, *We Look and See*—part of the classic "Dick and Jane" series first published by Scott, Foresman and Company in the 1930s—contained only 17 different words: "come" "Dick," "down," "funny," "go," "Jane," "jump," "look," "oh," "Puff," "run," "Sally," "see," "Spot," "Tim," and "up." Having mastered those, budding readers would move on to *We Work and Play*, *We Come and Go*, and—the ultimate, marking the passage into readership—*Fun With Dick and Jane*.

Oh, no, said Flesch. No, no, no. Instead, he argued, there should be a return to the "phonics" reading method, in which children learn relationships between letters and sounds, as in this example from a 1963 textbook, *Let's Read*: "Dad had a map. Pat had a bat. Tad had a tan cap. Nan had a tan hat."

Flesch's persuasive arguments wreaked havoc in teaching circles, where Dick and Jane's recognition was matched only by that of Cubby and Karen. During the mid-1950s, Dick and Jane had close to 85 percent of the reading market. But by the end of the decade, a wide variety of alternative solutions had been posed, all debated bitterly at a fall 1959 National Conference on Reading in English held at Syracuse University.

By the early 1960s, nearly every teacher in the land had adopted a "basal-reading system," a reading program that included a teaching system (contained in a teacher's manual), a collection of stories (contained in books for students), and practice exercises (in student workbooks). Among the innovations of basal was an emphasis not just on words but on their *meanings*. In the workbooks, students were asked to answer questions about the text, and to interpret the accompanying illustrations.

The innovations didn't stop there. In the mid-1960s, several new texts were designed specifically for the urban and "ethnically different" child, using an urban setting (instead of Dick and Jane's white-picket-fence suburb) and more minorities. And the debates over the "best" method continued. And continue.

So, whatever happened to baby Jane—and Dick and Sally and Spot?

They became casualties of the times. As the American family changed, they did, too. For starters, Mike and his twin sisters moved in next-door to Dick and Jane. Mike's family was black. But that wasn't enough. Feminist and civil rights groups began to point out that the middle-class families of Dick, Jane, and Mike—with a mother who kept house, a father who worked, a couple of kids, and some pets—no longer had relevance in the turbulent, changing 1960s. In 1965 the Dick and Jane books endured their final revisions. By 1980 most were out of print.

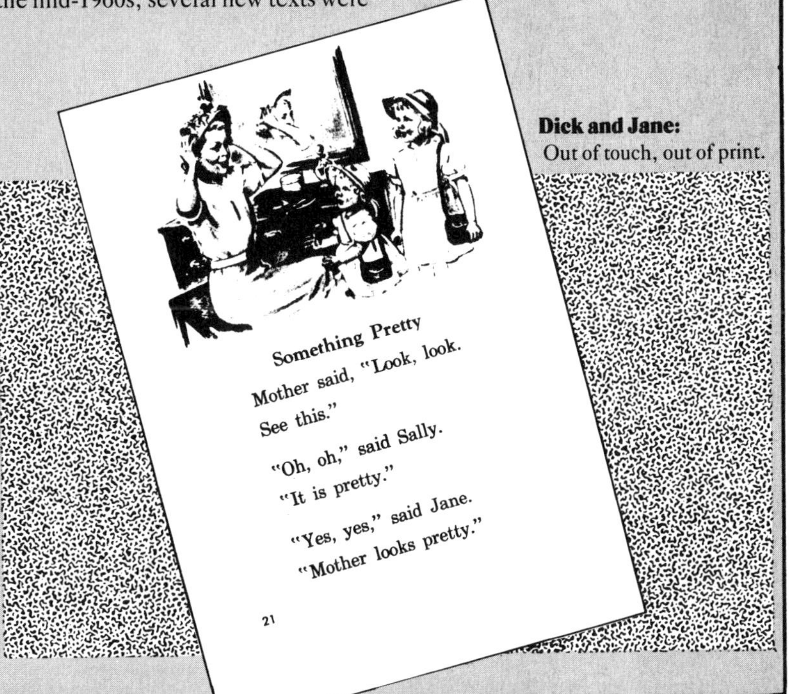
Something Pretty

Mother said, "Look, look.
See this."

"Oh, oh," said Sally.
"It is pretty."

"Yes, yes," said Jane.
"Mother looks pretty."

21

Dick and Jane: Out of touch, out of print.

never expected it to last six weeks." She will ask for their two children, half of their $20 million TV production interests, their mansion, two station wagons, and her plot at Forest Lawn Cemetary.

Luci, Desi: Divorce Court.

The Birds: A flap over icy blonds.

Mystery Man

JUNE 16, 1960. *Psycho*, directed by Alfred Hitchcock, opens and will create a sensation among movie-goers. Among other things, *Psycho*, one of many Hitchcock hits since the 1930s, is a return to black and white, following a string of very successful color films in the 1950s, including *Rear Window*, *North By Northwest*, and *Vertigo*. Hitchcock's reputation as the master of suspense will be matched only by his reputation for involvement with his leading ladies, including Tippi Hedren, whom he allegedly will proposition during shooting of the 1964 film *Marnie*; she will turn him down and Hitchcock will never speak to her again, addressing her for the remainder of the shoot through crew members and cast. Hitchcock will have a life-long obsession with icy blonds, using Grace Kelly, Eva Marie Saint, Kim Novak, and many others in his films. They have become as much a mark of his films as his own cameo appearances. Although with *Psycho*, Hitchcock will inscribe his name indelibly among filmdom's greats, creating one of the most imitated films ever, it will mark the beginning of his creative decline, which will reach its nadir with his final film, *Family Plot*, four years before his death in 1980. Meanwhile, *Psycho* will traumatize countless people against taking showers and its star, Janet Leigh, will never again shower with the curtain closed.

Twilight Zone: Serling success.

Another Dimension

JUNE 20, 1960. Rod Serling's year-old show "The Twilight Zone" has brought television into another dimension, and his writing is honored with an Emmy award.

Film Flashbacks

Suspense

The Birds
Blow-Up
Diabolique
Don't Look Now
Klute
Night of the Hunter
North By Northwest
Psycho
Rear Window
Repulsion
Seance on a Wet Afternoon
Touch of Evil
Vertigo
Wait Until Dark

Early Bird

AUGUST 12, 1960. The world's first telecommunications satellite, Echo I, is put in orbit. It will make possible satellite and telephone communications across the Atlantic Ocean.

The Medium is the Message

SEPTEMBER 26, 1960. Seventy-five million Americans—the largest TV audience to date—tune in the first of four debates between presidential candidates John F. Kennedy and Richard M. Nixon. The Chicago debate puts the power of TV in focus: radio listeners rate the event a draw; TV viewers, noting that Nixon looks tired and Kennedy looks bright, give JFK the edge. Despite the medium's impact on politics, televised presidential debates won't be used again until 1976.

Flashback

Kids' Classics

A Friend is Someone Who Likes You	Joan Walsh Anglund	1958
And to Think That I Saw It on Mulberry Street	Dr. Seuss	1939
The Borrowers	Mary Norton	1953
Caddie Woodlawn	Carol Ryrie Brink	1935
The Cat in the Hat	Dr. Seuss	1957
The Cat in the Hat Comes Back	Dr. Seuss	1958
Charlotte's Web	E.B. White	1952
Curious George	H.A. Rey	1940
Facts of Life and Love for Teen-agers	Evelyn W. Duvall and Sylvanus Duvall	1950
Five Chinese Brothers	Claire H. Bishop	1938
The 500 Hats of Bartholomew Cubbins	Dr. Seuss	1950
Freckles	Gene Stratton Porter	1904
The Girl of the Lumberlost	Gene Stratton Porter	1909
Good-night Moon	Margaret Wise Brown	1947
Henry Higgins	Beverly Cleary	1959
Homer Price	Robert McCloskey	1943
Johnny Tremain	Esther Forbes	1943
Laddie	Gene Stratton Porter	1913
Lassie Come Home	Eric Knight	1940
The Little Engine That Could	Watty Piper	1929
The Little House in the Big Woods	Laura Ingalls Wilder	1932
The Little Prince	Antoine de St.-Exupery	1943
Love Is a Special Way of Feeling	Joan Walsh Anglund	1959
Madeline	Ludwig Bemelman	1939
Make Way for Ducklings	Robert McCloskey	1953
Mary Poppins	P.L. Travers	1932
Mike Mulligan and His Steam Shovel	Virginia Lee Burton	1942
Mr. Popper's Penguins	Richard and Florence Atwater	1938
Misty of Chincoteague	Marguerite Henry	1946
The Moffats	Eleanor Estes	1941
My Father's Dragon	Ruth Gannett	1947
My Friend, Flicka	Mary O'Hara	1941
National Velvet	Enid Bagnold	1935
Pat the Bunny	Dorothy Kunhardt	1940
Pippi Longstocking	Astrid Lindgren	1950
Pollyanna	Eleanor H. Porter	1913
Rebecca of Sunnybrook Farm	Kate Douglas Wiggins	1904
Seventeen	Booth Tarkington	1916
The Story About Ping	Marjory Flack	1933
The Story of Babar	Jean de Brunhoff	1933
Stuart Little	E.B. White	1945
Winnie the Pooh	A.A. Milne	1926
The Witch of Blackbird Pond	Elizabeth George Speare	1958
Wonderful Wizard of Oz	Frank L. Baum	1900
The Yearling	Marjorie Kinnan Rawlings	1952

Rock of Ages

SEPTEMBER 30, 1960. Fred and Wilma take to the air with

Flintstones: Prime-time prehistory.

the arrival of "The Flintstones." The show is the first animated prime-time offering and will make it into the top 20 on the Nielsen chart in its first season. It will inspire other prime-time cartoons, most notably "The Jetsons," a sort of Flintstones in reverse, which will help audiences imagine what life will be like in the Space Age.

No Thanks

NOVEMBER 25, 1960. CBS broadcasts "Harvest of Shame." The Thanksgiving Day documentary, reported by Edward R. Murrow, details the plight of the migratory worker and will make a major impression on the American public.

Feeling His Oats

JANUARY 5, 1961. The naysayers predict that a show about a talking horse will never leave the gate, but "Mr. Ed" proves them wrong. The show debuts as a syndicated series, but by October CBS will put it in the prime-time network schedule, where it will remain for four years before being put out to pasture in September 1965.

> *"They say that 90 percent of TV is junk. But 90 percent of everything is junk."*
>
> **Gene Roddenberry**
> **"Star Trek" producer**

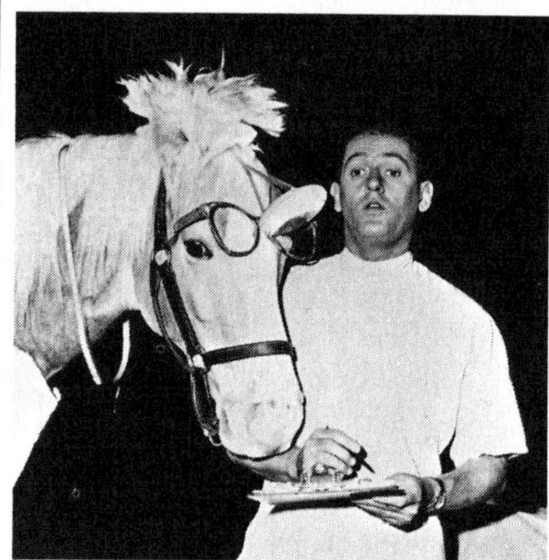

Mr. Ed: Mane attraction.

There's Nothing Wrong With Your Picture

MAY 9, 1961. FCC chairman Newton Minnow, sworn in just two months ago, stuns the broadcasting industry as he declares TV programming "a vast wasteland." In a speech at the annual convention of the National Association of Broadcasters, Minnow says: "I invite you to sit down in front of your television set when your station goes on the air, and stay there. You will see a vast wasteland—a procession of game shows, violence, audience participation shows, formula comedies about totally unbelievable families . . . blood and thunder . . . mayhem, violence, sadism, murder . . . private eyes, more violence, and cartoons . . . and, endlessly, commercials—many screaming, cajoling, and offending . . . ." Two years later, Minnow will resign.

Loose Moose

SEPTEMBER 24, 1961. Following in the footsteps of his pal Rocky the Flying Squirrel, Bullwinkle the Moose gets his own show. "The Bullwinkle Show" will continue the Saturday morning antics of a cast of animated characters that will reach near-cult status: Natasha Fataley, Boris Badenov, Mr. Big, Dudley Do-right, and Mr. Peabody, along with his boy Sherman and the Time Machine.

Doctor's Smock

OCTOBER 2, 1961. Vince Edwards will prove to be just what the doctor ordered for ABC's ailing lineup, as "Ben Casey" begins a four-and-a-half-year run. Drs. Casey and Zorba (Sam Jaffe)—along with their medical-show competition, Drs. Kildare (Richard Chamberlain) and Gillespie (Raymond Massey)—will

Drs. Gillispie, Kildare: Fashion setters.

leave a lasting imprint on the national fabric: for months, "Ben Casey" smocks will be all the rage.

Dynasty

OCTOBER 3, 1961. "The Dick Van Dyke Show" debuts, starring Van Dyke, Mary Tyler Moore, Rose Marie, and Morey Amsterdam. Considered one of TV's classic comedies, it will enjoy a successful five-year run before spinning off a host of other sit-coms. Mary Tyler Moore will move to Minneapolis, where she will work at the fictitious TV station WJM. The "Mary Tyler Moore Show" will, in turn, spin off "Rhoda" (Valerie Harper, Mary's neighbor and closest friend), "Lou Grant" (Ed Asner; Mary's boss at WJM), and "Phyllis" (Cloris Leachman, Mary's landlady and resident busybody).

Van Dyke, Moore: A host of spin-offs.

Heartthrobs

JANUARY 5, 1962. "The Twilight Zone," well into its third TV season, airs a two-person episode titled "Nothing in the Dark." The subordinate role, that of Mr. Death, is played by an unknown actor named Robert Redford, who turns in a wooden performance. Redford will break into movies the following year with a part in *War Hunt*, although he won't make another appearance on film for three years. Through most of the 1960s he will appear in a series of pleasant, albeit undistinguished roles before breaking through when he teams up with Paul Newman in the 1969 hit, *Butch Cassidy and the Sundance Kid*. One of the biggest heartthrobs of the 1970s, Redford will appear in films with fellow hunk Newman so often they will become referred to as "America's favorite couple." Eventually, Redford will become powerful enough to insist on his own roles, often choosing characters he believes reflect the pioneer spirit of his native Colorado. Few, however, will be hits.

Fat Chance

JANUARY 23, 1962. Citing violations of the Food, Drug, and Cosmetic Law, the Food and Drug Administration (FDA) seizes 1,600 copies of Dr. Herman Taller's bestseller, *Calories Don't Count*, which urges overweight people to cut out carbohydrates and increase consumption of certain fats. Published last fall, it has been through nine printings and

Book Flashback
Bestsellers—1961-65

The Autobiography of Malcolm X	Malcolm X
The Bell Jar	Sylvia Plath
Big Sur	Jack Kerouac
Black Like Me	John Griffin
Candy	Terry Southern and Mason Hoffenberg
Catch-22	Joseph Heller
Cat's Cradle	Kurt Vonnegut
A Clockwork Orange	Anthony Burgess
A Confederate General From Big Sur	Richard Brautigan
Demian	Herman Hesse
Fail-Safe	Eugene Burdick and Harvey Wheeler
The Feminine Mystique	Betty Friedan
The Fire Next Time	James Baldwin
Franny and Zoey	J.D. Salinger
Games People Play	Eric Berne
God Bless You, Mr. Rosewater	Kurt Vonnegut
The Golden Notebook	Doris Lessing
The Gutenberg Galaxy	Marshall McLuhan
Happiness is a Warm Puppy	Charles M. Schulz
In His Own Write	John Lennon
Kandy-Kolored Tangerine-Flake Streamline Baby	Tom Wolfe
Little Big Man	Thomas Berger
The Making of the President 1960	Theodore H. White
The Man With the Golden Gun	Ian Fleming
Manchild in the Promised Land	Claude Brown
A Moveable Feast	Ernest Hemingway
Nobody Knows My Name	James Baldwin
One Day in the Life of Ivan Denisovich	Alexander Solzhenitsyn
One-Dimensional Man	Herbert Marcuse
One Flew Over the Cuckoo's Nest	Ken Kesey
Profiles in Courage	John F. Kennedy
A Proper Marriage	Dorris Lessing
The Psychedelic Reader	Timothy Leary
Run River	Joan Didion
Seven Days in May	Fletcher Knebel and Charles Bailey
Sex and the Single Girl	Helen Gurley Brown
The Source	James A. Michner
The Spy Who Came in From the Cold	John Le Carre
Thunderball	Ian Fleming
To Kill a Mockingbird	Harper Lee
Travels With Charley	John Steinbeck
Tropic of Cancer	Henry Miller
Understanding Media	Marshall McLuhan
Up the Down Staircase	Bel Kaufman
You Only Live Twice	Ian Fleming

more than 300,000 copies. But the book was attacked by nutrition experts, who have called Taller's advice harmful, fraudulent, and worthless. In response to its success, a New York vitamin company in which Taller has a financial interest has marketed capsules of safflower oil, which is low in polyunsaturated fats; in his book, Taller recommends taking the oil in capsule form daily to "soften your body fat and help get it out of your system." The FDA seizure is but one of many legal actions that have or will surround the book. In 1963 the Federal Trade Commission will charge Taller and others with making false claims. The Justice Department will indict Taller, the vitamin company, and others for false labeling and conspiracy. There will be four civil lawsuits among Taller, Simon & Schuster (publisher of Taller's book), and the vitamin company. Finally, in 1967 a jury will find Taller guilty of mail fraud, conspiracy, and violations of the FDA law.

No Place Like Home

FEBRUARY 14, 1962. First Lady Jacqueline Kennedy gives "A Tour of the White House With Mrs. John F. Kennedy," broadcast simultaneously over CBS and NBC with nine tons of equipment and 54 harried technicians. After six months of preparation, 46 million people—three out of four people watching TV at that hour—watch Mrs. Kennedy stroll gracefully through the executive mansion, demonstrating her detailed knowledge of the valuable paintings and the White House redecoration project. The show

Jackie: Rave reviews.

will get reviews ranging from ecstatic ("She was to prove a virtuoso among guides," *New York Times*) to merely enthusiastic ("an example of television at its best," *Chicago Daily News*), and will generate tens of thousands of congratulatory telegrams praising the show's achievement.

Cronkite: Hey, Mr. Spaceman.

Uncle Walter Takes Off

FEBRUARY 20, 1962. John Glenn soars into orbit and the networks voraciously cover his voyage. On earth, Walter Cronkite's coverage shines brightest. Uncle Walter will become a sort of national spokesman for the Space Age; his enthusiasm for the burgeoning technology will be infectious.

Soup's On

APRIL 13, 1962. "Soupy Sales" goes off the air after seven funny but controversial years, having begun in 1955 as a summer replacement for "Kukla, Fran and Ollie." Sales (real name: Milton Hines; his brothers called him Soupbone to match their nicknames, Hambone and Chickenbone) ran a one-man, three-ring circus of puns and puppets, including Marilyn Monwolf, White Fang, Black Tooth, Pookie the Lion, and Hippy the Hippo. Sales cavorted in top hat and polka-dot tie, frequently throwing pies in the faces of stars like Dean Martin and Frank Sinatra. In four years Sales will take his show to New York's WNET-TV, where he will be suspended for his on-air antics. At one point, he will ask his young viewers to look in their parents' purses and wallets for the "green paper" inside, and mail it to him. Rumors will claim that he netted millions from the response, but he will put the number at $80,000 or $90,000—"all in Monopoly money or fake cash."

Sales: One man, three rings.

That Cosmo Girl

MAY 23, 1962. *Sex and the Single Girl*, by Helen Gurley Brown, 38, is published. The first frank guide to catching a man, the book will become an instant bestseller, launching Brown into a spotlight that will lead to her becoming editor of *Cosmopolitan* magazine in 1966. There she will transform a once-humdrum magazine into a breathless, sex-filled monthly, focusing largely on self-improvement and the dearth of available males.

Blonde Bombshell

AUGUST 5, 1962. Marilyn Monroe is found dead, an apparent suicide. Details of her death will remain obscure, however, and various conspiracy theories will evolve, sparked in part by a missing diary and phone records and reports of her involvement with President John Kennedy. All of this will add to the larger-than-life aspect of Monroe's persona as Hollywood's symbol—of sex and glamor to some, of exploitation to others. Monroe, born Norma Jean Baker in 1926, worked during World War II as a paint sprayer, where she was discovered by an Army photographer who turned her into a GI pinup girl. By the end of the war, her brown hair had been dyed blonde, she had divorced, and she had decided to become a model. She appeared on magazine covers and was signed by Fox Studios for $125 a week. First came a few tiny roles, many of which were cut from the final films. But her career really took off when she took off her clothes. In the late 1940s, out of work, Monroe was paid $50 to pose as centerfold in the premiere issue of *Playboy*. In 1950, re-signed by Fox, she began her climb to stardom, playing in such films as *Gentlemen Prefer Blondes*, *Bus Stop*, *Seven Year Itch*, and *Some Like It Hot*. Her last film was *Misfits*, which was also Clark Gable's last film. Moody throughout, almost unable to function, she collapsed from a pill overdose on the movie set of a subsequent, unreleased movie and was ultimately fired. Monroe has ushered in the genre of the busty, silly blonde that will be imitated, with varying degrees of success, by Jayne Mansfield, Zsa Zsa Gabor, Mamie Van Doren, June Wilkinson, and Diana Dors, among others.

Hix Pix Stix

SEPTEMBER 26, 1962. "The Beverly Hillbillies" debuts on CBS and will quickly become

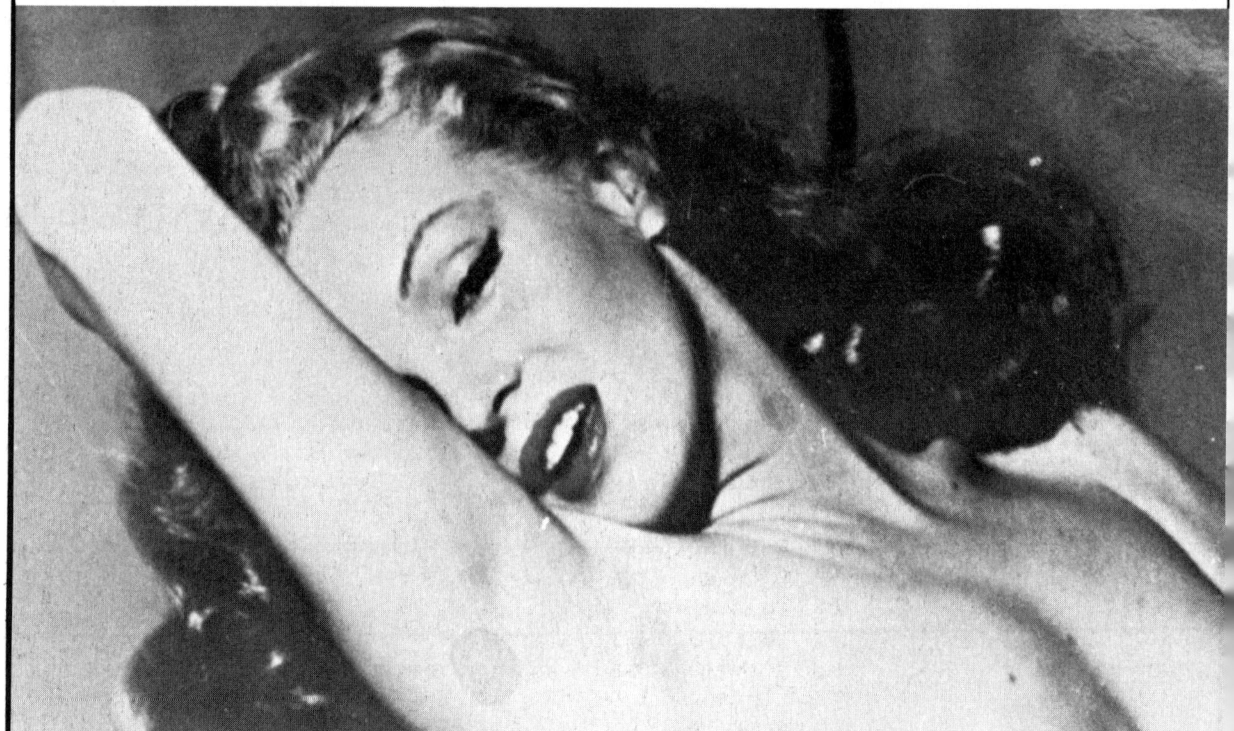

Monroe: Sex, glamor, exploitation.

the first show since "I Love Lucy" in 1956-57 to knock the westerns out of the number-one spot in the Nielsen ratings. It will hold the top spot through the 1963-64 season before "Bonanza" reclaims the spot for the gunslingers. "The Beverly Hillbillies" theme song, "The Ballad of Jed Clampett," was composed by bluegrass legends Lester Flatt and Earl Scruggs; in 1963 the song will make the pop charts.

Heeere's Johnny

OCTOBER 1, 1962. Following in the footsteps of Steve Allen and Jack Paar, Johnny Carson takes over as host of "The Tonight Show" with sidekick Ed McMahon, NBC orchestra bandleader Skitch Henderson, and guests Joan Crawford, Tony Bennett, Rudy Vallee, and Mel Brooks. Carson will become king of late-night TV with regular features like Stump the Band, Carnac the Magnificent, and the Mighty Carson Art Players. McMahon will remain faithfully as "Tonight Show" announcer; bandleader Henderson will soon be replaced by Milton Delugg and, in 1967, by Doc Severinsen. One of the show's more memorable events will take place on December 17, 1969, as aging vaudeville performer Tiny ("Tiptoe Through the Tulips") Tim marries 17-year-old Miss Vicki on the show.

Poison Pen

NOVEMBER 5, 1962. *Silent Spring* by biologist Rachel Carson,

TV Flashback
Sit-Coms

Dobie Gillis

Addams Family (1964-66)
Adventures of Ozzie and Harriet (1952-66)
All in the Family (1971-83)
Andy Griffith Show (1960-68)
Bachelor Father (1957-62)
Beverly Hillbillies (1962-71)
Bewitched (1964-72)
Car 54, Where Are You? (1961-63)
Danny Thomas Show (1953-71)
Dennis the Menace (1959-63)
Dick Van Dyke Show (1961-66)
Donna Reed Show (1958-66)
Father Knows Best (1954-63)
Flying Nun (1967-70)
Get Smart (1965-70)
Gilligan's Island (1964-67)
Gomer Pyle, U.S.M.C. (1964-78)
Green Acres (1965-71)
Happy Days (1974-84)
Hazel (1961-66)
Hogan's Heroes (1965-71)
Honeymooners (1955-71)
I Dream of Jeannie (1965-70)
I Love Lucy (1951-61)
Leave It To Beaver (1957-63)
Lucy Show (1962-74)
M*A*S*H (1972-83)
Many Loves of Dobie Gillis (1959-63)
Mary Tyler Moore Show (1970-77)
Maude (1972-78)
McHale's Navy (1962-66)
Mr. Ed (1961-65)
Monkees (1966-68)
Mork & Mindy (1978-82)
Munsters (1964-66)
My Favorite Martian (1963-66)
My Mother the Car (1965-66)
My Three Sons (1960-72)
Odd Couple (1970-75)
Our Miss Brooks (1952-56)
Partridge Family (1970-74)
Patty Duke Show (1963-66)
Petticoat Junction (1963-70)
Phil Silvers Show (1955-59)
Real McCoys (1957-63)
Rhoda (1974-78)
Sanford and Son (1972-77)
That Girl (1966-71)
Topper (1953-56)

an assessment of the dangers of pesticides and insecticides, tops the nonfiction list. The text appeared originally as a four-part series in the *New Yorker* before being published by Houghton Mifflin. Like Carson's earlier book, *The Sea Around Us*, this one has received considerable attention. In 1964 Fawcett Crest will publish a paperback edition of the book which, in seven years, will see 17 printings and sales of more than 1.6 million copies. *Silent Spring* will be looked back upon as the first book to create a truly national and international uproar about ecology. Next June, in an article taking note of the first anniversary of publication, *Publishers Weekly* will write that "Few books have ever accomplished so much in a single year."

The Big Chill

JANUARY 7, 1963. Reflecting the Cold War chill being felt nationwide, *Fail-Safe* and *Seven Days in May* are numbers one and two on the fiction bestseller list.

Bon Appetit

FEBRUARY 11, 1963. Julia Child prepares Boeuf Bourguignonne on Boston educational TV station WGBH, beginning a series of cooking demonstrations called "The French Chef." Child, 50, a native of Pasadena, Calif., enrolled in the Cordon Bleu when her husband Paul joined the Foreign Service and went to Paris after World War II. Last year, the couple left Paris for Cambridge, Mass., where Child began writing a cooking column for the *Boston*

Child: Cheap wine and cigarettes.

Globe. The column led to the TV series, which will soon appear throughout the country on public television and will help create a national appetite for gourmet cooking. Despite her haute cuisine image, in real life Child is said to smoke cigarettes between courses, seldom spend more than $1.25 on a bottle of wine, and top off a lunch of flaky cheese quiche with a piping hot cup of Nescafe.

Wives and Lovers

FEBRUARY 9, 1963. *The Feminine Mystique*, by Betty Friedan, is published. It is not the first book addressing issues of feminism, but it will be the first to have a major impact beyond a core group of feminists. Friedan charges that since World War II, American women have been victimized by a set of ideas—a "feminine mystique"—in which female happiness is defined as total involvement as a wife and mother, manipulated by advertisers, women's magazines, psychiatrists, and politicians, among others. The result, she says, is a "comfortable concentration camp" of home life. *The Feminine Mystique* will be credited with revitalizing the women's movement and driving its key points home, literally, to millions of women.

Friedan: "Comfortable concentration camp."

Career Change

MARCH 8, 1963. Richard Nixon, who four months ago lost the California governor's race, plays an original piano composition on "The Jack Paar Program."

Roll 'em

APRIL 1, 1963. New York City's 114-day-old newspaper strike finally ends, following a bitter battle over pay and automation. For the city's four morning papers—the *Times, Daily News, Mirror, and Herald Tribune*—their own reappearance will be the main story; the tabloid *Mirror's* headline reads "Alive Again!" But by the time afternoon papers come out, the strike will have been relegated to back pages. The pay raises won by the New York Typographical Union, and their resulting newsstand price hikes, will lead to the demise of three of the papers by the end of the decade.

No Talkin'

MAY 12, 1963. Bob Dylan refuses to appear on "The Ed Sullivan Show" after CBS informs him that he can't sing "Talkin' John Birch Society Blues" on the air. The song will not be included on any of the albums released by Dylan's label Columbia, which is owned by CBS, but will show up on one of Dylan's better-known bootleg records, "Great White Wonder."

Everlasting Bond

MAY 29, 1963. *Dr. No* premieres, ushering in the James Bond era and an enduring public fascination with the world of espionage. The film resulted almost by chance. NBC producer Hans Morganthau III had suggested to writer Ian Fleming an action-adventure series to be set in Jamaica called *Commander Jamaica.* Fleming prepared a 28-page script, but nothing came of it. So Fleming, who already had published several James Bond novels, turned the script into a novel. (An earlier Fleming effort, *Casino Royale*, had been made into a little-watched 1954 CBS show, and Fleming later sold *Casino Royale's* movie rights for a piddling

Dr. No: Kennedy loves Connery.

$6,000.) *Dr. No* is the first in what will become the most popular movie series ever. Bond's popularity has grown substantially since President Kennedy admitted that he enjoys the character. Fleming thought the best choice for the suave Agent 007 would be David Niven, but the first Bond is the relatively unknown Sean Connery, an actor whose previous jobs have included modeling swimming trunks (made possible by his body-building hobby). His identification with the British spy will be so effective that he will spend years trying to shake the Bond image. Connery will be succeeded by George Lazenby, who will appear in *On Her Majesty's Secret Service* (1969), then by Roger Moore, who will take over in 1973 with *Live and Let Die.* Bond movies will be legendary for their expensive look and scale, gadgetry, bizarre villains, exotic women and imaginative opening credits. Eventually, Bond will fade in popularity—although he will make a comeback in the late 1970s—but not before creating a small industry of James Bond-film clones.

The Liz-and-Dick Show

JUNE 12, 1963. *Cleopatra* opens, after production costs of

Cleopatra: $40 million affair.

more than $40 million—which, adjusted for inflation, will make it one of the most expensive films in Hollywood history, as well as perhaps the most anticipated film of the decade. The film and its publicity will strongly affect the careers of Elizabeth Taylor and co-star Richard Burton, although it will nearly bankrupt Twentieth

Century-Fox. *Cleopatra* was originally intended to be a $2 million vehicle for actress Joan Collins, but Collins was busy at the time. On a hunch producer Walter Wanger called Taylor on set of *Suddenly Last Summer.* Taylor, on a lark, decided to do it, but asked $1 million, an unheard-of fee, which she will get. *Cleopatra* will be followed by a string of "Liz-and-Dick" films, most of which will bomb, with the exception of *Who's Afraid of Virginia Woolf?*, in which they caricature themselves. Over the years, Taylor and Burton will marry, divorce, remarry, and redivorce.

Like Taking Candy From a Baby

JULY 12, 1963. Advertisers have discovered that the 40 million American children aged two to 12 influence the spending of one consumer dollar in seven, reports *Time* magazine, and the rush is on to market products to kids beyond toys and candy. One recent success is Colgate-Palmolive's "Soaky"—several pennies' worth of bubble bath in a cartoon-character plastic toy container, retailing for 69 cents. Soaky illustrates how well kids respond to animated symbols, evident also with the advent of the Bosco Bear, the Campbell Kids, Chock's use of TV puppets Kukla and Ollie, and sneakers sellers Kedso the Clown and Captain Keds. Kids' fickle tastes are a problem, though. Popeye is currently out, as are tuna fish, electric trains, and Doctors Kildare and Casey. Currently in are Mr. Magoo, electric toothbrushes, army toys, English bikes, kosher foods, pizza, and Frankenstein.

Kukla, Fran, Ollie: Chock full of hype.

Max'd Out

JULY 22, 1963. California's conservative superintendent of public instruction, Max Rafferty, has opened a new front in his battle to maintain decency in the public schools. His most recent target is the *Dictionary of American Slang*, a 669-page reference book Rafferty calls "a practicing handbook of sexual perversion." As a result, some schools will require that students using the book be accompanied by a librarian.

Banned Books

JULY 29, 1963. Two years after the Justice Department dropped a futile 27-year ban on importing the Paris edition of Henry Miller's *Tropic of Cancer*, a New York State Supreme Court rules that John Cleland's 18th-century novel, *Memories of a Woman of Pleasure*, better known by the name of its heroine, "Fanny Hill," is, indeed, obscene. Proponents of the book—the tale of a 15-year-old Lancashire lass who arrives in London and falls into the clutches of a local brothel before finding true love and quitting the oldest profession—say that Fanny's escapades are nowhere near as unsavory as the boy-meets-boy encounters in James Baldwin's *Another Country*, or the climatic sexual passage in John Updike's *Rabbit Run*. What's

more, they say, Ms. Hill never uses dirty words. No matter, says the court: "Neither the quality of the writing nor the so-called literary worth of the book prevents the book from being adjudged obscene." In March 1966 the U.S. Supreme Court will overturn the decision, ruling that *Fanny Hill* is not obscene. The controversy will place *Fanny Hill* in the same ranks as Terry Southern's *Candy* and D.H. Laurence's *Lady Chatterly's Lover* (the latter was cleared by the courts in 1960), which have been widely circulated among teens for years, with dog-earred copies typically disguised in William Saroyan book jackets.

Save the Last Dance for Me

AUGUST 30, 1963. After six years, "American Bandstand" ends its daily run. Audiences can still dance to it, but only on Saturday afternoons.

30 Minutes

SEPTEMBER 2, 1963. "The CBS Evening News" expands from 15 minutes to a half-hour. It takes NBC only one week to follow suit.

Before Big Bird

SEPTEMBER 9, 1963. "Romper Room" begins its 10th season, with more than five million daily preschool-aged watchers. Started by vaudeville impresario Bert Claster in Baltimore, the first "Romper Room" teacher was his wife Nancy. As its success became apparent, CBS offered to run the program nationally, but the Clasters opted to expand as a series of local programs. When a Norfolk, Va., TV station manager asked if he could imitate the show, Bert Claster trained a teacher, sent her to Norfolk with a kit of sets and props, and kept her supplied with scripts and new materials. Now Claster has trained more than 200 teachers, including those in Canada and Japan. The show, which features a new crop of six five-year-olds each day, combines skill-building (alphabets, numbers) and basic knowledge (can a whale get a sunburn?) with play time. It has become such a part of growing up that many kids, faced with the terror of a first day of real-life kindergarten, dry their tears when told by their moms that "it will be just like 'Romper Room.' "

Flashback
Saturday Morning Cartoons

Adventures of Superman
Alvin and the Chipmunks
Beany and Cecil
Bullwinkle
Bugs Bunny
Casper, the Friendly Ghost

Crusader Rabbit
Daffy Duck
Felix the Cat
Flash Gordon
Flintstones
Gerald McBoing-Boing

George of the Jungle
Gumby and Pinky
Heckle and Jeckle
Huckleberry Hound
King Leonardo and His Short Subjects
Jetsons
Looney Tunes
Magilla Gorilla
Mighty Mouse Playhouse
Mr. Magoo
Popeye

Porky Pig
Quick Draw McGraw
Road Runner
Rocky and His Friends
Ruff and Reddy
Sergeant Preston of the Yukon
Superman

Sylvester and Tweety
Terrytoons
Tom and Jerry
Tom Terrific
Top Cat
Woody Woodpecker
Yogi Bear

It's My Parody

OCTOBER 1, 1963. *MAD* magazine turns 10. In 1953, after suffering three money-losing issues, publisher William Gaines, a 250-pound chain-smoker of 40 cigars a day, featured a parody of the Lone Ranger. The enthusiastic response turned *MAD* into a monthly poking fun at just about anything and everything. With the help of editor Alfred Feldstein and a dedicated readership of more than a million teenagers and college students, *MAD* has become one of the most profitable humor magazines ever. Moreover, its popularity has spread beyond U.S. borders; in England alone, *MAD* sells 20,000 copies a month. One reason for the British enthusiasm may be the magazine's constant portrayal of young Prince Charles as a twitching, unhappy, disobedient boy, drawn to resemble the magazine's own imbecilic mascot, Alfred E. Neuman. But *MAD*'s universal appeal derives primarily from its universal themes: growing up, politics, the inanities of life in general. Among *MAD*'s recent innovations are bound-in playable 45-RPM records, such as "It's a Gas," a bouncy tune whose lyrics consist entirely of belches.

Newman: *Mad* man.

First Take

OCTOBER 23, 1963. *Dementia 13* opens on double bill with *X—The Man With the X-ray Eyes.* Although it will not receive rave reviews—a *New York Times* critic will call it "stolid"—its young director, Francis Ford Coppola, will be encouraged to try again. Coppola wrote the screenplay while working in Ireland as a sound man for Roger Corman's *The Young Racers*. Corman had hoped to do the film himself, but had returned to Hollywood to make *The Raven*; he gave Coppola $22,000 to direct the film. Coppola, who two years ago directed a nudie film called *Tonight For Sure*, will go on to make *You're a Big Boy Now*, which he will present as his master's thesis at UCLA film school. *Big Boy* will

Coppola: From nudies to nukes.

Film Flashbacks
Sci-fi and Fantasy

The Blob

A Boy and His Dog
Angry Red Planet
Barbarella
The Blob
Dark Star
Earth vs. the Flying Saucers
Fahrenheit 451
Five Million Years to Earth
The Fly
Forbidden Planet
Godzilla
Hercules
I Married a Monster From Outer Space
Incredible Shrinking Man
Invasion of the Body Snatchers
The Mysterians
Plan Nine From Outer Space
Panic In Year Zero
Planet of the Apes
Rodan
Seventh Voyage of Sinbad
Silent Running
Them
Time Machine
2001, A Space Odyssey
Village of the Damned
Westworld
World, The Flesh and the Devil
X, the Man With the X-Ray Eyes

lead to a big-budget musical, *Finian's Rainbow* (1968), and *Rain People* (1969), neither of which will be commercial successes. Not deterred, the persistent Coppola will form his own company, San Francisco-based American Zoetrope, and in 1972 will make *The Godfather*, an Oscar-winning smash hit. In 1973 will come *American Graffiti*, directed by film-school buddy George Lucas, followed in 1974 by *Godfather II*. By the mid-1970s Coppola will begin to waste money on several ventures, including a city magazine in San Francisco and several money-losing films, among them *Apocalypse Now* and *One From the Heart*.

That Was the Show That Was

NOVEMBER 10, 1963. NBC introduces America to the British satire on the news, "That Was the Week That Was," known also by its initials, "TW3." Next January, an American version hosted by David Frost will premiere, offering a controversial mixture of political satire and general slapstick based on the week's headlines—which will center around the Vietnam war, civil rights, the population explosion, and President Johnson. The show will serve as a vehicle for launching or furthering the careers of many of its writers—including Buck Henry, Herb Sargent, Gloria Steinem, and Calvin Trillin—and actors—including Henry, Phyllis Newman, Alan Alda, and Henry Morgan. The show will have a dedicated but limited following and in May 1965, it will become the show that was.

Point Blank

NOVEMBER 24, 1963. Jack Ruby's live TV murder of President Kennedy assassin Lee Harvey Oswald features use of the instant replay. Its success during this macabre setting will spur network producers to make the technique a staple of sports programming.

Basket Cases

DECEMBER 30, 1963. "Let's Make a Deal" premieres. The show begins with normally dressed contestants, but later a man will show up in the parking lot dressed as a vegetable in the hope of attracting the producer's attention. He will, and before long a flood of life-sized fruits—sometimes entire busloads of them—will descend on the show. In May 1967, "Let's Make a Deal" will move to prime-time.

The Big-Bang Theory

JANUARY 29, 1964. *Dr. Strangelove* opens, based on a book called *Two Hours to Doom* by Peter George, writing under the pseudonym Peter Bryant, a straightforward novel on preventive nuclear war (it has been published in the U.S. as *Red Alert*). George sold movie rights for this unlikely book to Stanley Kubrick, a regular reader of *The Bulletin of Atomic Scientists*, among other things, with a strong interest in the problem of nuclear war. Deciding to make a serious film on the subject, Kubrick has discovered how absurd the problem seems to be. The result is *Strangelove*, subtitled "How I Learned to Stop Worrying and Love the Bomb." As Kubrick will put it: "What could be more absurd than the very idea of two megapowers willing to wipe out all human life because of an accident, spiced up by political differences that will seem as meaning-

Strangelove: "Is nothing sacred?"

Film Flashbacks
Politics

Slaughterhouse Five

Apocalypse Now
The Battle of Algiers
Bed Sitting Room
Dirty Dozen
Dr. Strangelove
Fail Safe
Gay Deceivers
Great Escape
Green Berets
Hell Is For Heroes
Hearts and Minds
How I Won the War
In The Year Of the Pig
King of Hearts
La Chinoise
M*A*S*H
Medium Cool
Milhouse
On the Beach
Night and Fog
The Parallax View
Paths of Glory
Patton
Pork Chop Hill
Slaughterhouse Five
The Sorrow and the Pity
The War Game
Z

less to people a hundred years from now as the theological conflicts of the Middle Ages appear to us today." Kubrick made the film in London because its star, Peter Sellers, was in the midst of a divorce and couldn't leave England for an extended period. Sellers plays three parts in the film and has been permitted to improvise whole scenes. *Strangelove* will be a ground-breaking film: it makes vicious fun of the military, the President, and many U.S. ideals, including private property. *New York Times* movie critic Boseley Crowther will be moved to write three articles about the movie; one will be headlined, "Is Nothing Sacred?" Kubrick, whose previous hit was *Lolita*, will later make several classics, including *A Clockwork Orange* and *2001: A Space Odyssey*.

But She Buys Detergent

FEBRUARY 1, 1964. The first of a two-part series written by feminist author Betty Friedan begins in *TV Guide*. In "Television and the Feminine Mystique," Friedan says that television's image of the American woman "is a stupid, unattractive, insecure little household drudge who spends her martyred, mindless boring days dreaming of love—and plotting nasty revenge against her husband."

A Breath of Fresh Air

FEBRUARY 3, 1964. The Government Printing Office reports that its hottest title is *Smoking and Health*, the Surgeon General's grim report on the link between cigarettes and lung cancer. Superintendent of Documents Carper W. Buckley says that nearly 10,000 copies of the 387-page book were sold the day the book was released.

All I Have to Do Is Scream

FEBRUARY 9, 1964. Ed Sullivan has a really, really big shoooooo, as 60 percent to 70 percent of American homes tune in to watch the Beatles' American debut. The TV audience will have one advantage over the lucky few who have made it into the studio audience: it will be able to hear the Beatles over the screaming.

Sullivan, Fab Four: No quiet on the set.

Fighting MAD

MARCH 13, 1964. *MAD* magazine has the last laugh on songwriter Irving Berlin after winning a copyright infringement case filed by Berlin in the U.S.

Court of Appeals. Berlin had charged that *MAD*'s parody of some of his best-known hits—part of *MAD*'s periodic feature, "Sing Along with *MAD*"—violated copyright law. (Example: Berlin's "A Pretty Girl Is Like a Melody" became *MAD*'s "Louella Schwartz Describes Her Malady.") Said the opinion written by Judge Irving R. Kaufman: "We believe that parody and satire are deserving of substantial freedom—both as entertainment and as a form of social and literary criticism."

Winning Kiss

APRIL 13, 1964. Millions of viewers are shocked when Ann Bancroft not only presents Sidney Poitier with a best actor Oscar for *Lilies of the Field*, but gives him a congratulatory kiss on the cheek. Poitier is the first black man to win an Oscar; it is cap to a career in which he has become the first black to establish a name in film without singing or dancing. His major roles have included *Blackboard Jungle*, *Defiant Ones*, *Raisin in the Sun*, *Patch of Blue*, and *To Sir With Love*. Among his most famous films is *In the Heat of the Night* in which, insulted by a southern bigot, he slaps him back, marking a change in black-white relations in film. By the time he makes *Guess Who's Coming to Dinner?* in 1967, about interracial marriage, the times will finally have caught up with Poitier. The film will be seen as fatuous (there had been several braver efforts in the early 1960s, including *One Potato, Two Potato*) and Poitier will begin to seem a bit like an Uncle Tom. His efforts to reverse the image with tougher roles—as in *They Call Me Mr. Tibbs*—won't be entirely successful.

Still No Channel 1

APRIL 30, 1964. Starting today, all new TV sets must be equipped to receive UHF channels 14 through 83.

In the Heat of the Night

Mass Media

JULY 13, 1964. The TV networks descend in force on the Republican National Convention; for the first time, convention delegates (1,308) are outnumbered by accredited representatives of the networks (1,825). By 1980 the press-to-delegate ratio will approach two to one.

The Strong, Silent Type

SEPTEMBER 12, 1964. *A Fistful of Dollars* opens, directed—sometimes by telephone, according to reports—by Sergio Leone. An immense success, it will prompt a stampede of brutal, updated "oaters," so-called spaghetti westerns filmed in Italy or other low-cost locations. This one stars Clint Eastwood, otherwise known for his TV role in "Rawhide." In *Fistful*, Eastwood plays a quiet but powerful Man With No Name, a character he will expropriate later in other films he will produce himself.

'Place' Kick

SEPTEMBER 15, 1964. "Peyton Place" debuts on ABC and is an instant hit. The show will air twice, sometimes three times, each week for the next four years, finally settling into a weekly time slot in February 1969, just four months before its demise. Steamy subplots keep the action moving in the small New England town of Peyton Place. Among cast members who will achieve longer-lasting recognition are Mia Farrow and Ryan O'Neal.

Rock Video

SEPTEMBER 16, 1964. Sam Cooke stars in the opening shows of "Shindig," hosted by Jimmy O'Neill on ABC. The show will feature most of the big names in rock music, as will NBC's clone "Hullabaloo," which will air in January.

Hullabaloo: A shindig for NBC.

Thrush Busters

SEPTEMBER 22, 1964. Napoleon Solo (Robert Vaughn) and Illya Kuryakin (David McCallum) communicate over Channel D for the first time as "The Man From U.N.C.L.E." joins the NBC lineup. U.N.C.L.E. ("United Network Command for Law and Enforcement") spends most of its time fighting off THRUSH, an

TV Flashback

Drama and Adventure

The Adventures of Superman

Adam 12 (1968-75)
Adventures of Rin Tin Tin (1954-59)
Adventures of Superman (1952-57)
Alfred Hitchcock Presents (1955-65)
Batman (1966-68)
Ben Casey (1961-66)
Charlie's Angels (1976-81)
Columbo (1971-77)
Dr. Kildare (1961-66)
Dragnet (1952-70)
F.B.I. (1965-74)
Fugitive (1963-67)
Hawaii Five-O (1968-80)
I Spy (1965-68)
Ironside (1967-75)
Kojak (1973-78)
Lassie (1954-71)
Lost In Space (1965-68)
Man From U.N.C.L.E. (1964-68)
Mannix (1967-75)
Marcus Welby, M.D. (1969-76)
McCloud (1970-77)
Medical Center (1969-76)
Mission: Impossible (1966-73)
Mod Squad (1968-73)
National Velvet (1960-62)
Outer Limits (1963-65)
Perry Mason (1957-74)
Peter Gunn (1958-61)
Peyton Place (1964-69)
Playhouse 90 (1956-61)
Police Woman (1974-78)
Quincy, M.E. (1976-83)
Rockford Files (1974-80)
Room 222 (1969-74)
Route 66 (1960-64)
Secret Agent (1965-66)
77 Sunset Strip (1958-64)
Star Trek (1966-69)
Streets of San Francisco (1972-77)
Tarzan (1966-69)
Twilight Zone (1959-65)
Untouchables (1959-63)
Voyage to the Bottom of the Sea (1964-68)
Waltons (1972-81)

Vaughn, McCallum: A pen mightier than the sword.

international crime gang with an implied connection to the Soviet Union. The show will make Kuryakin into a teen-age heart-throb and will inspire millions of people, young and old, to talk furtively into partly disassembled ballpoint pens. A spinoff, "The Girl From U.N.C.L.E.," starring Stefanie Powers, will debut in 1966; the viewing public won't buy the premise, although Powers will go on to star in such other bland vehicles as "Hart to Hart" and countless mini-series.

First in a Series

OCTOBER 7, 1964. John Forsythe and Jane Wyatt star in "See How They Run," the first made-for-TV movie. The NBC/Universal Studios presentation runs well back in the ratings, establishing a trend other made-for-TV movies will follow for years.

"In America, you watch TV and think that's totally unreal. Then you step outside and it's just the same."

Joan Armatrading

Z-Z-Z-Z-Z-Z-Z

NOVEMBER 2, 1964. The American Academy of Pediatrics reports on a new phenomenon, "the tired-child syndrome," brought about by an overdose of TV. The finding results from a study of 30 patients, aged three to 12, who had two things in common: they lived on U.S. Air Force bases and they were suffering from nervousness, continuous fatigue, headaches, loss of sleep, bellyaches, and occasional vomiting. After tests for the usual childhood illnesses turned up nothing, medics looked at the kids' lifestyles. After several interviews, the truth emerged: the youngsters spent from three to six hours a day watching TV on weekdays, and from six to 10 hours on weekends. After parents cut TV time to two hours a day, the symptoms vanished in five to six weeks.

You Heard It Here First

APRIL 19, 1965. New York radio station WINS becomes the first all-news station, although competition will heat up as WCBS follows suit. Soon, all-news stations will appear in most major cities, as the trend continues toward specialization in radio broadcasting.

All the World's a Stage

AUGUST 11, 1965. The crew of KTLA, an independent Los Angeles television station, equips a helicopter with a special camera and provides sensational shots of rampaging mobs during the Watts riots. All three networks use the dramatic footage, and helicopters will soon become state-of-the-art in the TV news business.

Radical Rag

AUGUST 13, 1965. The *Berkeley Barb* is founded, a child of

Barb: Radical rag.

Berkeley's year-old Free Speech Movement. Emphasizing sexual freedom as much as radical politics, it will soon encounter legal harassment for its frank language and semipornographic pictures. In 1968 staffers frustrated with the *Barb's* politics will quit and form a rival paper, *The Berkeley Tribe*. Both papers, along with the *Los Angeles Free Press*, will serve as models for dozens of alternative and underground papers that will sprout up in coming years.

Give Us a Brake

SEPTEMBER 14, 1965. In one of the stranger premises for a situation comedy, CBS parks "My Mother the Car"—starring Jerry Van Dyke, with Ann Sothern as the voice of Van Dyke's maternal Model T—in its Tuesday night lineup. It will sputter along for a year before being relegated to the video junkheap.

...Nor Dark of Night

NOVEMBER 9, 1965. A massive power failure blacks out New

Flashback
Underground and Alternative Papers

Argus	Ann Arbor, Mich.
Berkeley Barb	Berkeley, Calif.
Bay Guardian	San Francisco
Black Panther Party Paper	Oakland, Calif.
Daily Flash	St. Louis
Daily Planet	Miami
Distant Drummer	Philadelphia
Dock of the Bay	San Francisco
East Village Other	New York
Express-Times	San Francisco
Fifth Estate	Detroit
Free Press	Columbus, Oh.
Free Press	Los Angeles
Free Press	Philadelphia
Free Press	San Diego
Free Press	Washington, D.C.
Great Speckled Bird	Atlanta
Helix	Seattle
Independent Eye	Cincinnati
Insight	Nashville
Juche	Cambridge, Mass.
Kaleidoscope	Milwaukee
Kudzu	Jackson, Miss.
Logos	New Orleans
NOLA Express	New Orleans
Northwest Passage	Bellingham, Wash.
Notes	Dallas
Off Our Backs	Washington, D.C.
Old Mole	Cambridge, Mass.
Open City	Los Angeles
Oracle	San Francisco
Orpheus	Phoenix
Other Voice	Hartford, Conn.
Outlaw	St. Louis
People's Voice	Dallas
Queen City Express	Cincinnati
Quicksilver Times	Washington, D.C.
Rag	Austin, Tex.
SDS New Left Notes	Chicago
Second City	Chicago
Seed	Chicago
Space City	Houston
Street Journal	San Diego
Sun	Detroit
Tribe	Berkeley, Calif.
Yipster Times	New York

York City and much of the East Coast. The major networks will broadcast the evening news to the rest of the nation by candlelight, using emergency generators. Without TV to watch, East Coast couples will find other things to do, and nine months later maternity wards will be overflowing.

Em-Barris-ing

DECEMBER 20, 1965. "The Dating Game," produced by Chuck Barris, makes its entrance on ABC; the following October it will move to prime-time. A sequel, "The Newlywed Game," will be added to ABC's lineup next July; by the following January it too will run in prime-time. Barris will outdo even himself in the schlock department when he later dreams up "The Gong Show."

No Stars in Space

DECEMBER 29, 1965. Stanley Kubrick begins production on his new film, *Journey Beyond the Stars*. Kubrick has based his script on Arthur C. Clarke's 1951 story, "Sentinal of Eternity." Kubrick and Clarke have been working for months on the script, and Kubrick has spent additional months assembling a cast and crew. By the time the film opens in April 1968, it will be retitled *2001: A Space Odyssey*, and times have changed so that the film will represent a psychedelic experience unexpected when Kubrick started planning the film four years earlier. Notable as the first major production without a single bankable performer, *2001* will be shortened by 19 minutes after it opens, an action some will say saved the film at the box office. As it is, *2001* will open to mixed reviews, including many pans, the sole exception being Penelope Gilliatt in *New Yorker*, who will herald the film as "some kind of masterpiece."

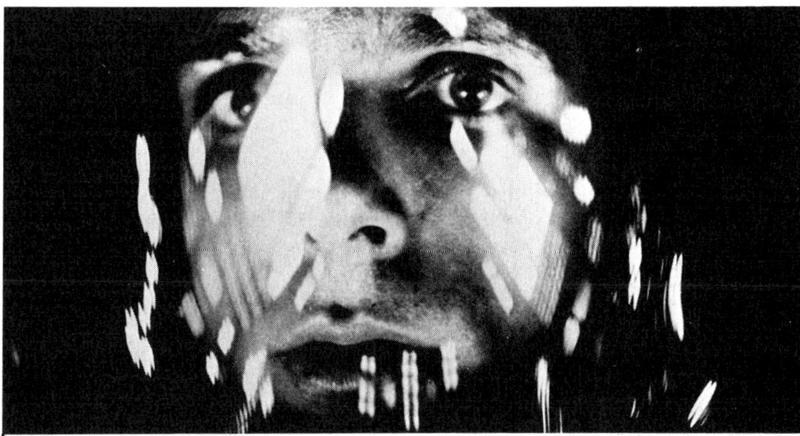

2001: A Space Odyssey

Crime Capers

JANUARY 12, 1966. Holy hits, Robin, "Batman" is here! The age-old comic book hero comes to prime-time, with Adam West playing The Caped Crusader and Burt Ward playing his sidekick Boy Wonder. The two will work and live in a secret crime lab under "the Wayne mansion" where they will hide the Batmobile and other crime-fighting paraphernalia. Their near-slapstick adventures will hook them up with the likes of The Penguin (Burgess Meredith), The Joker (Cesar Romero), Egghead (Vincent Price), and King Tut (Victor Buono), and will create a national passion for black capes and masks. But after two years of successfully fending off video villains, the Dynamic Duo will be beaten by their own ratings, which will go *CRUNCH!*

G.M.'s Nadir

MARCH 9, 1966. General Motors Corporation admits harassing Ralph Nader following publication of Nader's controversial book, *Unsafe at Any Speed*. The book, published last November, is a heavily documented indictment of the automobile industry and the existing traffic safety establishment for massive failures in protecting the public from hazardously designed cars, and of the government itself for its failure to set adequate safety standards for the manufacture of cars. Nader's thesis wasn't exactly new—articles on the topic have been published regularly for the past five years—but the book received tremendous publicity, which brought considerable embarrassment to the industry. Among the most embarrassed was G.M., whose car, the 1960 through 1963 Corvair, was a main focus of Nader attacks on what he declared to be lethal design deficiencies in the car. Following the book's publication, G.M.'s lawyers investigated Nader's personal life in the hope of discrediting him. They trailed him for several weeks, made late-night phone calls to Nader at his Washington,

Nader: Unsafe.

D.C., boarding house, hired attractive young women to seduce him, and interviewed friends and associates, trying to determine his sources of income, his friends, whether he drove a car (and, if so, what kind), whether he was a homosexual, an anti-Semite, or a Communist. But G.M.'s often less-than-subtle investigators made Nader suspicious, and when he found himself trailed into a Senate office building, he related the incident to a *Washington Post* reporter, resulting in a small story about Nader's being trailed. The *Post* piece was followed in early March by a longer article in *The New Republic*, which began a flurry of publicity about who was investigating Nader. Reporters hounded the four major auto makers; Ford, Chrysler, and American Motors all issued firm denials of involvement, with G.M. declining comment until it had no choice but to admit that its lawyers had done a "routine" investigation on the auto safety advocate.

Between the Covers

APRIL 18, 1966. Although it was written for the medical-scientific community, the just-published William Masters and Virginia Johnson book, *Human Sexual Response*, is already on its way to bestsellerdom. Within days of publication, people will clamor for often hard-to-get copies, much as they did for Alfred Kinsey's *Sexual Behavior in the Human Male* and the corresponding female volume, which have sold close to 300,000 and 200,000 copies, respectively. The Masters and Johnson book, based on 11 years of research at their Reproductive Biolgy Research Foundation in St. Louis, provides extraordinarily detailed accounts of the female's arousal to orgasm, based on observations and color movies of some 10,000 orgasms by 382 women and 312 men under laboratory conditions.

A Cult Is Born

SEPTEMBER 8, 1966. The Starship U.S.S. *Enterprise* blasts off as "Star Trek" boldly goes where no TV series has gone before. For the next three years, Captain James T. Kirk, Mr. Spock, Dr. McCoy, Mr. Scott and the rest of the crew will do battle with Klingons, Romulans, and other alien forces. Although NBC will cancel the series in 1969 after only 78 episodes, the show's hardcore fans—"Trekkies," as they will become known—will keep the concept alive with conventions, fan clubs, and pressure on local TV stations for reruns. A decade after the show's demise, the

Masters and Johnson: 10,000 orgasms.

Trekkers: Romulans and reruns.

first of the "Star Trek" movies will open in theatres.

Fu*k Censorship

NOVEMBER 15, 1966. Local police continue an apparent censorship campaign as they raid the Psychedelic Shop in San Francisco's Haight-Ashbury district, arresting a clerk for selling *The Love Book*, a collection of erotic poetry by local poet Lenore Kandel. Kandel's poems, which make liberal use of four-letter words (sample: "I love you/your cock in my hand/stirs like a bird/in my fingers") have already appeared in print elsewhere, but her descriptive cosmic love scenes will become a focus for San Francisco's police, who will bust the City Lights Bookstore two days later for a similar *Love Book* offense. Another police censorship target has been *The Beard*, a play by Michael McClure, which fea-

Book Flashback
Bestsellers—1966-70

Armies of the Night	Norman Mailer
The Andromeda Strain	Michael Crichton
The Back Country	Gary Snyder
Caught in the Quiet	Rod McKuen
The Crying of Lot 49	Thomas Pynchon
Do It!	Jerry Rubin
The Electric Kool-Aid Acid Test	Tom Wolfe
Everything You Always Wanted to Know About Sex	David Reuben
Fahrenheit 451	Ray Bradbury
The Godfather	Mario Puzo
The Greening of America	Charles Reich
Hell's Angel	Hunter Thompson
Human Sexual Response	William Masters and Virginia Johnson
A Hundred Years of Solitude	Gabriel Garcia Marquez
I Know Why the Caged Bird Sings	Maya Angelou
In Cold Blood	Truman Capote
Islands in the Stream	Ernest Hemingway
Jonathan Livingston Seagull	Richard Bach
The Kingdom and the Power	Gay Talese
The Late Great Planet Earth	Hal Lindsey and C.C. Carlson
Linda Goodman's Sun Signs	Linda Goodman
Listen to the Warm	Rod McKuen
The Love Machine	Jacqueline Susann
Love Story	Erich Segal
The Making of a Counter Culture	Theodore Roszak
Myra Brekenridge	Gore Vidal
The Naked Ape	Desmond Morris
Narcissus and Goldmund	Herman Hesse
Player Piano	Kurt Vonnegut
Play It As It Lays	Joan Didion
Portnoy's Complaint	Philip Roth
Quotations of Chairman Mao	Mao Tse-Tung
Radical Chic and Mau-Mauing the Flak Catchers	Tom Wolfe
The Selling of the President 1968	Joe McGinniss
The Sensuous Woman	"J"
Sexual Politics	Kate Millett
Slaughterhouse Five	Kurt Vonnegut
Soledad Brother	George Jackson
Soul On Ice	Eldridge Cleaver
The Teachings of Don Juan	Carlos Casteneda
Unsafe at Any Speed	Ralph Nader
Valley of the Dolls	Jacqueline Susann
The Whole Earth Catalog	Stewart Brand, ed.
Welcome to the Monkey House	Kurt Vonnegut
Why Are We in Vietnam?	Norman Mailer

tures a scene that simulates cunnilingus. Local citizens will protest the police actions, pointing out that topless—and, soon, bottomless—dancing in North Beach bars is perfectly legal. Soon a group of San Francisco State College professors will hold a protest—a reading of *The Love Book* and the controversial sex scene from *The Beard*—hoping to attract police for a mass arrest. The cops, by now winding down their sex-in-litera-ture campaign, won't bother to show up.

$16,666 a Second

JANUARY 15, 1967. The first AFC-NFC championship—dubbed "Super Bowl I" by Texas millionaire and Kansas City Chiefs' owner Lamar Hunt—is broadcast by both CBS and NBC. While Vince Lombardi's Green Bay Packers are beating up the Chiefs, CBS easily outdistances NBC in the Nielsen ratings. The next year, however, the two networks will begin alternating coverage of the game, which will become so popular that advertising time eventually will reach $1 million a minute.

O'er the Ramparts We Watched

FEBRUARY 1, 1967. CIA and IRS officials meet to discuss ways to harass *Ramparts*, the leading magazine of the left. The intelligence community had long been interested in *Ramparts*, but advance word of the magazine's planned expose of the CIA's relationship with the National Student Association has required that drastic action be taken to discredit the publication. This meeting will result in an IRS investigation into *Ramparts*' financial backers, looking especially for ties to foreign intelligence agencies. It will find no such ties.

Medicine Man

MARCH 8, 1967. At the suggestion of *Berkeley Barb* editor Max Scherr, Dr. Eugene Schoenfeld, staff physician at the University of California, Berkeley, student clinic, begins writing a weekly health column under the byline "Dr. HIPpocrates." Soon, some 15 underground newspapers—including the *Barb*, *East Village Other*, and *Los Angeles Free Press*—will carry the column, which answers readers' letters on a wide range of subjects. (For example, "Will any harm come to our nursing baby if my wife smokes marijuana?" Answer: "Your baby is on a good trip anyway at its mother's breast. Why take a chance?") "Dr. Hip," as he will come to be called, will become something of a surgeon general for the Now Generation, liberally dispensing information on everything from acne to acid. He will warn against the impurities of street drugs, but won't dismiss recreational drugs altogether; harangue readers to get regular VD checkups; explain pelvic examinations to girls fearful of them; and, to a reader worried about getting cancer of the armpits from spray deodorants, recommend an alternative: daily bathing.

How I Got That Story

MAY 15, 1967. On the eve of an anticipated invasion of long-hairs for the much-publicized "Summer of Love," the *San Francisco Chronicle* begins a week-long "investigative" series, "I Was a Hippie," in which otherwise straight-laced *Chronicle* reporter George Gilbert reports on his recent assignment: "to live as

Exclusive Report

'I WAS A HIPPIE'

THE WEATHER

103rd Year No. 135

San Francisco Chronicle

THE VOICE OF THE WEST

FINAL

MONDAY, MAY 15, 1967

10 CENTS GArfield 1-1111

'I Was a Hippie'

Reporter George Gilbert mingled with Hippieland's "Love Generation"

A Month on the Scene

Report From Haight-Ashbury

Riot Police Battle Mob At Playland

San Francisco police wielding nightsticks broke up a crowd of some 500 youths after a fist fight turned into a wild brawl at Whitney's Playland-at-the-Beach on Ocean Beach last night.

Soviet Roar For Far-Out U.S. Jazz

The Gallup Poll

Extreme Views Of the Viet War

Action Over North

U.S. Jets Score A Triple Kill Of Red MIGs

American pilots blazing away with new rapid firing cannon and air-to-air missiles shot down three more MIG jets over North Vietnam's industrial heart yesterday in a series of fierce fights.

Chronicle: Underground journalism.

a hippie for a month." As Gilbert tells it: "I shunned my barber, grew a beard, donned a black turtle neck sweater, white levis with mod belt and Navy pea jacket. From my neck hung a lead pendant." In the series Gilbert will reveal, among other things, what life is like at crash pads; how marijuana is bought, sold, and smoked; the sexual mores of hippies; and "the High Life at a hippie party."

Hello, Mr. Briggs

JUNE 3, 1967. "Mission: Impossible" wins its first Emmy. Although the show will never make it into the top 10, it will develop a loyal following. The team of agents seems able to slip in and out of any situation in any foreign country; Barney Collier (Greg Morris) can build a rocket launcher out of cardboard and toothpicks if necessary. Each week, following the self-destruction of the instructional tape, the audience will see glossy photos of the men and women in charge of the operations against which the I.M. Force is pitted. In September 1973 CBS will decide to disavow any knowledge of the show's existence.

I.M. Force: Anything's possible.

Bonnie and Clyde

The Second Time Around

AUGUST 13, 1967. *Bonnie and Clyde* debuts and almost immediately closes after a week of bad reviews and bad business. But co-star Warren Beatty will threaten to sue Warner Bros. over the handling of the film, and after critic Pauline Kael writes a 9,000-word rave in the *New Yorker*, Warner will rerelease the film in late September. Upon its second appearance, *Bonnie and Clyde* will experience an astonishing turnaround, hailed by both movie-goers and critics, many of whom will rereview the film favorably. Ultimately, Beatty and co-star Faye Dunaway will make *Time* magazine's cover.

But Who Shot J.R.?

AUGUST 29, 1967. Nearly three-quarters of all TV viewers tune in to see the final episode of "The Fugitive." After four years of running from Lt. Gerard, Dr. Richard Kimble (David Janssen) finally tracks down the elusive one-armed man. For weeks theories have abounded about the final episode; everyone, it seems, has a distant relative who has seen a copy of the script and knows who *really* killed Kimble's wife. With Gerard in pursuit, Kimble and the one-armed man will slug it out on top of a tower after a thrilling chase scene; Gerard will realize he has been tracking the wrong person and will kill the one-armed man. (Unfortunately, only Kimble will hear the confession, and he now is back in custody.) Kimble will be exonerated, though, when a witness steps forward, and his cross-country rambles come to a end, along with the ABC series.

Name That 'Toon

OCTOBER 3, 1967. *Zap No. 0*, the first issue of what will become the first continuing underground comic magazine, is published by Apex Novelty Company, formed earlier this year by Robert Crumb and three other cartoonists. Crumb, 24, who ventured from Cleveland to New York in 1963 to "meet the heroes of my youth—mostly the little group of cartoonist geniuses who kept satire alive through the otherwise vacuous 1950s," as he will later tell the tale—came to San

Fritz: 'X' marks the cat.

Francisco two years ago, attracted by the burgeoning Haight-Ashbury community. The first four *Zap* issues, 0 through 3, will garner near-immediate cult status, enhanced by the Berkeley police's impounding of issue No. 4 for obscenity as it comes off the presses. Crumb will run into additional legal problems next year, when the premiere of his new publication *Snatch* runs up against obscenity laws, with virtually all 800 copies confiscated; the few copies that escape police clutches will become valuable comics in collectors' markets. In the late 1960s, Crumb will create some of the more memorable characters of underground comics, including Fritz the Cat, the basis for a 1972 movie of the same name that will be the first X-rated cartoon, and Mr. Natural, who will help make the phrase "Keep On Truckin' " a generational anthem and will be featured on a brand of tablets of LSD that bears his name.

Film Flashbacks

Bang, Bang

Goldfinger

A Fistful of Dollars
Billy Jack
Bonnie & Clyde
Bullit
Butch Cassidy and the Sundance Kid
Cheyenne Autumn
Cool Hand Luke
Death Wish
Dirty Harry
El Topo
French Connection
From Russia With Love
The Godfather
Goldfinger
The Good, the Bad, and the Ugly
Hud
Kiss Me Deadly
Long Riders
Magnificent Seven
McCabe and Mrs. Miller
Man Who Shot Liberty Valence
Mean Streets
The Misfits
Once Upon a Time in the West
One-Eyed Jacks
Our Man Flint
Point Blank
Ride the High Country
The Searchers
Soldier Blue
The Sting
Straw Dogs
The Wild Bunch

Lean On the Left

OCTOBER 19, 1967. Liberation News Service sets up an "underground" wire service, providing news of the political left to alternative newspapers and magazines. But the news service will be subject to a wide range of FBI surveillance and trickery, part of the bureau's counterintelligence program against the New Left. Among other things, the FBI will direct the IRS to comb through the organization's tax records and will send anonymous letters to New Left organizations in an attempt to discredit the news service. Similarly treated will be the Alternative Press Syndicate (formerly the Underground Press Syndicate), founded in 1966, which by 1970 will serve publications reaching a combined readership of 20 million. In 1969 Phoenix police will raid the organization's office, looking unsuccessfully for illicit drugs. In the process, police will steal the organization's subscription lists, destroy its files, and damage its library.

That Boy

NOVEMBER 6, 1967. *Is the caller there?* "The Phil Donahue Show" debuts on WLWD in Dayton, Oh., where Donahue has been a radio newsman and talk show host before making the jump to television. In June 1969 the show will become syndicated, then move to Chicago and, ultimately, New York. Within a decade it will be a national staple of morning TV. Donahue, married to Marlo "That Girl" Thomas, will emerge as the consummate "man of the '80s": caring, sensitive, etc.

Gonzo to Gotham

NOVEMBER 9, 1967. The first issue of *Rolling Stone* is published in San Francisco by entrepreneur Jann Wenner, 21. Wenner has started the rock 'n' roll newspaper with an initial investment of $8,000, most of it borrowed, and a staff made up largely of part-time volunteers. Its first edition will have a press run of 40,000 copies, of which only 6,000 will sell. Slowly, however, it will catch on, becoming the bible of the antiestablishment rock world, carrying news of music, drugs, the New Left, and the youth culture. By the early 1970s, the paper will begin running long investigative pieces, many winning journalism awards. Its reputation will attract a lengthy list of counterculture writers and promote the "New Journalism" of the late 1960s. Among those writers will be Hunter S. Thompson, the self-proclaimed "doctor of Gonzo journalism," whose reports on everything from national politics to Hell's Angels will create a cult following. By 1973 *Rolling Stone's* circulation will grow to 400,000, which will more than double a decade later. In 1967, in response to San Francisco's fading cultural and music scene, the paper will go from Gonzo to Gotham, setting up shop in New York City.

Wenner: Gathering no moss.

Antihero

DECEMBER 21, 1967. *The Graduate*, starring Dustin Hoffman and Katharine Ross, opens. Hoffman fell into the lead role by accident. Director Mike Nichols, fresh from a success with *Who's Afraid of Virginia Woolf?*, discovered him performing in *Eh?*, a British stage farce playing in New York. A smash success, *The Graduate* will quickly gain favor among a

The Graduate

fast-growing counterculture by questioning the value of college, accusing the establishment of hypocrisy, and suggesting that ultimately everything's a pointless compromise. (The movie will, however, proffer some sound advice: "plastics," a field suggested to the Hoffman character, will become one of the boom industries of the 1970s and 1980s.) An undersized antihero, Hoffman will emerge as one of the biggest stars of 1970s, with leading roles in *Midnight Cowboy, Little Big Man, Straw Dogs, Lenny, All the President's Men, Marathon Man, Kramer vs. Kramer*, and *Tootsie*. Despite his apparent "overnight success," he has spent years struggling, unable to break in even off-Broadway, supporting himself with such jobs as janitor and mental ward attendant.

Veeerrrry Interesting

JANUARY 22, 1968. "Rowan & Martin's Laugh-In" debuts and quickly takes the nation by storm. Dan Rowan and Dick Martin, along with announcer Gary Owens, are joined by a troupe of outrageous guests; many of the comedy routines they concoct will become American classics. Among those who will help catapult the show to number one in the ratings are Lily Tomlin, as the nasal telephone operator; Ruth Buzzi, as the little old lady with the umbrella; Goldie Hawn, the dumb but funny blonde; and Arte Johnson, whose himself will introduce a wide range of characters. Among the phrases the show will make part of the national heritage include "Here come de judge," "Look that up in your Funk and Wagnall's," and "You bet your bippy." In May 1973 NBC will subject the show to the Fickle Finger of Fate.

Rowan, Martin: Bippy betters.

That's the Way It Is

FEBRUARY 27, 1968. Walter Cronkite, in a half-hour CBS News special from Vietnam, concludes: "It seems now more certain than ever that the bloody experience of Vietnam is to end in a stalemate." The statement reportedly will convince President Johnson not to seek re-election, thinking that if he had lost Cronkite, he had lost Middle America.

High Class, Low Ratings

MARCH 4, 1968. "The Dick Cavett Show" premieres on ABC. The former gag writer, who drops names like the Mets' Marv Thornberry drops baseballs, has a 90-minute talk show that will combine comedy and "seri-

TV Flashback
Comedy/Variety

- Andy Williams Show (1958-71)
- Candid Camera (1948-67)
- Carol Burnett Show (1967-78)
- Dean Martin Show (1965-74)
- Ed Sullivan Show (1948-71)
- Garry Moore Show (1958-67)
- Jack Benny Show (1950-77)
- Jackie Gleason Show (1952-70)
- John Davidson Show (1969-76)
- Johnny Cash Show (1969-76)
- King Family Show (1965-69)
- Lawrence Welk Show (1955-71)
- Milton Berle Show (1948-67)
- Original Amateur Hour (Ted Mack) (1948-60)
- Paul Winchell-Jerry Mahoney Show (1950-54)
- People Are Funny (1954-61)
- Perry Como Show (1948-63)
- Red Skelton Show (1951-71)
- Rowan & Martin's Laugh-In (1968-73)
- Sing Along With Mitch (1961-66)
- Smothers Brothers Comedy Hour (1967-75)
- Sonny and Cher Comedy Hour (1971-77)
- Spike Jones Show (1954-61)
- Steve Allen Show (1956-61)
- That Was the Week That Was (1964-65)
- Walt Disney (1954-83)
- You Asked For It (1950-59)
- You Bet Your Life (1950-61)
- Your Hit Parade (1950-74)

Red Skelton

ous" guests. The show begins on weekday mornings, but in May 1969 will be moved to prime-time, and seven months later will be moved to late night, where Cavett will replace the fading Joey Bishop. The critics will love the intellectual Cavett, but audiences will be lukewarm. Among the highlights of the show's run is former Georgia governor Lester Maddox storming off the set when called on his segregationist views. In another historic moment, nutrition guru J.I. Rodale will say, "I'm so healthy I expect to live on and on." Minutes later, he will drop dead of a heart attack.

Womenspeak

MARCH 12, 1968. *Voice of the Women's Liberation Movement*, the first independent radical women's newsletter, is published in Chicago. By 1971 there will be more than 100 women's journals, newsletters, and newspapers published in the U.S. In June, *Notes From the First Year*, a collection of writings and reports on radical feminism, will become the first radical feminist journal.

Food for Thought

MAY 21, 1968. "CBS Reports" broadcasts "Hunger in America," a hard-hitting documentary focusing on malnutrition among American Indians in the Southwest and tenant farmers in Virginia. The show is a followup on Edward R. Murrow's classic "Harvest of Shame" broadcast of 1960 and will force U.S. Secretary of Agriculture Orville Freeman to defend the government's hunger policy.

Cooley High

Black is Profitable

JULY 8, 1968. *Story of a Three Day Pass* opens in movie theaters, the American release of a French film entitled *La Permission*. Directed by an expatriate American black man, it is, remarkably, the first black-directed feature ever to have a commercial release in the U.S. It is based on a French novel by the director, Melvin Van Peebles. His film about a black soldier on leave with a French woman will create an opening through which a gush of black exploitation films—"blaxploitation," as they will be termed—will soon rush. Van Peebles, for one, will be signed by Columbia Pictures to make *Watermelon Man*, a comedy starring Godfrey Cambridge as a middle-class white man who suddenly turns black. Van Peebles will be unhappy with his experience with large studios and will invest his earnings in a film he will direct, produce, edit, score, and star in: *Sweet Sweetback's Baadasssss Song*, which he will film in three weeks at a cost of $500,000, $50,000 of which will come from Bill Cosby. The film—which ends with the message, "A BADASS NIGGER IS COMING BACK TO COLLECT SOME DUES"—will take the film world by surprise. Although the media, including the black press, will pan the film, black audiences will be enthusiastic, promising audiences hungry for black heroes for years to come. Among the resulting films: *Shaft, Superfly*, *Blackenstein*, *Blacula*, and *Cooley High*.

Film Flashbacks
Blacks and Whites

- Blacula
- The Cool World
- The Defiant Ones
- Cooley High
- Cotton Comes to Harlem
- For Love of Ivy
- Friday Foster
- Guess Who's Coming to Dinner?
- Imitation of Life
- In the Heat of the Night
- Island in the Sun
- Lady Sings the Blues
- No Vietnamese Ever Called Me Nigger
- Nothing But A Man
- One Potato, Two Potato
- Shaft
- Sounder
- Superfly
- Sweet Sweetback's Baadasssss Song
- Up Tight
- Watermelon Man

Carnaby Cops

SEPTEMBER 24, 1968. "The Mod Squad" appears on ABC. For the next four years, Captain Adam Greer will have the services of three hippies-turned-criminals-turned-cops. Pete, Linc, and Julie, using long hair and beads as disguises, will slip in and out of the counterculture, identifying adult criminals who are co-opting the young. The youth squad will draw the line, though: it never rats on its hip "brothers and sisters."

Tick-Tick-Tick-Tick

SEPTEMBER 24, 1968. "60 Minutes," the CBS news magazine, makes its debut. For three years, the show will alternate with

Wanted: Equality

AUGUST 9, 1968. Following an effort spearheaded by the National Organization for Women, the Equal Employment Opportunity Commission issues guidelines forbidding separate male and female want-ad listings. A year ago, NOW had picketed the *New York Times* to protest its policy of separate male-female "help wanted" listings.

And So We Did

SEPTEMBER 16, 1968. Richard Nixon says "Sock it to me!" on "Laugh-In."

Mod Squad: Defenders of wild life.

"CBS News Hour"; in January 1972 it will move to its own Sunday evening time slot, where it will begin to develop a strong following, by 1979 becoming the nation's highest-rated series. Using extreme close-up camera shots of squirming interviewees, the show will conduct some of the most important investigative reporting in TV history, exposing corruption, crime, and scandal; it also will treat viewers to in-depth profiles of the famous and infamous. With the tick-tick-tick of the stopwatch in the background, the show's correspondents will become well-known figures: Mike Wallace, Harry Reasoner, and Morely Safer, and later arrivals Dan Rather, Ed Bradley, and Diane Sawyer. Conservative James Kilpatrick will square off against liberals Nicholas Von Hoffman and, later, Shana Alexander in the "Point Counterpoint" segment; in the summer of 1978, Andy Rooney will arrive to spread his gospel.

'A' Is for Awful

OCTOBER 7, 1968. The film industry unveils its new ratings system, a long-awaited replacement for the laughably outdated Production Code of the 1930s. The U.S. has been among the few countries in the world that doesn't classify films, and this is the route the film industry will choose. The new system includes four ratings: "G" is for "general" audiences; "M" is for "mature" audiences; "R" means "restricted," requiring those 16 and under to be accompanied by an adult; and "X" means that no one 16 or under is allowed. "M" will be changed to "PG," for "parental guidance." Some major titles will be given "X" ratings, including *Midnight Cowboy*, but that rating will soon be reserved for really dirty stuff. Several producers will argue that their films should be "downgraded" from "M" or "PG" to "R," in the hope that the raunchier rating will bring bigger audiences.

Funny Papers

OCTOBER 11, 1968. FBI director J. Edgar Hoover writes a memo to his Indianapolis office, describing the publication of *Armageddon News*, an FBI-created "underground" newspaper. This will be the first of two FBI ventures into underground publishing. Early next year, the bureau will create *Longhorn Tales*, published in San Antonio. Both papers will attempt to promote the view that most students are not participating in antiwar protest movements.

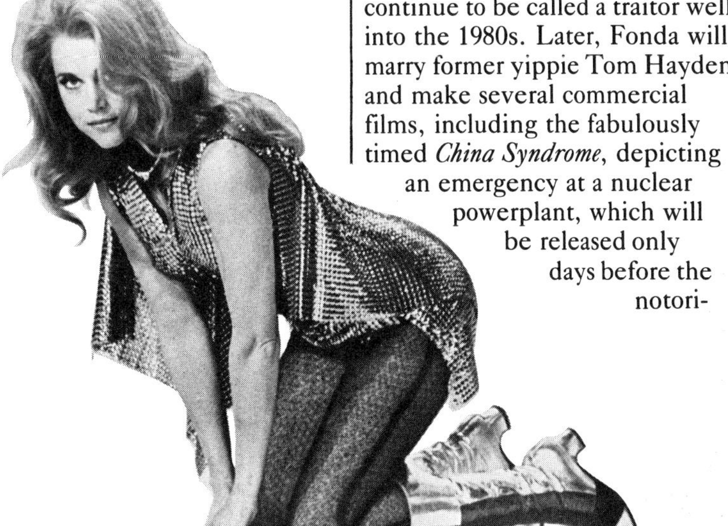

Fonda: Bardot, no.

See Jane Run

OCTOBER 11, 1968. *Barbarella* opens, starring sex kitten Jane Fonda, wife of director Roger Vadim, the man who turned Bridgitte Bardot into an international sex star. Vadim will try to make Fonda a sex kitten, too. She will soon appear on magazine covers and in cheesecake photos, culminating in *Barbarella*, a bizarre amalgam of sci-fi, sex, and the absurd written by Terry Southern, author of *Candy*. But Fonda ultimately will reject the sex image, opting instead for liberal politics, speaking out against the Vietnam war and touring military posts there with a show called "FTA" for "Free the Army," written and produced by Fonda and Donald Sutherland. In 1974 Fonda will visit Hanoi, an event that will embitter many, especially Vietnam vets, against her forever; she will continue to be called a traitor well into the 1980s. Later, Fonda will marry former yippie Tom Hayden and make several commercial films, including the fabulously timed *China Syndrome*, depicting an emergency at a nuclear powerplant, which will be released only days before the notorious 1979 accident at Three-Mile Island.

The Write Stuff

OCTOBER 13, 1968. The crew of Apollo 7—Walter Schirra, Donn Eisele, and Walt Cunningham—treat American TV viewers to the first live transmission from space. The trio hold up cards reading, "Keep those cards and letters coming in, folks."

School's Out

November 4, 1968. *Summerhill: A Radical Approach to Child Rearing* by A.S. Neill, published four years ago, experiences a resurgence, with sales at an all-time high of 12,000 copies a month. The book's publisher attributes the phenomenon in part to the growing interest in alternative child rearing as the "flower children" of the 1960s begin having children of their own.

Tools for Living

NOVEMBER 12, 1968. *The Whole Earth Catalog* is born, a skinny 68-page hodgepodge that its founder Stewart Brand calls the inspiration of Buckminster Fuller and L.L. Bean. The 29-year-old Brand, trained as a scientist via the Army and IBM, has come to the publication by way of the San Francisco hippie scene. Among other things, he helped organize the Trips Festival in 1966 and, following an investigation of the peyote traditions of southwestern American Indians, founded an organization called America Needs Indians. *The Whole Earth Catalog*, published with the help of the nonprofit Portola Institute, describes itself as "an evaluation and access source, providing the user with information about tools...." At first it will be published quarterly, with each issue bigger and better-selling than the one before; the fall 1969 issue will sell more than 160,000 copies. Its format will be both a blessing and a curse; so much information will be crammed into every page that it will be called "amateurish and confusing" by publishing industry gurus. But format will matter little to what will become a hard-core following of *The Whole Earth Catalog* junkies, who will swear by its evaluations of "tools" ranging from geodesic domes to the *Wall Street Journal*. The format will become so overwhelming, in fact, that Brand's nonprofit Portola Institute will publish *The Last Whole Earth Catalog* in 1971, followed three years later by *The Updated Last Whole Earth Catalog* and *The Whole Earth Epilog*, and, finally, *The Next Whole Earth Catalog*, a 608-page behemoth published in 1980.

Brand: *Whole Earth* in his hands.

The Show Must Go On

NOVEMBER 17, 1968. A made-for-TV production of *Heidi* interrupts a football game between the Oakland Raiders and the New York Jets on NBC. The Jets are comfortably ahead with less than a minute to play, so the network decides to cut away for the movie. But the Raiders score twice in the final minute for a breathtaking win. The highlights will be shown later on evening newscasts and the following morning on "Today," but that won't appease football fans, thousands of whom flood NBC and local stations with irate phone calls. The networks get the message: football games will forever run intact, no matter how long they take.

Heidi: Clipping penalty.

Not a Creature Was Stirring

DECEMBER 24, 1968. Apollo 8, the first manned spacecraft to orbit the moon, brings Christmas Eve TV viewers a black-and-white, close-up shot of the lunar surface. With a panoramic shot of the moon, astronauts Frank Borman, Jim Lovell, and Bill Anders read from "Genesis," closing with "God bless all of you on the good Earth."

All the News That's Left

JANUARY 14, 1969. Army intelligence operatives join the FBI in a search of the Washington, D.C., offices of the *Free Press*, part of a coordinated monitoring program conducted by military and civilian intelligence organizations against underground newspapers published by Americans in the U.S., Japan, and West Germany. Another part of the FBI's "counterintelligence program," as spelled out in a 1968 FBI memo, involves "the use of articles from student and 'underground' newspapers to show the depravity of New Left leaders and members." The memo suggests that "articles showing advocation of the use of narcotics and free sex are ideal to send to university officials...and parents of students who are active in New Left matters." In another recent memo, FBI director J. Edgar Hoover asks regional FBI officers to prepare a "detailed survey concerning New Left-ty publications being printed and circulated in your territory...." The FBI previously has alerted local offices to use "friendly news media to vividly portray the revolutionary-type actions and militant nature of the New Left movement...."

Hoover: Counterintelligence.

Grin and Bare It

FEBRUARY 5, 1969. As a representative from *Playboy* magazine enters the room to speak on a "Sex Education Series" forum at Grinnell College in Iowa, six women and four men stage a "nude-in" to protest *Playboy* magazine's demeaning attitude toward women.

That's Not Chopped Liver

MARCH 24, 1969. *Portnoy's Complaint* by Philip Roth tops the fiction bestseller list. The novel, a semiautobiographical tale of a sexually frustrated and generally confused Jewish adolescent, has reached the top in spite of—or because of—controversy about the plain sexual language and graphic images it contains. (Example: young Alexander Portnoy regularly relieves his pent-up sexual frustration with the aid of a piece of raw beef liver.) By mid-April, the book will have sold more than 330,000 copies, making it the fastest-selling hardback novel in history. At the library system of Miami, where 30,000 teenagers recently staged a Rally for Decency at the Orange Bowl, there is a long waiting list for the 159 copies of the book. Through most of the summer, *Portnoy* will wage a seesaw battle with Jacqueline Susann's *The Love Machine* for the number-one bestseller position.

Roth: Raw sex.

Brothers Smothered

APRIL 4, 1969. CBS cancels "The Smothers Brothers

Show" after two years of censorship battles. The last straw, says CBS, is a proposed Easter Sunday show with an "offensive" monologue in the form of a "sermonette" by satirist David Steinberg, in which he explains that in the story of Jonah, "the gentiles, as is their wont from time to time, threw the Jew overboard." But the brothers Smothers insist that the Steinberg gag is simply the excuse CBS has been looking for. "They've harassed us and want us off the air because they think we're a threat to them," says Tommy Smothers. The show has encountered periodic censorship by CBS since 1967, when the network snipped an antiwar, anti-LBJ ballad, "Knee Deep in the Big Muddy," by Pete Seeger. Last year, CBS toned down the presidential "campaign" of comedian Pat Paulsen, a "Smothers Brothers" regular, fearing it would prompt equal-time demands from other candidates. Just last month CBS blue-penciled part of Joan Baez's dedication of a song to her draft-resister husband David Harris. Next year ABC will give the show a brief reprieve as a summer fill-in, but it will fail to garner much interest. NBC will give the brothers yet another shot, but by then, the political climate will have cooled, TV's decency standards will have relaxed, and the Smothers Brothers' humor will seem innocuous, looking more and more like just another comedy-variety show.

Smothers: Not ready for prime-time.

Big Bucks Bikes

JULY 14, 1969. *Easy Rider* opens. Last year, Jack Valenti, head of the Motion Picture Association, spoke to Canadian filmmakers, calling for fewer films about drugs and more family fare such as *Dr. Dolittle.* But Peter Fonda, in the audience, decided it was time to do a great film about bikers. One of Hollywood's bad boys—he was cast in several early-1960s pictures but has dropped out since his recent LSD experiences—Fonda sat in his hotel after Valenti's speech. By chance, he saw an ad showing a couple of bikers and envisioned an entire movie plot in

Easy Rider

Film Flashbacks
Underground

- Chelsea Girls
- Dog Star Man
- Flaming Creatures
- Flicker
- Relativity
- Sleep
- Scorpio Rising
- Wavelength

his mind. Although it was 3 AM, he called friend and fellow drop-out Dennis Hopper to tell him about it. Hopper, a method actor thrown out of Hollywood after *From Hell to Texas*—during which director Henry Hathaway told him he'd "never work in this town again"—had remained out of film work for eight years. He and Fonda had worked together in Roger Corman's *The Trip* (written by Jack Nicholson) and had shot some film depicting an LSD trip, an idea expanded on in *Easy Rider*. Making *Easy Rider* became a terrible experience—Fonda had to hire a bodyguard to protect him from Hopper—but the film will be timed right and the $550,000 budget will be recouped in a matter of days.

Battle of the Sexists

AUGUST 9, 1969. *Penthouse* magazine begins publication, the first to compete with *Playboy's* 16-year monopoly of the skin-magazine market. The magazine was started by Robert Guccione, 38, in London four years ago and is now being introduced to Americans. Guccione, a transplanted Brooklynite, will initially take on archrival *Playboy*, buying full-page newspaper ads declaring, "We're going rabbit hunting," a reference to *Playboy's* bunny rabbit logo. Guccione plans to capitalize on what he calls "the new liberalism," which, translated, will result in a more graphic version of *Playboy*. As it will turn out, Guccione's new venture will invigorate the skin-trades market; a decade later, both publications will be in the pink.

Skyrocketing Sales

AUGUST 18, 1969. *Publishers Weekly* reports that in response to the recent moon landing, more than two dozen books on space travel and the moon will soon be published. Titles range from three "instant books" detailing the historic mission to a dictionary of 6,000 technical terms compiled by the International Academy of Astronautics.

Neurotic Comedy

AUGUST 18, 1969. *Take the Money and Run* opens, written, directed, and produced by comic Allen Konigsberg, using the name Woody Allen. Allen, a joke writer for TV and newspaper columnists, has long performed his own material as a stand-up comic at clubs in Greenwich Village. The stage appearances will launch TV exposure, which has led to his film writing. His first effort was

Allen: Bananas.

the 1965 film *What's New Pussycat?* The following year, he took footage from a James Bond-clone Japanese spy film and dubbed in his own lines, creating a whole new plot. That film, *What's Up Tiger Lily?*, became a cult classic. Allen will soon become one of the most prolific and successful screenwriters—and actors and producers—in the business, introducing a style of neurotic comedy that will dominate in the 1970s.

Film Flashbacks

Comedy

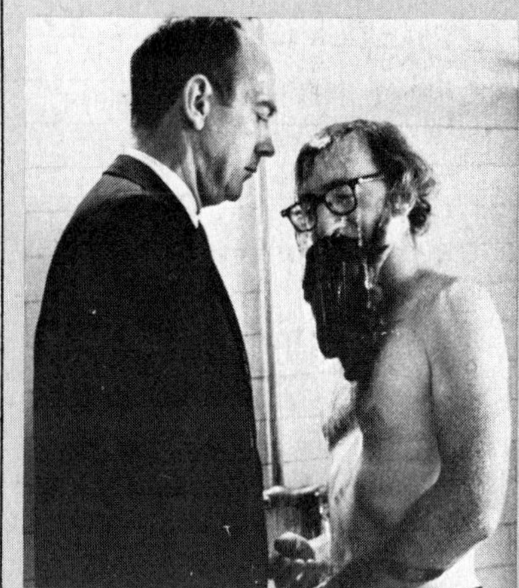

Bananas

- A Shot in the Dark
- Bananas
- Bedazzled
- Cat Ballou
- I'm All Right, Jack
- Kind Hearts and Coronets
- Ladykillers
- Lavender Hill Gang
- Make Mine Mink
- The Pink Panther
- Sleeper
- Some Like it Hot
- Take the Money and Run
- That Man From Rio
- Tom Jones

Not Our Scene

SEPTEMBER 22, 1969. "The Music Scene," a rock version of "Your Hit Parade," airs on ABC. The show has six rotating hosts, including David Steinberg and Lily Tomlin; by November, Steinberg will become permanent host. The first show features the Beatles, Three Dog Night, James Brown, Buck Owens, Tom Jones, and Crosby, Stills, Nash, and Young; most major rock stars will appear on the show, which also will feature an improvisational comedy group, but the idea won't catch on, and by January Steinberg will be un-Scene.

Giving Teachers the Bird

NOVEMBER 10, 1969. "Sesame Street" debuts. Designed by the Children's Television Workshop of Boston and funded by the Ford Foundation, the Carnegie Corporation, and the U.S. Office of Education, "Seasame Street" will teach preschool children letters and numbers with the same techniques used in commercial TV programs such as "Captain Kangaroo." "Seasame Street" will introduce characters that become bona fide TV "stars": Oscar the Grouch, Big Bird, the Cookie Monster, Ernie, and Grover. Some school teachers will complain that the "Sesame Street" cast has so excited young children about the process of learning that they will find standard classroom settings with only humans—no birds, bears, or cookie monsters—dull by comparison.

Sesame Street: Better than real life.

Vice Squad

NOVEMBER 13, 1969. Vice President Spiro Agnew lashes out against the "small and unelected elite" of TV news producers, commentators, and anchors who "decide what 40 to 50 million Americans will learn of the day's events in the nation and in the world." Impetus for the attack was the media analysis of President Nixon's speech on Vietnam 10 days ago, which Agnew now describes as Nixon's attempt to "rally the American people to see the conflict through to a lasting and just peace...." But, says the vice president, "his words and policies were subjected to instant analysis and querulous criticism." Agnew's speech will bring national reflection on American's love-hate relationship with TV news, particularly the "Eastern Establishment" of the networks, which broadcast nightly from New York and Washington. Agnew will continue his attacks on the media in coming weeks, in some speeches ominously reminding audiences that TV is "licensed" by government. Not long ago, the outspoken vice president called Vietnam war critics "an effete corps of impudent snobs." In a forthcoming speech he will call TV commentators "nattering nabobs of negativism."

Clearing the Airwaves

JANUARY 1, 1970. A three-year phasing out of cigarette ads on radio and TV begins, the effect of a plan formulated by the National Association of Broadcasters last July. Cigarette ads on TV

Banzhaf: Fired up.

have been the target of critics led by John Banzhaf II, 29, a Washington, D.C., lawyer. In 1966 Banzhaf, then a law clerk, wrote a letter to WCBS-TV in New York, criticizing ads that present smoking as "socially acceptable and desirable, manly, and a necessary part of a rich, full life." In 1967 Banzhaf left his New York law firm to start Action on Smoking and Health (ASH), which soon filed a formal complaint against WCBS. The station tried to comply with the complaint by running a program dealing with the effects of smoking on health, but the Federal Communications Commission deemed such programs inadequate and required all cigarette ads on TV to carry a notice warning of the dangers of smoking. It also ruled that Banzhaf could invoke the Fairness Doctrine in requesting equal time for antismoking public service announcements to counter the station's cigarette commercials. Finally, the industry gave up, removing all ads from radio and TV.

That's All She Wrote

JANUARY 26, 1970. Feminists stage a coup d'etat at *Rat*, a New York-based underground newspaper that mixes radical politics with pornography. It will remain a collectively run women's paper, although some will criticize it for not being "feminist" at all. One woman involved in the coup will express disappointment: "It's now just a radical paper that happens to be run by women."

Booked Up

FEBRUARY 9, 1970. The Department of Commerce reports that the number of "major publishers" has increased from 993 in 1963 to 1,050 in 1969. During the same period, the number of titles produced annually has increased from 25,784 to an estimated 35,000.

Laughing All the Way to the Bank

MARCH 30, 1970. The *National Lampoon* is launched from a Madison Avenue office, the literary scion of the *Harvard Lampoon*. Its first six issues will bomb, nearly bankrupting the publication, before it begins to catch on among college campuses. Within three years circulation will jump from 165,000 to 685,000 and annual profits will exceed $1 million, coffered with parody issues on topics such as "Greed," "Fraud," "Paranoia," "Women," and "Religion for Fun and Profit." The *Harvard Lampoon*, meanwhile, will make headlines in 1972 with a parody issue on *Cosmopolitan* magazine—with articles such as "Myth of the Male Orgasm" and "How to Tell if Your Man Is Dead"—including a centerfold depicting Henry Kissinger sprawled in the buff, a fictitious photomontage of a recent Burt Reynolds pictorial.

Pressing Matters

APRIL 15, 1970. Nine members of the Women's Liberation Front break into a CBS stockholders' annual meeting in San Francisco and charge CBS, and the media in general, with downgrading and distorting the role of women in commercials and programming. The effort is one part of a growing movement to change the way media portray women. Last month, 200 woman staged an 11-hour sit-in at *Ladies' Home Journal* protesting the image of women portrayed by that and other women's magazines; the magazine will allow the group to put out a "women's liberation" supplement to its August issue. In May nearly 150 women will complain to the New York State Attorney General's office, charging Time Inc.'s four magazines, *Time, Life, Fortune*, and *Sports Illustrated*, with sex discrimination. In June a group of feminists will invade the *San Francisco Chronicle*, presenting a list of demands on the'paper's "sexist" writings. Another group will confront *New York Times* managing editor A.M. Rosenthal to protest the tone of the paper's editorial against the Equal Rights Amendment. Also in June *Washington Post* executive editor Benjamin Bradlee will issue a memo to the editorial staff, instructing reporters and editors not to use words such as "brunette," "divorcee," and "grandmother" to describe women, unless the same kinds of words would be applied to men.

Signing Off

JULY 31, 1970. "Goodnight, David" is heard for the last time, as Chet Huntley ends his tenure at NBC News. Before signing off, Huntley expresses to viewers his hope that "there will be better and happier news, one day, if we work at it."

Counter Revolutionary

SEPTEMBER 12, 1970. *Five Easy Pieces*, starring Jack Nicholson, premieres. The film features what will become one of the best-remembered moments in modern film, as Nicholson attempts to order toast from a waitress in a truck-stop cafe, a scene that emerged from a real-life event while the film was being made. *Five Easy Pieces* will secure Nicholson's *Easy Rider* success. He will later appear in such memorable films as *Carnal Knowledge, One Flew Over the Cuckoo's Nest* (for which he'll receive a best-actor *Oscar), Chinatown*, and *Terms of Endearment*.

Nicholson: Hold the toast.

Film Flashbacks
Antiestablishment

- A Summer Place
- Alice's Restaurant
- American Graffiti
- Easy Rider
- Five Easy Pieces
- Getting Straight
- The Graduate
- Harold & Maude
- If . . .
- Mean Streets
- Putney Swope
- Riot on Sunset Strip
- RPM
- Ruling Class
- Shampoo
- Strawberry Statement
- Thunder Road
- Weekend
- Wild in the Streets
- The Wild Rebels
- Zabriskie Point

West Side Story

Character Actor

SEPTEMBER 17, 1970. "The Flip Wilson Show" debuts on NBC and quickly becomes a hit. Wilson, a former "Laugh-In" regular, introduces a variety of his own characters, including sassy Geraldine Jones and the hustling Rev. Leroy, from the Church of What's Happenin' Now. Wilson is the first black entertainer whose own variety show attracts a large audience; in fact, during its first two years only "Marcus Welby, M.D." and "All in the Family" will keep Wilson's show out of the number-one spot.

Monday Night Kick-Off

SEPTEMBER 21, 1970. ABC's "NFL Monday Night Football" debuts, as Roone Arledge brings professional football back to prime-time after an absence of two decades. Howard Cosell and Keith Jackson do play-by-play commentary, with former Dallas Cowboy quarterback "Dandy" Don Meredith providing color. The games will become prime-time fixtures and will be credited with reviving the Monday night bar business all across America. Before he leaves the program in 1984, Cosell will become one of the most loved and hated personalities in TV history.

Cosell: The mouth that bored.

Boone's Boon

SEPTEMBER 27, 1970. After 22 years "The Original Amateur Hour" signs off. Ted Mack's show, which aired on ABC, CBS, NBC, and the DuMont network, proved that even kazoo players can entertain TV audiences. Among those contestants who went on to bigger and better things were Frank Sinatra and the man with the white bucks, Pat Boone.

Up With Smut

OCTOBER 5, 1970. *Argus*, a magazine published by students at the University of Maryland, announces "the first annual national creative pornography competition," with a first prize of $100. Says editor Dave Bourdon: "The quality of American pornography is going downhill, and we want to return to the American heritage of fine filth."

Panther Clause

OCTOBER 15, 1970. *Soledad Brother: The Prison Letters of George Jackson* is published, two days after the arrest of Jackson's friend Angela Davis for allegedly providing guns to help Jackson's brother Jonathan escape from the Marin County Courthouse near San Francisco last August; Jonathan Jackson was among four killed in the incident. George Jackson, a Black Panther imprisoned originally 10 years ago for stealing $70 from a gas station, is still at Soledad, now accused with two others of killing a prison guard. His letters—to Davis, among many others—will be described by one reviewer as "often poetic, often strained and awkward, always peppered with the tight, excoriating rhetoric of the revolutionary"—high praise for a writer who was never graduated from high school and is almost completely self-educated.

Davis: A woman of letters.

Stop the Presses

DECEMBER 8, 1970. The Women's National Press Club changes its name to the Press Club of Washington and votes to admit male members. Next month, the all-male National Press Club will follow suit, voting to admit women members.

Bunker Mentality

JANUARY 12, 1971. "All in the Family," based on the British series "Till Death Do Us Part," makes its debut. Produced by Norman Lear, the show will cause immediate controversy; Archie Bunker's blunt comments about minorities are new to TV viewers. But Archie, Edith (Dingbat), Gloria, and Meathead will soon be adopted by the American public, who make the show the nation's highest-rated for several years.

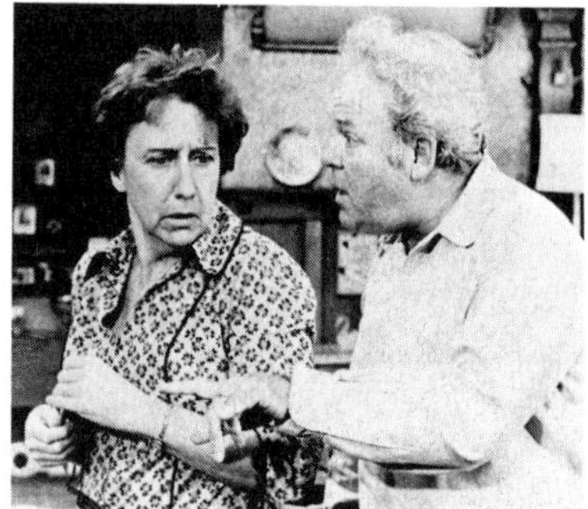

Edith, Archie: Redneck chic.

Sex and Violence

JANUARY 14, 1971. After selling nearly a million copies in hardback, the paperback edition of *Everything You Always Wanted to Know About Sex...And Were Afraid to Ask* is now on sale, with a first printing of more than two million copies. Within eight days, eight new printings will bring the in-print figure to more than 4 million copies. Bantam, publisher of the

All in the Families

The American TV families of the 1950s lived in homes with white picket fences, but no toilets.

The model American family of "Father Knows Best" lived in the fictitious midwestern town of Springfield. Jim Anderson (Robert Young), the father, was into insurance, and his wife Margaret (Jane Wyatt) was into housekeeping. Their three kids, Betty, Bud, and Kathy, were into going to school and growing up. The Andersons so embodied wholesome America that the Treasury Department once commissioned an episode to promote democracy and U.S. Savings Bonds. The episode, never aired but widely used as a teaching tool, depicted the Andersons living under an oppressive dictatorship for a day.

Father Knows Best

The Cleaver family of "Leave It to Beaver" had a bit less whitewash. The show centered around the world of Theodore "Beaver" Cleaver (Jerry Mathers), seven years old when the show began in 1960. The Beave had a brother (Wally; Tony Dow), parents (June and Ward; Barbara Billingsly and Hugh Beaumont), teachers (Miss Canfield and Miss Landers), and, most memorably, Wally's friend Eddie Haskell (Ken Desmond), the prankster who oozed politeness when he spoke to adults. Over the six-year course of the series Beaver matured from a kid who thought girls led to "mushy stuff" to an adolescent beginning to date.

Leave It to Beaver

Unlike many real-life Americans, both the Cleaver and the Anderson families remained intact throughout their respective series. The Williamses of "The Danny Thomas Show" (called "Make Room for Daddy" in its first three seasons) went through many transformations. At the outset in 1953, the family consisted of daddy Danny, wife Margaret (Jean Hagen), and their kids Terry (Sherry Jackson) and Rusty (Rusty Hamer). When Hagen quit the show in 1956, she left the family without a wife and

Danny Thomas Show

mother. In the scripts, Margaret died, daddy spent a season dating, then married Clancey (Marjorie Lord) in an off-camera ceremony before the fall 1957 season.

The kids came and went, too. Clancey brought a six-year-old daughter Patty (Lelani Sorenson), although when the show switched from ABC to CBS in 1957, Clancey's daughter became Linda, played by Angela Cartwright. Daughter Terry was sent off to college in 1958, then returned for a spell in 1960, played now by Penny Parker; she then married a nightclub performer (Pat Harrington), then vanished from the show. Only Rusty stayed put throughout.

The Nelsons, of "The Adventures of Ozzie and Harriet," changed on screen as they matured in real life,

Ozzie and Harriet

playing themselves from 1952 to 1966. Little Ricky Nelson launched a singing career and grew up to become a teen idol, performing songs on the show and turning them into real-life hits. His recording of Fats Domino's "I'm Walkin'," introduced in 1957, sold more than a million copies. (The two children on "The Donna Reed Show," played by Shelly Fabares and Paul Petersen, also introduced hit songs on the show, although their stardom was fleeting.)

Although David and Ricky Nelson grew from boys to men, the creators of "Lassie" decided that the collie's master should remain young. For the show's first three years, Lassie lived

Lassie

on the Miller's farm outside the town of Calverton, and "her" master (Lassie was actually played by a series of male dogs) was Jeff Miller (Tommy Rettig). In 1957, when it seemed he had outgrown the role, Jeff moved to The Big City with Gramps and his widowed mother Ellen. They left poor Lassie in Calverton with a recently adopted orphan named Timmy Martin. For one season Cloris Leachman and John Shepodd played his parents, Ruth and Paul Martin. Then June Lockhart and Hugh Reilly stepped in, still playing Ruth and Paul.

Lassie was orphaned again in 1964, when the Martins "moved" to Australia, leaving their pet with a forest ranger named Cory Stuart (Robert Bray). Freed from the constraints of family life, the pup embarked on a wider range of adventures in various parts of the country. In 1968 Cory was "injured" fighting a fire and two new rangers, Scott and Bob (Jed Allen and Jack De Mave), took custody. Gradually, Lassie became more autonomous; by the series' end, she was something of a freelance. In the final season, Lassie fell in love with a male collie and, through the miracle of TV, bore him pups.

Like "Lassie," "My Three Sons" survived many cast changes, but the premise—Fred MacMurray as a gentle, upstanding widower, the father of three boys—remained intact. The three sons came and went. By 1969—the series' 10th season—one of the original three sons, Robbie (Don Grady, formerly Don Agrati, an ex-Mouseketeer), had married one of his TV steadies, Katie (Tina Cole), who miraculously gave birth to triplets—three sons—who helped see the series through to its demise in 1972.

Although "My Three Sons" spanned the entire decade, the 1960s were virtually absent from the show's plots. During a decade of heated political debate, the series presented essentially 1950s middle-class fare with

My Three Sons

light, domestic situations. Perhaps appropriately, "My Three Sons" was replaced by a show that would deal with changing American values, "All in the Family."

Finally, a household with a toilet.

paperback version, reports that "the really interesting thing...is the strength it's showing in the smaller cities all around the country." Bantam thinks it has the fastest-selling book in publishing history, but that claim is disputed by Fawcett, which says that its more than seven million paperback copies of *The Godfather*, which went on sale early last year, is the record-setter. *The Godfather* will win in the end: next year, when the movie is released, Fawcett will print more than a million more copies, raising the total to more than 10 million.

No Reservations

MARCH 14, 1971. Dee Brown's *Bury My Heart at Wounded Knee: An Indian History of the American West* makes the bestseller list, with more than 50,000 copies in print after its publication on January 28. This is Brown's 15th book on the American West—he also wrote three on other subjects—but the first to make it big.

Public Screwtiny

MARCH 22, 1971. *Screw* magazine publisher Jim Buckley, 26, and executive editor Al Goldstein, 35, are convicted on obscenity charges surrounding their hard-sex tabloid. Surprisingly, the charges stemmed not from the sexually explicit articles and photos but from the many ads offering dildos and other paraphernalia, and from classified ads seeking participants in sex acts that violated New York's penal laws. Their sentences—fines of

$1,500 each—will be relative slaps on the wrists, and the two will continue their three-year-old publication, which generates annual revenues of $1 million and has inspired countless imitators throughout the country.

The War of Words

MARCH 28, 1971. In an unprecedented move, the *New York Times Book Review* section devotes an entire issue to books about the Vietnam war, masterminded by *Times* reporter Neil Sheehan, who read and reviewed 33 books on the subject.

The Last Picture Shoo

JUNE 6, 1971. "The Ed Sullivan Show" gets the hook after 23 years. The final hour features Carol Channing, Sid Caesar, Robert Klein, and Gladys Knight and the Pips.

Sullivan: The show must go off.

On Recycled Paper

AUGUST 16, 1971. *Publishers Weekly* reports a boom in ecology books brought about by last year's Earth Day and the growing consciousness about environmental issues. The top seller is Dr. Paul Erlich's *The Population Bomb*, with more than 2.25 million copies in print, the first "eco-book" to make the bestseller list since Rachel Carson's *Silent Spring. The Population Bomb* was published almost by chance: Friends of the Earth president David Brower heard Erlich on the radio, secured some mimeographed copies of his public addresses, and passed them along to Ian Ballantine, head of the company that published Erlich's book in 1968. The book already had gone through 12 printings before Erlich appeared on "The Tonight Show." The next day, Ballantine printed 400,000 more copies to respond to the demand. According to *Publishers Weekly*, eco-books are the bestselling titles on college campuses, with sex-related titles providing the only other real campus competition.

The Last Waltz

SEPTEMBER 4, 1971. After 16 years, Lawrence Welk blows his last bubble—at least on ABC. But the accordions continue to play, as Welk generates enthusiasm when he syndicates the show.

Book Flashback

Bestsellers—1971-75

All the President's Men	Bob Woodward and Carl Bernstein
Another Roadside Attraction	Tom Robbins
August, 1914	Alexander Solzhenitsyn
The Best and the Brightest	David Halberstam
The Book	Alan Watts
The Book of Daniel	E.L. Doctorow
Breakfast of Champions	Kurt Vonnegut
Burr	Gore Vidal
Bury My Heart at Wounded Knee	Dee Brown
The Day of the Jackal	Frederick Forsyth
The Exorcist	William P. Blatty
Fear and Loathing in Las Vegas	Hunter Thompson
Fear and Loathing on Campaign Trail '72	Hunter Thompson
Fear of Flying	Erica Jong
The Female Eunuch	Germaine Greer
Fire in the Lake	Frances Fitzgerald
The Floating Opera	John Barth
The Foxfire Book	Eliot Wigginston
Future Shock	Alvin Toffler
Getting Even	Woody Allen
Gravity's Rainbow	Thomas Pynchon
The Gulag Archipelago	Alexander Solzhenitsyn
Honor Thy Father	Gay Talese
How to Be Your Own Best Friend	Mildred Newman et al.
Humboldt's Gift	Saul Bellow
I'm O.K., You're O.K.	Thomas Harris
Jaws	Peter Benchley
Journey to Ixtlan	Carlos Castaneda
The Joy of Sex	Alex Comfort
Looking for Mr. Goodbar	Judith Rossner
The Prisoner of Sex	Norman Mailer
The Population Bomb	Paul Erlich
Rabbit Redux	John Updike
Ragtime	E.L. Doctorow
The Sensuous Man	"M"
Shogun	James Clavell
Tales of Power	Carlos Castaneda
The Terminal Man	Michael Crichton
Tinker, Tailor, Soldier, Spy	John LeCarre
The Total Woman	Marabel Morgan
TM: Discovering Energy and Overcoming Stress	Harold H. Bloomfield
Trout Fishing in America	Richard Brautigan
Watership Down	Richard Adams
The Winds of War	Herman Wouk

Look No More

SEPTEMBER 16, 1971. *Look* magazine, the mass circulation biweekly, announces it will cease publication with the October 19 issue. The announcement comes as a surprise to most in the industry, although *Look* has had financial difficulties for the past two years, as has its chief competitor, *Life*. *Look's* founder and editor-in-chief, Gardner Cowles, blames network television, which has sapped advertising revenue, and postal rates, which will rise 142 percent over the next five years, as the primary reasons for the decision to fold. Founded in 1937, *Look* originally sold for 10 cents a copy, and the first issue sold more than 700,000 copies. Within 10 months it had grown to 1.7 million, with circulation peaking in 1967 at 7.75 million.

What Articles?

OCTOBER 9, 1971. *Playboy's* publisher invites the magazine's more eminent contributors to Chicago for the 1971 Playboy International Writers' Convocation. To the surprise of everyone, including Hefner, an all-star list of 65 literati shows up, including John Cheever, Jules Feiffer, John Kenneth Galbraith, Arthur Schlesinger, Jr., Tom Wicker David Halberstam, Murry Kempton, and sexologist William Masters. But the panels—which cover "The Future of Sex," "The New Journalism," and "The New Urban Life Style"—produce nothing but cliches.

T.A. Takes Off

OCTOBER 12, 1971. *Born to Win*, the first book to apply the theories of Transactional Analysis to problems in everyday life, is published. It will sell only modestly for its first months in print, but will suddenly take off as T.A. becomes a fast-rising trend. Next year it will sell 110,000 copies, with sales hitting one million by early 1976.

The Evening Stars

OCTOBER 13, 1971. The Pittsburgh Pirates beat the visiting Baltimore Orioles 4-3 in the first World Series night game. NBC instigated the later start, figuring it could garner higher ratings at night than during the day, an argument that easily persuaded Major League Baseball, which has seen TV ratings and stadium attendance dropping over the years. Within a few years, night games will be the rule.

The Midas Touch

NOVEMBER 13, 1971. "Duel" is broadcast on ABC-TV, a thriller starring Dennis Weaver, who plays a driver being followed by a gigantic 18-wheeler truck. The film will make a name for the director, Steven Spielberg, whose first film production was *Escape to Nowhere*, a 40-minute amateur war film he made at age 13 to accolades in his native Cincinnati. In a second effort, the ambitious teenager made a two-hour film entitled *Firefight*. Later, as a student at Cal State College, he made a short called *Amblin'*, shown at the Atlanta Film Festival, which led to a Universal Studios contract and a shot at TV work. The result was "Duel," which will be deemed good enough for release in European theaters. In 1974, at age 27, he will direct *Sugarland Express*, followed the next year by one of the all-time blockbusters, *Jaws*. Additional blockbusters will follow, including the "Indiana Jones" series.

A Writer's Sentence

JANUARY 9, 1972. Billionaire recluse Howard Hughes holds a telephone news conference from the Bahamas to disclaim a purported "autobiography" that McGraw-Hill has bought from writer Clifford Irving, 35, for more than $750,000. Irving has claimed to have assembled the autobiography on the basis of more than 100 meetings with Hughes, none of which actually occurred. In coming weeks it will be revealed that Irving's wife, Edith, a Swiss citizen, has withdrawn the funds from a specially established Zurich bank account by countersigning checks "H.R. Hughes." In March, Irving will be charged with forgery, mail fraud, conspiracy, and grand larceny. In June, he'll receive a two-and-a-half-year jail term; his wife will receive a two-month sentence; and Irving's researcher, Richard Suskind, will receive a six-month sentence.

> *"No one who has read it can doubt its integrity, or upon reading it, that of Clifford Irving."*
> **McGraw-Hill spokesman**

Irving: Novel approach.

The Odd Couple

JUNE 17, 1972. Following a break-in at the Democratic National Committee headquarters at the Watergate office complex in Washington, D.C., *Washington Post* "Metro" reporter Bob Woodward, 29, receives an early morning call from the *Post's* city editor. Woodward, reluctantly, will accept the assignment to cover the break-in, although, as he will later put it, he "was always looking for a good Saturday assignment, but this didn't sound like one." Within hours, it will emerge that James McCord, one of the Watergate burglars, was security coordinator for the Com-

Woodward, Bernstein: Toast of the *Post.*

mittee for the Re-election of the President. Another *Post* reporter, Carl Bernstein, 28, will be assigned to profile McCord. Although most observers have yet to consider Watergate significant, at least one, *Post* district editor Barry Sussman, sees a larger story and decides to keep Bernstein on it, although primary responsibility still belongs to Woodward. Soon, they will be working together, the Odd Couple of journalism: college dropout Bernstein, talented but unreliable, who wrote rock reviews and was beginning to consider applying for a job with *Rolling Stone*, and the up-and-coming Woodward of Wheaton, Ill., modest and pleasant, a darling of *Post* editors. The two had never worked together—they hadn't really been introduced—but will soon spend the next several years covering the downfall of Richard Nixon for the *Post* before turning to books and a movie about their serendipitous assignment.

A Magazine of One's Own

JUNE 26, 1972. *Ms.* magazine begins publication, with former *McCall's* editor Patricia Carbine as publisher and feminist Gloria Steinem as editor. The publication made its debut as a 44-page

Steinem: Women's issues.

supplement to the 1971 year-end issue of *New York* magazine, then as a prototype "Spring '72" issue. In the interim, it has attracted a $1 million investment from Warner Communications. Focusing on feminist issues, the magazine will attract a solid corps of readers—and advertisers, who are increasingly discovering the buying power of the "female market"; a rum ad in the first issue will ask, "Why shouldn't a woman make a good daiquiri?" The magazine will be an instant success: all 300,000 copies of the sample spring issue were sold in eight days. By January circulation will exceed 500,000.

High Flier

AUGUST 13, 1972. *Jonathan Livingston Seagull* by aviation writer Richard Bach sets a publishing record as Avon Books purchases the paperback rights from Macmillan for $1.1 million. *Seagull* is a tale about a bird who turns an enlightened wing upon his garbage-scrounging and angst-stricken contemporaries to test his mettle against the rigors of high flight. It's seen as an allegory, dealing with such matters as individuality, spirituality, and freedom. Published exactly two years ago, the 93-page, $4.95 book has sold nearly two million copies in hardback. Sales will be helped by a November cover story in *Time*, following which sales will zoom from 35,000 copies to 60,000 copies per week. In February Avon will issue the paperback edition with a first printing of 1.6 million copies, although sales will reach 6.5 million copies by year-end. It

BOOM! MEDIA

The Really Big Shoo

If someone with a snappier personality could have made a variety show endure for 23 years, no one has. Ed Sullivan's woodenness and lack of charisma made him an easy target for critics and impressionists. As Jack Benny described an upcoming Sullivan appearance on his TV special: "He's going to talk and everything."

A journalist by training, Sullivan had an instinct for signing the right act at the right time. He culled his guest performers from a broad range of sources. At his daughter's suggestion, he booked Dean Martin and Jerry Lewis for his premier broadcast, the young comedy team's first appearance on national TV. At Carl Sandburg's request, he signed an act called the Australian Woodchoppers. A cab driver recommended a magician, whom Sullivan invited on his show.

Yet Sullivan gets virtually sole credit for the success of "The Ed Sullivan Show," which first aired on CBS in 1948 as "Toast of the Town." For one thing, he didn't just present "acts"; he presented entertainment for America, hand-picked, screened, and choreographed just right. To the end, he stood fast on matters of decency. His

Sullivan

cameras censored Elvis' pelvis and covered cleavages by shooting busty performers from the shoulders up.

Sullivan's stiffness was another asset: the corny incongruity of doing gags with an Italian mouse-puppet named Topo Gigio went over big with American viewers. But his stony front didn't prevent him from dancing with Gene Kelly, singing with Roberta Peters, or hamming it up—in a blond wig and evening gown—with Soupy Sales.

Ironically, the program that introduced the Beatles and so many other acts to millions of hysterical teenagers—and adults—fell victim to the widening generation gap. By the late 1960s, the diverging tastes of older and younger viewers made attracting a mass audience increasingly difficult. CBS pulled the plug on Ed Sullivan in 1971, and TV variety shows would never be the same. No one else could fill his "really big shoe."

won't be the year's bestseller, however: its sales will be eclipsed by those of Xaviera Hollander's *The Happy Hooker*, which will hustle sales of 6.6 million copies.

Hard to Swallow

August 17, 1972. *Deep Throat* is seized from the World Theater in New York. Although it will later be found obscene in New York and other states, the film has become a *cause celebre*, a major breakthrough in pornography. *Throat* is seen to be something new, an entertaining film that is also porno. It will soon become acceptable for couples to attend such films together; numerous porno filmakers will gain some semblance of respectability. Porno "stars" will emerge, including Marilyn Chambers, star of *Behind the Green Door*, whose photo will

Chambers: Porn to be wild.

be removed from boxes of Ivory Snow detergent, on which she's pictured holding a baby, the product of an earlier modeling job. In rendering his verdict, Judge Joel T. Tyler stated that "This is one throat that deserves to be cut."

War is Swell

SEPTEMBER 17, 1972. "M*A*S*H" debuts on CBS. The antiwar comedy, set during the Korean War, will run for a decade and make Hawkeye (Alan Alda) and his sidekicks at the 4077th Mobile Army Surgical Hospital well-known faces—both in prime-time and on reruns.

Joy to the World

SEPTEMBER 28, 1972. *The Joy of Sex* by Alex Comfort is published in hardbound. It will rank number-three for the year, behind *Jonathan Livingston Seagull* and *I'm O.K., You're O.K.*, but will take off when released in paperback next year. By the end of 1975 total paperback sales will exceed three million copies.

Filthy Business

OCTOBER 10, 1972. Accusing the Supreme Court of "mocking the Constitution," publisher Ralph Ginzburg, 42, is paroled from federal prison in Allenwood, Pa., after serving eight months of a three-year sentence for porno-pandering by mail. The sentence resulted from Ginzburg's 1962 mail-order solicitations for *Eros*, one of many periodicals he has published, including the artistically innovative *Avant-Garde*, *Fact*, and *Moneysworth*. *Eros*, a slick publication produced "quarterly on the joys of love," as Ginzburg put it, was launched quietly with a companion newsletter, *Liason*, and a mail-order treatise called *The Housewife's Handbook on Selective Promiscuity*. Contributing to the 35,000 complaints received by the post office were *Eros*' photos of a black man and a white woman embracing in the nude. In 1963 Ginzburg, a former *Esquire* editor, had been convicted of violating an 1872 law prohibiting the mailing of obscene material; his appeals all the way to the Supreme Court delayed imprisonment until early this year. Although Ginzburg—whose case is part of an ongoing struggle to define "obscenity"—maintained that *Eros* had artistic and literary merit, the Court ruled that it "appealed to prurient interest" and was "utterly without redeeming social value." Ironically, by the time Ginzburg entered prison, the offensive material in *Eros* seemed relatively tame. In 1976, with copies of *Eros* worth up to $100 apiece, Ginzburg will donate the remaining 3,216 copies of the magazine to the American Civil Liberties Union.

Ginzburg: Clearing the *Eros*.

Film Flashbacks
Sex and Drugs

- And God Created Woman
- Baby Doll
- Behind the Green Door
- Bob & Carol & Ted & Alice
- The Boys In the Band
- Carnal Knowledge
- Cisco Pike
- Death In Venice
- Deep Throat
- The Devil in Miss Jones
- Emmanuelle
- Fritz the Cat
- I Am Curious (Yellow)
- Immoral Mr. Teas
- Killing of Sister George
- La Dolce Vita
- Last Tango In Paris
- Midnight Cowboy
- Peyton Place
- Splendor in the Grass
- Trash
- The Trip
- Vixen

I Am Curious (Yellow)

NHL on HBO from MSG

NOVEMBER 8, 1972. Time Inc.'s Home Box Office cable TV system begins operating with a National Hockey League game from Madison Square Garden, followed by a movie, *Sometimes a Great Notion*. Starting with 365 subscribers in the Wilkes-Barre, Pa., area, HBO will turn out to be a great notion, indeed, becoming the largest pay-TV network after going national via satellite in September 1975.

The End of Life

DECEMBER 29, 1972. After a 36-year *Life* span, the pioneer of news photojournalism in America ceases publication. With the demise of *Life* following the folding of *Look*, *The Saturday Evening Post*, and *Collier's* over the past 15 years, this is the first time since before World War II that the nation does not have a mass-circulated, general interest, text and picture magazine. Over the past two years, *Life* tried to improve its financial picture by changing its circulation strategy, reducing total circulation from 8.5 million to 5.5 million. But as with *Look*, postal rate hikes dealt the final blow, as *Life* anticipated increases of more than 170 percent over five years.

Rock in the Wee Hours

FEBRUARY 2, 1973. Nine weeks after ABC introduces "In Concert," Don Kirshner's Friday night platter of taped rock acts, NBC counters with "The Midnight Special." The show, hosted by well-known DJ Wolfman Jack, runs from 1:00 AM to 2:00 AM.

An Offer He Could Refuse

MARCH 27, 1973. Marlon Brando refuses an Oscar for his performance in *The Godfather*, sending in his place a native American woman. This has been Brando's comeback film after years in professional limbo; the Oscar is the industry's welcome. That he refuses it is yet another sign of his antipathy toward the industry. An advocate of Native American rights, Brando has become—along with Jane Fonda, Donald Sutherland, Jack Nicholson, and a few others—a stalwart of political Hollywood. As a result of Brando's theatrics, the Academy Awards will become an annual contest to see who can get away with what controversial message before Hollywood's best and brightest—and one of the largest TV audiences of the year.

Brando: Indian giver.

> *"All right, Edith, you go right ahead and do your thing . . . but just remember that your thing is eggs over-easy and crisp bacon."*
>
> **Archie Bunker**

A Real-Life Soap

JULY 13, 1973. As a full week of congressional Watergate hearings ends, the Nielsen ratings reveal that the televised proceedings were the top daytime TV show. NBC's coverage ranked number one for the week, eclipsing, perhaps ironically, "Let's Make a Deal." ABC's coverage took third placc, and CBS' came in eighth, just behind "As the World Turns" and ahead of "All My Children."

At the Hop

AUGUST 11, 1973. *American Graffiti* opens, written by University of Southern California film school grad George Lucas about growing up in his hometown of Modesto, Calif. Already Lucas has made a short feature about a popular Los Angeles disc jockey

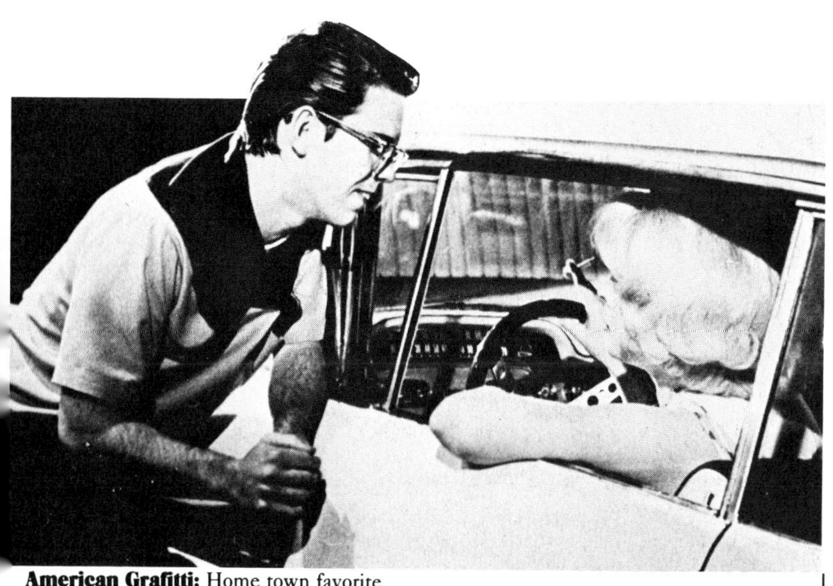
American Grafitti: Home town favorite.

called *The Emperor*, which previewed many of the themes that appears in *Graffiti*. Lucas' major work at USC, a sci-fi short called *THX-1138-4EB*, later was expanded into his first feature. His career will be intertwined with that of Francis Ford Coppola, whom Lucas met at USC and with whom he worked on Coppola's *Finian's Rainbow*; Coppola, in turn, produced Lucas' *Graffiti*. In 1977 Lucas will mix pulp sci-fi, movie serial, and western nostalgia into the wildly popular *Star Wars* brew.

Film Flashbacks

Rock 'n' Roll

A Hard Day's Night (Beatles)
American Graffiti (various)
Beach Blanket Bingo (Frankie Avalon)
Beach Party (Frankie Avalon)
Concert for Bangladesh (various)
Don't Knock the Rock (various)
Don't Knock the Twist (Chubby Checker)
Don't Look Back (Bob Dylan)
Easy Rider (various)
Elvis on Tour (Elvis Presley)
Farewell of the Cream (Cream)
Gimme Shelter (various)
The Girl Can't Help It (Little Richard)
The Harder They Come (Jimmy Cliff)
Having a Wild Weekend (Dave Clark Five)
Help! (Beatles)
How to Stuff a Wild Bikini (Frankie Avalon)
Jailhouse Rock (Elvis Presley)
King Creole (Elvis Presley)
The Last Waltz (various)
Let It Be (Beatles)
Let's Rock (various)
Lonely Boy (Paul Anka)
Love Me Tender (Elvis Presley)
Loving You (Elvis Presley)
Magical Mystery Tour (Beatles)
Monterey Pop (various)
Performance (Rolling Stones)
Rock Around the Clock (various)
Rock Around the World (various)
Rock, Pretty Baby (various)
Sgt. Pepper's Lonely Hearts Club Band (Beatles)
Soul to Soul (various)
Sympathy for the Devil (Rolling Stones)
The T.A.M.I. Show (various)
Tommy (Who and others)
Wattstax (various)
Woodstock (various)
Yellow Submarine (Beatles)

Yellow Submarine

Talk Dirty to Me

OCTOBER 30, 1973. In an early afternoon broadcast on the contemporary use of language, Pacifica radio station WBAI in New York plays a George Carlin comedy album containing a 12-minute sketch called "Filthy Words." Carlin's monologue, about "the seven words you can't say on the public airwaves" (the words are "shit," "piss," "fuck," "motherfucker," "cocksucker," "cunt," and "tits"), includes Carlin's repeating the words over and over. Despite the station's warning that the broadcast might be offensive, the Federal Communications Commission will receive a complaint from a man who heard

Carlin: Expletive delighted.

the broadcast while driving in his car with his 12-year-old son. The FCC will file charges against Pacifica, citing the broadcast as "patently offensive," although admitting it was not "obscene." Pacifica will challenge the action, and in 1978 the Supreme Court will reverse the FCC, stating that it violated the First Amendment.

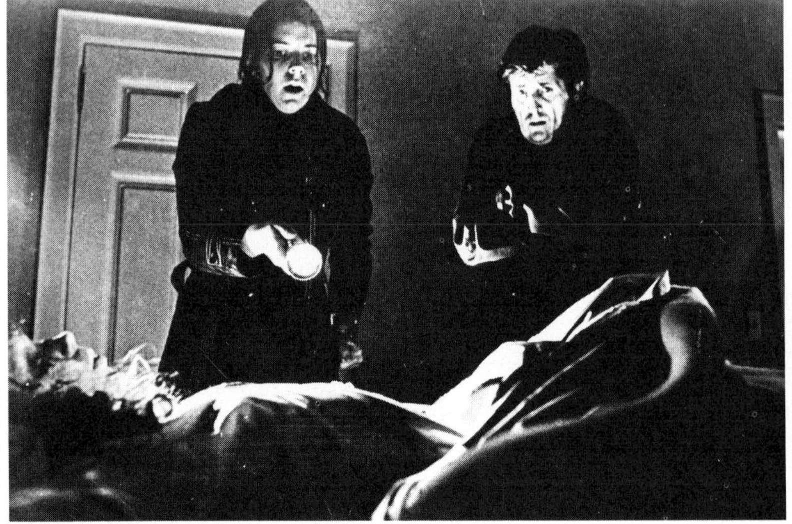
The Exorcist

The Devil Made Him Do It

DECEMBER 26, 1973. *The Exorcist* opens in movie theaters, based on a 1971 book by William Peter Blatty. The book came from a real-life story Blatty read while attending Georgetown University in Washington, D.C. A never-identified 12-year-old boy in Mount Ranier, Md., near Washington, exhibited signs that led some to believe he was possessed by a devil. The resulting book and film will cause some of the greatest hysterical outcries ever generated by Hollywood. There will be widespread reports of viewers becoming ill at screenings, developing fears of the devil, coming to believe that they are possessed, and even of exorcisms. Interest in satanism will grow significantly, and an onslaught of possession films will begin. *The Exorcist*, which will become one of the most profitable films ever, will succeed at horrifying its audience through a variety of graphic effects and shocking, discomfiting images. The film was directed by William Friedken, who has also made the enormously popular *French Connection* and the groundbreaking *Boys in the Band*.

Film Flashbacks
Horror

Abominable Dr. Phibes
Curse of the Demon
Curse of the Werewolf
The Exorcist
Homocidal
House That Dripped Blood
House of Usher
I Was a Teenage Frankenstein
Little Shop of Horrors
Night of the Living Dead
Pit and the Pendulum
Rosemary's Baby
Taste the Blood of Dracula
The Texas Chain Saw Massacre
The Tingler
Tomb of Ligeia
What Ever Happened to Baby Jane?
Willard

...Are Here Again

JANUARY 15, 1974. '50s nostalgia is big, and ABC capitalizes by introducing "Happy Days." Within two years it will be the second-most-watched series, behind only "Laverne & Shirley," a "Happy Days" spinoff.

Fish Story

JANUARY 18, 1974. *Jaws*, by Peter Benchley, is published in hardbound. It will sell just over 200,000 copies during 1974, making it only the third bestselling title of the year, but it will receive the highest-ever advance for a paperback reprint: $1.85 million, beating the $1.5 million paid last year for the reprint rights to *The Joy of Cooking*. When published next year, the gamble will pay off, as *Jaws* becomes 1975's hit movie and sells more than nine million copies in paperback.

Wail Til Next Year

FEBRUARY 4, 1974. *Publishers Weekly*, summarizing the 1973 publishing year, reports that the Watergate affair has been a bust for publishers. "There was a flurry of activity...to cash in on the scandal," says *PW*, "but without much apparent success." But the scandal will soon become big industry business, with nearly three dozen Watergate-related titles published over the next two years. *PW* also reports that sales of *Charlotte's Web* passed the three-million mark during 1973.

Making Book On Nixon

MAY 7, 1974. The first copies of Bantam's *The White House Transcripts*, based on taped conversations held in Richard Nixon's Oval Office, go on sale at 9:30 AM at Trover Gift Shop in Washington, D.C., only seven days after the transcripts are released by the White House. The race between Bantam and Dell (which had its version, *The Presidential Transcripts*, available only hours later), has been the book-publishing news event of the year, widely covered by print and broadcast journalists. Dell's version, despite losing the race, is deemed the better of the two, because it includes interpretive material by four *Washington Post* reporters, including Bob Woodward and Carl Bernstein. Within two weeks Dell will have printed 1.7 million copies of the book, just over half of the three million copies it predicts it will eventually sell.

> *"You can't be a revolutionary today without a television set."*
>
> **Jerry Rubin**

A Minute a Day

JULY 4, 1974. CBS airs the first of more than 200 60-second "Bicentennial Minutes." The network will broadcast one each night for more than two years.

Transcript: Paper chase.

Signing Off

AUGUST 8, 1974. Without acknowledging wrongdoing in the Watergate affair, President Nixon appears on live TV to announce his resignation. In the three networks' commentary following the historic broadcast, most journalists—who have spent the past weeks and months in an unprecedented investigation of the President's activities—will appear uncharacteristically somber and sympathetic. But CBS' Roger Mudd will chastise Nixon for his inability to admit guilt.

I Am Not a Book

AUGUST 29, 1974. The book industry has been busy during the first weeks following President Nixon's resignation.

Film Flashbacks
Cult Films

A Clockwork Orange
All About Eve
Annie Hall
Altered States
Barbarella
Bedtime for Bonzo
Behind the Green Door
Casablanca
Citizen Kane
Deep Throat
The Devils
Easy Rider
Eraserhead
Fantasia
Five Easy Pieces
Freaks
The Harder They Come
Harold and Maude
King Kong
King of Hearts
The Last Picture Show
Last Tango in Paris
The Man Who Fell to Earth
Midnight Cowboy
Mondo Cane
Monty Python and the Holy Grail
Night of the Living Dead
The Pawnbroker
Pink Flamingoes
The Producers
Rebel Without a Cause
Reefer Madness
Rocky Horror Picture Show
Seventh Seal
Taxi Driver
Texas Chain Saw Massacre
Two-Lane Blacktop
2001 : A Space Odyssey
Where's Poppa?
Wizard of Oz

Fantasia

Two "instant" paperbacks came out within a week of the resignation, one produced by the staff of the *Washington Post*, the other by the rival *New York Times*; two publishers have announced joint publication of the three-hour oral argument before the Supreme Court in which the Court upheld Judge John Sirica's subpoena of the White House tapes; another publisher has announced a new campaign for a biography of Gerald Ford, originally published in June; reorders for Bob Woodward and Carl Bernstein's *All the President's Men* have reached 35,000 in the past four weeks. And just 20 days after resigning as President, Nixon has let it be known, through an intermediary, that he "would entertain an offer of $2 million" for the rights to publish his memoirs. The former President reportedly would like the sum spread over a 10-year period at $200,000 a year.

Hams Across the Water

OCTOBER 6, 1974. Britain's "Monty Python's Flying Circus" crosses the Atlantic, where it finds a new home on public television stations.

Python: The Empire strikes back.

Beauty and the Beast

FEBRUARY 3, 1975. *Publishers Weekly* reports that the top-selling hardbound nonfiction for 1974 was *The Total Woman* by former beauty queen Marabel Morgan, a how-to for improving and revitalizing life and marriage. It sold just under 370,000 copies, at least 100,000 more than the runner-up, Bob Woodward and Carl Bernstein's *All the President's Men.*

That Was the War That Was

APRIL 29, 1975. All three networks broadcast specials on the fall of Saigon. CBS airs "Vietnam: A War That Is Finished"; NBC offers "7,382 days in Vietnam"; and ABC offers "Vietnam: Lessons Learned, Prices Paid."

High Noon

SEPTEMBER 1, 1975. After two decades, the Cartwright clan lopes off into the sunset as CBS yanks "Bonanza." After enjoying immense popularity—from 1968 through 1972, the ratings were dominated by "Bonanza," "Gunsmoke," "Wagon Train,"

James Arness: "Gunsmoke" shot down.

and "Have Gun, Will Travel"—westerns bite the dust on prime-time.

Not Necessarily the News

OCTOBER 20, 1975. "The Robert MacNeil Report" debuts on PBS, a daily half-hour feature on a single subject of current interest. Next year, Washington reporter Jim Lehrer will receive co-billing, creating what will become "The MacNeil-Lehrer Report."

Parting Shot

NOVEMBER 17, 1975. More than a decade after the Warren Commission Report, a fresh wave of Kennedy assassination books has further undermined the conclusion that Lee Harvey Oswald acted alone. The newest title to piece together the facts has been released today: *They've Killed the President!* by Robert Sam Anson, a former correspondent for *Time* and *New Times* magazines. Anson postulates that those responsible for Kennedy's death were members of the Central Intelligence Agency, the Mafia, and anti-Castro Cubans who believed that Kennedy abandoned them with the Bay of Pigs fiasco. Another recent title, *Appointment in Dallas: The Final Solution to the Assassination of JFK* by Hugh C. McDonald, former chief of detectives of the Los Angeles County sheriff's department, claims that a former CIA agent, now deceased, confessed to him of the assassination plot, including a second man hired to kill the President. Other recent or forthcoming titles include *The Politics of Conspiracy* by the Boston-based Assassination Information Bureau; *Coup D'Etat in America: The CIA and the Assassination of John F. Kennedy* by Michael Canfield and Alan J. Weberman; and *The Assassination Tapes* by George O'Toole, a former CIA computer specialist who has run the tape recordings of testimony before the Warren Commission through a psychological stress-evaluating device and decided that many witnesses were lying.

TV Flashback
Westerns

- Bonanza (1959-73)
- Daniel Boone (1964-70)
- Gunsmoke (1955-75)
- Have Gun, Will Travel (1957-63)
- Life and Legend of Wyatt Earp (1955-61)
- Lone Ranger (1949-57)
- Maverick (1957-62)
- Rawhide (1959-66)
- Rifleman (1958-63)
- Roy Rogers Show (1951-57)
- Virginian (1962-71)
- Wagon Train (1957-65)
- Wanted: Dead or Alive (1958-61)

Wyatt Earp

ACID • BARBIE • BEATNIKS • BIRTH CONTROL • LENNY BRUCE • C
CANDY • CARNABY STREET • WILT CHAMBERLAIN • CHRISTO • CA
COLLEGE MAJORS • COMPUTERS • CULTS • DATING • DAVY CROCK
DISNEYLAND • ELEPHANT JOKES • ESALEN • FRISBEES • HAIR STY
HALLUCINOGENS • THE HOG FARM • HULA HOOPS • HIPPIES • JUN
KRISHNAS • DON LARSEN • TIMOTHY LEARY • LEVIS • MANSON • M
ROGER MARIS • PETER MAX • MCDONALD'S • MINISKIRTS • MOON
NAMATH • THE NEW MATH • NEW YORK METS • NUREYEV • OLYMP
PHREAKS • POLIO SHOTS • SEX EDUCATION • MARK SPITZ • SPUT
STREAKING • SUMMER OF LOVE • SUPER BOWL • TEFLON • THALI
TINKERTOYS • TOPLESS • TOYS • TWIGGY • ANDY WARHOL • YO-Y
BARBIE • BEATNIKS • BIRTH CONTROL • LENNY BRUCE • CAMPING
CARNABY STREET • WILT CHAMBERLAIN • CHRISTO • CASSIUS CLA
MAJORS • COMPUTERS • CULTS • DATING • DAVY CROCKETT • DIS
ELEPHANT JOKES • ESALEN • FRISBEES • HAIR STYLES • HALLUCIN
HOG FARM • HULA HOOPS • HIPPIES • JUNK FOOD • KRISHNAS • D
TIMOTHY LEARY • LEVIS • MANSON • MARIJUANA • ROGER MARIS •
MCDONALD'S • MINISKIRTS • MOONWALKS • JOE NAMATH • THE N
ACID • BARBIE • BEATNIKS • BIRTH CONTROL • LENNY BRUCE • C
CANDY • CARNABY STREET • WILT CHAMBERLAIN • CHRISTO • CA
COLLEGE MAJORS • COMPUTERS • CULTS • DATING • DAVY CROCK
DISNEYLAND • ELEPHANT JOKES • ESALEN • FRISBEES • HAIR STY
HALLUCINOGENS • THE HOG FARM • HULA HOOPS • HIPPIES • JUN
KRISHNAS • DON LARSEN • TIMOTHY LEARY • LEVIS • MANSON • M
ROGER MARIS • PETER MAX • MCDONALD'S • MINISKIRTS • MOON
NAMATH • THE NEW MATH • NEW YORK METS • NUREYEV • OLYMP
PHREAKS • POLIO SHOTS • SEX EDUCATION • MARK SPITZ • SPU
STREAKING • SUMMER OF LOVE • SUPER BOWL • TEFLON • THAL
TINKERTOYS • TOPLESS • TOYS • TWIGGY • ANDY WARHOL • YO-

BOOM! CULTURE

M-m-m-m, Good

APRIL 4, 1955. Campbell's Soup Company announces it has acquired control of C.A. Swanson & Sons, originator of the "TV dinner." Campbell's, already the largest producer of canned and frozen soups and the second largest packager of pork and beans, will expand the Swanson line of 11 TV dinners to 65 varieties.

Billions and Billions

APRIL 15, 1955. Paper cup and milkshake machine salesman Ray Kroc opens the first McDonald's restaurant, in Des Plaines, Ill., outside Chicago. The restaurant was franchised from Richard and Maurice McDonald, owners of a fast-food emporium in San Bernardino, Calif., that was using several of Kroc's milkshake machines. They had purchased so many machines that Kroc paid them a visit; as he will later explain, "I had to see what kind of an operation was making 40 [milkshakes] at one time." Kroc's first location will do so well that he'll open two more this year. Eventually, he will buy the McDonalds out and turn out new locations like french fries. Hamburgers will sell like hotcakes: by 1960, there will be 228 locations, and 7,500 after 25 years; by 1963 McDonald's will have sold more than a billion hamburgers. Kroc will build a half-billion-dollar empire, including a chain of Hamburger Universities and the San Diego Padres baseball team. Also opening this year is the first Kentucky Fried Chicken outlet, started by Colonel Harland Sanders, a seventh-grade dropout who has previously been in the hotel and restaurant business. McDonald's and KFC will spur a fast-food industry capitalizing on the nation's mushrooming suburbs. By 1980 the top 10 fast-food chains will have a combined total of nearly 30,000 locations.

McDonald's: Turning out McProfits like hotcakes.

King of the Wild Frontier

APRIL 25, 1955. America is in the grip of a Davy Crockett craze, reports *Life* magazine, with coonskin caps and toy rifles among the hottest-selling toys. The frontier fever started with the Walt Disney TV show starring Fess Parker as the legendary pioneer. A million-dollar industry has sprouted around the legend, with some 200 items ranging from Crockett baby shoes to Crockett wallets—and, of course, several million coonskin caps.

Disneyland: Walt's Fantasyland come true.

No Mickey Mouse Operation

JULY 17, 1955. Disneyland opens at Anaheim, 25 miles south of Los Angeles. Entertainment mogul Walter E. Disney, 54, has mortgaged his life insurance policy, stock holdings, house, and furniture to acquire an orange grove, clear it, and finance construction of the Jungle River Ride, the Mark Twain paddle-wheeler ride, and other attractions of "Adventureland," "Frontierland," "Fantasyland," and "Tomorrowland." The $17 million, 244-acre amusement park's opening marks a major financial turnaround for Disney, who only 15 years ago was $4.5 million in debt. But after World War II, Disney's fortunes turned as he began to diversify from cartoons to adventure films. Starting with a seven-part True Life Adventure series of 30-minute films, Disney stretched out with a full-length movie, *The Living Desert*, which will make as much money, at less cost, as any previous Disney production. Another big money-maker has been Mickey Mouse: a license to U.S. Time Corp. has resulted in sales of more than nine million Mickey Mouse watches to date. TV, including "Davy Crockett," one of the top-rated TV shows ever, has generated about $2 million annually in sideline products. (Spurred by the show's success, Disney this fall will debut a five-night-a-week TV show, "The Mickey Mouse Club.") The success of Disneyland will lead to Disney's ultimate dream, an "Experimental Prototype Community of Tomorrow," or EPCOT for short. In October 1982, 16 years after Walt Disney's death, EPCOT—a $900 million project that also includes a Disneyland clone called Walt Disney World—will debut on a 27,500-acre parcel near Orlando, Fla.

Pay Day

AUGUST 12, 1955. The federal minimum wage jumps from 75 cents per hour to $1 per hour.

Sabin and Salk

OCTOBER 1, 1955. The Department of Health, Education, and Welfare reports preliminary findings that children aged five to nine inoculated for polio show 25 percent to 50 percent fewer cases of the disease. The report, coupled with the release last April of the first batches of a new vaccine perfected by Dr. Jonas Salk, will lead to a massive antipolio drive involving close to 70 million persons over the next two years. The "Salk vaccine" drive will have dramatic results: total U.S. cases of polio will drop to 29,000 this year, half the number in 1952; next year, the number will again be halved, with only 15,000 cases reported. In 1961 another antipolio drug, an oral vaccine developed by Dr. Albert Sabin, will be introduced; more than 100 million Americans will take the "Sabin vaccine" within three years, many through a massive drive orchestrated by public schools involving a series of three treatments of vaccine-laden sugar cubes. By 1962, total annual polio cases will drop to less than 1,000, and to less than 200 by 1964.

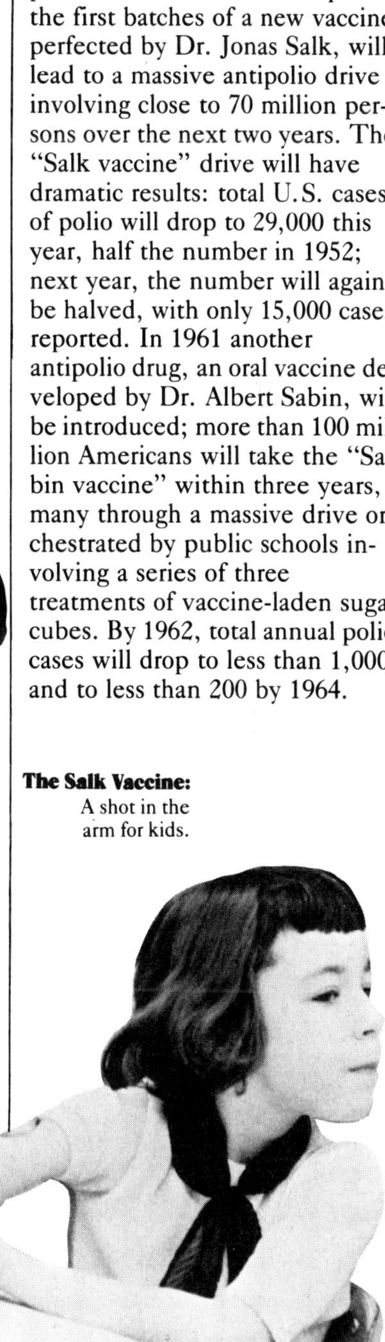

The Salk Vaccine: A shot in the arm for kids.

Perfect

OCTOBER 8, 1956. With the World Series tied at two games apiece, the New York Yankees' Don Larsen has retired batter after batter without any Brooklyn Dodgers reaching base. Sportscaster Mel Allen has tried to avoid jinxing Larsen—who was shelled by the Dodgers in the second game of the Series—by acknowledging only that "the Yankees have all the hits in the game." Finally, with two outs in the top of the ninth and the Yanks leading 2-0, Larsen slides a called strike past Dodger Dale Mitchell. He has pitched a perfect game, the first in World Series history. As the stadium erupts, Yankee catcher Yogi Berra runs to the mound and leaps into Larsen's arms, a scene that will be captured forever on film.

A Better Idea

FEBRUARY 4, 1957. Ford Motor Company announces plans to market a "remarkable new automobile" called the Edsel, a quarter-billion-dollar investment to produce the first new line of Ford cars in two decades. But when its four models—Ranger, Pacer, Corsair, and Citation—are introduced in September, Edsel sales will stall, then sputter, then run out of gas. Initially, the Edsel will seem to have all the right features: a revamped V-8 engine, Ford's patented Teletouch Drive push-button automatic transmission, and "a dial that lets you select temperature, quantity, and direction of air with one twist of the wrist," as an ad proclaims. But such innovations will fall victim to a poorly orchestrated advertising, distribution, and sales effort that will leave dealers fuming and customers yawning. Ultimately, the Edsel will represent one of the biggest marketing failures ever, causing a widespread questioning of the effectiveness of market research, and "Edsel" will become synonymous with "lemon" in the American vernacular.

Steady As She Goes

SEPTEMBER 9, 1957. *Life* magazine reports on the "Debate About Going Steady," which "became a nationally noticed teenage custom several years ago." At first, says the magazine, it was looked upon with approving clucks as a romantic phenomenon of youth, but now is "being

Edsel: The wrong stuff.

viewed with much alarm." One problem is the jump in steady dating among 13- and 14-year-olds; the concern is that a teenager "may not meet a suitably large cross section of the opposite sex before marriage." (Moreover, "it might encourage sexual intimacies.") *Life* also reports that "The newest way a few couples have of calling attention to their steady status is identical hair-dyeing. The idea is for the boy and girl to pick a shade different from their natural hair and then color each other with it. This marks them irrevocably for each other—at least until new hair grows in."

Teens: The facts of *Life*.

Star Wars

OCTOBER 4, 1957. The space age takes off as Sputnik I, the world's first man-made earth satellite, is launched by the Soviet Union. Sputnik II will lift off in November, carrying a live dog. The Soviet's jump in the "space race" will lead to a frantic effort by Americans to catch up, including a major infusion of federal dollars into public school systems for improvements in teaching math, science, and reading. In just under four months, the U.S. Army's Jupiter-C rocket will fire Explorer I, the first U.S. earth satellite, into orbit.

Places in the Heart

NOVEMBER 5, 1957. With growing concern over the increased death rate from heart attacks among young people, a debate rages at the annual meeting of the American Heart Association over the role of nutrition in causing cardiovascular diseases. For the past several years, doctors have advised patients that a diet rich in fats causes atherosclerosis—hardening of the arteries—and that reducing fats will reduce the risk of heart problems. But several recent studies have disputed that assumption, including a recent AHA study concluding that "there is not enough evidence available to permit a rigid stand on what the relationship is between nutrition...and coronary heart disease." At the annual meeting, speakers propose other causes for the rise in heart attacks, including heredity, liver inefficiency, disordered metabolism, and tension.

Hoop-La

MARCH 30, 1958. Blessed with publicity from the likes of Dinah Shore, the Wham-O Manufacturing Company struggles to produce sufficient Hula Hoops to meet an incredible demand. Richard Knerr and Arthur "Spud" Melin, co-founders of the 10-year-old company, which previously had made mostly sling shots, have been setting up Hula Hoop factories frantically in California, New Jersey, Illinois, Canada, England, and Germany, producing up to 100,000 hoops daily from a single location. Competitors, meanwhile, have churned out thousands more unauthorized knock-offs. Knerr and Melin lifted the idea for the Hula Hoop from the Australians, who use rattan hoops as exercise equipment. Using a new polyethylene plastic compound, Wham-O went into production and began demonstrating Hula Hoops in department stores. In a six-month period the two entrepreneurs will sell nearly 100 million hoops worldwide, but the fad will soon fade, leaving Wham-O buried under a mountain of unsold Hula Hoops. Although the product will put Wham-O on the map, the company will earn only $10,000 profit from all the Hoopla.

Stamp Act

AUGUST 1, 1958. First-class postage rises to 4 cents; it has been 3 cents since 1932.

Back to the Lab

SEPTEMBER 6, 1958. President Eisenhower signs a bill requiring all new food additives to be subjected first to animal tests; if they cause cancer in laboratory animals, they will be assumed to pose a threat to humans. The "Delaney clause," as it will be known (named for New York congressman James Delaney, who introduced the measure as an amendment to an existing Food, Drug, and Cosmetic Act), will be used in coming years to ban several suspected cancer-causing additives, including Red Dye No. 2 and cyclamates. Among those responsible for passage of the new law is actress Gloria Swanson, who has lectured senators and their wives on the hazards of additives. Swanson also has waged campaigns against sugar—which she equates roughly with cyanide—and has campaigned for increased federal spending for research to combat heart disease.

Flashback
Candy

- Baffle Bars
- Big Hunks
- Black Jack gum
- Chiclets
- Chocolate babies
- Chuckles
- Chunky
- Clark bars
- Cracker Jacks
- Dots
- Double Bubble Bubble Gum
- Fireballs
- Fizzies
- Good and Plenty
- Heath bars
- Hollywood bars
- Jawbreakers
- Juicyfruit gum
- Jujubees

Hula Hoop: Plastic fantastic.

People Are Funny

OCTOBER 18, 1958. Shirley Sanders and Robert Kardell, both 26, are married at the First Presbyterian Church in Hollywood, Calif., the first couple to be matched by a computer. The blushing bride and groom have been brought together as a stunt concocted by the producers of Art Linkletter's "People Are Funny" TV program, who will present them with a Honolulu honeymoon. Soon, the computer-as-matchmaker notion will yield to sensibility and computers will

- Life Savers
- Lik-em-aid
- Necco Wafers
- Pay Day
- Pez
- Pop Rocks
- Red Hots
- Rock candy
- Rocky Road
- Screaming Yellow Zonkers
- Sizzle Sticks
- Sugar Daddies
- Sweet Tarts
- Teaberry gum
- Tootsie Roll Pops
- Turkish Taffy
- Uno bars
- Walnettos
- Wax lips
- Whopper Malted Milk Balls
- Zagnut bars
- Zero bars

henceforth be used for the more mundane task of arranging *dates*.

Space Cadets

NOVEMBER 7, 1958. Sputnik has launched a new popularity in space toys, reports the *Washington Post.* For Christmas this year there's a Cape Canaveral Rocket Research Center ($6), which has a central headquarters building topped by a plastic radio transmitting tower and antenna unit on the roof, all surrounded by three rocket launching pads. Also popular are an ICBM Vanguard satellite launcher ($7) that includes a radar screen to "track" the satellite's progress; a moon spaceship, with a translucent blue globe that beeps as it rolls around in orbit and automatically adjusts its course when it bumps into unidentified objects ($5); and a 40-power telescope that reportedly can spot Jupiter and Saturn ($15). Down-to-earth little girls, who have yet to enter the space race, can look forward to a $6 washer-dryer combo that actually washes and dries.

Go, Johnny, Go

DECEMBER 28, 1958. In a game that will consummate the lucrative marriage of TV and pro football, Johnny Unitas leads the Baltimore Colts to a dramatic 23-17 overtime victory over the New York Giants in the National Foot-

Unitas: Cool Colt.

Flashback
Junk Foods (store bought)

- Beef Jerky
- Beeman's gum
- Berry pies
- Bosco
- Bugles
- Cheeze-Its
- Devil Dogs
- Dreamsicles
- Eskimo Pies
- Fiddle Faddle
- Fig Newtons
- Good Humor bars
- Hostess Cupcakes
- Hostess Twinkies
- Hot Tamales
- Jay's Potato Chips
- Kool-Aid
- Miller's pretzels
- Moon pies
- Nestle's Quik
- Nutty Butty
- Oreos
- Ovaltine
- Pringles
- Reese's Peanut Butter Cups
- Rocket Push-ups
- Slim Jims
- Yoo Hoo

(homemade)

- Banana and marshmallow sandwiches
- Chex party snack
- Chocolate Cokes
- Egg creams
- Fluffernutters (peanut butter and marshmallow spread)
- Gorp
- Hash brownies
- Mayonnaise sandwiches
- PB&J
- Smores
- Rice Krispie bars
- Squashed banana sandwiches
- Toasted marshmallows
- Toll-House cookies

ball League championship. Eschewing a potentially game-winning field goal, Unitas directs a masterful 80-yard drive, ending with Alan Ameche's one-yard touchdown plunge. For perhaps the first time the game will captivate a huge television audience and, in the process, the 25-year-old Unitas, already known for his crew cut and coolness under fire, will become a national sports hero.

Making the Circuit

MARCH 24, 1959. The integrated circuit makes its debut at the Institute of Radio Engineers convention in New York City. The circuit—or, as it will soon become known, the "chip"—is a flat, half-inch-long electronic component that contains resistors, capacitors, and transistors integrated on a single piece of silicon. The chip is the brainchild of Jack Kilby, a Kansas-born inventor who, working for Texas Instruments, created the first working model last September. (A similar chip has been created this month by Robert Noyce at Fairchild Semiconductor Labs, which will result in a decade-long patent suit over who really invented the component; Noyce will win.) The chip won't garner much attention at the convention—it is but one of 17,000 electronic products being exhibited—but the invention will be looked back upon as one of the most significant in human history, on a par with Thomas Edison's light bulb and Alexander Graham Bell's telephone. Over the next two decades, tiny integrated circuits containing hundreds of thousands of transistors will appear in computers, watches, toys, appliances, cars, space programs, medical devices, and countless other products.

Flashback
16 Ways to Not Get High

- Aerosol cans
- Aspirin and Coke
- Banana peels
- Catnip
- Cigarettes dipped in paregoric
- Ether
- Helium
- Morning-glory seeds
- Nitrous oxide
- No Doz
- Nutmeg
- Robitussin
- Sniffing freon
- Sniffing glue
- Sunflower seeds
- Turnip greens

A Different Drummer

SEPTEMBER 21, 1959. In an article titled "Squaresville, U.S.A. vs. Beatsville," *Life* magazine portrays two contrasting lifestyles—"a happy home" in Hutchinson, Kan., and a "hip family's cool pad" in Venice, Calif., "the seedy capital of the bearded bohemians called beatniks." The article tells of three Hutchinson teenage girls who invited Lawrence Lipton, Venice's beatnik leader and author of *The Holy Barbarians*, and his friends to quaint Hutchinson to brief locals on the essence of "cool." Lipton accepted their invitation, but when the Hutchinson town fathers found out, the invitation was rescinded. When rumors spread that the beatniks had been reinvited by other teenagers, the police passed the word that a "beatnik doesn't like work, any man that doesn't like work is a vagrant, and a vagrant goes to jail around here." Life, reports *Life*, isn't exactly cool in Venice, either. The town's "squares" complain about the incessant pounding of bongo drums emanating from such places as the Gas House, a defunct bingo parlor turned beat hangout. At a public hearing on the subject, the beatniks' lawyer argued that "a bongo drum is a way of dissolving your antagonisms toward other people."

Flashback
Types of LSD

Blotter	Orange wedge
Blue cheer	Owsley
Blue dots	Purple barrels
Clear light	Purple haze
Green flats	Sandoz
LSD-25	Sunshine
Mr. Natural	Window pane

It Gets On Your Nerves

FEBRUARY 24, 1960. The anti-anxiety drug Librium is approved by the Food and Drug Administration for sale and will quickly become one of the nation's most frequently prescribed drugs, far outselling the meprobamates, which have been the bestselling relaxation medications. But the real sleeper will be Valium, created by Roche labora-

The Search for the Legal High

Seedy Business: Summer 1965. Gardening stores have a run on morning-glory seeds, said to produce hallucinations. Indeed, the U.S. Food and Drug Administration admits, some such seeds contain drugs chemically related to d-lysergic acid diethylamide, better known as LSD. But most users report not much more than a mild buzz followed by a less-than-glorious morning-after headache. The two appropriately named favorite seed variaties are "Heavenly Blue" and "Pearly Gates."

Grate Stuff: Summer 1966. Two students at the University of North Carolina, having heard stories about the hallucinogenic effects of nutmeg, each ingest two tablespoons—the powder equivalent of two grated nutmegs—in a glass of milk. Within hours, their feet and legs feel heavy, their heads light and airy. Their hearts begin to pound and their faces turn beet-red. A doctor administers a strong laxative, but the effects will persist for more than two days.

Unapeeling: Summer 1967. Donovan Leitch's song "Mellow Yellow" begins a sudden craze for "electrical bananas," better known as smoking banana peels. Chemists reveal that bananas contain serotonin, a neurochemical closely related to psilocybin. The process involves baking the white fibers from inside the peels; the resulting dark brown ash is smoked in joints or in pipes. But the fad will soon fade, as thousands of young people try it—once—with few encouraging results. One side effect: T-shirts brandishing the blue logo of the United Fruit Company, one of the fruit industry's top bananas, will become popular apparel.

tories, which also developed Librium. Valium will be many times more potent than Librium as a muscle-relaxant and anticonvulsant, with fewer unwanted side effects. It will eventually outsell Librium.

Birdie: What's the matter with kids?

Watch the Birdie

APRIL 14, 1960. *Bye Bye Birdie* opens on Broadway. The show, depicting an Elvis Presley-like pop singer, Conrad Birdie, who (like Elvis) must relinquish stardom temporarily to serve Uncle Sam, is the first musical about modern teens. Starring Dick Van Dyke, Paul Lynde, Maureen Stapleton, and Ann-Margaret, it is the story of a Birdie-stricken teenage girl torn between her idol and her steady, Hugo. The show will ask, then answer, "what's the matter with kids today?"

Pale Pink Pill

MAY 9, 1960. The Food and Drug Administration gives G.D. Searle & Co. approval to market Enovid-E, a pale pink birth-control pill. "The pill," as it will generally become known, contains as little as one thirty-thousandth of an ounce of chemical—a synthetic hormone related to those that cause both ovulation and menstruation—but it will change and liberate sex and family life as never before and usher in the "sexual revolution." By 1967 there will be 12 varieties of FDA-approved pills, divided into two main classes, although all have two principal effects: they regulate a woman's monthly cycle so she has her "period" every 26 to 28 days, and they prevent the release of an egg from a woman's ovaries during the cycle in which the pills are taken, making it virtually impossible for her to conceive. Over the years the pill will be found to have several side effects but generally will be preferred over other contraceptives, including condoms, which will remain the bestselling contraceptive in the U.S. throughout the 1960s. One early problem with the pill will be its cost—about 50 cents each, or $11 a month—although costs will drop considerably within five years.

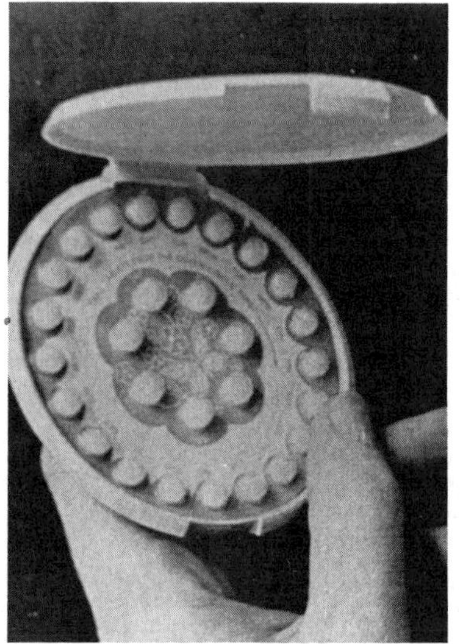

Pill: Just what the doctor ordered.

On the Beam

JULY 7, 1960. Hughes Aircraft announces achievement of the first laser action. The term (short for "light amplification by stimulated emission of radiation") was coined three years ago by a Columbia University inventor, but Hughes scientist Theodore Maiman has perfected the technique, for which a wide range of applications is anticipated, including precision cutting of materials, delicate surgery, and microscopic welding. In less than two decades, lasers will become a billion-dollar-a-year business, used for everything from information storage to telecommunications to eye surgery.

Etch A Sketch: Drawing power.

Before Video Games

JULY 12, 1960. Etch A Sketch makes its U.S. debut. Invented in France, it is an innovative drawing device that uses a metal stylus activated by two separate links of monofilament line connected to two turning knobs. The stylus removes the powdered aluminum and tiny plastic beads from the glass window, which is covered by a tough protective mylar film. Soon the Ohio Art Company will produce 8,000 of the $4 toys a day, and more than a million a year, its television-tube shape contributing to its popularity among members of the TV generation.

On the Right Track

SEPTEMBER 3, 1960. A slender student from Tennessee A&I named Wilma Rudolph becomes the first woman to win three Olympic gold medals as she anchors the U.S.' 400-meter relay team to a first-place finish. Earlier in the Rome Olympics, Rudolph, one of 19 brothers and sisters, became the first American woman to win both the 100-meter and 200-meter dashes.

Amazing Maz

OCTOBER 13, 1960. A smooth-fielding second baseman named Bill Mazeroski hits one of the most dramatic home runs in World Series history, giving the Pittsburgh Pirates their first major league championship in 35 years. Mazeroski's long fly ball over the left field wall at Forbes Field comes in the bottom of the ninth of Game Seven, with the New York Yankees having tied the score at 9-9 in the top of the inning. The loss is particularly humiliating to the Yanks because they have just set World Series records for team batting (.338 average), runs (82), and hits (151).

Maz: Yankees go home.

After the game, Yankee manager Casey Stengel will tell reporters, "I'll never make the mistake of being 70 years old again."

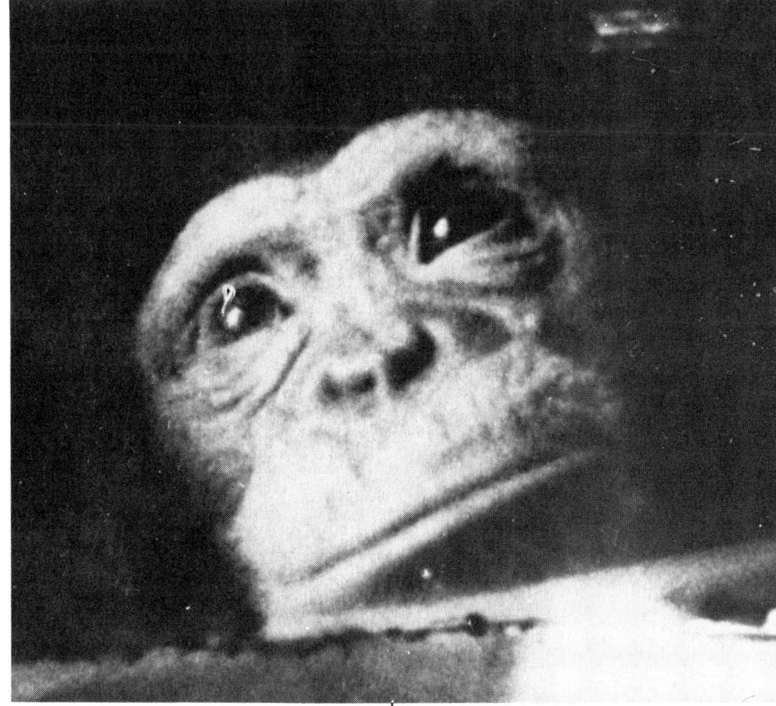

Ham: One small scep for chimp-kind.

Slick Stuff

DECEMBER 15, 1960. The first Teflon-coated pots and pans go on sale, at Macy's in New York, for $6.94 each. Although the substance was invented in 1938, this is its first application for consumers; its use until now has been in manufacturing gaskets that resist the viciously corrosive uranium hexafluoride used in producing U-235, the key ingredient in nuclear bombs. Discovered by Roy J. Plunkett, a young chemist at a Du Pont lab in New Jersey, it will soon become part of a Du Pont product, "Silverstone," a revolutionary line of pots and pans to which little, if anything, sticks. Later, it will be used in such things as John Glenn's space suit, wire insulation, and artificial corneas, aortas, and knees.

Chimp Thrills

JANUARY 31, 1961. Ham, a 37-pound chimpanzee, survives the first American experimental space shot, following an 18-minute, 420-mile ride over the Caribbean from Cape Canaveral. The flight is one of the final tests of a Mercury space capsule that will soon be used by astronaut Alan Shepard. One problem is that Ham's capsule overshot its landing target by 130 miles.

Barbie's Beau

MARCH 1, 1961. Mattel Inc. introduces a boyfriend named Ken for its highly successful Barbie doll. The svelte, foot-high Barbie (measurements: 5¼″-3″-4¾″) bombed when she debuted at the 1958 Toy Fair; baby dolls were then the rage and toy store buyers thought the busty Barbie was too "developed." The buyers proved wrong: Mattel will sell nine million Barbies by 1963 and more than 200 million by the mid-1980s. Ken is the first of a Barbie "family" Mattel will introduce, including Barbie's younger sister Skipper, her twin brother and sister Todd and Tutti, and a petite, flat-chested cousin Francie, designed for parents who don't want children playing with "mature" dolls. (Francie, however, will be the only Barbie family member to fail in the marketplace.) Ken's debut will be greeted with mild controversy, criticized by some for being anatomically incorrect, due to his lack of genitalia. (In 1978 a competitor will market an anatomically correct Gay Bob, the world's first homosexual doll, complete with flannel shirt, jeans, cowboy boots, and a closet from which he can come out.) In addition to the dolls, Mattel will make a small industry out of Barbie and friends' wardrobes and wigs (blonde bubble cut, brunette page boy, redhead flip), making Mattel the largest manufacturer of "women's wear" in the world, with more than 20 million Barbie fashions sold annually. As early Barbie owners reach adulthood, the Barbie phenomenon will take on new proportions: by the early 1980s there will be Barbie auctions, an illustrated *Barbie Price Guide*, and an annual Barbie collectors' convention, complete with Barbie and Ken dress-alike competition. The original Barbies, meanwhile, will become hot items. A first-run 1959 Barbie NRFB—Never Removed From Box—will garner $1,500 to $1,800; a used first-run Barbie, a mere $500 or so.

Barbie: Dubious debut.

Shape Up, America

MARCH 23, 1961. President Kennedy establishes a national program for physical fitness, naming University of Oklahoma athletic coach Charles "Bud" Wilkenson as special consultant on "youth fitness." The effort stems in part from America's perceived weakness and lack of self-discipline compared to the Soviets, illustrated most recently by the U.S.S.R.'s jump in the space race. Kennedy will call for "vim and vigor," set up fitness testing programs in elementary through high schools, and encourage such events as one-day, 50-mile walks, which will be organized in more than 100 cities.

Wilkenson: Vim and vigor.

Flights of Fancy

APRIL 12, 1961. Soviet cosmonaut Yuri Gagarin, 27, becomes the first human in space, orbiting the earth in 89.1 minutes in the space capsule Vostok I. Three weeks later Navy Commander Alan B. Shepard, Jr. will become the first American in space, flying 116.5 miles up in a 15-minute, 302-mile trip. Shepard is one of seven volunteers chosen two years ago from a list of 110 military test pilots. The seven were required to pass a grueling battery of tests, walking on endless treadmills, sitting with their feet in ice water, enduring two hours in a room heated to 130 degrees and three more hours in a soundproof, totally dark chamber. On May 5, after being plucked from the Atlantic Ocean by helicopter and deposited on the deck of the carrier *Lake Champlain*, Shepard will exult, "Boy, what a ride!" In late May President Kennedy will respond to the Soviet's three-week jump in the space race by calling for a vastly enlarged space effort, including landing a

Shepard & Co.: "Boy, what a ride!"

Flashback
Dolls

Baby Bumpkins	Betsy Wetsy	Madame Alexander dolls	Scooba Doo
Baby Magic	Chatty Cathy	Magic Lips	Shirley Temple
Baby Pattaburp	Charmin' Chatty	Miss America	Tammy
Babie Teenietalk	Ginny	Patty Play Pal	Tiny Tears
Barbie and friends	Katie Kachoo	Raggedy Ann and Andy	Tressy

man on the moon by 1970, a goal that will be achieved in July 1969.

Ups and Downs

MAY 22, 1961. *Newsweek*, reporting on the yo-yo craze, reveals that over a two-month period, Donald F. Duncan Inc., which controls 90 percent of the market, has sold more yo-yos in Nashville (350,000) than there are people (322,000). Yo-yos have been popular in the U.S. since the late 1920s, but sales lagged for years until Duncan tried TV advertising two years ago. (Until then Duncan had hired troops of Filipino demonstrators to tour playgrounds and neighborhood centers, dazzling onlookers with yo-yo tricks such as "walking the dog" and "rocking the baby.") Thanks to TV, Duncan sales will jump from under $2 million this year to nearly $7 million in 1962. By the mid-1980s, more than a half-billion yo-yos will have been sold in the U.S., their popularity bolstered periodically by such events as Abbie Hoffman's contempt-of-court citation in 1968 for "walking the dog" during hearings of the House Un-American Activities Committee, and Richard Nixon's yo-yoing on stage at the Grand Ole Opry in 1974. In 1985 the crew of the space shuttle Challenger will carry a Duncan Imperial yo-yo—as well as a spin-

Walking the dog: Winning spinner.

ning top, a gyroscope, a Slinky, jacks, marbles, and a toy mouse—to conduct experiments in a zero-gravity environment.

Type Casting

MAY 27, 1961. IBM introduces a $450 "Selectric" typewriter, the creation of industrial designer Eliot Noyes, the first radically new typewriter design since the introduction of the first electric model 40 years ago. Among its biggest innovations is a removable golf-ball-like type element that eliminates the need for a moving carriage and replaces the levers used traditionally to bring typing elements into contact with paper; type elements can be interchanged to produce different type sizes and styles. In three years, the Selectric will be able to connect to a magnetic card or tape device, enabling secretaries to produce similar documents repeatedly without actually retyping them. By 1975 various Selectric models will account for about three-fourths of all typewriter sales.

What's Camp

MAY 31, 1961. With summer vacation officially underway, the National Park Service predicts record crowds throughout the country as a camping craze sweeps America. More than 16 million Americans are expected to head for the hills this year, about two million more than last year. One reason for the growth is that the number of campsites has almost doubled since 1950, from about 3,000 to nearly 6,000. Sears, Roebuck reports that camping equipment sales are up 40 percent since 1956; its sales of rubber air mattresses alone have risen 700 percent in a single year. Coleman Co. of Wichita, Kans., a manufacturer of lanterns, stoves, and other camping equipment, recently reported its best four months in history.

Jetway Jete

JUNE 16, 1961. Breaking the grip of two Soviet strongarms,

Flashback

Girls' Hair Styles

Artichoke
B-52
Beehive
Bouffant
Cher
Corn rows
Dorothy Hamill
Fall
Farrah Fawcett
Flip
French twist
Frosted
Ironed hair
Jackie Kennedy
Long, straight hair
Page boy
Pixie
Ratted
Sassoon cut
Shag
Streaked
Teased
Toni permanent
Twists

Boys' Hair Styles

Afro
Beatle
Butch
Collegiate
Crew cut
D.A.
Flat top
Kookies
Mutton chops
Pompadour
Prince Valiant
Razor cut
Shag
Sidewalls
Square back
The Brylcreem look
The dry look
The wet look

ballet dancer Rudolf Nureyev, 23, races away from a Soviet plane at a Paris airport, defecting to the West. Screaming "Protect me! Protect me!" Nureyev will demand political asylum and be taken to Paris, smiling. Within weeks he will perform in Paris and London and will study in Copenhagen. In January he will arrive in New York to make his first U.S. appearance—with American ballerina Maria Tallchief on NBC-TV's "Bell Telephone Hour."

Music to Our Ears

AUGUST 11, 1961. *Time* magazine reports that transistor radio fever has hit Americans. Introduced in late 1954, the device has dropped in price to less than $10, and sales last year jumped to more than eight million. The miniscule music box has brought consternation to many, says *Time*, as students tune out teachers while listening to rock 'n' roll through earplugs and reluctant husbands listen to boxing matches while accompanying their wives to the symphony. One observer, University of Illinois sociology professor Peter Klassen, suggests that transistor radios offer an "appeal to bodily comfort which is related to the desire to go back to the womb, the mother, and the breast."

For the Record

OCTOBER 1, 1961. New York Yankee right fielder Roger Maris hits a record-setting 61st home run of the season against Red Sox pitcher Tracy Stallard, breaking the immortal Babe Ruth's long-standing record. For most of the season, Maris has battled with teammate Mickey Mantle for the home-run crown; by September, Maris had 51 four-baggers to Mantle's 48. Maris' 60th homer came in the 159th game of the season. Because Ruth had reached that total in 154 games, purists will claim Maris' feat is tainted. Indeed, baseball commissioner Ford Frick will yield to pressures from Ruth boosters and decree that an asterisk be placed next to Maris' name in the record book explaining this fact. Nearly two decades later Maris will complain, "They acted as though I was poisoning the record book or something."

Maris: Ruthless record.

See Me, Feel Me, Touch Me

OCTOBER 10, 1961. The Esalen Institute is founded near Big Sur, Calif., by Michael Murphy and Richard Price. Murphy's grandfather had purchased 375 acres in 1910, intending to use the beautiful site and natural hot springs as a health spa, but had died before they could ever finish the project. Murphy's grandmother had managed the land, which she leased to an odd assortment of evangelicals, hippies, and petty outlaws. Murphy and Price will turn the site into a trend-setting laboratory for psychological and spiritual development, sprung largely from the encounter-group therapy influenced by psychologist Carl Rogers. Over the next few years, Esalen will become a magnet for those on the cutting edge of psychological theory and social change: Fritz Perls, William C. Schutz, Aldous Huxley, Arnold Toynbee, Ken Kesey, Linus Pauling, George Leonard, Rollo May, Virginia Satir, Bishop James A. Pike, B.F. Skinner, and Carlos Casteneda, among others. By the mid-1960s, Esalen will offer a wide range of programs—from Gestalt therapy to Rolfing, Tai Chi, meditation, and "nude encounters"—helping to spur a national interest in "interpersonal relations," including numerous

Esalen imitators. By 1967 even the federal government will be sending officials to sensitivity classes.

Creating New Interest

JANUARY 1, 1962. The Federal Reserve raises the maximum interest on savings accounts to 4 percent.

Home Away From Home

JANUARY 5, 1962. Federal, state, and local civil defense officials decide to emphasize fallout shelters over evacuation in all future civil defense planning. Their reasons, they say, are the short warning time that would probably be available in a nuclear attack and the risk of widespread fallout immediately following the attack. The announcement will spur development of public and private fallout shelters throughout the country.

Glenn: Round-the-world whirl.

Globe Trotter

FEBRUARY 20, 1962. Marine Corps Lt. Col. John Glenn, 40, riding the Mercury capsule Friendship 7, becomes the first American to orbit the earth, circling the globe three times in just under five hours.

Reaching New Heights

MARCH 2, 1962. Philadelphia 76ers' seven-foot center Wilt "the Stilt" Chamberlain reaffirms his status as the dominant offensive player in National Basketball Association history by scoring a record 100 points in a

Major Interests
Undergraduate College Degrees, 1959-1978

The impact of the baby boom on the college system resulted in a near tripling of degrees between 1960 and 1980. Also evident from the figures below are the trends in learning: some subjects, such as business, psychology, and political science, saw dramatic increases in enrollment; old standbys, including English, history, and math, did not grow nearly as fast as the college-age population.

Year	All BAs	Bus/Mgt	Econ	Educ	Eng/Lit	History	HomeEc	Math	Psych	PolSci
1959-60	392,440	52,110	7,453	89,421	20,128	14,737	4,370	11,399	8,061	6,596
1961-62	417,846	52,139	8,366	96,954	24,334	17,340	4,246	14,570	9,578	8,362
1963-64	498,654	59,198	10,583	112,209	32,614	23,668	4,843	18,624	13,258	12,126
1965-66	519,804	63,639	11,555	117,185	39,015	28,612	5,655	19,977	16,897	15,242
1967-68	632,289	80,592	15,193	134,905	47,977	35,291	7,350	23,513	23,819	20,387
1969-70	792,316	106,054	17,197	165,453	56,400	43,386	10,217	27,442	33,606	25,713
1971-72	887,273	122,009	15,231	191,172	55,991	43,695	12,072	23,713	43,093	28,135
1973-74	945,776	132,384	14,285	185,181	47,343	37,049	13,533	21,635	51,821	30,744
1975-76	925,746	143,436	14,741	154,758	35,432	28,400	17,409	15,984	49,908	28,302
1977-78	921,204	161,271	15,661	136,079	29,732	23,004	17,621	12,569	44,559	26,069

Wilt: Always a bridesmaid, never a bride.

game against the New York Knicks. Chamberlain has controlled the game from the outset, taking 63 shots from the floor and making 36. Although he is generally an erratic foul shooter, he makes 28 of 32 free throws. Chamberlain will win the NBA scoring title this year, as he will for the next four seasons. Ironically, Chamberlain will never play on an NBA championship team, nor will his popularity ever match his ability. As he will explain: "Nobody loves Goliath."

Flashback
Basketball Heroes

Kareem Abdul-Jabbar (Lew Alcindor)
Red Auerbach
Rick Barry
Elgin Baylor
Bill Bradley
Wilt "The Stilt" Chamberlain
Bob Cousy
Walt Frazier
John Havlichek
"Pistol" Pete Maravich
Earl "The Pearl" Monroe
Willis Reed
Oscar Robertson
Bill Russell
Bill Walton
Jerry West

In Bad Form

AUGUST 18, 1962. Rebuffed by U.S. doctors, Sherri Finkbine of Arizona gets a Swedish abortion of her baby deformed by thalidomide, a "miracle" tranquilizer used by thousands of pregnant women to control "morning sickness." Originally marketed in Germany, it was deemed the perfect drug: a sleeping pill, it is not a barbituate, seldom leaves a hangover, and is virtually impossible to commit suicide with—nearly 200 people are known to have tried and failed. Five years ago, thalidomide was judged so safe in Germany that it was approved for sale without a prescription; in fact, its German manufacturer boasted that it "is especially well suited for calming down anxious, nervous and restless children.... Excellent for babies." In the U.S., the drug has been kept off the market pending government approval, but many Americans like Sherri Finkbine have purchased it from European or Canadian sources. Increasing evidence has linked the drug with a host of birth defects, however, including one hitherto rare condition: phocomelia, also known as "seal limbs," so called because infants' hands and feet are more like flippers than human limbs, attached close to the body with little or no arm or leg. In Germany alone, where up to 15 million thalidomide pills had once been consumed each month, as many as 3,000 deformed babies are linked to their mothers' intake of the drug during pregnancy, with a total of 8,000 thalidomide babies worldwide. The problem prompted President Kennedy to lead off a press conference two weeks ago with a demand for "additional protection to American consumers from harmful or worthless drug products."

Flashback
Baseball Heroes

Hank Aaron
Ernie Banks
Johnny Bench
Yogi Berra
Lou Brock
Roberto Clemente
Don Drysdale
Whitey Ford
Harmon Killebrew
Sandy Koufax
Mickey Mantle
Juan Marichal
Roger Maris
Willie Mays
Willie McCovey
Stan Musial
Brooks Robinson
Pete Rose
Tom Seaver
Duke Snider
Warren Spahn
Willie Stargell
Casey Stengel
Ted Williams
Maury Wills
Carl Yastremski

Flashback
Football Heroes

George Blanda
Terry Bradshaw
Jim Brown
Dick Butkus
Billy Cannon
Larry Csonka
"Mean" Joe Green
Bob Griese
Sam Huff
John Mackey
Joe Namath
Ray Nitshke
Gale Sayers
Don Shula
O.J. Simpson
Bart Starr
Roger Staubach
Fran Tarkenton
Tim Taylor
Y.A. Tittle
Johnny Unitas

Fair Well

NOVEMBER 18, 1962. As the 538-bell carillon atop the 600-foot-high Space Needle plays "Auld Lang Syne," the Seattle World's Fair closes after a highly successful six-month run. Among its other distinctions, this is the first single-year world's fair ever to finish in the black; in fact, the original $2.5 million seed money advanced by private underwriters was repaid within three months. After the last fair-goer departs, the city of Seattle will be left with the impressive Space Needle as well as $30 million worth of new downtown buildings, including an opera house, a playhouse, a Coliseum, an International Fountain, and a Federal Science Pavilion.

Altered States

MAY 27, 1963. Harvard University dismisses psychologists Richard Alpert and Timothy Leary, both Ph.D.s, for their experiments involving psilocybin and LSD. Operating through the university's Center for Research in Personality, Alpert and Leary have carried on wide-ranging experiments with mind-altering psychedelic drugs, including administering some 3,500 doses of LSD and psilocybin to 400 subjects, mostly grad students in psychology and theology. The drugs have been obtained legally from Sandoz Pharmaceuticals of Basel, Switzerland, under the supervision of the U.S. Food and Drug Administration, which permits importing the drugs for investigational use only by licensed professionals. But the two psychologists' work has been criticized by psychiatrists, who claim that the drugs are too potent for such campus experiments. Previous experiments have found that doses of LSD too

Ram Dass: Ivy League guru.

small to be visible can be sufficient to throw an emotionally unstable person into a mental hospital. Leary and Alpert will be unconcerned about their dismissals; calling themselves the International Federation for Internal Freedom, they already have set up an office in a modern Boston medical center, where they plan to continue their work. Says Leary: "This is much more important than Harvard." Alpert will move west to Stanford, where he will teach while serving as a director of the *Psychedelic Review*, a magazine Leary will start in 1965. Alpert will soon discover Eastern religion and change his name to "Baba Ram Dass," producing a mind-expanding book, *Be Here Now*.

Where No Woman Has Gone Before

JUNE 17, 1963. Russian Valentina Tereshkova becomes the first woman in space. The first American woman in space, Sally Ride, won't make her journey until 1983.

Greasy Kids' Stuff

JUNE 27, 1963. A survey released by Scholastic Magazines Inc. concludes that American boys and girls age 12 through 17 are becoming big buyers of personal-care products. It finds that 90 percent of all boys surveyed use a hair dressing, two-thirds of them daily, and that half the boys who shave use after-shave lotion. Scholastic also finds that deodorants are used by 93 percent of the girls and 66 percent of the boys; 85 percent of the girls use hair spray; 84 percent use nail polish (with an average of 3.3 shades owned per person); and 87 percent use lipstick.

Mail Chauvinism

JULY 1, 1963. ZIP codes appear, amid confusion about how to use the new five-digit numbers. The U.S. Post Office has designed the ZIP (for "Zone Improvement Plan") system to speed up sorting and delivering a growing burden of first-class mail, now nearing 70 billion pieces a

Mr. Zip: First-class male.

year. Recently, the Post Office sent 72 million postcards—the largest single mailing in history—to every mailing address in the country, informing businesses and residents about the new appendage to their address. The Post Office will soon use other promotional gimmickry to promote the system, including a cartoon character—"Mr. ZIP"—and a bouncy TV and radio jingle sung by Ethel Merman to the tune of "Zip-a-Dee-Doo-Dah" ("Wel-come the ZIP code/Learn it to-day/Send your mail out/The five-di-git way..."). The Post Office claims that the new system will speed up delivery of first-class mail by a day or more.

Flashback
Drug Paraphernalia

- Automatic rollers
- Bongs
- Chillums
- Cleaning machines
- Hookahs
- Papers
- Roach clips
- Rollers
- Stash boxes
- Water pipes

Flashback

Boomer Rumors

It's Simply Not True That. . .

- ☐ a woman once tried to dry her wet poodle using a microwave oven, during which the poodle exploded;
- ☐ Jerry Mathers, star of "Leave It to Beaver," died in Vietnam;
- ☐ Ken Osmond, who played Eddie Haskell on "Leave It to Beaver," later became a porno film star;
- ☐ Paul McCartney died in 1966 after he "blew his mind out in a car";
- ☐ James Dean *didn't* blow his mind out in a 1955 car crash but is being kept alive artificially in a hospital;
- ☐ you'll get horny if you eat green M&Ms;
- ☐ Soupy Sales once gave the finger on his TV show;
- ☐ someone once bit into a piece of Kentucky Fried Chicken to discover it was really a Kentucky fried rat;
- ☐ you can get VD from touching dirty doorknobs;
- ☐ cigarette makers have trademarked brand names for marijuana in case it is ever legalized;
- ☐ the moon landings were staged.

Man on the moon: Hollywood hoax?

Up From Slavery

AUGUST 2, 1963. *Time* magazine reports on the slang of American blacks, asserting that "Since slavery days, Negroes have created an ever-changing argot of their own, full of ambiguities, tinged with humor and sorrow." Some examples: *butter head, chili bowl, ditty bob*—terms of contempt, used to refer to blacks whose behavior embarrasses other blacks; *wheels*—civil rights leaders; *upside-downers*—militants who reject the idea of nonviolence; *untouchables*—demonstrators who have never been jailed; *shot through the grease*—made a fool of; *brotherhood hustle*—civil rights rally; *stallion*—a man who is handsome or husky or prosperous; also a buxom woman; *greys, whities, paddies, Mr. Charlie, Miss Ann*—various names for whites.

Smoke Scream

JANUARY 11, 1964. Surgeon General Luther L. Terry issues a report linking cigarette smoking to lung cancer. The report will set off a long battle between health professionals and the American tobacco industry about whether evidence linking cigarettes with cancer—or anything else—is conclusive. But the news will shock many American smokers, who now consume 524 billion cigarettes a year—more than 4,300 for every American over age 18. Later this year, public pressure will persuade tobacco companies to stop advertising to college students through campus publications, radio stations, and sporting events. The government proclamation will have an effect on the cigarette industry: within a month of the report, three of the largest tobacco companies will cut back work schedules to three- and four-day weeks, as sales slump 5 to 15 percent, with the sharpest declines in nonfiltered brands. But over the next decade, lung cancer rates among U.S. men, presently 30 cases per 100,000 population, will increase to 50 per 100,000, and rates for women, now lower than 5 per 100,000, will more than double. By 1974, in spite of reduced consumption and new popularity in "low-tar" cigarettes, death rates related to smoking will soar to more than 250,000 per year.

The Mouth That Roared

FEBRUARY 25, 1964. Cassius Clay wins the world heavyweight boxing crown, beating Charles "Sonny" Liston, who will be unable to leave his corner when the bell announces Round Seven. The flamboyant 22-year-old Clay has become known for his fast feet, which never stop dancing in the ring, and his fast tongue, which never stops chattering out of the ring. Before this

Flashback
Boxing Heroes

Muhammed Ali (Cassius Clay)
Joe Frazier
Emile Griffith
Sonny Liston
Floyd Patterson
Sugar Ray Robinson

American flags
Army jackets
Ankle bracelets
Beads
Bell bottoms
Ben Casey shirts
Bermuda shorts
Bicycle dresses
Boatneck shirts
Bobby socks
Boots
Buster Brown shoes
Chemise dresses
Chinos
Clam diggers
Clogs
Colored socks over nylons
Crinolines
Culottes
Dashikis
Davy Crockett hats
Desert boots
Dickies
Down jackets and vests
Dirndl skirts
Earth shoes
Felt skirts
Fishnet stockings
Fruit loops on shirts
Go-go boots
Granny dresses
Granny glasses
Halter tops
Huarachi sandals
Headbands
High-top shoes
Hip huggers
Hoop skirts
Hot pants
Hush Puppies
ID bracelets
Inside-out swea
Jean jackets
Jean skirts
Love beads
Macrame belts
Madras
Mary jane shoe
Maxiskirts
Mickey Mouse e
Micromini skirt

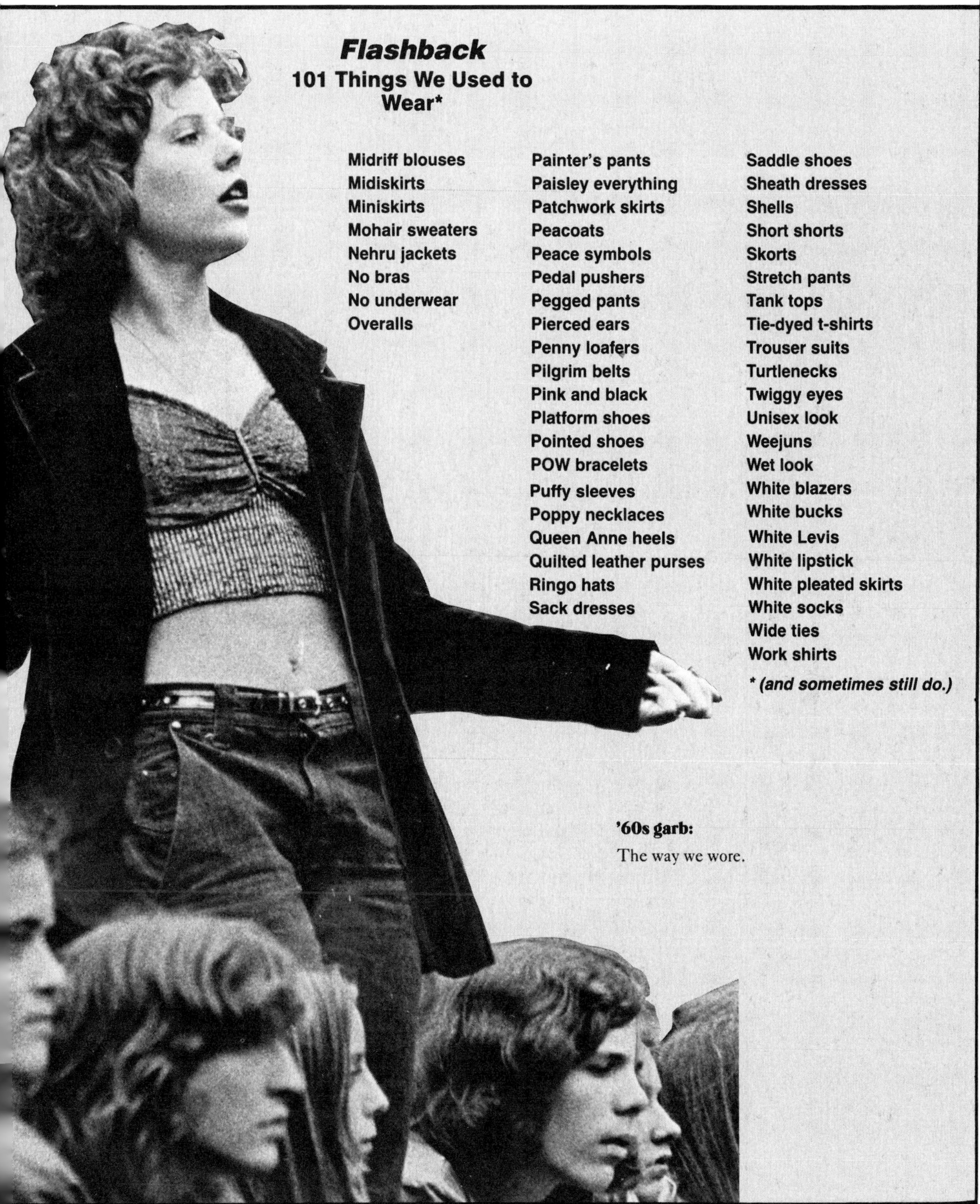

Flashback

101 Things We Used to Wear*

Midriff blouses
Midiskirts
Miniskirts
Mohair sweaters
Nehru jackets
No bras
No underwear
Overalls
Painter's pants
Paisley everything
Patchwork skirts
Peacoats
Peace symbols
Pedal pushers
Pegged pants
Pierced ears
Penny loafers
Pilgrim belts
Pink and black
Platform shoes
Pointed shoes
POW bracelets
Puffy sleeves
Poppy necklaces
Queen Anne heels
Quilted leather purses
Ringo hats
Sack dresses
Saddle shoes
Sheath dresses
Shells
Short shorts
Skorts
Stretch pants
Tank tops
Tie-dyed t-shirts
Trouser suits
Turtlenecks
Twiggy eyes
Unisex look
Weejuns
Wet look
White blazers
White bucks
White Levis
White lipstick
White pleated skirts
White socks
Wide ties
Work shirts

** (and sometimes still do.)*

'60s garb: The way we wore.

fight he told reporters, "I am the greatest," a phrase that will become his calling card and the title of his autobiography. "I am also the prettiest," he went on. "I am so pretty that I can hardly stand to look at myself. I am the fastest. I

Clay: Fighting words.

am the fastest heavyweight that you ever did see. Next to me, Liston will look like a dump truck." Within coming weeks, Clay will drop his middle name, Marcellus, in favor of the Black Muslim "X"; cut a rock 'n' roll record for Columbia; then change his name again—to Muhammad Ali.

Pay Less

MARCH 15, 1964. The Labor Department reports that one in three U.S. women work, a 50 percent increase over the past 15 years. Moreover, the 25 million-woman labor force is growing at a rate of 2.5 percent annually, compared to a 1.4 percent growth rate for men. But the average woman's salary is only 60 percent of a man's—$3,300 a year compared with $5,500. Twenty-two states already have passed equal-pay laws for women, and Congress has passed a law taking effect in June aimed at guaranteeing equal pay for women, but the 60 percent pay discrepancy will remain for at least two decades.

Barely Chic

JUNE 8, 1964. The topless bathing suit is modeled in the flesh for the first time, to clothing store buyers in New York. The suit, later called a "monokini," is the creation of designer Rudi Gernreich and will immediately generate a swell of of controversy. Hess' Department Store in Allentown, Pa., will face picket lines of women protesting the daring new suit. A clergyman in San Francisco, where sales of topless suits are brisk, will warn that "nakedness and paganism go hand in hand." New York's posh Lord & Taylor will order the suits, then change its mind even before they arrive. Store president Melvin Dawley will announce that "They will be sealed up immediately and shipped to the poor." *Life* magazine will note that "Breasts of course are not absurd; topless swimsuits are. Lately people keep getting the two things mixed up." Despite the avowed absurdity, *Life* next month will feature a two-page spread on the Gernreich design, with text by staff reporter Shana Alexander. Later this month, dancer Carol Doda will make entertainment history by dancing in a Gernreich-designed topless suit at the Condor club in San Francisco's North Beach district, the first of dozens of topless—and later bottomless—North Beach establishments.

Avant-Garde Meets the Old Guard

JUNE 16, 1964. Comedian Lenny Bruce goes on trial in New York City criminal court for alleged obscenity in his night club act. The controversial Bruce already has been arrested and tried nine times on a variety of charges, including vagrancy and narcotics addiction; this is his third for obscenity. Some critics suspect that this trial is part of a larger effort by New York power broker Robert Moses to "clean up" the city before its World's Fair. Part of a school of avant-garde comedians that includes Mort Sahl, Shelley Berman, Elaine May, and Bob Newhart, Bruce has become notorious for his "dirty" language that pokes fun at race, sex, religion, politics, and social mores. But in this courtroom, avant-garde will meet the old guard, as a humorless assistant district attorney will try to prove that Bruce's performances at the Cafe Au Go Go in lower Manhattan offended prevailing community standards. During the trial, Bruce's attorney will offer a parade of witnesses attesting to his humor's redeeming values, including *Newsweek* drama critic Richard Gilman, cartoonist Jules Feiffer, critic Nat Hentoff, Episcopal minister Sidney Lanier, and Hearst gossip columnist

Carol Doda: A swell of controversy.

Dorothy Kilgallen. In the end, Bruce will be acquitted of obscenity charges, but these and other legal proceedings will begin to take their toll. Bruce will increasingly become obsessed with his First Amendment rights, often

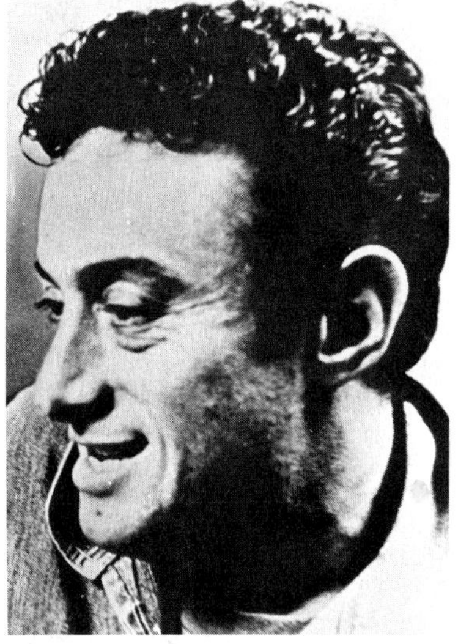

Bruce: Tragi-comic.

turning night club routines into readings from transcripts of recent trials, turning off all but his devoted followers. His last public performance will be a Bill Graham production at San Francisco's Fillmore Auditorium, performing with the Mothers of Invention. Bruce's life will end much as it was led—tragically—when he is found dead of a narcotics overdose in his Los Angeles home in 1967 at age 40.

Flashback
Illicit Substances

Cocaine
Codeine
DMT
Downers
Afghan hash
Black beauties
Black hash
Blonde hash
Butyl nitrate
Crystal meth
Green-beenies
Hashish
Hash oil
Heroin
Ketamine
LSD
Magic mushrooms
MDA
Mescaline
Methadone
Morphine
Opiated hash
Opium
PCP (angel dust)
Peyote
Poppers (amyl nitrate)
Psilocybin
Quaaludes
Reds
Seconol
Soapers
STP
Speed
THC
White cross speed
Yellow jackets

LET'S FREAK OUT TOGETHER

A Nation Going to Pot
Percent of Marijuana Smokers by Age

Age	1962	1967	1972	1977	1982
12-17	1%	7%	14%	28%	27%
18-25	4	13	48	60	64
26-34	2	3	3	7	12
Adults 18+	2	5	16	25	32

Source: National Institute on Drug Abuse

Living Dolls

JUNE 17, 1964. Mattel Inc., the nation's largest toy maker, introduces this year's playthings. Highlights include the V-room bicycles that emanate a loud motor sound from a battery-operated device; a new line of "weapons you'll need behind enemy lines," including a burp gun, a commando knife, a Special Forces green uniform, and a (harmless) plastic booby trap; a Charmin' Chatty doll, which can utter 200 expressions in six languages by means of record inserts; a new line of Barbie doll clothes and furniture; and two beatnik dolls, capable of spouting such phrases as "Hey, like you're way out—play it cool, don't be a square."

Flagging Interest

JUNE 26, 1964. *Time* magazine reports that Fieldcrest, a manufacturer of towels and linens, has introduced a line called "Three Cheers"—red, white, and blue stars and stripes in the style of an American flag. Years later, American youths will be arrested and tried in landmark legal cases over whether they have the right to wear American flags or sew them onto their clothes.

Sticks That Stuck

SEPTEMBER 12, 1964. Tinkertoys celebrates its golden anniversary. Made since 1914 in Evanston, Ill., by the Toy Tinker Division of A.G. Spalding & Bros., it was invented by

Flashback

Boomer Toys

Balsawood gliders
Banana seat bikes
Bean shooters
Cap guns
Chemistry sets
Cootie
Crayola crayons
Daisy Air Rifle
Easy Bake Oven
Electric baseball and football
Erector Sets
Etch A Sketch
Finger painting
Flexible Flyer wagons
Frisbees
G.I. Joe
Gumby and Pokie
Handy Andy tools
H.O. trains
Hot Wheels
Hula Hoops
Jacks
Kaleidoscopes
Kites
Legos
Lincoln Logs
Lionel trains
Marbles
Matchbox cars
Mexican jumping beans
Mr. Machine
Mr. and Mrs. Potato Head
Nerf balls
Pick-up sticks
Play Doh
Pogo sticks
Revell models
Scooters
Silly Putty
Skate boards
Sleds
Slingshots
Slinky
Soap bubbles
Squirt guns
Stingray bikes
Suzy Homemaker toys
Superballs
Ten-speed bikes
Tinkertoys
Tonka Trucks
Twister
Vacuform
ViewMaster
Visible Man and Visible Woman
Visible V-8
V-room Engines
Whiffle ball
Yo-yos

Toys for tots: How boomers spelled boredom.

Charles Pajeau, a tombstone maker who had watched children playing with sticks and spools. Spalding bought rights to the product—virtually unchanged—in 1952 and little has changed since. In fact, four years ago, Spalding asked the Arthur D. Little consulting firm to analyze Tinkertoys. The analysis: don't tinker with a thing. Increasingly, Tinkertoys' uses transcend age. At the Illinois Bell Telephone Company, for example, an employee's craft level is determined in part by the ability to make given items from Tinkertoys spools and rods. A more sophisticated Tinkertoys game purportedly detects management potential.

Hair Razing

OCTOBER 1, 1964. Hair styles inspired by the Beatles are causing problems between teenagers and their parents, according to a variety of reports. At a Catholic high school in the Bronx, a dean used a pair of shears to lop off students' long locks. A young man was kicked out of Houston's Lamar High School for refusing to get a "proper haircut." And in Kenosha, Wisc., 175 boys were refused admission to public schools because of their long hair.

Golden Boy

OCTOBER 15, 1964. At the Tokyo Olympics Don Schollander, 18, swims to a world record in the 400-meter freestyle, becoming the first swimmer to win four Olympic gold medals. Two days ago, he set another record, in the 100-meter freestyle; the day before he anchored the U.S. team to gold medals and world records in the 400- and 800-meter relays.

Rags to Riches

DECEMBER 14, 1964. Raggedy Ann turns 50. Created in 1914 for his terminally ill eight-year-old daughter by comic strip artist John Gruelle, she has become a childhood classic. After his daughter died in 1916, Gruelle began writing Raggedy Ann stories as a memorial to his child. The first Raggedy Ann book was published in 1918, and over the years Ann settled down with a male friend, Raggedy Andy, and acquired a dog, Raggedy Arthur. She has multiplied 50-million-fold during the past half-century, despite an increasing sophistication in doll technology. Joining her in the world of dolls this Christmas season, for example, will be Baby Pattaburp, who belches when patted on the back; Scooba-Doo, who utters "jive talk" ("I dig that crazy beat, yeah."); and Tressy, with hair that grows and can be washed, sprayed, set, and cut.

Broadway Joe

JANUARY 1, 1965. University of Alabama quarterback Joe Namath, the number-one draft choice of the New York Jets, leads the Crimson Tide to a 21-17 victory over the University of Texas Longhorns, despite a recurring knee injury. The 6′2″ 195-pound passing star will soon sign a contract for a record $389,000 over three years, making him the highest-paid rookie in pro football.

Home Sweet Dome

APRIL 9, 1965. The $31 million, 44,500-seat Harris County Domed Stadium, better known as the Astrodome, is host to the first indoor pro baseball game. The world's largest indoor arena, the Astrodome will create a revolution in baseball and football stadiums. Among its innovations are Astroturf, a synthetic playing surface that looks like—but doesn't feel like—grass, which will be installed in 1966; a temperature always set at 72 degrees; and a $2 million, 474-foot-long, three-panel scoreboard, capable of display-

For What It's Worth

If You Had Only Saved . . .	*. . . It May Now Be Worth*
An original 1959 Barbie Doll ($3)	$500 - $1,800
The October, 1952 premier issue of MAD magazine (25 cents)	$60 - $300
A Topps 1955 Willie Mays baseball card (5 cents)	$20 - $130
A 1950 Girl Scout uniform, circa ($4)	$10 - $15
A 1957 Chevy Corvette ($3,465)	$15,000 - $25,000

ing animation and between-inning commercials as well as a wide range of information that interferes with the enjoyment of sporting events, according to critics. Some fine-tuning will be needed—for example, the dome's opaque glass panels will be painted green after a number of dropped fly balls that cost the Houston Astro baseball team several games—but the stadium generally will be highly praised. Today, with President and Mrs. Johnson looking on, the Astros will inaugurate their new home with a 2-1 victory over the New York Yankees. In addition to the Astros, the stadium will host in its first year such diverse acts as Judy Garland, University of Houston football games, the Ringling Brothers circus, a bullfight, and a Billy Graham crusade.

Namath: Rich rookie.

> *"The baby boom generation has not sold out; it is just achieving and waiting to take over."*
>
> **Jerry Rubin**

Pop Goes the Easel

APRIL 6, 1965. The guest list at the black-tie gala at the Metropolitan Museum of Art in New York reads like a high society *Who's Who*, from Lady Bird Johnson to Harry Guggenheim to Mrs. Vincent Astor. But all eyes are on Andy Warhol and Edie Sedgwick—"Andy and Edie," as they are referred to by the cognoscenti.

Warhol: "Anything you can get away with."

Warhol has been lionized by the Met set for the past three years, ever since Pop Art popped forth. Already, he has been described as a "legend," an unlikely destiny for someone who arrived in New York just seven years ago as a struggling artist with little training and even less money. Warhol, 30, now finds himself at the center of the flourishing Pop Art scene, a movement devoted to celebrating the Packaging of America—food packages, to be sure, but also movie star packages and politician packages. Like the products inside the packaging, pop paintings and photos are mass-produced—as photographs, lithographs, or silkscreens, for example. Warhol, for one, catapulted to fame with his true-to-life paintings of such household staples as Campbell's Tomato Soup and Brillo pads. Among his Pop Art compatriots—including Roy Lichtenstein, Tom Wesselman, Claes Oldenburg, Jasper Johns, Robert Rauschenberg, and Richard Estes—images have ranged from street scenes to nudes to shopping-cart-as-still-life. "Art," as Warhol likes to put it, "is anything you can get away with."

The White Stuff

JUNE 3, 1965. Edward White becomes the first American astronaut to walk in space.

Small Change

JULY 23, 1965. President Johnson signs a bill to replace silver quarters and dimes with alloy versions, the first major change in U.S. coinage since 1792. The new coins will have copper-and-nickel exteriors with copper interiors; the materials will be worth about half the coins' face values.

The Gang's All Here

AUGUST 7, 1965. Ken Kesey and friends host a party for the local Hell's Angels at Kesey's six-acre spread in the hills south of San Francisco. Kesey, already recognized for his novel *One Flew*

Thompson: On the wing with Angels.

> *"It is perhaps indicative that LSD was invented in the same decade as the atom bomb."*
> **Timothy Leary**

Over the Cuckoo's Nest, has assembled a group of locals who've dubbed themselves the Merry Pranksters, known for promoting theatrical cosmic jokes on the straight world. Kesey has recently been introduced to some local Angels by another Bay Area writer, Hunter Thompson, who will soon produce *Hell's Angels*, a book based on his motorcycle adventures with the gang. Now, the Pranksters and the Angels are partying together. The Angels, no strangers to drugs, will soon be introduced to acid by Kesey and friends and they all will trip merrily for more than two days in a mind-bending and -boggling sex-and-drug orgy.

Sounds Reasonable

OCTOBER 1, 1965. "Hi-fi" audio equipment is dropping to within the price range of most Americans with the advent of all-in-one transistorized equipment, being debuted at this week's High Fidelity Music Show in New York. Until now music buffs had to assemble a system of separate components: an amplifier, preamplifier, turntable, tuner, and speakers, all of which could cost up to $1,500. Now KLH, Shure, Fisher, and other manufacturers have designed compact systems that fold up like suitcases. Price: a very sound $200 to $400.

Dressed for Excess

OCTOBER 8, 1965. "The muu muu has gone mod and turned into a granny," reports *Time* magazine, referring to the hot new ankle-length "granny dress" that is sweeping women's fashion. It began, naturally, in California, which borrowed the Hawaiian muu muu, then trimmed off material above the breasts and added ruffles and flourishes. Says one 14-year-old quoted by *Time*: "They make you feel so dressed up."

Pie in the Sky

NOVEMBER 1, 1965. Wham-O, the company that brought America the Hula Hoop, files for a patent on the Frisbee. The product isn't new; its origins date back some 40 years. Although the specifics are subject to controversy, some facts are known. Frisbees originated with the Frisbie Pie Company of Bridgeport, Conn. Depending on the version of the story, either the company's empty pie tin or the round lid from a tin of its sugar cookies was the inspiration for the toy. In the mid-1940s Walter Morrison, son of the inventor of the automobile sealed-beam headlight and former prisoner of war in Stalag 13, made a plastic version of the pie tin he played with as a child. In 1951

Frisbee: Flights of fancy.

that version served as the design for Wham-O's Pluto Platter. Wham-O's founders, Richard Knerr and "Spud" Melin, found Morrison hawking his wares in downtown Los Angeles and talked him into letting them produce the product from their San Gabriel, Calif., factory. The Pluto Platter became the Frisbee, which started flying off the production line in January 1957. By the early 1960s, Wham-O's marketing geniuses helped turn the toy into a sport, aided with the introduction last year of a "Professional Model" Frisbee. Wham-O vice president Ed Headrick personally formed an International Frisbee Association, which has sponsored tournaments and demonstrations. In 1969 the U.S. Navy will invest $375,000 to study how to adapt Frisbees to carry flares for combat and rescue use. The Navy will test Frisbees in wind tunnels, follow their flights with computers and special cameras, and build a special Frisbee-launching machine on top of a Utah cliff to test a prototype flare launcher. But instead of soaring gracefully over the ground, the flaming Frisbee will shoot into the air. The project, like the Navy's Frisbee, won't fly.

The Big Turn-Off

NOVEMBER 9, 1965. Cascading west, south, and east from Niagara Falls, a massive power failure blacks out New York City and parts of eight northeastern states and two Canadian provinces beginning at about 5:30 PM, throwing 30 million people into darkness for up to 12 hours. In Manhattan, 800,000 commuters will be trapped in subways overnight, with thousands more stuck in elevators. Rumors will be rife; in a stalled electric-powered Long Island commuter train, a conductor will announce that "Some Commie's pulled the switch from here to Canada!" But overall, cooperation and calm will prevail. At unlit intersections throughout the region, countless volunteers will direct traffic. Acting on their own, groups of men and youths will patrol neighborhoods to prevent looting. Amazingly, only two people will die from the incident, one falling down stairs, the other collapsing of a heart attack after walking up 10 flights. When the lights come back on, Consolidated Edison will assure the public that no more blackouts will occur, but New York will suffer an even worse power failure in the summer of 1977.

This is Only a Test

NOVEMBER 27, 1965. Ken Kesey and his Merry Pranksters host the first public Acid Test in Santa Cruz, Calif. It is a test in the real sense: never before has anyone publicly advertised an LSD party. The event, which costs participants $1 each, is uneventful, short of the electronic gadgets Kesey and friends have strewn on the premises. Hidden microphones and speakers send sounds of people, instruments, and synthesizers emanating from trees, furniture, just about anything. It will be the first of several "tests" in coming weeks, each attracting a growing constituency, from college kids to beat poets to musicians such as Jerry Garcia, a former bluegrass player whose group, the Warlocks, will soon change its name to the Grateful Dead. The Dead will perform at what will be one of the largest tests, at the Fillmore Auditorium in January. More than 2,000 people will come to sip from a bathtub filled with acid-spiked "electric Kool-Aid," which will become the source for the title of a Tom Wolfe book on the subject. The ultimate test, however, will take place a few weeks later at the Trips Festival, held at San Francisco's Longshoremen's Hall, a weekend-long music-and-acid affair through which nearly 6,000 participants will pass.

"Hippies create police. Police create hippies."

Baba Ram Das (Richard Alpert)

Flashback

Marijuana Arrests, 1965-82

Year	Arrests
1965	18,815
1970	188,903
1975	416,100
1980	405,600
1982	455,600
Total 1965-82:	5,312,639

Source: FBI Uniform Crime Reports

Short Subjects

DECEMBER 10, 1965. The miniskirt raises hemlines and eyebrows in London, introduced by designer Mary Quant, who opened London's first boutique, on the King's Road, in 1955. Quant has been experimenting with dress styles for 10 years, ever since she was unable to find designs appropriate for London's changing youth population. By 1961, having opened a second store, she has found a following among the fashion-conscious mods. Soon traffic jams clogged King's Road, as crowds gaped at gawky mannequins whose angular faces and long limbs proclaimed the new look. As Carnaby Street, a dusty Soho back street lined with empty warehouses, became a new center for London's young, Quant's outrageous designs encouraged the trendy chic to abandon Paris for London. "We suddenly didn't want to be chic—we just wanted to be ridiculous," Quant will later explain. Now Quant's designs—dubbed "the Look" in smart London circles—have reached American shores, imported by Puritan Fashions, a U.S. firm. In coming months Quant will become a known quantity in America thanks to a 14-day, 30-outfit whirlwind tour of fashion shows best described as "happenings," with miniskirted models literally stopping traffic as they display their fashions in the middle of New York's Times Square. The mini will become an instant success, as women of all shapes hoist their hems to heretofore unconscionable heights, eventually dwindling to "micro-mini" lengths, then dropping midcalf to "midi," then finally to floor-length "maxi" lengths. Like a stock market gone haywire, skirt lengths will fluctuate so dramatically that in 1968 designers will create the ultimate: the "mini-maxi," a short skirt onto which a separate piece can be added. The prolonged period of thigh-high fashions will be a boon to the nascent pantyhose industry, which will stretch from almost nothing in 1965 to more than 600 million pairs sold annually in the U.S. alone by 1969. Quant, too, will prosper, as her organization becomes an international conglomerate of fashion, cosmetics, fabrics, bed linens, books, dolls, and wine. Among the styles she will introduce later this decade are the bicycle dress, the trouser suit, op art prints, curtain lace suits, and "the wet look"—clothing made from shiny, petroleum-based polyvinyl chloride.

Miniskirts: Reaching new heights.

Playing With Fire

JANUARY 1, 1966. Starting today, all cigarette packs sold in the U.S.—and all advertisements promoting them—must carry the following notice: "Warning: Cigarette Smoking May Be Hazardous to Your Health." The message will not have a significant impact on cigarette consumption, however.

Warning: No lark for smokers.

For the Head of the House

JANUARY 3, 1966. The Psychedelic Shop opens on Haight Street in San Francisco's Haight-Ashbury district, the first store devoted entirely to the needs of the counterculture. During its 20-month lifetime it will become a hip general store, featuring everything from records, books, and underground newspapers to rolling papers, hookahs, and bongs, and serving as a meditation center for the community. The store will survive administrative assaults by police and city officials, hoping to find drugs that will justify the store's closing; strict rules about turning on in the store will thwart such efforts. Despite international publicity and earning a place on the Gray Line tour route, The Psychedelic Shop will close in October 1967 during the "hippie funeral" because of its inability to make a profit.

You Put Your Right Hand Here

MARCH 10, 1966. Twister is introduced to the world on Johnny Carson's "Tonight Show." Thanks to Carson the game—which requires players to move a hand or foot into a different colored circle on a vinyl game "rug," usually resulting in players twisting themselves into peculiar contortions—will soon become a college rage. After additional exposure on the "Mike Douglas Show" and again on "Tonight," Milton Bradley, Twister's creator, will deposit Twister games on the beach in Ft. Lauderdale during Easter week, where they will be "discovered" by vacationing students. The game will make a small comeback in 1977, when Milton Bradley's marketing moguls concoct a National Twister Team Competition hosted by Dick Clark.

Cheap Frills

MARCH 18, 1966. Scott Paper introduces a $1 paper dress.

Twister: College contortions.

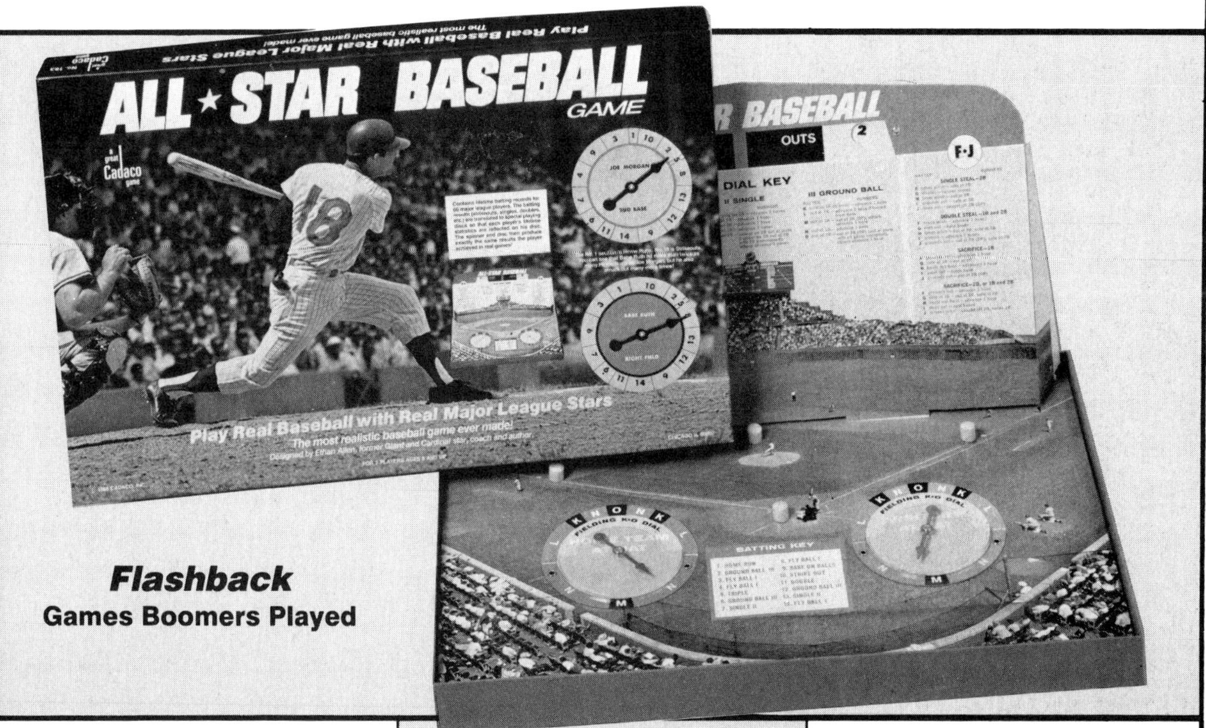

Flashback
Games Boomers Played

All Star Baseball
Candy Land
Careers
Chutes and Ladders
Clue
The Game of Life
Game of the States
Go to the Head of the Class
Monopoly
Parcheesi
Password
Rack-O
Risk
Scrabble
Sorry
Twister
Yahtzee

Goal Mettle

APRIL 2, 1966. Chicago Black Hawk forward Bobby Hull, feared for his vicious slapshot, sets a National Hockey League record by scoring his 54th goal of the season. No previous NHL player has ever scored 50 goals in a season, but Hull's feat will soon become a benchmark for scoring prowess. On this day, however, Hull's effort is wasted as the Black Hawks lose to the Montreal Canadiens in the NHL championship game.

You Gotta Believe

APRIL 8, 1966. In its cover story *Time* magazine asks "Is God Dead?" and explores the trend away from organized religion. But the magazine answers its own question with a remarkable statistic: according to a 1965 Lou Harris poll, 97 percent of all Americans say they believe in God.

Cymbals of Our Times

JULY 11, 1966. The International Society for Krishna Consciousness is incorporated in New York. The group was begun a year ago by His Divine Grace A.C. Bhaktivedanta Swami Prabhupada, a retired businessman from Bengal who, his followers believe, is the direct descendent of the first Hindu "Spiritual Master"—a disciple of God—an unbroken chain of spiritual teachers dating back 5,000 years. The swami arrived in New York with $50 in rupees and a pair of cymbals, determined to spread the teachings of Lord Krishna, a supreme Hindu deity. Over the next few years, Swami Prabhupada will attract several thousand saffron-clothed devotees, who will dance in daily processionals through the streets of American cities, and several thousand more interested outsiders who will show up at Krishna ritual feasts. In 1971 the Krishna society will set up a school for the young children of sect members, financed largely by the $1 million annual income generated by its incense factory. By 1974 there will be 27 Krishna ashrams—religious communities—across the U.S.

Fleet Feet

JULY 17, 1966. Runner Jim Ryun, a 19-year-old University of Kansas student, returns the mile world record to the United States for the first time in 32 years. Running in a meet in Berkeley, Calif., Ryun clips a substantial 2.3 seconds off the record held by Frenchman Michel Jazy, finishing the mile in 3.513 minutes. Despite his heroics, Ryun will never win an Olympic gold medal. In his last attempt, at the 1972 Olympics, he won't even make the finals; during a qualifying heat for the 1,500-meter run, he will collide with another runner and tumble to the track.

In a League By Himself

SEPTEMBER 19, 1966. Timothy Leary, out on bail following a drug arrest, holds a press conference in Greenwich Village to announce formation of a new religion called the League for Spiritual Discovery, to be known by its initials, LSD. Leary will argue, unsuccessfully, that the drug LSD should be legalized for his church members because it is a religious sacrament.

Leary: Getting religion.

Reel Fun

OCTOBER 10, 1966. At its annual meeting, GAF Corporation announces it has purchased View-Master, a popular 3-D viewing toy created in the late 1930s. The toy, a binocular-like device into which users insert reels containing tiny color transparencies, has become a childhood institution. In the 1950s View-Master was the largest single user of Kodachrome film, which may have prompted its purchase by archrival GAF. Despite the fast-growing electronic media explosion, View-Master will continue to sell for years—in 116 countries and 17 languages. In 1981 the company will be sold to

Viewmaster: Moving pictures.

New York City businessman Arnold Thaler, who will update the reels to include "Sesame Street," Michael Jackson, and Cabbage Patch dolls.

Keeping Busy

OCTOBER 18, 1966. The "beep line" is the newest teen fad, reports *Time* magazine. It works like this: because dialers who get busy signals are all shunted off onto the same massive phone line where the busy signal is produced, it is possible for everyone getting the same busy signal to communicate between "beeps" on a kind of giant conference call. Often one local number—the weather recording, for example—is designated as the local beep line. When a suburban weekly columnist in Fall River, Mass., wrote about the phenomenon recently, reporting that a local radio station's weather-reporting service was the new beep line, the number of "busy" calls to the station increased in one week from 1,495 to 27,928. Reports *Time*: "It just might be the greatest social game since kissing."

A Man and a Woman

NOVEMBER 21, 1966. Johns Hopkins, one of the nation's most reputable medical institutions, opens a Gender Identity Clinic and performs the first sex-change operation in the U.S. Such operations were first performed 14 years ago when an ex-GI named George Jorgensen went to Denmark for surgery to become female, but most American doctors have considered castration an act of mutilation, opting instead for treating patients psychiatrically. Now experts at Hopkins and an increasing number of other institutions have concluded that psychotherapy doesn't work in all cases. By early December Hopkins' doctors will have "converted" two men into women; the clinic has been screening two applicants a month for some time. Says Hopkins plastic surgeon Dr. John Hoopes: "If the mind cannot be changed to fit the body, then perhaps we should consider changing the body to fit the mind."

Flashback
Elephant Jokes
(circa 1963)

Q. Why are elephants gray?
A. So you can tell them apart from blueberries.

Q. What did Tarzan say when he saw the elephants coming?
A. Here come the elephants.

Q. What did Jane say when she saw the elephants coming?
A. Here come the blueberries. (She was color-blind.)

Q. Why do elephants wear sneakers?
A. To creep up on mice.

Q. Why do elephants wear green sneakers?
A. To hide in tall grass.

Q. Why do elephants wear red sneakers?
A. Because their green ones are in the laundry.

Joe's Woes

DECEMBER 20, 1966. Sales of war toys are de-escalating, report the nation's retailers, the result of Americans' disenchantment with the war in Vietnam. Sales of tanks, cannons, and soldiers are down as much as 40 percent, although old standby toy guns and rifles remain popular. One casualty will be Hasbro's GI Joe, a foot-high soldier doll introduced in 1964. To counter slipping sales, Hasbro will "reposition" GI Joe from a "soldier" to an "adventurer," including a "Kung-Fu" grip and a bionic "Atomic Man." GI Joe will be discontinued in 1978 but will be re-enlisted by Hasbro in 1982 as "GI Joe, A Real American Hero," albeit as a demoted, four-inch-high shadow of his former self.

G.I. Joe: No tanks.

It's About Time

JANUARY 6, 1967. *Time* magazine's "Man of the Year" is "the 25-and-under generation." Says the magazine: "In the closing third of the 20th century, that generation looms larger than all the exponential promises of science or technology: it will soon be the majority in charge." Among the magazine's other upbeat predictions and revelations about the prototypical member of this generation: "Untold adventure awaits him. He is the man who will land on the moon, cure cancer and the common cold, lay out blight-proof, smog-free cities, enrich the underdeveloped world and, no doubt, write finis to poverty and war....The vast majority of the Now Generation has little time for the far-out revels of the beatniks. In consequence, perhaps, its leisure time Happenings have an imaginative opulence that far transcends the entertainments of its parents....Indeed, Viet Nam has given the young—protesters and participants alike—the opportunity to disprove the doom criers of the 1950s who warned that the next generation would turn out spineless and grey-flannel-souled."

No Nudes Were Noticed

JANUARY 14, 1967. San Francisco's Haight-Ashbury community holds a "Human Be-In" in Golden Gate Park's polo grounds. Subtitled "A Gathering of the Tribes," it draws nearly 20,000

S.F. scene: Circumambulation, celebration.

people for a four-hour celebration in the sun. Earlier in the day, to ensure the event's proper religious status, a group of people led by poet Allen Ginsberg has performed a Hindu religious rite at the Polo Grounds known as circumambulation, which involves walking clockwise around a sacred spot chanting a blessing. With the Hell's Angels guarding the stage, the day's entertainment will include the Quicksilver Messenger Service, the Grateful Dead, the Jefferson Airplane, jazz trumpeter Dizzy Gillespie, Ginsberg, and radical Jerry Rubin, who passes the hat to help raise money for his legal defense. A local communal group, the Diggers, gives away fruit and vegetable stew. The *San Francisco Chronicle* will dutifully report that "No nudes were noticed." In midafternoon, LSD apostle Timothy Leary, garbed in white for the occasion, will make a speech advising young people to "turn onto the scene; tune into what is happening; and drop out—of high school, college, grad school, junior executive, senior executive—and follow me, the hard way." An abbreviated version—"turn on, tune in, drop out"—will soon become an anthem for the hippie movement. The event will inspire similar "be-ins" in New York, Los Angeles, and London and will spur 1967's "Summer of Love."

"Turn on, tune in, drop out."
Timothy Leary

Super I

JANUARY 15, 1967. Hardly suggestive of the spectacle it will become, the first Super Bowl is played before a crowd of 62,000 at the Los Angeles Coliseum. After a sluggish start, the NFL champion Green Bay Packers hit their stride in midgame and pummel the AFL champion Kansas City Chiefs, 35-10. Their victory is sparked by stalwarts Bart Starr, Jim Taylor, and Elijah Pitts, plus an unlikely hero, second-string wide receiver Max McGee, who catches seven passes for two touchdowns. The winning players are thrilled with their $15,000 spoils, but not nearly as much as subsequent Super Bowl participants, who by 1980 will each receive checks in excess of $36,000.

Rats!

MARCH 16, 1967. *Science* magazine reports that rats that took LSD suffered chromosome changes that could lead to abormalities in their offspring. In another recent research project at the University of Oregon, eight Portland hippies who had taken LSD several times donated blood samples, which was compared with samples from non-LSD users. Six of the eight hippies had a significant excess of broken chromosomes.

No Kidding

APRIL 4, 1967. The Food and Drug Administration announces plans to study the effects of smoking dried banana peels. Three months later it will report that it could find "no detectable quantities of known hallucinogens," a fact most banana-smokers had already discovered.

The Out-of-Towners

APRIL 5, 1967. The Gray Line Bus Company begins a "Hippie Hop" tour of San Francisco's Haight-Ashbury neighborhood, "the largest hippie colony in the world," as drivers will tell spellbound passengers. Gray Line will advertise the experience as "the only foreign tour within the continental limits of the United States." Passengers will be given a "Glossary of Hippie Terms" and a tour monologue from drivers who will explain that "Among the favorite pastimes of the hippies, besides taking drugs, are parading and demonstrating; seminars and

Flashback
Boomer Kitsch

- Ant farms
- Black lights
- Day-Glo paints
- God's eyes
- Gum wrapper chains
- Incense
- Lava lamps
- Mood rings
- Pet rocks
- Pop-top chains
- Strobe candles
- 3-D glasses and movies
- Troll dolls
- Waterbeds

group discussions about what's wrong with the status quo; malingering; plus the ever-present preoccupation with the soul, reality, and self-expression, such as strumming guitars, piping flutes, and banging on bongos." In June a hippie will board a Gray Line bus and proclaim that "This bus has been taken over by the Diggers." He will "hijack" the bus to the Grateful Dead's house and hand out avocados to passengers. As a result, the house will become part of the regular tour.

On the bus: Love-Haight relationship.

The Inside Skinny

APRIL 15, 1967. *Vogue* captures Twiggy's influence on fashion. Born Lesley Hornby, the 17-year-old Cockney became the hottest model in London last year and her stick-figure fashion is now taking America by storm as well. A fragile blonde with grey-blue eyes, she measures 5′6-½″ tall and a gaunt 31-22-32. In February 1966 she went to her London hairdresser to have her long locks lopped off. A *London Daily Express* fashion editor happened to be on hand and ran photos of her cutting the next day. That incident began exposure that within a year led to Twiggy Enterprises, Ltd., including Twiggy boutiques, a Twiggy line of clothes, and a Twiggy perfume. In 1984, a fuller-figured Twiggy will be trilling and high-stepping in the Broadway musical, "My One and Only."

Twiggy: When you're haute, you're hot.

Summer of Love

JULY 7, 1967. According to a variety of reports, the "Summer of Love" is in full force, as hippies stage a wide range of activities. In New York City, for example, they recently brought their tambourines and guitars to support dog owners protesting a leash law in Greenwich Village's Washington Square Park, chanting "What is *dog* spelled backward?" At Seal Beach, Calif., 2,500 conducted a "love-in"; in Dallas, 100 gathered at a local hangout—appropriately called Stone Place Mall—to protest a law prohibiting gatherings there. And several dozen hippies recently staged a "smoke-in" in Lafayette Park, across the street from the White House, to lobby for marijuana legalization.

Plastic Fantastic

JULY 15, 1967. Interbank Card Association mails out its first batch of MasterCharge cards. The association of banks, formed last year, is trying to muscle in on the Bank of America's eight-year-old BankAmericard, which started a revolution by offering credit cards to middle-class Americans with annual incomes as low as $5,000. MasterCard is but one of many new "all-purpose" credit cards. Recent months have seen an explosion of plastic, bearing names such as "Plastic Fantastic," "Supercard," and "Everything Card." But MasterCharge will be a big winner; its growth will be four times faster than expected. By the end of next year it will match BankAmericard with 17 million cardholders, causing banking experts to predict a "cashless society" by the end of the 1970s.

Serious Business

AUGUST 8, 1967. The *San Francisco Chronicle* reports that "an Eastern crime syndicate is

trying to gain control of LSD and marijuana traffic in Haight-Ashbury district...." One grim piece of the puzzle came with the recent discovery of the body of William Thomas, better known as "Superspade," in a sleeping bag on a cliff at Point Reyes. Superspade was a notorious narcotics dealer who, police report, had recently been told to join "The Organization" or suffer the consequences. This was the second hippie-dealer murder in less than a week.

Flashback
Fun and Games

- Capture the flag
- Chicken
- Chinese fire drills
- Cruising
- Dodge ball
- Drag racing
- Kick the can
- Mother, may I
- Mooning
- Name game
- Red light, green light
- Red rover
- Scavenger hunts
- Seven minutes in heaven
- Slumber parties
- Sock hops
- Spin the bottle
- Stickball
- Streaking
- Submarine races
- Truth or dare

Where Have All the Flowers Gone?

AUGUST 24, 1967. "Flower Parents Anonymous," a group formed "to help parents understand the problems and ideals of runaway youth," opens its doors in Washington, D.C.

R.I.P.

OCTOBER 6, 1967. Officially ending the "Summer of Love," the Haight-Ashbury community stages a "funeral" for the hippie movement. The ceremony, held in Golden Gate Park, in-

> *FUNERAL NOTICE*
>
> **HIPPIE**
>
> *In the Haight Ashbury District of this city, Hippie, devoted son of Mass Media*
>
> Friends are invited to attend services beginning at sunrise, October 6, 1967 at Buena Vista Park.

cludes a 15-foot "casket" filled with such things as beads, flowers, charms, flags, hash brownies, and money—all surrounding a reclining "corpse" clutching a zinnia. Hippies "died," say the event's organizers, from media overexposure, the misuse of drugs, the spreading of venereal disease, and the swelling ranks of "plastic" part-time hippies. Ironically, the event will be one of the most widely covered media events of the summer.

Seeds of Knowledge

OCTOBER 23, 1967. The University of California police begin a search in Berkeley for the person who planted marijuana in the university chancellor's front yard.

All Americans

NOVEMBER 20, 1967. The U.S. census clock passes 200 million people. It reached 100 million in 1915.

Heart to Heart

DECEMBER 3, 1967. The world's first successful heart transplant takes place in Capetown, South Africa, by surgeon Christiaan Barnard, 45, as the heart of a 25-year-old female bank clerk replaces the dying heart of a 55-year-old Jewish grocer. Louis Washkansky, who will soon tell a nurse, "I am a new Frankenstein," will live only 18 more days—his body will essentially reject the new heart—but the pioneer procedure will become used increasingly, more than 250 times in the next seven years, although only one in five patients will live for more than a year after the operation.

Bombed at Pearl Harbor

DECEMBER 4, 1967. Eleven crewmen have been involved with marijuana aboard the aircraft carrier *Kitty Hawk*, according to a statement released today by the Pacific Fleet headquarters at Pearl Harbor, Hawaii.

New Genes

DECEMBER 14, 1967. Artificial life is created for the first time as Stanford University scientists announce that they have produced in a laboratory the active, infectious inner core of a virus. The active virus core material is DNA, or deoxyribonucleic acid, the principal building-block chemical of all life and the substance that determines the heredity of every living thing. Dr. Arthur Kornberg, Nobel Prize winner and senior member of the Stanford research team, says he believes the material can be used to synthesize other viruses and to produce and modify the hereditary material of some living cells. He also believes the method can be used to find a possible cure for cancer.

The Acid King

DECEMBER 21, 1967. Federal agents raid a home in Orinda, Calif., outside San Francisco and arrest Augustus Owsley Stanley III, 32, grandson of a U.S. senator from Kentucky, reputed to be the millionaire kingpin of the LSD industry. This isn't his first bust; Owsley was arrested by state narcotics agents in 1965 for operating a methedrine lab, but was released when no methedrine could be found. Owsley got into the LSD-making business in 1965. "Owsley" acid has long been considered to be the cream of the psychedelic crop, although its reputation has been diminished recently by "bootleg" drugs bearing his name but manufactured by others. Owsley tablets are smaller than most, slightly larger than saccharin, and come in three colors: white, purple, and orange. According to recent reports, Stanley had been developing a new product, a super-hallucinogen called "FDA," in honor of the Food and Drug Administration.

Flashback

31 Flavors of Marijuana

Acapulco Gold
Black Gungeon
Bolivian
Chiba-Chiba
Colombian
Culican
Domestic
Guadalajara Green
Guatemalan
Guerrero Gold
Hawaiian Blue
Home-Grown
Jamaican Blue Mountain
Kali
Kauai
Kona Gold

Machu Picchu
Mad Jag
Malawi
Maui Wowie
Michoacan
Molokai Magic
Oaxacan
Panama Red
Popo Oro
Sinaloan
Sinsemilla
Sumatran
Thai Sticks
Vietnamese
Zacatecas Purple

Fleming: Perfect figure.

Cold Comfort

FEBRUARY 10, 1968. Figure skater Peggy Fleming wins the United States' only gold medal of the 1968 Winter Olympics.

Pop Gun

JUNE 3, 1968. Valerie Solanis, founder of an organization called SCUM—the Society for Cutting Up Men—shoots pop artist Andy Warhol twice through the stomach, liver, spleen, and lungs, critically wounding him. Warhol hasn't known Solanis well. "She once brought a script...and gave it to me to read—it was called *Up Your Ass*," Warhol will write later. After five hours on the operating table—at one point, doctors will later tell him, he was considered lost—Warhol will pull through. But this may be the only time in his high-profile career that Warhol

Flashback

Top-Selling Candy Bars, 1960

1. Mounds
2. Almond Joy
3. Hershey Milk Chocolate
4. Hershey with Almonds
5. Mars Bar
6. Wayne Bun
7. Marsettes
8. Rolo
9. PowerHouse
10. Baby Ruth
11. Nestle Crunch
12. Seven Up
13. Milky Way
14. Pay Day
15. Hershey Krackel
16. Nut Goodies

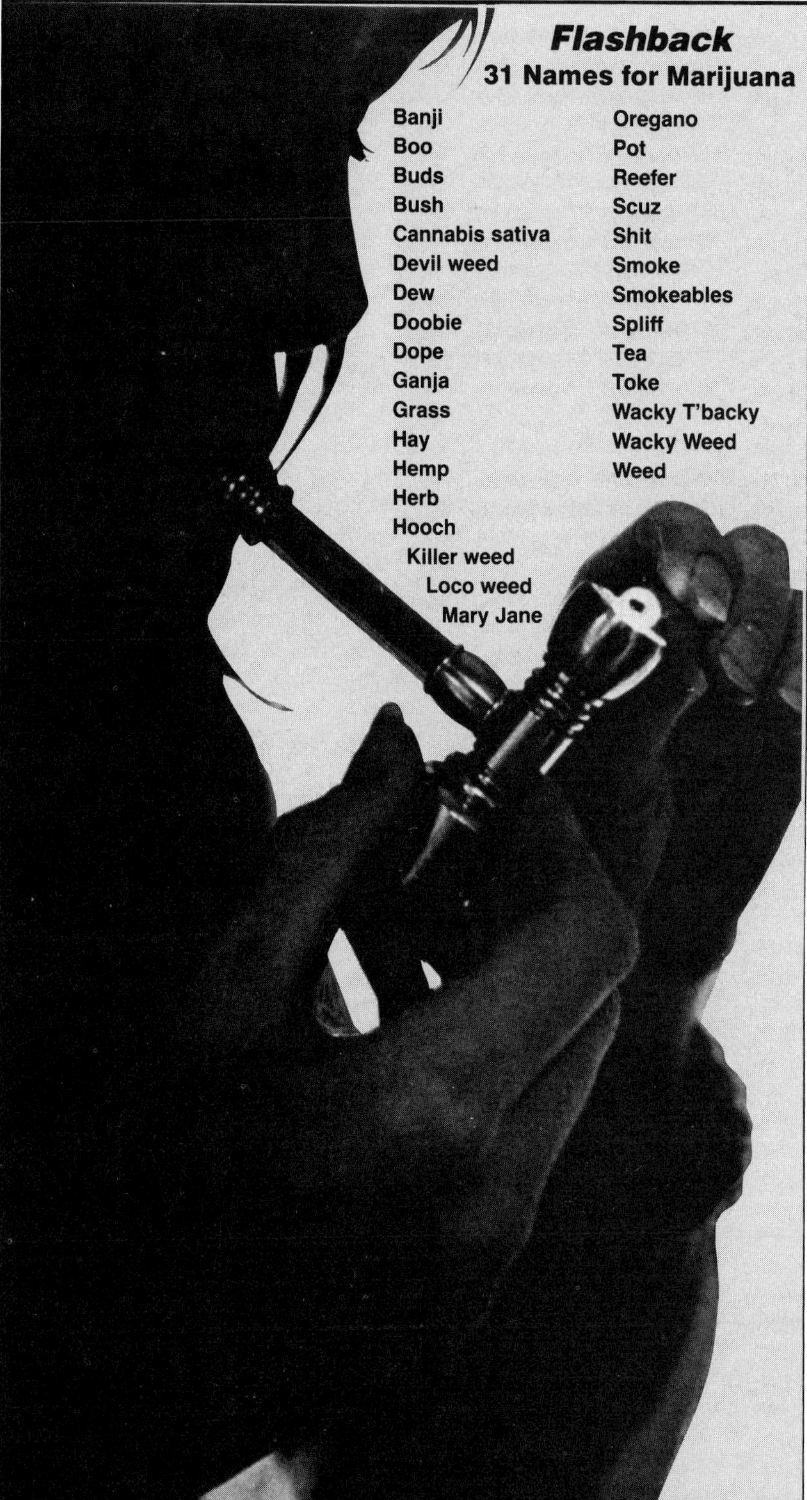

is upstaged: Tomorrow, Sen. Robert Kennedy will be assassinated in Los Angeles, and Warhol's name will vanish from the news.

The China Syndrome

JULY 13, 1968. Researchers at the Albert Einstein College of Medicine in New York announce that they have discovered the cause of "Chinese Restaurant Syndrome," the malady that grips some people after eating Chinese food. The cause, they say, is MSG—monosodium glutamate—also sold under the product names Accent and Ajinomoto. The syndrome was first recognized by the medical community in a report last May in the *New England Journal of Medicine.* Afterward, one scientist began eating Chinese food for breakfast, lunch, and dinner, eliminating ingredients one by one until MSG was deemed the culprit. In 1960 MSG was removed from baby foods after a medical researcher in St. Louis reported that it had produced brain lesions in mice using the same dosage found in baby foods.

Ms. America

SEPTEMBER 7, 1968. Two hundred radical women stage "guerrilla" actions at the Miss America Pageant in Atlantic City, crowning a live sheep "Miss America" and setting up a "Freedom Trash Can" in which women discard items symbolic of traditional ideas of feminity. A leaflet distributed for the event has instructed participants to "throw bras, girdles, curlers, false eyelashes, wigs, and representative issues of *Cosmopolitan*, *Ladies' Home Journal*, *Family Circle*, etc.—bring any such woman-garbage you have around the house." Based on this document, some media will report tales of "bra-burnings," although no such event will have taken place. More accurately, however, newspapers will report the following day, as the *New York Daily News* will put it, that "some women who think the whole idea of such contests is degrading to femininity took their case to the people....During boardwalk demonstrations, gals say they're not anti-beauty, just anti-beauty contests."

Curve Ball

SEPTEMBER 19, 1968. Detroit Tigers pitcher Denny McLain becomes the first 31-game winner since Dizzy Dean in 1931. McLain will finish the season with an outstanding 31-6 record, winning handily the league's Cy Young Award. But his fortunes will begin to turn in the World Series against the St. Louis Cardinals, when he wins only one of three games he pitches; teammate Mickey Lolich will record victories in the three wins needed to ensure the championship. Two years later, McLain will be suspended by Commissioner Bowie Kuhn for betting on games. As McLain will put it: "My biggest crime was stupidity."

Welch: Sexless.

Feminists: Sheep thrills.

The Birch and the Bees

SEPTEMBER 25, 1968. The Christian Crusade of Tulsa publishes a pamphlet titled "Is the School House the Proper Place to Teach Raw Sex?" as part of a growing controversy over the teaching of sex education in public schools. Although teaching the birds and the bees has been approved by many school boards and PTA's, conservative groups—such as the Christian Crusade and the John Birch Society, whose founder, Robert Welch, has called sex education a "filthy Communist plot"—have become better organized and increasingly vocal. In the next few months, communities in 35 states will become embroiled in disputes over sex education courses, led by groups with names such as Sanity of Sex (SOS), Parents Against Universal Sex Education (PAUSE), and the Movement to Restore Decency (MOTOREDE). Their principal charge will be that such courses are too specific, too early, and too stimulating.

A Day at the Races

OCTOBER 17, 1968. Civil rights takes center stage momentarily at the Mexico City Olympics as two American sprinters, each wearing black sweatsuits, black socks, and a single black glove, raise their fists in a "black power" salute during the playing of the "Star-Spangled Banner." The runners, Tommie Smith, winner of the 200-meter dash in world-record time, and bronze medalist John Carlos, will be immediately suspended from the games and ordered to leave Mexico City within 48 hours. Tomorrow, American long-jumper Bob Beamon will soar an amazing 29 feet, 2-1/2 inches, nearly two feet farther than the existing world record. When the distance is announced, Beamon will fall to his knees and begin to cry with joy. Later, track experts and physiologists will surmise that Beamon's leap may have reached the limit of human potential, aided by the games' high-altitude location.

Spacing Out

DECEMBER 21, 1968. Apollo 8 launches from Cape Kennedy for a week-long mission. In addition to the voluminous flight documents and other materials carried aboard by the American astronauts, all three also bring a sterling silver eggshell containing Silly Putty, which they will use to alleviate boredom and to help fasten down tools during the weightless period. Down on earth, Silly Putty has alleviated boredom for nearly 20 years. The product was born by accident at a General Electric silicone lab in 1945 during experiments to produce synthetic rubber for the American war effort. Engineer James Wright tossed a bit of boric acid into some silicone oil. When he lifted the substance from the test tube, he found that it bounced when he threw it on the floor. As the strange bouncing stuff made the rounds at cocktail parties, it drew the attention of marketing expert Peter Hodgson, who began selling it in 1949 as Silly Putty. The $2 product quickly took off, helped by an article in *New Yorker* magazine. At first, purchasers were 80 percent adults, 20 percent children, but the figures reversed in the early 1950s, when the first Silly Putty TV commercials aired during the "Howdy Doody" show.

Smith, Carlos: Run out of town.

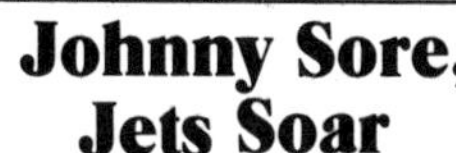

Johnny Sore, Jets Soar

JANUARY 12, 1969. The New York Jets, behind their cocky quarterback "Broadway" Joe Namath, stun the heavily favored Baltimore Colts in Super Bowl III and earn instant respect for the much-maligned American Football League. Three days earlier, Namath, during a poolside interview at a Miami hotel, had flatly predicted, "We'll win Sunday. I guarantee it." He went on to say that the Jets were a better team

Flashback
Comedy Albums

Big Bambu	Cheech and Chong
Bill Cosby Is a Very Funny Fellow Right!	Bill Cosby
Class Clown	George Carlin
Craps	Richard Pryor
Don't Crush That Dwarf, Hand Me the Pliers	Firesign Theatre
The First Family	Vaughn Meader
How Can You Be in Two Places at Once When You're Not Anywhere at All?	Firesign Theatre
I Started Out As a Child	Bill Cosby
Lemmings	National Lampoon
Let's Get Small	Steve Martin
Matching Tie and Hankerchief	Monty Python
The Night Club Years	Woody Allen
Occupation: Foole	George Carlin
Radio Dinner	National Lampoon
The Real Lenny Bruce	Lenny Bruce
Stan Freberg Presents the United States of America	Stan Freberg
Thank You, Masked Man	Lenny Bruce
That Nigger's Crazy	Richard Pryor
That Was the Year That Was	Tom Leher
To Russell, My Brother, Whom I Slept With	Bill Cosby
The 2,000-Year-Old Man	Carl Reiner
Why Is There Air?	Bill Cosby

than the Colts—who were favored by almost three touchdowns—and that Colts starting quarterback Earl Morrall would be no better than the third-string QB on the Jets. Most fans expect Namath to eat his words, but he responds with a pinpoint passing attack that sparks a 13-0 half-time lead. In desperation, Colts coach Don Shula calls on a sore-armed Johnny Unitas, but he has no miracles left in his career. The Jets land a sweet 16-7 victory. Their win, the first for an AFL team, will provide major impetus toward the eventual merger between the two leagues.

Afro-Didie

MARCH 6, 1969. Black-power consciousness has caught up with the toy industry, as manufacturers unveil new lines of black dolls at this year's Toy Fair. Ideal Toy Corp., for example, is displaying, along with its Tearie Betsy Wetsy—"a doll that cries and wets"—a Negro Tearie Betsy Wetsy. It also has a Crissy, "the hair-growing doll," and a Negro Crissy. Mattel is distributing a black doll named Baby Nancy, manufactured by Shindana Toys, a self-help black organization in Los Angeles; "shindana" is Swahili for "competitor."

Altered Jeans

MARCH 12, 1969. Levi Strauss begins marketing bell-bottom jeans. It is a major development for the 116-year-old company, which rarely tampers with its true-blue products; among the few innovations made to its original "501" model jeans have been zippers, introduced in the early 1950s; preshrunk jeans in 1959; "White Levi's" and corduroys in 1963; and hip-huggers for "gals" just last year. Within the next 15 years, as company management passes to a younger generation, the San Francisco-based Levi Strauss & Co. will grow into an international fashion conglomerate, producing vast lines of men's and women's clothing.

Take It to the Max

APRIL 5, 1969. Artist Peter Max has turned Pop Art into a new vehicle of expression as his series of posters begin to appear on 20,000 buses, subways, and trolleys throughout the U.S. The "Transit Art"—which includes brightly colored Max posters expressing "Love," "Dove," "Hello," and "Great Big Beautiful Smile"—is part of a deal with

Metro Transit Advertising to bring new interest to the space it has to sell. In two years, Max, 29, has become the nation's most prolific—some would say overexposed—American artist, with his swirly Day-Glo designs populating countless posters as well as a growing list of consumer products. In the process, Max has become one of the first hippie millionaires. Born in Berlin, raised in Shanghai, and schooled in Israel, he now lives in New York with his wife and their two children, Adam Cosmo and Libra Astra. A strict vegetarian, he studies weekly with his guru, Swami Satchidananda, a regime to which he credits inspiration for his art and philosophy. "Before I was searching for where I came from and where I was at," he recently told *Newsweek*. "Now I'm really dealing with the future and what makes it all revolve....It's cosmic art." His art has extended recently to the cosmos of bed linens, puzzles, stationery, belts, decals, and ashtrays, all of which bear Peter Max designs. Among his innovations is a series of numberless psychedelic children's clocks designed for General Electric. "I want people to get hung up on design, not time," he said recently. "What does '3:15 and time to go' mean to a kid? He'd rather say it's half past a daisy and quarter to a nose." As Max's designs become increasingly imitated, demand for his work will drop precipitously and he will soon slip into quiet but comfortable obscurity.

Max: Every picture tells a story.

Boys and Girls Together

APRIL 20, 1969. Princeton announces that it will join Yale by going coed in the fall. The news will spur a flood of applications by young women throughout the U.S. and more than a dozen foreign countries, both recent high school grads and transfers from other colleges. The pioneering first-year women will be but a drop in Princeton's bucket: 130 women among 3,250 men.

Oh, What a Night

MAY 9, 1969. More than 2,500 college youths invade the mining town of Zap, N.D., (pop. 300) for a Mother's Day "Zap-Out," part of a plan promoted by the North Dakota State University newspaper to turn Zap—with its two bars and one cafe—into "the Fort Lauderdale of the North." But what starts as a springtime put-on will turn into a nighttime terror, as students dismantle an abandoned building and start a bonfire, then smash windows, loot, and fight. The owner of the town's cafe, which rings up an impressive $150 in student business on Friday night will suffer $2,000 in damage on Saturday.

Armstrong: Fifth Avenue fete.

side Los Angeles by Wavy Gravy, a.k.a. Hugh Romney, now 33, once a therapist in a California State College program for neurologically handicapped children. Gravy arranged to take care of 33 acres of unfarmed property for an earth-moving contractor who had raised pigs in his spare time but could no longer afford the taxes. Within a year, Gravy had attracted 40 others to what became one of the many communes sprouting up throughout California in the mid-1960s. But sitting still wasn't enough for Gravy, whose previous incarnations include Greenwich Village beat poet and Ken Kesey Merry Prankster. Last year the Hog Farm purchased and renovated a school bus, departed the farm, and put the commune on wheels. Soon there were several Hog Farm buses, all based at a new farm in the outlands of New Mexico, but mostly on the road, doing good deeds—such as hauling away 200 tons of garbage in

Flashback
Diets

- Fasting
- Fruitarian
- Grapefruit
- Herbs and grains
- High-protein
- Juice fasting
- Junk food
- Lacto-ovo
- Lacto-vegetarian
- Low-carbohydrate
- Macrobiotic
- Meat and potatoes
- Organic
- Rice
- Scarsdale
- Stillman
- Vegetarian
- Water

Stepping Out

JULY 20, 1969. Climbing out of a four-legged lunar module near the arid Sea of Tranquility, Neil Armstrong becomes the first human to walk on the moon. His well-crafted first words—"That's one small step for man, one giant leap for mankind"—will be watched and heard live by some 600 million TV viewers around the world.

Helping Out

AUGUST 8, 1969. One hundred members of the Hog Farm commune arrive at the site of what in a week will be the Woodstock Music and Art Fair; they represent two-thirds of the 150-person security force that will seek to control the festival's estimated half-million attendees. The Hog Farm had been formed in 1966 in the San Gabriel Mountains out-

Communers: Wavy Gravy's babies.

Cincinnati, "just to help out." At Woodstock the group was flown in on a chartered 727 to help out once again. The Hog Farm will feed the hungry, heal the sick, and keep the peace. Gravy's peace-keeping strategy will be brilliant in its simplicity: made into a policeman for the occasion, he will deputize everyone; because everyone will be a peacekeeper, there will be no laws broken and no trouble with the law.

Charlie's Angels

AUGUST 10, 1969. Actress Sharon Tate Polanski, 26, is murdered at her Bel-Air, Calif., home, along with coffee heiress Abigail Folger, 25, her common-law husband, Wojiciech "Voytek" Frykowski, 32, Hollywood hair stylist Jay Sebring, 35, and delivery boy Steven Jay Parent. Later that day supermarket chain president Leno LaBianca, 44, and his 38-year-old wife Rosemary will be murdered in nearby Los Angeles. L.A. police will initially deny connections between the two multiple slayings, but both will soon be connected to Charles M. Manson, 32, and his hippie-cult family. Manson, an illegitimate child who has spent 17 years in prison, has had a long-time interest in Scientology, although he never joined the movement, and claims to have direct communications with cosmic forces, which he has interpreted as a battle plan for the coming apocalypse. During the 1967 Summer of Love, he recruited fellow drifters and San Francisco hippies, who became mesmerized by psychedelic drugs, sex, and Manson's satanic religion—leading to the ritualistic murders. In late 1970 a jury will find Manson and his "family" guilty of all seven murders.

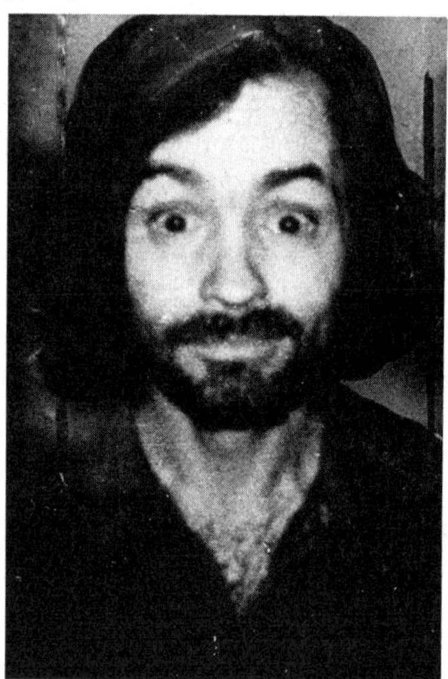

Manson: Family man.

Do You Believe in Magic?

OCTOBER 6, 1969. New York's "Miracle" Mets, a team that had once been the laughingstock of major league baseball for never finishing higher than ninth place, finishes its Cinderella season by beating the Baltimore Orioles 5-3 to win the World Series. With the exception of 25-game winner Tom Seaver, the Mets have no stars in their lineup, but still managed to win the National League East pennant and defeat the Atlanta Braves in the league's first year of divisional playoffs. The Mets lost the first game against the Orioles, then responded with three straight victories. In this, the fifth game, they fell behind 3-0, then tied the score on homers by Donn Clendenon, the eventual series MVP, and Al Weis, a light-hitting second baseman who has never before hit a homer at Shea Stadium. In the eighth inning, they will take the lead for good on back-to-back doubles by Cleon Jones and Ron Swoboda. After pitcher Jerry Koosman holds off the Orioles in the top of the ninth, the entire city of New York will believe in miracles—at least for a day.

Bitter Memory

NOVEMBER 24, 1969. Hershey discontinues its 5-cent chocolate bar, citing rises in chocolate and sugar prices. With this move, the Hershey Bar will set the pace for a steady rise in candy-bar prices, which will take a bite out of consumers' change purses by skyrocketing to 30 cents and higher within a decade.

Not-So-Super Bowl

JULY 23, 1970. Breakfast cereals come under fire as Robert B. Choate, Jr. testifies before a Senate subcommittee on the nutritional value of the $700 million-a-year dry cereal industry. Choate, a former Nixon administration hunger consultant, has ranked 60 cereals by their content of nine nutrients. Surprisingly, at the bottom of the heap are such childhood standbys as General Mills' Cheerios and Wheaties, Kellogg's Sugar Frosted Flakes, and Nabisco Shredded Wheat, all of which are said to provide "empty calories" and little else. The cereal industry, fearing that Choate will become the Ralph Nader of breakfast, refute his charges, but the day's impact will be felt from Checkerboard Square to Battle Creek and will inspire a trend toward improving morning nutrition.

Is Nothing Sacred?

APRIL 1, 1971. The Boy Scouts of America announce that the Explorer Scout Division, consisting of scouts aged 15 to 20, will begin to admit girls.

It Figures

AUGUST 20, 1971. Texas Instrument introduces the first pocket calculator. Priced at $149, it is intended to be a kind of executive toy but will have instant appeal to diverse consumers. Within a year more than 50 U.S. firms will manufacture pocket calculators, and prices will begin to drop to $60, with expectations that by next summer some cheaper models will plummet to as little as $35. One growing debate will be whether such devices are a tool or a crutch for students. Several universities will ban calculators for test-taking students.

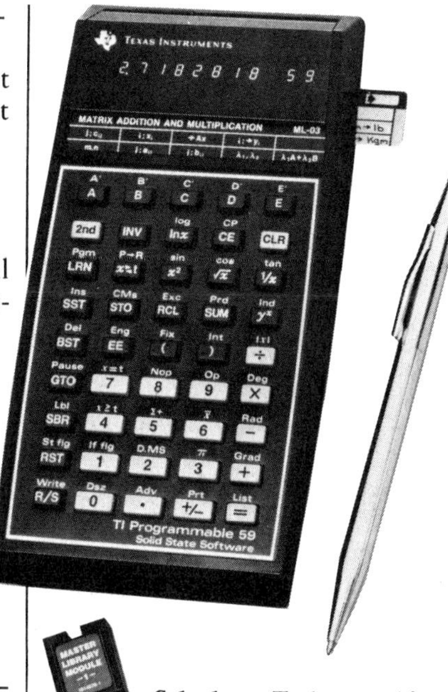

Calculator: Tool or crutch?

They Call Him the Wrapper

OCTOBER 16, 1971. A 400-foot-high, 1,250-foot-wide Day-Glo orange curtain is temporarily installed across Rifle Gap in remote western Colorado, the brainchild of artist Christo Javacheff, better known by his first name. It is the latest in a series of multimillion-dollar "wrapping" art projects by the 36-year-old Bulgarian-born artist. Over the past seven years, Christo has wrapped Chicago's Museum of Contemporary Art with 62 pieces of brown tarpaulin tied down with two miles of brown rope; wrapped the Bern, Switzerland, Kunsthalle as

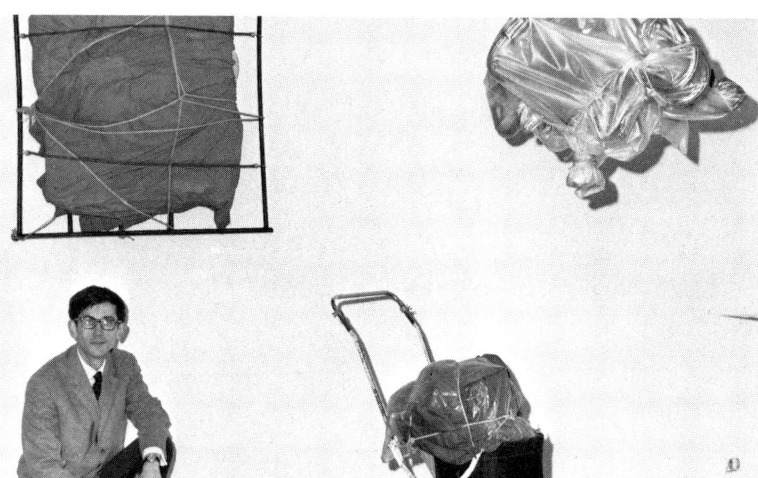

Christo: Bound for glory.

well as a medieval palace in Spoleto, Italy; wrapped a mile and a half of Australian seacoast; and built an "iron curtain" of 400 oil drums barricading a Paris street. Following the three-week exhibition of his Colorado "Valley Curtain," Christo will turn to his next project: an ambitious 100-mile-long "curtain" across the state of California.

Take the Money and Jump

NOVEMBER 24, 1971. A man with the presumably phony name of "D.B. Cooper" hijacks a Northwest Orient flight and parachutes from the jet somewhere between Seattle and Reno, carrying bags containing $200,000 in ransom money. Cooper, who will never be found, will become an instant legend. Over the next few months, hundreds of citizens will scour the landscape by foot, jeep, and air, looking for signs of the escapee. Only 72 hours after the skyjacking, a Portland manufacturer will have a T-shirt on the market asking "D.B. Cooper, where are you?" And by year-end, a record by a Seattle singer, "D.B. Cooper, Where Are You?" will be climbing the charts in California.

Games People Play

APRIL 28, 1972. *Life* magazine offers a special report on "The Marriage Experiments," a wide-ranging look at the changing institution of marriage. "From coast to coast," reports the magazine, "the ideas of women's liberation are convulsing families, and sometimes even leading wives... to ask for contracts in writing to make sure their husbands share the child-rearing and housework." Among other innovations, reports *Life*, are unmarried couples with children; collective marriages, in which several families under one roof share everything except sex; and the new interest in marriage counseling to save a growing wave of troubled relationships.

Flashback
Mindstyles

Arica
Astrology
Behavior modification
Bioenergetics
Biofeedback
Born Again Christians
Children of God
Church of Naturalism
Confucianism
Do'in
Encounter groups
Esalen
Est
Functional Integration
Gestalt therapy
Human potential movement
Hunger Project
Hypnotherapy
International Community of Christ
Jesus freaks
Jews for Jesus
Kinesiology
Krishna consciousness
Lao-tse
Lifespring
Living World Fellowship
Massage therapy
Mind Dynamics
Mind Expansion Training
More House
People's Temple
Primal therapy
Reality therapy
Reichian therapy
Rolfing
Satanism
Scientology
Sex therapy
Silva Mind Control
Synanon
Tarot
Transactional analysis
Transcendental Meditation
Unification Church
Universal Life Church
Yoga
Zen Buddhism

I'M FOR ME

$2 + 2 = 11_{three}$

Why 'The New Math' Didn't Add Up

Its very name inspired the inevitable question: what was wrong with The Old Math?

Plenty, it seemed. With their 1957 launch of Sputnik, the Soviets took an early lead in the space race and created a monumental public and government concern. Fueled by a flood of federal money The New Math sprang forth in response to the subsequent call for people trained in up-to-date science and mathematics to help the U.S. "beat" the Russians. The spread of automation also contributed. Everything from long-distance phone networks to ICBM guided missiles required complex calculations; so, too, did the programs that ran the new computing machines, capable of calculating "pi" to more than 3,000 decimal places in just minutes.

And so The New Math was born. Most widely used were materials of the School Mathematics Study Group, or SMSG, as it became known to a few million school kids in the early '60s. SMSG's approach taught theories of math at an early age, shunning mere memorization of arithmetic tables. Instead, there were *sets*—well-defined collections of like objects, or *members*. (For example, "the set whose members are all the commercial TV stations in Milwaukee.") Sets were enclosed in *curly brackets*. There were *subsets*, usually the *union* or *intersection* of two or more sets. All of this could be laid out in *Venn diagrams*, interlocking circles, in which unions and intersections could be identified through shading.

That was just for starters. There were *whole numbers* upon which *operations* could be made; *ordered pairs*; and *properties*—*closure*, *commutative*, *associative*, and *distributive* (as in "the distributive property of multiplication over addition").

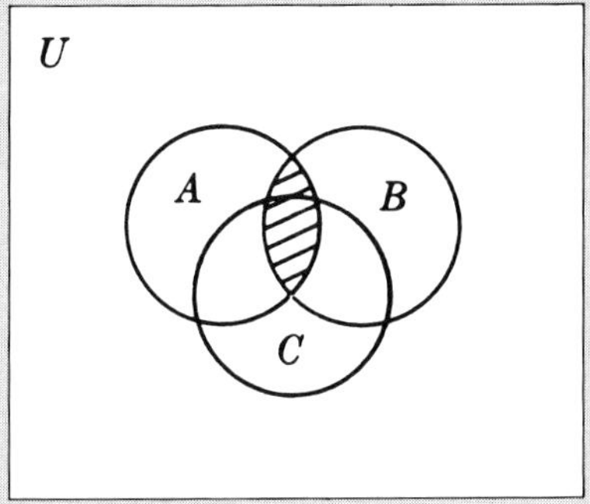

And then there were *bases*. Our everyday decimal system—using the 10 digits "0" through "9"—was dubbed "base 10." There were also "base two," "base three," and practically any other base you could name. Bases had no practical use of their own. As the SMSG folks explained in a 1961 introductory manual for parents: "Since, in using a new base, the pupil must necessarily look at the reasons for 'carrying' and the other mechanical procedures in a new light, he should gain deeper insight into the decimal system."

But The New Math turned out to be somewhat off base. In fact, reports a history published by the National Council of Teachers of Mathematics, "New math is generally perceived as being the cause of a decline in test scores in the late 1960s and through the 1970s." Among other things, mean math scores on Scholastic Aptitude Tests—used by most colleges to set admission requirements—decreased more than 30 points between 1960 and 1980. Another study found a trade-off: SMSG students had slightly lower arithmetic skills, but performed better in comprehension, analysis, and application. Another study found that SMSG helped those good in math to do better, but left slower students behind.

The resulting rebellion in the early 1970s brought back The Old Math with a new name: "Back to Basics," a program emphasizing addition, subtraction, multiplication, and division, using pencils on paper.

$A =$ { } $B =$ { }

$A \cup B =$ { }

Spitz: Golden boy.

Splish, Splash

SEPTEMBER 4, 1972. Mark Spitz, 22, turns a tight 400-meter medley relay into a U.S. victory and wins his seventh gold medal of the Olympic Games in Munich. Spitz' feat is made even more amazing by the fact that he has set world records in four individual events; the three gold-medal relay teams on which has swum also set records. After the games, Spitz, a tall, dark, and handsome Californian, will become even better known for a hot-selling poster of him clad in his sleek red, white, and blue swimsuit and his seven gold medals.

Supreme Decision

JANUARY 23, 1973. The Supreme Court delivers an historic ruling that strikes down nearly every antiabortion law in the country. Such laws, a majority of justices rule, represent an unconstitutional invasion of privacy that interferes with a woman's right to control her own body. The decision, upholding a challenge to Georgia's restrictive abortion law, will permit states to impose only minimal curbs on the right of women to seek abortion on demand. The Court's decision will be hailed by "pro-choice" advocates and January 23, the anniversary of the *Roe v. Wade* decision, will for years be an annual day of demonstrations for both "pro-choice" and "pro-life" groups.

Abortion activists: Whose rights are right?

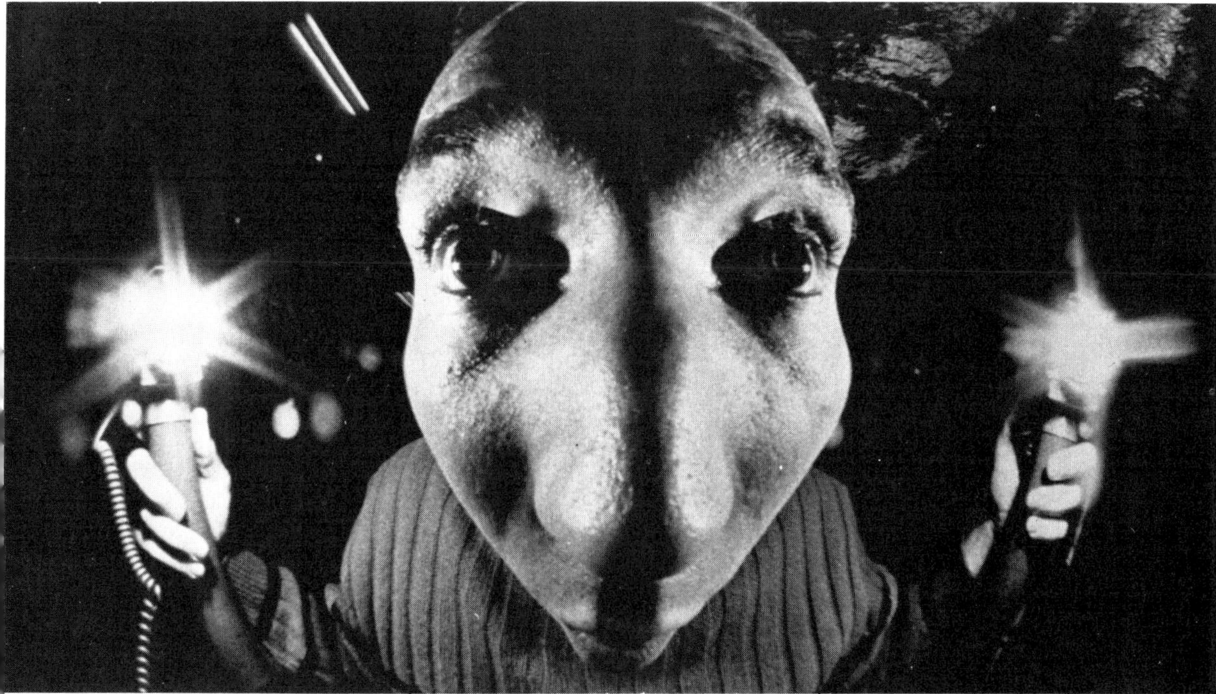

Pong pro: Tube tied.

Hot Seat

MAY 21, 1973. The Supreme Court rules that a young man convicted for wearing an American flag sewn to the seat of his pants was improperly charged under a 70-year-old Massachusetts criminal statute against anyone who "publicly...treats contemptuously" the U.S. flag. The justices say such laws are too vague.

Ride Your Pony

JUNE 9, 1973. Secretariat becomes the first horse to win the Triple Crown since Citation in 1948, by racing to an incredible 31-length victory in the Belmont Stakes. Jockey Ron Turcotte has ridden the steed to a track record, just as he had in the Kentucky Derby a few weeks earlier; an attempt for a record in the Preakness fell only two seconds short. By the time he retires at year's end, Secretariat will have winnings totaling more than $1.3 million, a sum that will be more than quadrupled in subsequent stud fees.

Turning On the Juice

DECEMBER 16, 1973. Running through the mud at Shea Stadium, the Buffalo Bills' O.J. Simpson gains more than 200 yards for the second game in a row, becoming the first National Football League back to gain 2,000 yards rushing in a single season. In doing so, he breaks Jim Brown's 10-year-old record of 1,863 yards. Simpson's record will stand for 11 years before being broken by Los Angeles Ram Eric Dickerson in 1984.

King Pong

DECEMBER 17, 1973. Pong has swept the nation, according to several media reports. The game, an electronic version of ping-pong, was created last year by computer engineer Nolan K. Bushnell, 29, under his new company, Atari. Three years out of the University of Utah, Bushnell founded Atari's forerunner, Syzygy Co., in 1971 with $250 in savings. To generate cash flow while he developed Pong, he leased

> *"Making bucks with computers in the '80s has become a viable replacement for making psychedelic waves in the '60s."*
>
> **Steven Levy, computer writer**

pinball machines from other manufacturers, which brought in $1,000 a month. When Atari (the name is a Japanese expression of warning) began marketing its new game, sales skyrocketed, with sales now reaching $1 million a month despite a instant rash of Pong imitators. Pong will whet Americans' appetites for increasingly sophisticated video games, opening the market for games played on personal computers. But Atari will soon lose almost everything in an attempt to develop a race-car game called Trak 10; it will be saved by Warner Communications, which will purchase Atari in 1976 for $28 million, netting its founder a cool $15 million. Bushnell will go on to other ventures such as Androbot, a "personal" robot; Chuck E. Cheese Pizza Time Theatres, a chain of pizza parlors featuring video games; and "Catster," one of a series of microprocessor-controlled robot "pets."

Where the Auction Is

DECEMBER 23, 1973. A federal arbitrator rules against major league baseball's reserve clause, giving birth to the era of high-priced "free agents." Specifically, the arbitrator has ruled that two pitchers, Dodger Andy Messersmith and Expo Dave McNally, are free to negotiate with the teams of their choice because their teams had allowed them to play a full season without signing them to contracts. The collapse of the reserve clause—which had bound a player to one team unless he was traded, released, or retired—will enable players to sell their services to the highest bidder, setting the stage for a wave of multi-million-dollar contracts.

Streaker: Stripped-down model.

That Was the Streak That Was

MARCH 19, 1974. Two men, yelling "Impeach Nixon!" run naked down Pennsylvania Avenue past the White House, the latest in the national "streaking" fad. Begun on college campuses, it has spread to every corner of the country, even to Europe. In coming weeks two male streakers will collide while running through a fashionable Detroit restaurant; a Los Angeles radio station will broadcast "streaker alerts" to warn when naked youths are on the loose; a young man will streak a New York Yankees game; and a young man will streak the Academy Awards just before Elizabeth Taylor mounts the stage to present the best actor award (Taylor will describe it as a "hard act to follow").

We've Got Your Number

MARCH 28, 1974. Singer Ike Turner is arrested at a Los Angeles recording studio and booked on charges of using a

Phone phreaks: No-Bell laureates.

"blue box" to make thousands of dollars of long-distance telephone calls without paying for them. Turner's arrest is among the most famous, but by no means the first. For years law enforcement officials have been stymied by a growing corps of "phone phreaks" who use homemade electronic gadgets to foil long-distance phone networks, thereby making phone calls internationally for free. "Phreaking" is largely the creation of Joe Engressia, a blind teenager with perfect pitch who learned how to whistle into the phone, imitating the electronic tones used when making long-distance calls. Another phreak, John Draper, discovered that the toy whistles that came in boxes of Cap'n Crunch breakfast cereal generated a perfect 2600-cycles-per-second tone, enabling users to break into long-distance lines and use them without detection. Officials at American Telephone and Telegraph Company have begun random checks to detect illegal long-distance usage; early next year AT&T will reveal that it monitored nearly two million long-distance calls between 1966 and 1970 in search of phone phreaks, resulting in hundreds of arrests and convictions. Among its victims will be former TV star Bob Cummings, who will be arrested with a blue box at his Los Angeles apartment late next year. (Ike Turner, meanwhile, will get off on a technicality.) By the late 1970s most phone phreaks will have tired of their wizardry, moving on to computer trickery that will become known as "hacking."

Brave New Record

APRIL 8, 1974. Facing Los Angeles Dodger's pitcher Al Downing, 40-year-old Hank Aaron knocks a fly ball over the left-field wall in Atlanta and shatters Babe Ruth's career record of 714 home runs. It takes Aaron 11,295 at-bats to break the record, compared to Ruth's 8,399. Aaron had tied Ruth four days earlier by homering on his first at-bat of the season against Cincinnati, although it wouldn't have happened had the Braves' management had its way. Recognizing the promotional value of having Aaron break the record at home in Atlanta, Braves' management wanted him to sit out the season's first three games. But baseball commissioner Bowie Kuhn interceded, ordering the team to use Aaron "in accordance with the pattern of his use in 1973, when he started approximately two of every three Braves' games."

Aaron: Bringing it all back home.

Memories Are Made of This

DECEMBER 19, 1974. The January issue of *Popular Electronics* hits the streets, complete with a story about the Altair "minicomputer kit." The Altair, the world's first personal computer, is the brainchild of Ed Roberts, an electronics tinkerer in Albuquerque, who turned to computers after designing a commercial $169 calculator in 1971; at the time, comparable devices cost around $500. Sales of the new computer will take off with the *Popular Electronics* publicity. The article—entitled "Project Breakthrough! World's First Minicomputer Kit to Rival Commercial Models...ALTAIR 8800"—will send hobbyists scrambling for the $397 machine. It contains 256 bytes of memory—1/4 kilobyte. One problem will be a lack of applications software for the new computer. Help will come from teenagers Bill Gates and Paul Allen, who will create a version of the BASIC programming language for Roberts; Gates and Allen will later form Microsoft, which will grow into a multi-million-dollar computer software company. Roberts' firm will sell $1 million worth of Altairs in 1975; when he sells the company in 1977, its annual sales will be $20 million.

A New Life

FEBRUARY 27, 1975. After four days of debate, 140 scientists gathered in a rustic church in Asilomar, Calif., come to an historic consensus on how to regulate their own work in the new and potentially hazardous field of genetic engineering. They have determined that research using "recombinant DNA" technology—the ability to cut and splice bits of genetic material from different organisms in combinations not found in nature—should go forward, but only under strict new safety guidelines. The meeting will later be hailed as a model of scientific self-regulation, although the research will become increasingly controversial, as some protest genetic engineering's role in furthering germ warfare and others question whether adequate precautions have been taken in creating new life forms.

Net Winnings

JULY 4, 1975. The reigning queen of tennis, Billie Jean King, celebrates the nation's 199th birthday by beating Evonne Goolagong Cawley in only 40 minutes to win her sixth straight Wimbledon singles title. It is her 19th Wimbledon title overall, making King the most prolific winner in the tournament's long history.

Come Together

JULY 15, 1975. In the first cooperative space mission, Apollo and Soyuz spacecraft take off for a joint U.S.-Soviet space mission. It is the first time that a Soviet liftoff has been televised. In two days, the two space capsules will link up about 140 miles above the Atlantic Ocean.

King: Wimbledon winner.

Ring of Fire

OCTOBER 1, 1975. In a brutal match fought outdoors before a huge crowd, Muhammad Ali wins the "Thrilla in Manila" when Joe Frazier's manager throws in the towel before the start of the 15th round. Frazier, who before the fight had said of Ali, "I want him like a hog wants slop," will protest violently, but will later agree that his manager made the right decision. After manhandling Ali in the middle rounds, Frazier had taken a beating and could barely see when he came to his corner at the end of Round 14. It has been the most grueling of the three fights between the two boxers—they had split the other two—and afterward, Ali will admit to reporters, "It was the closest thing to dyin' I know of."

Please, Mr. Postman

DECEMBER 31, 1975. First-class postage rises from 10 cents to 13 cents.

NEW • ASSASSINATIONS • BAY OF PIGS • THE BERRIGANS • BLAC
MBODIA • STOKELY CARMICHAEL • CASTRO • CHAPPAQUIDDICK
VEN • THE COLD WAR • ANGELA DAVIS • THE DRAFT • EARTH DAY
SENHOWER • ERA • SAM ERVIN • MEDGAR EVERS • FALLOUT SHELT
ORKERS • FEMINISTS • THE FREE SPEECH MOVEMENT • GOLDWAT
REAT SOCIETY • TOM HAYDEN • PATTY HEARST • ABBIE HOFFMAN
KENNEDY • KENT STATE • KHRUSHCHEV • MARTIN LUTHER KING •
AST • MY LAI • NADER • NIXON • OPEC • PEACE CORPS • THE PENT
APERS • PEOPLE'S PARK • PLUMBERS • POOR PEOPLE'S CAMPAIG
UBIN • SDS • BOBBY SEALE • KAREN SILKWOOD • SIT-INS • SNCC • T
T OFFENSIVE • GEORGE WALLACE • WATERGATE • WATTS • MALC
PPIES • AGNEW • ASSASSINATIONS • BAY OF PIGS • THE BERRIGA
OWER • CAMBODIA • STOKELY CARMICHAEL • CASTRO • CHAPPAQ
HICAGO SEVEN • THE COLD WAR • ANGELA DAVIS • THE DRAFT • E
SENHOWER • ERA • SAM ERVIN • MEDGAR EVERS • FALLOUT SHELT
ORKERS • FEMINISTS • THE FREE SPEECH MOVEMENT • GOLDWAT
REAT SOCIETY • TOM HAYDEN • PATTY HEARST • ABBIE HOFFMAN
KENNEDY • KENT STATE • KHRUSHCHEV • MARTIN LUTHER KING •
AST • MY LAI • NADER • NIXON • OPEC • PEACE CORPS • • THE PE
GNEW • ASSASSINATIONS • BAY OF PIGS • THE BERRIGANS • BLAC
AMBODIA • STOKELY CARMICHAEL • CASTRO • CHAPPAQUIDDICK
VEN • THE COLD WAR • ANGELA DAVIS • THE DRAFT • EARTH DA
SENHOWER • ERA • SAM ERVIN • MEDGAR EVERS • FALLOUT SHELT
ORKERS • FEMINISTS • THE FREE SPEECH MOVEMENT • GOLDWA
REAT SOCIETY • TOM HAYDEN • PATTY HEARST • ABBIE HOFFMAN
KENNEDY • KENT STATE • KHRUSHCHEV • MARTIN LUTHER KING •
ST • MY LAI • NADER • NIXON • OPEC • PEACE CORPS • THE PEN
PERS • PEOPLE'S PARK • PLUMBERS • POOR PEOPLE'S CAMPAI
BIN • SDS • BOBBY SEALE • KAREN SILKWOOD • SIT-INS • SNCC •
T OFFENSIVE • GEORGE WALLACE • WATERGATE • WATTS • MAL

BOOM! POLITICS

Gonna Take a Miracle

MAY 12, 1955. Secretary of State John Foster Dulles tells a background press conference that "The only government that can succeed [in Vietnam] is a government which is independent of foreign controls and which is really operating on a national basis." But only months earlier, training of the South Vietnamese army—fighting for the hearts and minds of a public besieged by the Communists to the north and revolutionaries from within—passed from the hands of the French to the Americans. By 1960 American aid to train South Vietnam's army will approach $300 million a year and the number of American "advisers" in Vietnam will swell to more than 4,000, and to 16,000 by the end of 1963.

Peoples' Parks

NOVEMBER 7, 1955. The Supreme Court rules that segregation of public parks, golf courses, and playgrounds is illegal, in a decision based on the landmark 1954 case, *Brown v. Board of Education*. That case concluded that "in the field of public education, the doctrine of 'separate but equal' has no place," making it illegal for schools to have separate classrooms for blacks and whites. *Brown v. Board of Education* will be cited increasingly in civil rights court cases.

The Bus Stops Here

DECEMBER 1, 1955. Mrs. Rosa Parks, a department store seamstress, refuses to move to the back of a Montgomery, Ala., bus when ordered to do so by the driver. Parks is not seated in any of the 10 spaces in the front of the bus reserved for whites, but is in the first unreserved section. Her refusal will lead to her arrest, followed by a trial four days later. That day, December 5, will mark the beginning of a lengthy black boycott of the Montgomery bus system, organized by Dr. Martin Luther King, Jr., president of the Montgomery Improvement Association. To the surprise of many, Montgomery's buses will travel empty, because blacks comprise about three-fourths of their riders. In coming months King will organize an efficient alternative transportation system, using more than 300 private cars, picking up and dropping off passengers from early morning through late evening. The $5,000-a-week cost will be covered through contributions from the community and, as word spreads, from throughout the world. In April King and 89 others will be arrested under a 1921 Alabama statute that makes it a misdemeanor for anyone to hinder lawful business without "just cause or legal excuse." He will be found guilty and fined, but the boycott will continue through the summer and into the fall.

Protesters: Separate, unequal.

United We Stand

DECEMBER 5, 1955. The American Federation of Labor and the Congress for Industrial Organizations merge to form the AFL-CIO after 20 years of discord between the two labor organizations. The combined organization will become the leading voice of American trade unionism. Its first battle will be the perceived antiunion policies of the Eisenhower administration.

Close Enough for Government Work

MAY 21, 1956. Taking elaborate precautions to "limit significant radioactive fallout," the first atmospheric hydrogen

bomb tests take place over the Bikini Islands in the South Pacific. In the first test, a B-52 will drop a bomb from 15,000 feet. The resulting flash reportedly will be equal to 500 suns, creating a four-mile-diameter fireball, although the bomb will miss its target by about four miles because of human error.

Truckin'

JUNE 29, 1956. Congress passes the Federal Aid Highway Act, authorizing construction of a 43,000-mile network of interstate highways linking major American cities, scheduled for completion in 1972. Under the act, the federal government will pick up 90 percent of the projected $33.5 billion price tag, although the system will cost the federal government almost three times that amount before completion. The act will indirectly subsidize intercity bus lines and trucking companies, among others, while abandoning passenger and freight railroad systems. The system's target completion date will prove unreachable, although 90 percent will be completed by the end of 1976.

Ike liker: Visions of the future.

We Like Ike

NOVEMBER 6, 1956. President Eisenhower wins re-election against Democrat Adlai Stevenson. The popular incumbent President wins 57 percent of the vote despite Stevenson's warnings that "Ike's" illness could lead to his death while in office, resulting in his being succeeded by controversial vice president Richard M. Nixon.

Fightin' Words

NOVEMBER 17, 1956. "History is on our side. We will bury you!" says Nikita Khrushchev to Western ambassadors at a reception at the Kremlin.

Red Scare

JANUARY 5, 1957. President Eisenhower asks a joint session of Congress to authorize him to use U.S. armed forces against "any Communist or Communist-dominated aggressor" in the Mideast area. In his first speech to Congress since his re-election, he promises to use this authority only if American troops are requested by nations under armed attack, only in "hour-by-hour" contact with Congress, and only in keeping with U.S. treaty obligations. But Eisenhower's promises are vague; he doesn't define "the Mideast area," for example, or state exactly when he will consult Congress. The "Eisenhower Doctrine," as it will be called, is markedly different from his campaign statements and will meet with objections from several congressmen, most notably Arizona's Sen. Barry Goldwater.

Yakity Yak

SEPTEMBER 9, 1957. A U.S. Civil Rights Commission is created through the first civil rights law since Civil War Reconstruction. The new commission, intended to end voting rights abuses, has been passed despite vehement opposition by southern legislators led by South Carolina's Sen. Strom Thurmond, who two weeks ago spoke against the bill on the Senate floor for more than 24 hours to set a new filibuster record. (That record will be broken in 1960, however, as senators filibuster for just over 82 hours against another voting rights bill. Both records will be eclipsed by a 75-day filibuster conducted to oppose what will become the Civil Rights Act of 1964.)

No Class

SEPTEMBER 24, 1957. President Eisenhower sends federal troops to Little Rock, Ark., to quell jeering mobs when school officials try to implement the Supreme Court's *Brown v. Board of Education* ruling by permitting nine black children to attend Little Rock's Central High School. Arkansas governor Orval Faubus

Little Rock: Class action.

is at the forefront of the protestors, but their efforts will fail, as troops restore order and allow the children to attend classes. Another year will pass, however, before all the legal wrinkles are ironed out when the Supreme Court meets in a special session to order that Little Rock must carry out the integration.

Deja Vu

JULY 15, 1958. Responding to an appeal by Lebanon's President Camille Chamoun, President Eisenhower orders 5,000 U.S. Marines and supporting air and sea power into Lebanon "to protect American lives" and to help the Lebanese government "defend its sovereignty and independence." Chamoun has feared being overthrown as a result of outside interference from Egyptian and Syrian governments, trying to settle long-term fighting between Druse and Phalangist factions—fights that will continue for more than a quarter-century. With Eisenhower's announcement, United Nations ambassador Henry Cabot Lodge will tell a Security Council meeting that the Marines will remain in Lebanon only as long as necessary to ensure that country's "continued independence." In a move that will be replayed with eerie accuracy more than two decades later, the Marines' first actions will be to occupy Beirut International Airport.

He's a Rebel

JANUARY 1, 1959. Fidel Castro, 32, achieves a long-fought victory by forcing Cuban dictator

Castro: Marx brother.

Fulgencio Batista and his supporters to flee the country, taking over the reins of government himself. Castro has been stirring up trouble in the Caribbean for years. At age 13, he organized a labor strike against his own wealthy father's sugar-cane plantation, asserting that the land belonged to the people. In 1947, he took part in a failed Cuban guerrilla mission aimed at toppling the government of the Dominican Republic. A year later he was involved in bloody antigovernment riots in Bogota, Colombia. Although Castro's revolution has held out the promise of a Marxist government, his supporters have included few known Communists, and his takeover will initially offer hope to the U.S. government, which last year halted arms shipments to Batista. But U.S. hopes will be crushed in two years when Castro will declare, "I am a Marxist-Leninist and will be a Marxist-Leninist until the day I die." Castro will then strengthen Cuba's ties with the Soviets, a move that will cause grave concern in Washington.

There's Something in the Air

JUNE 29, 1959. A new wave of "fallout scares" is sweeping the nation, reports *U.S. News and World Report.* The scares result largely from a lack of understanding of strontium-90, the radioactive element of fallout that settles in the soil and is passed along through the food chain. The misunderstanding is fueled by rumors, inaccurate press accounts, and general public panic. Other scares have stemmed from accounts of serious "fallouts" in such places as Belle Fourche, S.D. from A-bomb tests in Nevada during the summer of 1957. Two fallouts, occurring during rains, led to persistent radiation in Belle Fourche; on one occasion, the mayor ordered the streets hosed down. In another instance, 12 loaves of white bread purchased in New York City had a strontium-90 content four times that considered "safe" by scientists; similarly, whole-wheat flour milled in Broadview, Ill., exceeded the standards by sixfold.

Just the Two of Us

JULY 24, 1959. Vice President Richard Nixon meets with Soviet Premier Nikita Khrushchev in Moscow. The two men visit the United States National Exhibition in Moscow and wander into the kitchen of a model American house. There, the two leaders embark on a well-meaning, well-publicized argument about U.S.-Soviet relations. Khrushchev begins the exchange by referring to the shiny kitchen's new gadgets, claiming that "all our new houses have this kind of equipment." The conversation will go from household gadgets to military gadgets to references to Khrushchev's threat to place West Berlin under Communist control. Khrushchev waves a finger in Nixon's face and says, "If you want to threaten, we will answer threat with threat." Nixon replies: "We never engage in threats." The exchange continues. Khrushchev: "You wanted indirectly to threaten me. But we have means at our disposal that can have very bad consequences." Nixon: "We have too." Khrushchev's tone becomes friendlier: "We want peace with all other nations, especially America." Nixon, also relaxing: "We also want peace." Nixon then makes a reference to Soviet Foreign Minister Andrei Gromyko, "who looks like me but is better looking." Khrushchev replies, "Only outwardly," at which point the two men wander out of the kitchen, talking amicably. As a result of the exchange, Nixon's rating will skyrocket in Gallup polls, and the number of Americans favoring a U.S.-Soviet summit meeting also will increase. In early August President Eisenhower and Premier Khrushchev will announce reciprocal visits, to be opened by Khrushchev's visit to America in September.

Eisenhower, Khrushchev: Skipping Mickey.

You're an Honorary Mouseketeer

SEPTEMBER 15, 1959. Soviet Premier Khrushchev arrives in the U.S. only hours after Soviet scientists hit the moon with a missile that includes a Soviet hammer and sickle, which are implanted near the Sea of Tranquility. After being greeted by President Eisenhower, Khrushchev makes his first stop in California, where he hopes to visit Disneyland but is rebuffed for security reasons, to his extreme disappointment. Following visits to Los Angeles, San Francisco, and Des Moines (where he will consume his first hot dog), he will retreat with Eisenhower to Camp David, where the two leaders will talk for three days. Among other things, Khrushchev will decide during those three days to withdraw his threat about Berlin.

What If?

JANUARY 18, 1960. A joint congressional Committee on Atomic Energy releases a report detailing the probable effects of a surprise nuclear attack on the U.S. Assuming that the targets—the 71 largest cities, 21 atomic installations, and 132 key military installations—were hit by at least one nuclear weapon, the attack, says the committee, would endanger about half of all Americans directly, killing 50 million and seriously injuring 20 million more. The Northeast would be hardest hit: six million would die in New York; Boston would lose 75 percent of its population and Baltimore 80 percent. The safest place to be, says the report: Oregon, outside Portland. Next safest: the Dakotas.

Civil Defense: What to do if attacked.

In the Midnight Hour

Nothing may better symbolize the concern that has enveloped the past four decades than "The Doomsday Clock." Created in 1947, as the ashes from nuclear bombs dropped at Hiroshima and Nagasaki were still cooling, the clock is the brainchild of the *Bulletin of the Atomic Scientists*, a Chicago-based community of scholars dedicated to keeping the world acutely aware of the horrors of nuclear war.

In June 1947, the clock was set at seven minutes to midnight, the "zero hour" at which nuclear war is imminent. The clock "is intended to reflect basic changes in the level of continuous danger in which mankind lives in the nuclear age," says the *Bulletin's* co-founder. As world events dictate, the minute hand is moved. And it has moved several times, often coming within two minutes of the witching hour.

1947: Seven minutes to midnight. The clock first appears.

1949: Three minutes to midnight. The Soviet Union explodes its first atomic bomb.

1953: Two minutes to midnight. The U.S. and Soviet Union develop hydrogen bombs.

1963: Twelve minutes to midnight. The U.S. and Soviet Union sign the Partial Test Ban Treaty.

1968: Seven minutes to midnight. The nuclear "club" now includes France, China, Britain, the U.S., and the Soviet Union.

1972: Twelve minutes to midnight. Strategic Arms Limitations Talks (SALT) lead to a nuclear-arms agreement between the U.S. and U.S.S.R.

1974: Nine minutes to midnight. SALT reaches an impasse; India joins the nuclear "club."

1984: Three minutes to midnight. The arms race intensifies; arms control negotiations deadlock.

Walk Right In, Sit Right Down

FEBRUARY 1, 1960. In defiance of store policy, four black freshmen at A&T College sit down at a Woolworth's luncheon counter in downtown Greensboro, N.C. Over the next few weeks, the "sit-in," as the event will be called, will become a popular vehicle for civil rights activists, spreading to 15 cities in five Southern states over the next two weeks alone. Within a year some 50,000 Americans will have participated in sit-ins or other civil rights demonstrations in 100 cities, with more than 3,600 of them spending time in jail. In March, for example, police will arrest more than 350 students at lunch counter sit-ins in Orangeburg, S.C. Greensboro's lunch counters will be desegregated in July; by the end of next year, desegregation of several hundred additional lunch counters will follow.

Birth of a Notion

APRIL 14, 1960. The Student Non-violent Co-ordinating Committee (SNCC) is founded at a conference of sit-in leaders organized by the Southern Christian Leadership Conference (SCLC) in Raleigh, N.C. SNCC was created in part to satisfy the desire of young blacks to have their own organization, rather than fit into such existing "establishment" groups as SCLC and the Congress on Racial Equality (CORE). SCLC agreed, and will allocate SNCC a corner of its offices for the first few months. By the end of the Raleigh conference, SNCC organizers will have created their first statement of purpose, affirming "the philosophical or religious ideal of nonviolence as the foundation of our purpose...and the manner of our action." In coming months SNCC will be a spawning ground for new ideas and ideologies, many of which will filter—agonizingly slowly, for many SNCC leaders—into SCLC, CORE, and the various ad hoc organizations that will sprout for a time as the civil rights movement fluorishes. But even SNCC will face charges of discrimination—by its women members, who in 1964 will draft a paper charging that women are being given the same token status within the civil rights movement that blacks have been given in society at large. The paper will call for the "slow process of changing values and ideas so that all of us gradually come to understand that this is no more a man's world than it is a white world." SNCC leader Stokely Carmichael will ridicule the effort, responding that "The only position for women in SNCC is prone."

Jesse Jackson:
Are women minorities?

Powers Struggle

MAY 1, 1960. Soviet ground-to-air missiles shoot down American Francis Gary Powers, 30, flying at 60,000 feet in a U-2 supersonic spy plane. Powers, a CIA agent, was part of a Turkey-based group keeping tabs on the Soviet Union, Israel, Egypt, and Saudi Arabia. Powers is forced to parachute out of his plane and lands in a farm in the heart of Siberia. His airplane, with highly sophisticated electronic spying equipment, falls into Russian hands. Later this year Powers will be tried by his captors for espionage and sentenced to 10 years in Soviet prison, although he will be released in February 1962, in a Soviet-American spy exchange. The incident will cause Soviet Premier Khrushchev to cancel a summit conference with President Eisenhower. Powers, meanwhile, will die in a 1977 helicopter crash while working for a Los Angeles TV station.

There's a Riot Goin' On

MAY 13, 1960. Four hundred San Francisco police battle 200 student protesters outside House UnAmerican Activities Committee hearings into alleged Communist activities in northern California. The protesters claim they have been intentionally excluded from an ostensibly open hearing; they claim HUAC has packed the hearing chamber with members of right-wing groups such as Daughters of the American Revolution. While demonstraters sing "The Star-Spangled Banner," police will use nightsticks and fire hoses to disperse the crowd, and four students and eight police will suffer injuries (one policeman will be beaten with his own nightstick). More than 50 protesters will be arrested.

Kennedy, Nixon: JFK wins, no sweat.

Stand-off

JUNE 23, 1960. President Castro threatens to seize all American-owned property in Cuba in response to "economic aggression," a cutback in American imports of Cuban sugar—even though Cuba already has signed an agreement to sell the Soviet Union five million tons of sugar. Over the next few weeks the war of words will escalate, as President Eisenhower declares that the U.S. will never permit a government "dominated by international communism" to exist in the Western Hemisphere. Premier Khrushchev will respond with a threat to use Russian rockets to protect Cuba from American military intervention. By October Castro will have nationalized all Cuban banks and large commercial enterprises, including several U.S. oil refineries, forcing Eisenhower to impose an embargo on most exports to Cuba.

The Omen

SEPTEMBER 14, 1960. The Organization of Petroleum Exporting Countries (OPEC)—composed of charter members Saudi Arabia, Iran, Iraq, Kuwait, and Qatar—meets for the first time in Baghdad. Among its first items of business is to force Standard Oil of New Jersey to rescind its recent 14 cent rollback in the price of a barrel of oil.

You Say Yes, I Say No

SEPTEMBER 26, 1960. The first of four Kennedy-Nixon debates takes place in Chicago. Carried as a public service by all three TV networks and four radio networks, it attracts 60 million viewers, the largest audience ever for a single TV program. With Howard

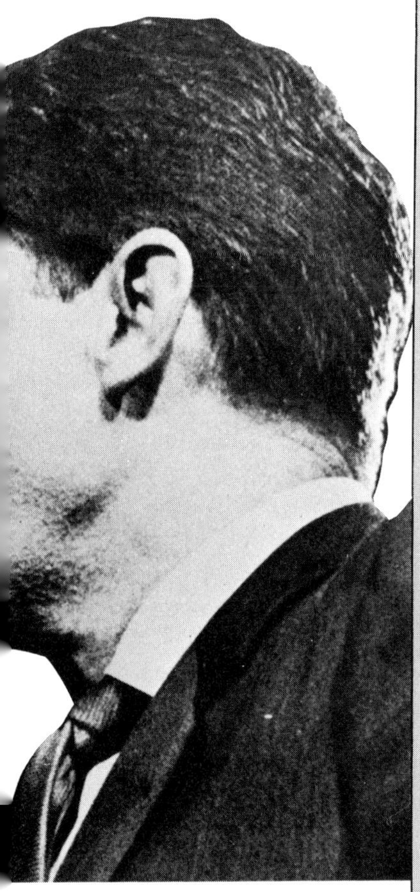

K. Smith of CBS serving as moderator, this exchange covers only domestic matters. Both candidates will demonstrate their ability to answer questions in a debate that is essentially issueless; it is their televised images that will make the big difference in this and subsequent debates. Nixon will come across poorly, looking tired and ill at ease. He had recently lost weight and his shirt appears to be too large. And he passed up a professional make-up job in favor of a dime-store Max Factor "Lazy Shave" treatment to cover up his five o'clock shadow. The telegenic Kennedy, on the

Is There a Boomer in the House?

Baby boomers began invading the halls of Congress in 1974, when four were elected to the House of Representatives. The first two boomers in the Senate, both Republicans, were elected in 1980. All told, 72 Americans born since the beginning of 1946 have become elected national officials in Washington. Thirty past or present members of Congress were born during the 1950s:

Name and Affiliation	Year Born	Year First Elected
John Wiley Bryant (D-Tex.)	1952	1982
James H.S. Cooper (D-Tenn.)	1954	1982
Michael Dewine (R-Oh.)	1952	1982
David T. Dreier (R-Calif.)	1952	1980
Dennis E. Eckart (D-Oh.)	1950	1980
Lane Evans (D-Ill.)	1951	1982
Jack M. Fields (R-Tex.)	1952	1980
Steve Craig Gunderson (R-Wisc.	1951	1980
John Patrick Hiler (R-Ind.)	1953	1980
John R. Kasich (R-Oh.)	1952	1982
Bob McEwen (R-Oh.)	1950	1980
John R. McKernan (R-Me.)	1950	1980
Donald L. Nickles (R-N.J.)	1953	1980*
Timothy J. Penny (D-Minn.)	1951	1982
Carl Perkins (D-Ky.)	1954	1984
John G. Rowland (R-Conn.)	1957	1984
Claudine Schneider (R-R.I.)	1947	1980
Bill Schuette (R-Mich.)	1953	1984
Charles E. Schumer (D-N.Y.)	1951	1982
James W. Shannon (D-Mass.)	1952	1978
Mark D. Siljander (R-Mich.)	1951	1980
Christopher H. Smith (R-N.J.)	1953	1980
Harley O. Staggers, Jr. (D-W.Va.)	1951	1982
Mac Sweeney (R-Tex.)	1955	1984
Michael L. Synar (D-Okla.)	1950	1978
Patrick L. Swindall (R-Ga.)	1950	1984
Thomas J. Tauke (R-Ia.)	1950	1978
Robert G. Toricelli (D-N.J.)	1951	1982
Vin Weber (R-Minn.)	1952	1980
Allan D. Wheat (D-Mo.)	1951	1982

* Elected to Senate.

other hand, will appear calm and professional. The debate's radio listeners will prove the power of the TV medium in politics: although TV viewers will give Kennedy the edge overwhelmingly, radio listeners will judge the debate a draw.

Sole Brother

OCTOBER 12, 1960. The U.N.'s 15th anniversary session is adjourned in pandemonium after Premier Khrushchev pounds his shoe on the table. The international body had just heard the Soviet leader deliver a speech denouncing colonialism. When Philippine delegate Lorenzo Sumulong responded that Eastern Europe was "deprived of political and civil rights" and had been "swallowed up by the Soviet Union," Khrushchev called Sumulong a "jerk" and a "lackey of Western imperialism." He then removed his shoe, brandished it at the Philippine delegation, and banged it on his desk. Khrushchev will bare his stockinged feet a second time, during a speech by U.S. Assistant Secretary of State Francis Wilcox.

Corps Group

OCTOBER 14, 1960. Presidential candidate John Kennedy addresses 10,000 students and faculty at the University of Michigan. He asks them, "How many of you are willing to spend 10 years in Africa or Latin America or Asia working for the U.S. and working for freedom? How many of you who are going to be doctors are willing to spend your days in Ghana...?" Each question brings a tumultuous response. Although the event will receive no significant media attention, it will later be viewed as the moment in which the notion for the Peace Corps was born.

JFK with volunteers: Corps group.

Convictions

OCTOBER 26, 1960. Two weeks before the presidential election, Robert Kennedy places a telephone call that helps secure Martin Luther King, Jr.'s release from a Georgia jail. King had been sentenced to four months of hard labor for driving with an out-of-state license. John Kennedy has already been warned that his support of King, the Teamsters' Jimmy Hoffa, or Nikita Khrushchev, could cost him three Southern states. Robert Kennedy decides to call the judge anyway, telling him, as he will later put it, that "if he was a decent American, he would let King out of jail by sundown." The judge complies. Days later, Martin Luther King, Sr. will announce that "I had expected to vote against Senator Kennedy because of his religion. But now he can be my president, Catholic or whatever he is....He has the moral courage to stand up for what he knows is right."

King, supporters: On the line against racism.

Camelot

NOVEMBER 8, 1960. John F. Kennedy and Lyndon Baines Johnson defeat Richard M. Nixon and Henry Cabot Lodge in the closest presidential election since 1884, with Kennedy receiving only about 113,000 votes more than Nixon out of nearly 70 million ballots cast. A single vote in each voting precinct would have changed the result.

So Close, Yet So Far

NOVEMBER 17, 1960. President-elect Kennedy is informed about the secret CIA operation to train Cuban exiles to overthrow Fidel Castro. In January, in the wake of worsening relations between the two countries, the U.S. will break diplomatic relations with Cuba.

Women's Issues

DECEMBER 14, 1961. President Kennedy establishes the President's Commission on the Status of Women, with Eleanor Roosevelt as its first chairwoman. It is the first time since the passage of the 19th Amendment giving women the right to vote that the federal government has formally addressed "women's issues."

Passing the Torch

JANUARY 20, 1961. John F. Kennedy is sworn in as the 35th President on a bleak, bone-chilling day. Dressed in a morning coat and top hat, Kennedy delivers a stirring inaugural speech, declaring, "Let the word go forth from this time and place, to friend and foe alike, that the torch has been passed to a new generation of Americans—born in this century, tempered by war, disciplined by a hard and bitter peace, proud of our ancient heritage." He concludes: "Ask not what your country can do for you—ask what you can do for your country." Earlier that morning, reading over his speech, Kennedy had scratched out the word "will" and replaced it with "can."

> *"Let the word go forth from this time and place . . . that the torch has been passed to a new generation of Americans."*
>
> **John F. Kennedy**

Mon Dieu!

FEBRUARY 13, 1961. France becomes the fourth member of the nuclear bomb "club"—joining the U.S., U.S.S.R., and Brit-

Kennedy inaugural: On the road to new horizons.

ain—by exploding its first atomic bomb over the Sahara Desert in Algeria.

Blood, Sweat, and Tears

MARCH 1, 1961. President Kennedy fulfills a campaign promise by recommending creation of a Peace Corps for Young Americans. The idea wasn't Kennedy's; it came early in the campaign from his brother-in-law, Robert Sargent Shriver. It will be Shriver who lobbies Congress to pass the measure, which the media will call "Kennedy's Kiddie Korps." The idea calls for young people to live in foreign countries, where they will help others to help themselves. In the Corps' early months, Communist leaders will call it "a nest of spies," although many countries will eagerly request that volunteers be assigned to them. Within two years, 7,000 Peace Corps volunteers will be in action in 44 countries. Within the next quarter-century, more than 100,000 volunteers will be sent to nearly 100 countries.

Peace Corps volunteers: Mission: possible.

Bad Move

APRIL 27, 1961. In what will come to be called "Kennedy's only defeat," CIA-trained forces invade Cuba's Bay of Pigs but are successfully repelled by Fidel Castro's Cuban forces. The plan has been in the making even before Kennedy's election; it was an Eisenhower project designed to eliminate the threat of Communist forces 90 miles off American shores—"eight jet minutes away," as defense experts liked to say. It is a classic CIA adventure: secret and dramatic—so secret that even Kennedy has not been fully informed. For months the CIA has recruited some 1,400 Cuban exiles, mostly in Florida, then trained them in a secluded mountain camp in Guatemala with a squadron of World War II B-26 bombers the CIA purchased for the mission, along with six old freighters for transport. An American destroyer is to lead the flotilla into the Bay of Pigs, about 120 miles from Havana, and let the Cuban exiles do the dirty work, with an American aircraft carrier standing by. Kennedy originally had considered it a contingency, not an operational, plan, but his Joint Chiefs of Staff have sold him on its merits and he has reluctantly approved it. It will later be said that Kennedy's bravado derives in part from his adminstration's apparent Midas touch: everything it touches seems to turn to gold. This time its touch is dross. As the invading ships near Cuban waters, they will encounter coral reefs that the CIA has failed to report. Many of the landing craft will never reach shore, their hulls cracking open on the reefs. Local beaches will unexpectedly be surrounded by swamps, making the invaders easy targets for Cuban planes. Despite Kennedy's orders, the first invaders to land will be Americans, not Cuban exiles. Over the next three days, it will become evident that the invasion

has been ill-planned and ill-executed; most of the 1,400 invaders will become trapped on the beaches while Castro's forces move in fast. There will be heavy loss of life, and more than 1,000 American prisoners will be taken; they will be returned by Castro on Christmas Eve 1962. Before news of the disaster arrives, some 15,000 wives, mothers, and friends of members of the wiped-out invasion forces will gather in Miami's Bayfront Park for a scheduled "Thank Kennedy" rally. But under the impact of the tragedy, the participants, faces wet with tears, instead will scream, "Kennedy! Help!" Kennedy will later call the Bay of Pigs episode "a tragedy...the most excruciating period of my life."

Kennedys:
Family matters.

Eight Miles High

MAY 1, 1961. National Airlines flight 337 from Miami to Key West is hijacked to Cuba by Antulio Ramierez Ortis, 35, in what will be the first of a rash of "skyjackings" of American planes. In September Congress will outlaw air piracy and the Federal Aviation Administration will take steps to initiate screening of passengers on selected flights, based on a character profile of typical skyjackers. But such efforts won't stem the tide, and the number of skyjackings will peak in 1969 at 44. In 1973 the FAA will begin metal detector searches of all U.S. airline passengers. Ortis will receive a 20-year jail sentence.

Common Ground

JUNE 3, 1961. President Kennedy and Premier Khrushchev meet at the American Embassy in Vienna. It isn't their first encounter; they met briefly in 1959 during Khrushchev's visit to the U.S. Although this meeting begins cordially, the two soon launch into a civil but tough debate over whether the U.S. is stifling Communism or the Soviet Union is stifling democracy. During lunch and for the rest of the next two days, they will discuss the space race, Laos, the Bay of Pigs, Cuba, Berlin, Iran, Poland, the test ban, and the need to maintain the balance of power. Later, at a state dinner hosted by the Austrian government, Jacqueline Kennedy will jokingly ask Khrushchev for one of the puppies born of a Soviet dog sent into space. Several months later, a terrified pup will be carried into the Oval Office, much to Jackie's—and her husband's—surprise. But the Kennedy-Khrushchev encounter will end grimly, as both hold fast to their positions—Khrushchev's that the U.S. is an aggressor against inevitable change among the governments of nations; Kennedy's, that the Soviets must decide whether Soviet aggression is worth the horror of nuclear war. Kennedy will leave the meeting feeling defeated, some will say humiliated.

The Wall

AUGUST 13, 1961. Responding to pressure from the Soviet Union and other Communist countries, East German authorities close the border between East and West Berlin, then erect a wall between the two sectors designed to halt a flood of East Berliners fleeing to the West.

Taking Cover

OCTOBER 6, 1961. In a speech to a New Jersey newspaper publishers' luncheon, President Kennedy pledges that nuclear fallout protection will be available to every American, but warns that "do-it-yourself" home shelters will be needed to supplement government-built group shelters. The cost for a home shelter, says the President, should run about $100 to $150; he adds that tax deductions for shelters probably won't be available.

Fallout shelter: No place like home.

No Ifs, Ands, or Butts

FEBRUARY 3, 1962. President Kennedy embargoes nearly all trade with Cuba. Hardest hit are American cigar smokers, who must do without the millions of Cuban cigars imported each year or rolled and wrapped in U.S. plants.

Firing Line

MARCH 9, 1962. The Defense Department verifies reports that U.S. pilots are flying combat missions in Vietnam. In a week Defense Secretary Robert McNamara will confirm that American troops are exchanging fire with the Viet Cong.

Sweet Talkin' Guy

OCTOBER 13, 1961. A charge by Sen. Margaret Chase Smith that the Kennedy administration lacks the will to use nuclear weapons brings a surprise counterattack from Nikita Khrushchev, who accuses her of being a warmonger: "It is hard to believe how a woman, if she is not the devil in the disguise of a woman, can make such a malicious, man-hating call. Even the wildest of animals, a tigress even, worries about her cubs, licks and pities them. Margaret Smith in her hatred of everything new and progressive has decided to beat all records of savagery."

Eve of Destruction

OCTOBER 29, 1961. The Soviet Union explodes a 50-megaton hydrogen bomb, the biggest in history. It creates a shock wave that circles the earth in just over 36 hours.

Combat Zone

DECEMBER 11, 1961. President Kennedy sends 425 helicopter crewmen, the U.S.' first combat troops, to Vietnam.

"There will not be, under any conditions, any intervention in Cuba by the United States armed forces."

John F. Kennedy

Bombs Away

APRIL 25, 1962. The U.S. resumes atmospheric testing of nuclear bombs. America hasn't exploded a nuclear bomb since a 1958 agreement with the Soviets to stop all such tests, a decision made after witnessing the horrible consequences of fallout on South Pacific residents following earlier tests. But the Soviets resumed atmospheric tests over Siberia last September and the disarmament talks recently broke down. Last month President Kennedy offered to hold off tests if the Soviets immediately halted theirs and signed a test-ban treaty; Premier Khrushchev declined the offer. As dawn breaks over Christmas Island in the Pacific, a new round of

ALWAYS FOLLOW THESE OFFICIAL CIVIL DEFENSE

AIR RAID INSTRUCTIONS

IF ATTACK COMES WITH **NO WARNING**	BE QUICK BUT CALM	IF YOU HAVE **WARNING**
Drop to floor. Try to get under a bed or heavy table.	AT HOME	Turn off stove burners. Go to shelter room you have prepared.
Drop to floor and try to get under desk or bench.	AT WORK	Go to assigned shelter, follow warden's orders.
Drop to floor and bury face in arms. Get out of line with windows.	IN SCHOOL	Go to assigned shelter, follow teacher's orders.
Drop to ground. If cover is close by, dive for it. Bury face in arms.	IN THE OPEN	Get in nearest approved building or shelter, obey CD wardens.
Drop to floor and bury face in arms.	STOP CARS, BUSSES OR TROLLEYS	Get out and go to nearest approved building or shelter, obey CD wardens.

OBEY INSTRUCTIONS AND

STAY PUT UNTIL THE ALL-CLEAR SOUNDS

Air raid instructions: Helter shelter.

American nuclear testing begins. In August 1963 the U.S., Soviet Union, and Britain will finally sign a test-ban treaty.

Change It or Lose It

JUNE 11, 1962. Students for a Democratic Society, a group of radical college students, begins a four-day national convention at a Port Huron, Mich., AFL-CIO camp. The group has formed in recent months as an information and support network for student civil rights workers, although it is interested in a wide range of issues, from nuclear disarmament to college dress codes. As SDS cofounder Tom Hayden will later put it, "We believed students could be the catalysts for change in the world." Much of the seed money for SDS has come from liberal labor union groups. At the Port Huron convention, several dozen SDS members will decide to draw up a document that expresses their ideas and visions. The 63-page "Port Huron Statement," as it will become known, will seem a remarkably tame document in retrospect, although it will become the most influential statement of SDS philosophy. "We are people of this generation," it will begin, "bred in at least modest comfort, housed now in universities, looking uncomfortably to the world we inherit." The statement will go on to "seek the establishment of a democracy of individual participation governed by two central aims: that the individual share in those social decisions determining the quality and direction of his life; that society be organized to encourage independence in men and provide the media for their common participation...."

Abbie Hoffman: Radical speak-out.

God, No

JUNE 25, 1962. By a vote of 6 to 1, the Supreme Court bans prayer in public schools, calling it "an establishment of religion" forbidden by the First Amendment. The ruling comes in a suit brought by five New York parents against the state's Board of Regents, which had drafted a 22-word nondenominational prayer in 1951 and recommended that it be used to start each school day.

Good Ole Boys

OCTOBER 1, 1962. In what will be called the gravest conflict between federal and state authority since the Civil War, President Kennedy calls on the U.S. Army to force Mississippi to allow James H. Meredith to enroll as the first black at the University of Mississippi at Oxford. Governor Ross Barnett has repeatedly

RFK, Meredith: 23,000 escorts.

ignored court orders to let Meredith enroll. With closing the university an undesirable alternative—and after using scores of state police to block Meredith's entrance—Barnett finally has been stymied in the face of U.S. Attorney General Robert Kennedy's insistence that Meredith "was going to be enrolled at the University of Mississippi." Ultimately, it will take tear gas and 23,000 U.S. troops to enforce one man's right to enroll in a public institution; 500 will remain on campus for the first months of Meredith's enrollment, fending off periodic violence by students that will leave several U.S. Marshalls injured and several students expelled.

Big Bad John

OCTOBER 15, 1962. President Kennedy is awakened at 6:30 AM and informed that intelligence photos confirm the installation of Soviet missiles in Cuba, threatening the entire East Coast. For the next week the news will remain secret among a handful of Kennedy's top advisers as they weigh the alternatives of invading Cuba, initiating a blockade against Soviet ships headed to Cuba, or taking no action and risking humiliation by Khrushchev's brashness. Following days of intense debates in Washington and solitude on the beach at Hyannisport, Kennedy will reject his advisers' recommendation to bomb Cuba and will instead appear on TV October 22 to announce a blockade. Within 10 days the first Soviet ships headed to Cuba will turn around and return home. In a few more days Kennedy will issue an ultimatum to Khrushchev to remove all existing missile bases within 24 hours or risk having them bombed. Khrushchev will opt to remove the missiles.

JFK: Block buster.

Wanna Bet?

NOVEMBER 7, 1962. Following his loss in the California governor's race to Edmund G. Brown, former vice president Richard Nixon—who is reportedly hung over from heavy drinking the night before—holds a press conference and tells reporters, "You won't have Nixon to kick around any more."

On a Clear Day

DECEMBER 11, 1962. The Second National Conference on Air Pollution is held in Washington, D.C. It opens on the heels of a tragic coincidence: a recent smog episode in London has claimed more than 300 lives. The conference will lead to an emphasis on air pollution in President Kennedy's national health message in February and to the introduction of several bills authorizing greater federal assistance to state and local pollution control efforts.

Bad Moon Rising

MAY 8, 1963. South Vietnam President Diem begins a campaign against Buddhist protesters by raiding pagodas throughout the country. Outrage is expressed in the form of suicides by Buddhist priests, who immolate themselves in gasoline-soaked pyres, many of which are broadcast in the U.S. on network news. The raids will become the focus for discontent with Diem, in both Vietnam and the U.S.

Ambushed

JUNE 12, 1963. Civil rights activist Medgar Evers, 37, walking to his house in Jackson, Miss., is murdered by a sniper hiding in a bush. The murder of Evers, whom Dr. Martin Luther King, Jr. will eulogize as a "pure patriot," will touch off mass protests in Jackson, resulting in 158 arrests; hundreds more will riot after Evers' funeral on June 15. In a rare show of unity, Gov. Ross Barnett will join with the NAACP to offer a reward for Evers' killer. Within a few days the FBI will charge Byron de la Beckwith, a 42-year-old fertilizer salesman, with the murder.

"One who breaks an unjust law must do so openly, lovingly, and with a willingness to accept the penalty."
Martin Luther King, Jr.

Flour Child

JUNE 26, 1963. President Kennedy, visiting the Berlin Wall, pledges his support for efforts to defend West Berlin from Communist takeover and to reunite Germany. He tells a cheering crowd as a sign of support, "Ich bin ein Berliner"—"I am a Berliner." Kennedy's German wasn't grammatically correct: his statement translates roughly as "I'm a donut," referring to an indigenous pastry known as a "Berliner." (The correct phrase should have been "Ich bin Berliner.")

Our Day Will Come

AUGUST 28, 1963. Martin Luther King, Jr.'s "I Have a Dream" speech concludes a highly successful "March on Washington for Jobs and Freedom," the first nonviolent black-organized event to attain national media coverage. A quarter-million black and white Americans have come to Washington to demonstrate support for civil rights and to demand passage of a civil rights legislative package "without compromise or filibuster": inte-

King: To the mountaintop.

marching. But it is King's speech that will be best remembered. After reading from a prepared text, King will launch into an impromptu sermon: "I have a dream that one day on the red hills of Georgia, the sons of former slaves and the sons of former slave owners will be able to sit down together at the table of brotherhood...I have a dream that my four little children will one day live in a nation where they will not be judged by the color of their skin, but by the content of their character...."

Dial 'M' for Moscow

AUGUST 30, 1963. A Washington-to-Moscow "hot-line," designed to reduce the risk of accidental war, opens.

Coup de Jour

NOVEMBER 1, 1963. South Vietnam's President Ngo Dinh Diem is overthrown and killed by his own generals, a coup organized in part, it will later be learned, by Americans. He will be replaced by Duong Van Minh, known because of his size as "Big Minh." But Minh's government will last only two months; it will be overthrown by Nguyen Khanh, who, in turn, will remain in office little more than a year.

gration of public schools, a federal job-training program, and a federal Fair Employment Practices Act barring all job discrimination. Equally important has been the coming together of a wide range of often-rival organizations in coordinating the event. Numerous other organizations have helped, ranging from the National Council of Churches, which made 80,000 box lunches for marchers, to the Washington Senators baseball team, which postponed two games so that baseball would not distract anyone from serious

Til Death Do Us Part

NOVEMBER 22, 1963. President Kennedy is assassinated as he rides in a motorcade through downtown Dallas. Kennedy has come to Texas partly because he is running behind Sen. Barry Goldwater in the polls for next year's presidential race. More immediately, though, Kennedy has come to honor his friend, Rep. Albert Thomas, for whom a testimonial dinner is being held. Kennedy's staff has put together a package of speeches, both political and nonpolitical, including a fundraiser in Austin. But it is the relatively insignificant ride through Dallas that will make history. As the motorcade passed the Texas Book Depository, the shots rang out. They will later be found to have been fired by Lee Harvey Oswald, 24, a Marine Corps veteran who has spent time in the Soviet Union; Oswald will be captured in a Dallas movie theater 80 minutes after the shooting. Oswald's third shot has torn off the top back of Kennedy's head, spewing blood over Jackie Kennedy's pink skirt. Jackie will stay with her husband until the very end; when they pull the white sheet over Kennedy's body, she will slip her wedding ring onto his finger.

Jackie, family: Together to the end.

Easier Said Than Done

NOVEMBER 23, 1963. President Lyndon Johnson is briefed on the Vietnam situation the day after becoming President. Without hesitation he proclaims, "I am not going to lose Vietnam. I am not going to be the president who saw Southeast Asia go the way China went." By the time he leaves office in January 1969, more than 300,000 American troops will be involved in a still-raging war.

See It Now

NOVEMBER 24, 1963. As millions of television viewers watch with disbelief, Dallas nightclub owner Jack Ruby murders Lee Harvey Oswald at point-blank range in the basement of the Dallas city jail. Next March, Ruby will be convicted of murder by a Dallas jury and sentenced to death, although his conviction will be reversed in 1966. Ruby will die of cancer in January 1967 before a second trial can be held.

One Man and a Gun

NOVEMBER 29, 1963. President Johnson appoints a commission headed by Chief Justice Earl Warren to investigate the assassination of President Kennedy. Next September, the Warren Commission will deliver its 295,000-word conclusion: that Oswald acted alone. The summary report alone will span 888 pages.

The conclusion will become a focus of controversy for decades.

War Declared

JANUARY 8, 1964. In his State of the Union address, President Johnson calls for a national "war on poverty." Within eight months Congress will enact a a key weapon in that war, the Economic Opportunity Act, aimed at a coordinated attack on multiple fronts: illiteracy, unemployment, and inadequate public services for minorities. The act and related legislation will commit nearly $1 billion for 10 different programs conducted by the Office of Economic Opportunity, including the Job Corps, work-training programs, work-study programs, small-business incentives, and VISTA (Volunteers In Service To America), a kind of domestic Peace Corps.

LBJ: A billion bucks for poverty.

Into the Mire

JANUARY 27, 1964. Defense Secretary Robert McNamara reports that the Vietnam war has claimed 101 lives. By November that number will have more than doubled; within 18 months the death toll will reach 500. In March, McNamara will report in a memo to President Johnson that

Viet soldiers: Sinking deeper.

"Substantially more can be done in the effective employment of military forces and in the economic and civic action areas. These improvements may require some selective increases in the U.S. presence...."

Can Sex Kill?

FEBRUARY 8, 1964. After a heated debate, the House of Representatives votes to add the word "sex" to Title VII of the proposed Civil Rights Act, joining race, color, religion, and national origin as outlawed forms of discrimination. Ironically, the "sex" amendment has been proposed by Rep. Howard Smith (D-Va.), an opponent of the civil rights bill; Washington observers feel that his amendment is a calculated maneuver to kill the bill entirely. To Smith's probable dismay, the entire bill, "sex" included, will pass the House tomorrow, with the Senate following suit in early July.

Pissed

APRIL 24, 1964. *Time* magazine reports that "Increasingly, local civil rights demonstrators seem to employ pointless, often destructive and sometimes dangerous tactics." Recently, for example, a New York chapter of the Congress on Racial Equality conducted a "stall-in" at opening day at Shea Stadium, creating a monumental traffic jam. In Berkeley, Calif., demonstrators have filled supermarket shopping carts with food, then abandoned them in the store, leaving the food to spoil. Another New York City protest threatened to waste water by orchestrating a massive running of faucets. And in Atlanta, blacks entered a segregated restaurant and urinated on the floor, causing Mayor William Hartsfield to pose a critical question: "Is urination nonviolent?"

Rights Stuff

JULY 2, 1964. President Johnson signs the Civil Rights Act of 1964, the nation's first broad-based civil rights bill, barring discrimination of all kinds. There had been rumblings about whether Johnson would maintain momentum on Kennedy's efforts to pass the bill, which was introduced in Congress last June; many thought Johnson would dilute the bill to ease its passage. But within days after Kennedy's death, Johnson summoned Martin Luther King, Jr., Roy Wilkins of the NAACP, and other civil rights leaders to the White House to assure them he would push the bill through. Johnson's major role was to shepherd the bill through without a great deal of time-wasting "horse-trading" that could weaken the bill and cause acrimony in Congress. After a long legislative fight, the House passed the bill in February and the Senate voted in June to end a filibuster, the first time a filibuster had been ended on a civil rights bill. There will be much skepticism over whether the act will be effective, but by the end of the first year, it will exceed even its writers' expectations, particularly in the South, which will be unalterably changed by the new law. The weakest section of the act will turn out to be Title I, aimed at protecting voting rights, but a 1965 law will close most of those loopholes. The strongest section will be Title VI, which will result in the desegregation of more schools during its first year than were integrated during all the years since the Supreme Court's 1954 ruling in *Brown v. Board of Education*. Title VII of the act will become a major tool in expanding women's rights; that section will provide women with a legal device to combat discrimination in hiring and job promotions.

Go With Goldwater

JULY 15, 1964. Sen. Barry Goldwater accepts the Republican presidential nomination at the party's convention in San Francisco. His running mate is Rep. William E. Miller, a seven-term congressman from western New York.

Goldwater fans: In your heart, you know he's right.

Running Scared

AUGUST 4, 1964. Following the second of two attacks by the Viet Cong against U.S. ships, President Johnson goes on national TV to announce retaliatory air strikes and military reinforcements. Within three days Congress will vote 88-2 to pass the "Tonkin Gulf Resolution" permitting the President "to take all necessary measures to repel any armed attack against the forces of the United States and to prevent further aggression." Although he continually emphasizes on the campaign trail that "the United States seeks no wider war," Johnson will later view the resolution as a virtual blank check to expand the war.

Half-Assed

SEPTEMBER 12, 1964. Students for a Democratic Society gives a qualified endorsement to President Johnson's re-election bid against Barry Goldwater. In its literature, SDS will modify Johnson's slogan, "All the way with LBJ," to suit its lack of enthusiasm with the Democratic Party and its candidate: "Half the way with LBJ."

Two-for-One

OCTOBER 15, 1964. Leonid I. Brezhnev and and Aleksei N. Kosygin replace Nikita Khrushchev as the Soviet Union's party secretary and premier, respectively. Khrushchev, whose last months in office will be marred by

The Free Speech Movement

As the fall semester began at the University of California at Berkeley, something was in the air. The students were returning to school after a summer that had seen civil rights demonstrations in the South and the Republican National Convention in San Francisco. Many of the students, in fact, had spent part of the summer at one or both locations, working for social change.

The entrance to campus, a 26-foot-wide concourse known as the "Bancroft strip," had long been a gathering place, a rallying spot, and an area where students set up card tables to distribute information. But off-campus political figures were not allowed to use the area, a rule that required both Richard Nixon and Adlai Stevenson to speak to students from sound trucks located on nearby city streets. By 1964 the rules had become somewhat more liberal, but freedom of speech was still a regulated commodity on campus.

The problems started when someone complained—that students were recruiting volunteers for Gov. William Scranton of Pennsylvania, the only serious opponent to Barry Goldwater at the Republican National Convention. During the last half of September 1964, student and campus administration representatives conducted often heated discussions, culminating in a ban on student activity directed at off-campus activities. On September 30 the situation escalated when card tables were once again set up in defiance of the rules. Eight students were summoned to the dean's office, but more than 300 showed up, occupying the administration building until 3 AM. On October 1 police arrested a former graduate student, Jack Weinberg, for distributing materials from the Congress on Racial Equality. Weinberg was led to a waiting police car, but hundreds of students followed and surrounded the car, holding it hostage—with Weinberg inside—for 32 hours. One protester, 21-year-old philosophy student Mario Savio, addressed the crowds from the roof of the police car. Savio would become the spokesman for what would come to be known as the "Free Speech Movement." The incident

Savio: Speaking freely.

ended with a six-point agreement between student leaders and the school administration.

But the trouble didn't end there. During the Thanksgiving recess, the university sent letters to four leaders of the demonstrations, charging them with violating university rules regarding order and safety and with inciting a crowd to detain a police car and an arrested man. Reactions to those charges led to a sit-in at Sproul Hall, the administration building, on December 2. Gov. Edmund G. Brown ordered police to arrest more than 800 people who refused to leave. More protests followed until December 7, when an extraordinary meeting was held to announce a peace proposal. The students had won the right to exercise free speech on campus, and colleges around the world would never be the same.

Sino-Soviet conflict, will be disgraced by his party two weeks after he has called for an historic change in Soviet economic policy, giving consumer needs priority over heavy industry and the military. Both Brezhnev, a Soviet technocrat, and Kosygin, an able economist and administrator, are considered somewhat pro-Western by U.S. observers, causing only minimal angst in Western capitals.

Power Play

OCTOBER 16, 1964. China explodes its first nuclear bomb, joining the U.S., Britain, France,and the Soviet Union in the "nuclear club." The Chinese hope that the successful experiment will give them much-needed diplomatic leverage, but their achievement will attain less than the desired results. Their clout will improve, however, when they successfully explode a hydrogen bomb in 1967, which the Peking government will proclaim to be "a splendid achievement of the Great Proletarian Cultural Revolution," adding ominously that "China's hydrogen-bomb test will give very great support to the people of Viet Nam fighting against the U.S., and to the Arab people, who are resisting the Israeli aggressors."

Wishful Thinking

OCTOBER 21, 1964. In a campaign speech two weeks before the election, President Johnson emphasizes his stand against expanding American involvement in Vietnam, stating, "We are not about to send American boys nine or ten thousand miles away from home to do what Asian boys ought to be doing for themselves."

Landslide

NOVEMBER 3, 1964. The Democrats have a landslide day at the polls, as Lyndon Johnson handily defeats Barry Goldwater for the presidency, winning 61 perecent of the popular vote, the largest vote plurality ever. Analysts will blame Goldwater's hawkish military stance; he is deemed to be too ready to use nuclear arms in a confrontation, and his suggestion to escalate the Vietnam war has not gone over with voters. Also elected today is Robert F. Kennedy, who will become the new junior senator from New York.

LBJ, family: Winning smiles.

Great Society

JANUARY 4, 1965. In the first State of the Union address of his second term, President Johnson calls for a vast national effort to achieve a "Great Society," which will become a Johnson catch-phrase for the next four years. Johnson has used the phrase publicly before, but this is his first comprehensive definition of the plan: a massive attack on crippling and killing diseases, a doubling of the War on Poverty, enforcement of the new Civil Rights Act, elimination of barriers to the right to vote, reform of immigration laws, a federal education program of scholarships and loans with a first-year authorization of $1.5 billion, and a "massive effort" to establish more recreational and open space areas. In spite of his ambitious plans, Johnson will in three weeks submit a budget of just under $100 billion, less than 15 percent of the gross national product, the lowest budget-to-GNP ratio in 15 years. The next 12 months will see the biggest flurry of major legislation since Franklin Roosevelt's New Deal: the Elementary and Secondary School Act, providing grants to school districts with needy children; implementation of a new Medicare system, designed to provide medical care for the elderly through the Social Security system; the Voting Rights Act of 1966, which will eliminate loopholes in previous civil rights legislation; the Omnibus Housing Act, establishing rent subsidies for low-income families; creation of a new Department of Housing and Urban Development, consolidating the missions of several federal agencies; creation of the National Endowments for the Arts and Humanities, providing financial assistance to scholars and artists; a Water Quality Act, setting new drinking water standards; and immigration laws, abolishing national quotas for foreigners emigrating to the U.S.

Malcolm X: "Chickens coming home to roost."

Family Affair

FEBRUARY 21, 1965. Malcolm X, 39, is assassinated at a rally in Harlem by Black Muslims from whom he had defected. Born Malcolm Little, he was the son of a Baptist preacher who was an enthusiast for Marcus Garvey's "Back to Africa" movement. Quitting school after the eighth grade, he turned mainly to hustling, pimping, and drug-dealing, before being sent to prison in 1946 for burglary. In prison, he copied a dictionary from A to Z to improve his vocabulary and learned about the Black Muslims, an extremist sect founded in Detroit in 1930 and led since 1934 by Elijah Muhammad. Paroled in 1952, he changed his last name to "X," replacing "the white slave-master name which had been imposed upon my paternal forebears by some blue-eyed devil," as he would later write. He soon proved a savage speaker and one of Elijah Muhammad's best recruiters, helping the Muslims grow to an estimated 250,000 members. Many of his speeches were to white civic groups and college audiences. But When Malcolm called John Kennedy's assassination a case of "the chickens coming home to roost," he was suspended from the Muslim movement, after which he quit to form his own Organization for Afro-American Unity. The rival group began leaking stories about immorality among Black Muslims, accusing Elijah Muhammad of having fathered eight illegitimate children. Today, as he rose to speak before 400 blacks at New

York's Audubon Ballroom, a seedy two-story building on Manhattan's upper Broadway, a disturbance broke out, during which three men rushed toward him, one blasting away at point-blank range with a sawed-off, double-barrelled shotgun. He will be buried in a suburban Westchester cemetery in a white robe that signifies his Muslim faith, his head pointed to the east, toward Mecca.

Lightning Strikes

FEBRUARY 7, 1965. Hours after the end of a cease-fire honoring Tet, the Vietnamese new year, eight Americans are killed and 126 wounded as mortar shells land in a U.S. military base at Pleiku. Within hours the U.S. will launch "Operation Rolling Thunder," a massive bombing of North Vietnam. On February 11, President Johnson will announce that "The people of South Vietnam have chosen to resist [North Vietnam]. At their request, the United States has taken its place beside them in this struggle." Later, evidence will emerge that President Johnson used the Pleiku incident as the excuse to launch a long-planned offensive.

Sunday, Bloody Sunday

MARCH 7, 1965. After weeks of futile efforts by blacks to register to vote, several hundred blacks march in protest through Selma, Ala., and are confronted by hundreds of helmeted and mounted state troopers and deputies, ordered by Gov. George Wallace to stop the march. Although blacks comprise nearly 50 percent of the city's 29,000 residents, they comprise only 1 percent of registered voters. For months hundreds of blacks have lined up daily at local courthouses, trying vainly to register to vote. On some days, fewer than one in 20 actually made it inside. The Selma protesters are attempting to replicate a successful march held two weeks ago in Montgomery, but this one will turn violent, as Wallace orders law enforcement officials to tear into a crowd of about 600 marchers with bullwhips, tear gas, and clubs. Nearly a score of marchers will be taken to hospitals with bone fractures and other serious injuries, and some 70 others will be treated for cuts, bruises, and the effects of

tear gas. But the event, later dubbed "Bloody Sunday," will have a major impact. The display of official brutality will electrify the nation and serve as a turning point for the civil rights movement and a major catalyst in passing the 1965 Voting Rights Act. Later this month, King will lead another March, this one from Selma to the state capitol in Montgomery, in a five-day, 54-mile trek.

New Wave

MARCH 8, 1965. Thirty-five hundred Marines land at Da Nang in the first deployment of U.S. ground troops in Vietnam, raising total U.S. troop strength to 27,000.

What Did You Learn in School Today?

MARCH 24, 1965. The first antiwar "teach-in" is staged by the University of Michigan. The teach-in will become an effective vehicle for the antiwar movement, although the Johnson administration will attempt, un-

successfully, to use teach-ins to gain support for its policies. On May 15 a teach-in will be held in Washington, D.C., with 122 college campuses connected by telephone lines. The early teach-ins will be academic in tone, including representatives from both the administration and its opponents, but future ones will become increasingly antiwar in tone. In mid-May another teach-in will be held, this one at the University of California at Berkeley, with speeches by Dr. Benjamin Spock and Free Speech Movement leader Mario Savio; more than 12,000 people will attend.

And Justice for All

MARCH 28, 1965. The U.S. Supreme Court issues two verdicts that give federal law enforcers new powers to prosecute on conspiracy charges persons sus-

Selma march: Voting with their feet.

pected of being involved in civil rights killings. The two cases reverse the decisions of cases in Georgia and Mississippi, in which murderers of both black and white civil rights workers had been let off without a conviction, or, in one case, without a trial. The rulings will give the Justicc Department a potent weapon for dealing with civil rights violence trials not settled in state courts.

Only the Beginning

APRIL 17, 1965. More than 25,000 people, mostly young, demonstrate in Washington, D.C., against the Vietnam war. The event, the first national mobilization organized by Students for a Democratic Society, is the largest protest to oppose American intervention in an ongoing foreign war. Its success will bring new media attention to SDS which, by late 1966, will have 265 chapters nationwide.

America, the Beautiful

MAY 24, 1965. President Johnson holds a White House Conference on Natural Beauty, intended to bring attention to environmental concerns for U.S. wilderness and recreation areas. The conference will spur an unprecedented wave of citizen action, as millions of Americans mobilize to work on projects involving community improvement, preservation of historic landmarks, and protection of natural resources.

Uncle Sam Wants You

JULY 21, 1965. Following Defense Secretary Robert McNamara's recommendation to send 200,000 American troops to Vietnam, President Johnson and close aides debate expanding the U.S. role. A week later, Johnson will announce his plan to send 50,000 troops to Vietnam immediately, and more later if needed, the largest deployment so far. Johnson also will ask for a doubling of draft calls. By July 28, U.S. troop involvement will total 125,000.

Boot camp: On to Nam.

That Championship Season

AUGUST 6, 1965. In what is turning into a flurry of legislative victories for the White House, President Johnson signs the Voting Rights Act of 1965. Congressional passage of the law will strengthen existing civil rights laws by eliminating stringent qualifications imposed on Southern blacks to "qualify" as voters—including reading tests that many whites could not pass—and continue Johnson's unmatched string of successes. By the end of this congressional year, Congress will have approved nearly 70 percent of the "Great Society" proposals submitted by Johnson, according to tabulations by *Congressional Quarterly*—the highest percentage since *CQ* started keeping tabs in 1954.

> *"The white man don't like nothing black but a Cadillac."*
>
> **H. Rap Brown**

In the Ghetto

AUGUST 13, 1965. Two thousand National Guardsmen are called in after three days of fierce rioting in the Watts section of Los Angeles. The weather has been unusually hot and smoggy, even for southern California. Two nights ago, the rioting began, precipitated by allegations of police brutality during arrest of a black man for drunk driving. Soon crowds of up to 5,000 gathered in a 20-block area, which was sealed off by some 400 L.A. police and sheriffs' deputies. Police will make only brief forays into the riot's center, opting instead to prevent its spread. Yesterday, civil rights leaders and black clergy toured the neighborhood, asking residents to stay inside, but their efforts have had little effect; by today the riots have spread to a 150-block region, including many white neighborhoods, which will suffer store looting and car burnings. By tomorrow the riots will spread farther, with 2,000 more Guardsmen called in and an 8 PM-to-dawn curfew imposed; the region will be declared a disaster area, and police from cities in four surrounding counties will be used. Police will declare that they have gained the "upper hand" by August 15th, although sporadic looting, sniping, and armed conflict will continue. By the 17th the curfew will end and as clean-up efforts will be under way. The final toll: 33 dead, 900 injured, 3,480 arrested, 200 buildings destroyed, 500 buildings damaged, total damage estimated at $200 million.

Watts: Taking it to the streets.

Grapes of Wrath

SEPTEMBER 16, 1965. The United Farm Workers (UFW) union votes to strike against grape

Chavez: Seeds of victory.

growers in the Central Valley district of Delano, Calif. The UFW is a three-year-old organization started by Mexican-American Cesar Chavez, who has been attempting to organize migrant farm workers against California's $170 million grape-growing industry. It has been a vicious battle, with Chavez orchestrating a highly successful campaign resulting in more than 1,500 of 2,000 workers voting for UFW representation, despite farmers having bused hundreds of "green-card" workers from Mexico to harvest their grapes. Chavez has charged that the federal Bureau of Immigration and Naturalization Service has cooperated with growers in letting the "green-carders" through U.S. borders. The strike will continue for five years, with mixed success. In April 1970 the UFW will sign agreements with two Coachella Valley, Calif., grape growers, the first labor contract ever covering grape pickers. Three months later 26 grape growers, representing 35 percent of the industry, will sign contracts with the UFW, ending the boycott. By the end of 1970 close to 300 growers will have signed contracts with the union.

A Movement Blossoms

OCTOBER 15, 1965. The first large antiwar rallies are held in four U.S. cities. At a rally in Berkeley, Calif., poet Allen Ginsburg introduces the term "flower power" to describe his philosophy of cooperation toward change.

We Shall Overkill

NOVEMBER 18, 1965. The Pentagon reports that 1,095 Americans have died in Vietnam, more than double the number only four months ago. Americans in Vietnam now total 170,000.

Who's Sorry Now?

DECEMBER 15, 1965. The AFL-CIO announces its "unstinting support" for the American effort in Vietnam.

Blackmail

JANUARY 11, 1966. Selective Service System director Lewis B. Hershey announces that students may properly be reclassified 1-A—the prime "draftable" category—if they demonstrate illegally against the draft. The decision could apply to draft-card burners and those participating in draft board sit-ins, says Hershey. The announcement will cause an immediate uproar from a wide range of fronts, most complaining about the announcement's chilling effects on First Amendment free speech. All told, few protesters will be prosecuted under this order.

Black Power

MAY 14, 1966. In a speech, Stokely Carmichael, chairman of the Student Non-Violent Co-ordinating Committee, introduces the term "black power" as a slogan. The term will immediately become controversial for its black separatist message. In separate national conferences in July, the Congress of Racial Equality will endorse the term, but the National Association for the Advancement of Colored People will reject it, although it will become increasingly acceptable to most blacks and some whites.

THE
VIET CONG
NEVER
CALLED ME
A
NIGGER

NOW or Never

JUNE 29, 1966. A group of 28 women at the Third National Conference on State Commissions on the Status of Women meets in Betty Friedan's hotel room to begin planning an organization that in October will become the National Organization for Women. Before departing the conference, the women will each chip in $5 toward startup costs and agree that the group's main purpose, as Friedan will later put it, will be "to take action to bring women into full participation in the mainstream of American society now, assuming all the privileges and responsibilities thereof

Friedan: Beginning of an ERA.

in truly equal partnership with men." Upon its incorporation in Washington in October, Friedan will be elected NOW's first president. By late next year the group will draw up a Bill of Rights for Women for 1968, to be presented to both political parties and major candidates for national offices in the upcoming 1968 election. It will include an Equal Rights Amendment to the Constitution, enforcement of sex discrimination laws, maternity leave rights at work, tax deductions for child care expenses, child care centers at work, equal educational and job-training opportunities, and "the right of women to control their reproductive lives," the repeal of all laws that restrict access to birth control information and devices. Within the next five years NOW's membership will grow from 300 members to 150 chapters and close to 10,000 members.

Summertime

JULY 12, 1966. The much-feared "long, hot summer" begins, as riots erupt in several U.S. cities. In Chicago's Near West Side neighborhood, roving gangs of blacks will toss Molotov cocktails at police cars and loot scores of stores. A bottle-throwing brawl will break out in New York's Coney Island at an interracial dance sponsored by the Young Men's Hebrew Association. More than 800 people, including poet LeRoi Jones, will be arrested during looting and riots in Newark, N.J. Later this month there will be outbreaks in East Harlem, Baltimore, Cleveland, Detroit, Waukegan, Ill., South Bend, Ind., Portsmouth, Va., and Phoenix, Ariz. The incidents will spur President Johnson to name a Presidential Advisory Commission on Civil Disorders—the Kerner Commission, named for its head, Illinois Gov. Otto Kerner—which in 1968 will blame "white racism" for the riots.

Road Scholars

SEPTEMBER 9, 1966. The National Traffic and Motor Vehicle Safety Act is signed into law, largely the result of years of attacks on the auto industry by consumer advocate Ralph Nader. The act, which sets up a National Highway Safety Bureau (which will later become the National Highway Traffic Safety Administration, part of a new Department of Transportation) has emerged from Nader's 1964 book, *Unsafe At Any Speed*, which told in frightening detail the hazards of American

Nader: Auto-crat.

automobiles and the unwillingness of auto makers to consider safety in their designs. By January the new Nader-inspired federal agency will be a target for Nader attacks, suffering his incessant criticism for its cozy relationship with the car makers. During the next two decades Nader will hound the agency to order recalls of unsafe cars and to monitor the industry. In 1970, realizing that even a strident federal watchdog would be insufficient, he will set up the Center for Auto Safety, which will become one of the most effective consumer-advocacy organizations ever.

An Oncoming Train

SEPTEMBER 21, 1966. President Johnson tells of U.S. progress in Vietnam, announcing that "there is a light at the end of what has been a long and lonely tunnel."

We're Number One

OCTOBER 15, 1966. For the first time, U.S. troops exceed regular Vietnamese forces at 320,000.

Act II, Scene I

NOVEMBER 8, 1966. Former grade-B movie actor Ronald Reagan, 55, is elected governor of California. He will serve two four-year terms.

Keeping Up With the Times

APRIL 25, 1967. Spurred by the women's movement as well as an increasing number of U.S. birth deformities caused by drugs such as thalidomide and a German measles epidemic, Colorado becomes the first state to liberalize its 19th century abortion laws. The new law will permit abortions if continuation of pregnancy would severely impair the physical or mental health of the mother, if the child would be born with severe physical or mental defects, or if the pregnancy resulted from rape or incest. Over the next three years 11 other states will follow suit.

Muhammad Speaks

APRIL 28, 1967. The World Boxing Association strips Cassius Clay, 25, also known as Muhammad Ali, of his heavyweight boxing title after Clay refuses to be inducted into the Army. Shortly after refusing to take the ceremonial step forward at the Armed Forces Entrance and Examining Station in Houston, Clay issued a statement saying, "I have searched my conscience and I find I cannot be true to my belief in my religion by accepting such a call." He has maintained throughout civil litigation that he should be granted exemption from the draft as an appointed minister of the Black Muslim sect.

Inciteful

MAY 16, 1967. Stokely Carmichael tells a Washington, D.C., audience that "there is no need to go to Vietnam and shoot somebody who a honky says is your enemy. We're going to shoot the cops who are shooting our black brothers in the back in this country. That's where we're going." Carmichael, who recently stepped down as head of the Student Non-violent Co-ordinating Committee, also announces that he will spend the summer in Washington organizing "black resistance" to the Vietnam war. In a separate incident later that night, black students, sniping from dormitory windows, will shoot three policemen, one fatally, at Texas Southern University. Some will attribute the shootings to the influence of Carmichael, who had delivered his fiery rhetoric at the University in April.

Six Days in June

JUNE 5, 1967. In stunning predawn air strikes across the face of the Arab world, Israeli jets wipe out most of the air forces of several Arab countries in the first day of what what will become known as the Six-Day War. Heaviest hit are four Egyptian air bases in the Sinai Peninsula, site of President Gamal Abdul Nasser's massive buildup against Israel in the past month. Some 200 of Nasser's Russian-built MIG-21 fighters are caught and destroyed on the ground. At almost the same time, Israeli jets hit Arab bases in Jordan, Syria, and Iraq. By the end of the first day, some 400 warplanes of five Arab nations will be destroyed; 19 Israeli planes and pilots also will be downed. The Israeli attack has come in response to the deployment of 80,000 Egyptian troops and equipment in the Sinai and Nasser's closing of the Gulf of Aqaba, Israel's maritime link with the Red Sea. When an offensive attack seemed inevitable, Israel mobilized tens of thousands of men and women soldiers and reservists, who in turn mobilized everything from laundry and ice cream trucks to taxis and private cars for use in the effort. All are part of a superbly organized system created by Major General Moshe Dayan between 1963 and 1966, when he was Israeli chief of staff. Israel's two main objectives in the coming days will be to break the back of the massed Arab armor on its borders, then to seize Sharm el Sheikh on the heights

Clay/Ali: Objection overruled.

that control access to the strategic Gulfs of Suez and Aqaba. On another front Israeli forces will capture the Golan Heights, the mountains to the north from which Syrian guerrillas have launched frequent attacks on Israeli villages. In the most vicious fighting, they will capture the West Bank of the Jordan River, including the divided holy city of Jerusalem. The fighting will end when Jordan breaks ranks with its Arab brethren by accepting the U.N. cease-fire that the Soviets will arrange in order to save the Arabs from total disaster.

Pennies From Heaven

AUGUST 24, 1967. Led by Jerry Rubin, a dozen Yippies (Youth International Party members) throw dollar bills from the

> *"I am not now nor have I ever been a member of the House Un-American Activities Committee."*
>
> **Abbie Hoffman**

visitors' gallery of the New York Stock Exchange onto the trading floor. Describing the incident two years later during testimony in the "Chicago Seven" trial, Abbie Hoffman will explain that "we wanted to make a statement that...money should be abolished. We didn't believe in a society that people had to interact with money and property, but should be on more humanitarian bases." Within three months the New York Stock Exchange will install bulletproof 1 3/16-inch-thick glass panels and a metal grillwork ceiling on its visitors' gallery.

Rubin: To market, to market.

Whatever Gets You Through the Night

SEPTEMBER 29, 1967. Despite a raging war, with 13,500 American soldiers killed, another 85,000 wounded, and 756 missing, President Johnson delivers an upbeat assessment of the Vietnam effort, telling a San Antonio, Tex., audience that "the tide continues to run with us."

Hell No, We Won't Go

OCTOBER 16, 1967. "Stop the Draft" week begins in Oakland, Calif., aimed at closing down the local Army induction center. Early tomorrow morning, about 3,000 demonstrators will gather outside the center, met by hundreds of armed police who will try to disperse the crowd by forming a "flying wedge." More than 200 demonstrators will suffer serious injuries and 119, including folksinger Joan Baez and her mother, will be arrested. Seven demonstrators—who will become known as the "Oakland Seven"—will be tried on conspiracy charges. The trial, which defense lawyer Charles Garry will turn into a teach-in on free speech, police brutality, and the Vietnam war, will acquit the seven of all charges.

Calling Out the Troops

OCTOBER 21, 1967. Approximately 55,000 antiwar protesters storm the Pentagon, sponsored by the National Mobilization Committee to End the War in Vietnam—known commonly as "the Mobe"—a coalition of 150 organizations, including church groups and labor unions. Nearly 7,000 police will be called in to protect the building, including 3,000 military police, the first time since 1932 that regular Army troops have been used to protect the nation's capital. The confrontations will be intense, with demonstrators twice breaching police lines; six demonstrators will enter

Pentagon protesters: Mobe mob.

the Pentagon, albeit briefly. There will be 250 arrests, including David Dellinger, chairman of the Mobe, author Norman Mailer, and Dagmar Wilson, founder of Women's Strike for Peace.

Emissions Omission

NOVEMBER 21, 1967. President Johnson signs the Air Quality Act of 1967, the first major legislation passed to improve the nation's deteriorating air. During the next three years, the new law will provide more money to combat air pollution than the U.S. has spent on the problem in its entire history. But Johnson will fail to pass through Congress a national emissions standard for cars and factories, leaving that to individual states.

It's Only Make Believe

JANUARY 7, 1968. San Francisco "underground" FM station KMPX holds a "grass ballot" presidential election. Bob Dylan and Paul Butterfield are elected president and vice president, respectively. Owsley Stanley, one of the kingpins in the LSD world, is elected Secretary of Commerce.

Sisterhood Is Powerful

JANUARY 15, 1968. A demonstration of women's peace groups is attended by 5,000 in Washington, D.C. In a pamphlet written by Kathie Amatniek, member of Radical Women, a New York group, the slogan "Sisterhood Is Powerful" is first used.

Release Me

JANUARY 23, 1968. North Korea seizes the American intelligence ship USS Pueblo and its 83-man crew after it comes within 12 miles of the Korean coast. The ship's commander, Lloyd M. Bucher, will deny that the ship violated North Korean waters, but he and his crew will be held for 11 months after the U.S. admits intrusion.

The Only Good Defense

JANUARY 30, 1968. The Viet Cong launch a massive military effort that will later be known as the "Tet offensive," reversing what little progress American troops have made in the war. It also causes political turmoil in the U.S., where President Johnson and Minnesota's Sen. Eugene McCarthy are battling for the Democratic presidential nomination. By early March General William Westmoreland will request an additional 206,000 American troops.

The Spoiler

FEBRUARY 8, 1968. Alabama governor George Wallace launches a third-party presidential campaign. Although his bid will prove unsuccessful, many will credit him with stealing enough Democratic votes to tilt the bal-

Wallace: Three's a crowd.

ance in favor of Richard Nixon, who will receive only .4 percent more votes than his principal opponent, Democrat Hubert Humphrey.

The Way We Wore

MARCH 4, 1968. The Supreme Court upholds the right of students to wear armbands at school under the First Amendment, considering it "closely akin" to "pure speech." The decision comes after a Des Moines, Ia., high school principal tried to force several students to remove armbands, worn to protest the Vietnam war. In another First Amendment case, the Court in June will overturn the conviction of a man who burned a personally owned American flag on a New York street corner while "talking out loud" to bystanders, saying that "We don't need no damn flag"; the Court will say the man "did not urge anyone to do anything unlawful," but that his action merely amounted to "excited public advocacy of [an] idea." In still another case, the Court will rule in 1974 that a college student who taped a black peace symbol on an American flag in protest over the Cambodia invasion and Kent State killings was only exercising his constitutional rights.

Poll-erized

MARCH 10, 1968. A Gallup Poll finds that one-half of all Americans believe that U.S.

involvement in Vietnam is a mistake.

Hat in the Ring

MARCH 16, 1968. Sen. Robert F. Kennedy of New York announces his candidacy for president.

Give it Up

MARCH 31, 1968. Facing mounting political pressure and an increasingly frustrating war, President Johnson goes on national TV to announce new air and naval attacks on North Vietnam and to renew previous offers to begin peace talks. In a surprise move he announces that, in an attempt to "not permit the presidency to become involved in the partisan divisions that are developing...I shall not seek, and I will not accept, the nomination of my party for another term as your president." Analysts will later cite antiwar Sen. Eugene McCarthy's strong showing in the New Hampshire Democratic primary last month as another factor in Johnson's decision.

LBJ: End of the line.

Flag waver and escorts (left): Bound for Old Glory.

Long Live the King

APRIL 4, 1968. Dr. Martin Luther King, Jr. is assassinated in Memphis. King, 39, had come to Memphis a week earlier to lead a march in support of striking sanitation workers, a march that began peacefully but ended in violence that left 62 injured, 200 arrested, and a 16-year-old boy dead. Another march was planned for April 8. The killing will send shock waves rippling across the nation, and violence will erupt throughout the country. Among the cities worst hit will be Washington, D.C., where looters will strike downtown, coming within six blocks of the White House. Other hard-hit cities will include New York, Nashville, Trenton, Tallahassee, Boston, Kansas City, Newark, Cleveland, Gary, Ind., Houston, Hartford, Jackson, Miss., and Chicago, where Mayor Daley will order police to "shoot to kill arsonists." Most black leaders will urge calm, although some, like Stokely Carmichael, will advise blacks to "go home and get your guns." In Baltimore, Gov. Spiro T. Agnew will meet with 80 black leaders and accuse them of not doing enough to help prevent riots in in that city. President Johnson will proclaim April 7 a national day of mourning for King, although it will be noted more for the violence that will continue through April 15. On April 10, with machine gun-carrying troops still ringing the U.S. Capitol, Congress will pass the Civil Rights Act of 1968, which Johnson will sign the following day. In two months King's alleged assassin, James Earl Ray, will be captured in England; he will plead guilty and be sentenced to 99 years in jail.

Takeover

APRIL 22, 1968. Mark Rudd, chairman of Students for a Democratic Society, and five others are placed on disciplinary probation for demonstrating inside a Columbia University building. The protesters are unhappy with the school's affiliation with the Institute for Defense Analysis, a consortium of universities engaged in Pentagon research. In addition, they express dissatisfaction with the university's policy of buying up nearby black neighborhoods and displacing residents for new university projects. Specifically, they object to a new $11 million gymnasium in Morningside Park. The following day, a rally led by black militants and the predominantly white SDS will move spontaneously to Hamilton Hall, a classroom building, then to Low Library, the administration building, to show solidarity with Rudd and the others. The protesters—who include such nonstudents as black militants H. Rap Brown and Stokely Carmichael and SDS co-founder Tom Hayden—will demonstrate inside the building, then stay there all night. Three other buildings will later be "liberated" by the students. Inside the buildings students will set up their own elected officials and perform an impromptu student marriage. The "wed-in," as it will be dubbed, will unite Andrea Burrow and Richard Egan in occupied Fayerweather Hall. A Columbia Protestant chaplain will declare the two to be "children of the new age," and they will share a cheesecake with other protesters. But not all will be festive. In the end 150 will be injured, more than 700 arrested, and classes will be suspended until May 5. The protest will become the basis for James Simon Kunen's 1969 book and 1970 movie, *The Strawberry Statement.*

Columbia Radical: No defense.

All Talk, No Action

MAY 3, 1968. After weeks of discussion, President Johnson announces that the U.S. and the North Vietnamese have broken a deadlock over meeting to begin peace talks, although he warns that there are "many, many hazards and difficulties ahead." One unexpected difficulty will be the shape of the conference table—whether it should be round, square, oblong, or whatever. As "a source in the American delegation" will tell the *New York Times*: "What may look like futile quibbling over protocol actually involves questions of political status, which will strongly influence the peace talks." The quibbling will delay the talks' opening for months.

Star Wars

MAY 10, 1968. The presidential campaign has turned into a star-studded event, reports *Life* magazine, as entertainers jump on candidates' bandwagons. Most opt for Democratic candidates. Singer Lesley Gore, for example, heads First-Time Voters for [Robert] Kennedy; other Kennedy stumpers are Sonny and Cher, Rod Steiger, Shirley MacLaine, Sammy Davis, Jr., Bobby Darin, and Peter Lawford, a Kennedy in-law. Hubert Humphrey has signed up Jimmy Durante, Frank Sinatra, Rudy

Valee, and Ginger Rogers. Eugene McCarthy, meanwhile, has lined up Tony Randall, Paul Newman, Dustin Hoffman, Robert Ryan, Elaine May, and Hal Holbrook. Waiting in the wings, undecided between Kennedy and McCarthy, are Barbra Streisand and Marlon Brando.

McCarthy backer: Campaigning in style.

Burn, Baby, Burn

MAY 17, 1968. Headed by brothers Philip and Daniel Berrigan, nine persons set fire to some 600 draft files at a Selective Service office in Catonsville, Md., near Baltimore. The group—six of whom, including the Berrigans, are present or former members of Roman Catholic religious orders—uses home-brewed napalm prepared from a recipe in a Special Forces handbook published by the federal government. Philip Berrigan, 44, already has been convicted of spilling duck blood on draft records in 1967. At the time of their arrest, Daniel Berrigan, 47, will explain that "We destroyed these records because they exploit our young men and represent misplaced power...." The nine will be charged with destruction of government property, mutilation of government records, impeding Selective Service processes, and conspiracy.

Bobby

JUNE 6, 1968. Moments after a speech celebrating a stunning victory in the California Democratic presidential primary, Sen. Robert F. Kennedy is shot twice in the head and critically wounded at Los Angeles' Ambassador Hotel. Although his condition initially will be listed as "stable," Kennedy will die two days later. His assassin, Sirhan B. Sirhan, 24, is apprehended immediately at the shooting. A Palestinian Arab, he is carrying a notebook stating that Kennedy, a supporter of Israel, must die be-

RFK: Rendezvous with destiny.

fore June 5, the first anniversary of the Arab-Israeli "Six-Day War"; the notebook also targets five others, including President Johnson. Fearing a reprise of the recent riots following Martin Luther King's death, Johnson will immediately put several thousand Army and Marine troops on alert across the country, although riots will not materialize. Sirhan will be placed under extremely tight security to prevent a repetition of the point-blank murder of John Kennedy assassin, Lee Harvey Oswald. Sirhan will plead "not guilty" to first-degree murder charges and, following a trial early next year, will be convicted and sentenced to die in California's gas chamber; his sentence will eventually be commuted to life imprisonment.

Where the Action Is

JULY 18, 1968. The National Student Association estimates that 221 demonstrations by more than 40,000 students at 101 campuses were held during the first six months of 1968.

Civil Disobedience

JUNE 23, 1968. The permit issued to leaders of the Poor People's Campaign to set up a "Resurrection City" on National Park Service land near the Lincoln Memorial expires, although the 500 or so camping there refuse to leave voluntarily. Several days earlier, demonstrators staged acts of civil disobedience as part of an otherwise peaceful week-long vigil outside the Department of Agriculture. When demonstrators began blocking traffic at major Washington intersections, police

"Yea though I walk through the valley of the shadow of death I fear no evil for I am the meanest motherfucker in the valley."

Inscription on Marine flak jacket, Vietnam

used tear gas and arrested 87. On June 24, a hot, humid summer day, riot-equipped police will close down Resurrection City, arresting 119 without resistance. But later that night looting and vandalism will break out in black neighborhoods in Washington, with police using tear gas to restore order. Just two days earlier, presidential candidate Richard Nixon called the D.C. crime rate "a national disgrace," promising to restore "freedom from fear" in Washington.

"A Nixon-Agnew administration will abolish the credibility gap and re-establish the truth, the whole truth, as its policy."

Spiro T. Agnew

Someday We'll Be Together

AUGUST 8, 1968. Former vice president Richard Nixon and Spiro Agnew, the formerly obscure governor of Maryland, are nominated as the Republican presidential ticket at the party's Miami national convention. Despite a strong showing by New York governor Nelson Rockefeller, Nixon wins on the first ballot, partially on the promise of a "secret plan" he has to end the Vietnam war. Nixon and Agnew will become the first president and vice president of the same administration both to leave office in disgrace.

Agnew, Nixon: A Rocky start.

Iron Hand

AUGUST 20, 1968. More than 200,000 Soviet troops invade Czechoslovakia following the threat of a revolution by an increasingly independent Prague government. The Soviet invasion comes after Czech Communist Party secretary Alexander Dubcek has declined invitations to attend party conferences in Warsaw and Moscow, a move for which he has received support from Yugoslavia's President Marshal Tito. But Soviet officials view the move as defiance of Moscow's iron-handed rule and move in. The invading troops include support from satellite nations, although Romania refuses to participate. In coming weeks Dubcek will be summoned to Moscow and will return to announce that several important Czech programs have ended and that a censorship system will be introduced.

Yippie

AUGUST 26, 1968. The Democratic National Convention opens in Chicago, greeted by some 10,000 demonstrators organized by "Yippies"—for "Youth International Party"—Abbie Hoffman and Jerry Rubin, among others. Hoffman, Rubin, and company have called for a half-million demonstrators to protest U.S. involvement in Vietnam and diverse domestic policies. At the center of activities is a "Festival of Life" scheduled for Grant Park and Lincoln Park, featuring speeches, concerts, smoke-ins, love-ins, and draft-card burnings. But the 10,000 or so demonstrators are outnumbered more than two to one by 12,000 Chicago police, 5,000 Illinois state police, and 6,500 National Guardsmen, all mobilized by Mayor Richard Daley to keep the radicals in line. Daley has refused the protesters permission to sleep in the parks and denied several permits for marches and demonstrations. One proposed march was to the convention hall, which has been so well protected by barbed wire and police that protesters have posted signs nearby that proclaim "Welcome to Prague" and "Czechago, Czechago," references to the Soviet's recent heavy-handed stifling of a Czechoslovakian revolt. The demonstrators, in turn, will taunt police and, in some of the more vicious incidents, hurl bricks, bottles, and nail-studded golf balls at police lines. The police will respond with tear gas and beatings of protesters and a frenetic bloodletting, in which police flail blindly into a crowd of 3,000, then roam the sidewalks to attack onlookers. In one instance, they will trap 150 people against the wall of a Hilton Hotel, causing a window to give way and spill protesters inside. Pursued by police, they will be beaten, as onlooking bunny-clad waitresses faint. Upstairs in the Hilton's 15th floor, campaign aides to Eugene McCarthy will set up a make-shift hospital. The final toll: about 200 arrested and hundreds injured, including many police. Hoffman, Rubin, and six others—to become known as the "Chicago Eight"—will be charged with conspiracy, among other crimes. Meanwhile, inside the convention hall, Vice President Hubert H. Humphrey will successfully fend off challenges by McCarthy and others to win the Democratic nomination with vice presidential running mate Edmund Muskie, the senator from Maine.

Born to Be Wild

OCTOBER 2, 1968. Jerry Rubin, bare-chested, body-painted, and dressed as a guerrilla, is one of 20 Yippies and their lawyers who walk out of a hearing by the House UnAmerican Activities Committee, investigating the disturbances at the Democratic National Convention. Another is Abbie Hoffman, who appears, as he will later describe it, "as an Indian with feathers, hunting knife, and a bullwhip." During the hearing, Rubin has shuttled in and out of the room, rattling his beads and bracelets. Guards relieved him of several rounds of ammunition but let him keep his toy M-16 rifle. The antics, relatively tame compared with previous congressional hearings of radicals, end when

Czechago, Czechago

As the Democrats gathered in Chicago in August 1968 to prepare for their 1968 national convention, several thousand demonstrators gathered there, too, organized by leaders of the Youth International Party, or "Yippies." They were met in Chicago with barbed wire and more than 20,000 city, state, and federal police, prompting Yippie leaders to liken the situation to Prague, Czechoslovakia, where the Soviet army was then suppressing a revolt against Soviet authority. The Chicago riots became the subject of a report submitted to the National Commission on the Causes and Prevention of Violence, which included this first-person account by "a federal legal official" of events on the evening of August 20:

> I then walked one block north where I met a group of 12-15 policemen. I showed them my identification and they permitted me to walk with them. The police walked one block west. Numerous people were watching us from their windows and balconies. The police yelled profanities at them, taunting them to come down where the police would beat them up. The police stopped a number of people on the street demanding identification. They verbally abused each pedestrian and pushed one or two without hurting them. We walked back to Clark Street and began to walk north where the police stoped a number of people who appeared to be protesters, and

cago: Police riot?

ordered them out of the area in a very abusive way. One protester who was walking in the opposite direction was kneed in the groin by a policeman who was walking towards him. The boy fell to the ground and swore at the policeman who picked him up and threw him to the ground. We continued to walk toward the command post. A derelict who appeared to be very intoxicated walked up to the policeman and mumbled something that was incoherent. The policeman pulled from his belt a tin container and sprayed its contents into the eyes of the derelict, who stumbled around and fell on his face.

committee chairman Richard Ichord orders Rubin and friends to sit down or leave the room. They leave.

Season of the WITCH

OCTOBER 31, 1968. A group of radical feminists use this Halloween to form a group called WITCH (Women's International Terrorist Conspiracy from Hell) that will perform Yippie-style street theater actions. Among its first events will be to "hex" the New York Stock Exchange, after which it will hex "the United Fruit Company's oppressive policy on the Third World and on secretaries in its offices at home"; WITCH's witches will chant "Bananas and rifles, sugar and death/War for profit, tarantulas' breath...." In Chicago a WITCH group will spook the University of Chicago's sociology department with a shower of hair cuttings and nail clippings after the firing of a radical feminist woman professor. WITCH members in several cities will disrupt bridal fairs, chanting "Always a bride, never a person." Within months WITCH covens will appear throughout the country and as far away as Tokyo. Many will redefine their acronyms as events dictate. One group will become Women Incensed at Telephone Company Harassment; a group of insurance company workers will form Women Indentured to Traveler's Corporate Hell; on Mother's Day, one coven will become Women Infuriated at Taking Care of Hoodlums and another, Women Interested in Toppling Consumption Holidays.

Try a Little Tenderness

NOVEMBER 1, 1968. The Defense Department reports that the U.S. has now dropped more bombs on Vietnam than were dropped during all of World War II.

Skin of His Teeth

NOVEMBER 5, 1968. Richard Nixon barely beats Hubert Humphrey for President, winning 43.4 percent of the vote to Humphrey's 43 percent; Alabama governor George Wallace has received the balance, carrying five Southern states and 45 electoral votes. All told, Nixon is elected by only 27 percent of the eligible voters. More than 40 percent of eligible voters have stayed away from the polls, the highest absenteeism rate in 12 years.

Great Balls of Fire

NOVEMBER 14, 1968. Dozens of demonstrations are held around the country as today is declared "National Turn In Your Draft Card Day." Several hundred cards are publicly burned.

Rip-Off

DECEMBER 2, 1968. Under police protection, classes resume at San Francisco State College, with former semantics

Hayakawa: Pulling the plug.

professor S.I. Hayakawa named as president. The school has been closed since November 19 because of a student strike over an open admissions policy and creation of a Third World Studies department. But Hayakawa's appointment won't restore order. Hayakawa will soon attempt to speak to students from a truck-mounted public-address system, but will be shouted down by angry students. In a fit of pique, he will dramatically rip out the speaker wires and unsuccessfully try to distribute copies of his statement on campus order.

Gusher

JANUARY 28, 1969. The first major U.S. oil spill occurs when Union Oil Company's Well A-21 blows out, within three days spewing oil over a 200-mile stretch of the Santa Barbara Channel off the California coast. Oil will cover miles of beaches and kill countless birds and fish, as emergency wildlife centers are set up along the coast to rescue threatened animals. The leak will take 11 days to be plugged, although it will continue to ooze oil for years. The next year will see a surge of oil spills, including five—off the coasts of Nova Scotia, Florida, California, and Australia—during a three-week period beginning Valentine's Day, 1970.

Class Action

FEBRUARY 12, 1969. Wisconsin's governor Warren P. Knowles orders 900 National Guardsmen and 400 riot-equipped police onto the University of Wisconsin's Madison campus after 3,000 students disrupt classes for the fourth day in support of student demands that the university increase black enrollment and set up an Afro-American Studies department.

Mind Over Matters

MARCH 21, 1969. A recently formed group of feminists calling itself Red Stockings holds a "speak-out" on abortion in New York City. Before an audience of 300, women will recount individual abortion experiences. The event will be the first public use of "consciousness-raising." Consciousness-raising groups will be-

Feminists: Up with consciousness.

come a key tool of the women's movement, and will be used by groups of men as well.

For Whom the Bell Tolls

APRIL 3, 1969. The U.S. death toll in Vietnam reaches 33,641, surpassing that of the Korean War, as U.S. troop strength peaks at about 550,000.

No More Pencils, No More Books

APRIL 9, 1969. Spring fever hits U.S. colleges and radicals spout new demands and lead demonstrations. The 154-year-old main Harvard University administration building is seized by 300 students, who manhandle and eject nine deans and lock the doors with bicycle chains. The takeover follows a rally by Students for a Democratic Society at which six "nonnegotiable" demands were issued, including abolishment of ROTC on campus and rollback of rent hikes on university-owned apartments. Until now, Harvard has largely avoided the serious political disruptions experienced at most other U.S. campuses. The next few days will see demonstrations at the predominantly black Southern University in New Orleans, Boston University, the University of Chicago, and Kent State University.

Student radicals: Movers and strikers.

A Lot of Trouble

MAY 15, 1969. One man is killed as Berkeley, Calif., police use shotguns in a battle for "People's Park." The battle began two days ago when the University of California, which owns the property, attempted to follow through on plans to turn the lot into a soccer field. Because the property has been abandoned for years, local residents have claimed it and transformed the glass-and-trash-strewn mess into a park. They have planted sod and flowers and installed swings and slides. A group once began to paint a sign to commemorate "Power to the People Park," but decided to shorten the name to "People's Park." The university, meanwhile, bolstered by Gov. Ronald Reagan's suspicion that the park was a ploy to whip up sinister antigovernment sentiment, ordered the university to reclaim the land, which it did yesterday, by constructing an eight-foot-high steel-mesh fence around the property, with signs declaring the area off limits. At a noon rally on campus, student body president-elect Dan Siegel suggested "We could go down there and take the park," a comment he will later deny as an outright incitement to riot. But 3,000 demonstrators do march to the park, confronting waiting police. Bottles and rocks are soon being thrown, countered by tear gas and, ultimately, bullets. More than 100 people are hurt, two seriously; one wounded man will die four days later. Protests and riots will continue, with nearly 500 arrested in just one day. Reagan has called in the National Guard, which will occupy the campus for 10 days. Fifteen years later, People's Park will remain, still used by local residents and still considered for development by university officials.

War Games

JUNE 8, 1969. After meeting with Nguyen Van Thieu, South Vietnam's president since

People's Park: (Left) Digging in for the long haul. **(Above)** Don't fence us in.

1967, at Midway Island in the Pacific, President Nixon announces a new policy of "Vietnamization," including the first withdrawal of U.S. troops. The new policy is aimed at helping the Vietnamese defend themselves, but will fall far short of its objectives.

Radical Chic

JUNE 17, 1969. The Michigan Regional Students for a Democratic Society issue a guide on what to wear during the demonstrations and possible riots expected this summer. Among their recommendations: (1) clothes should be loose-fitting for easy movement. Motorcycle jackets are particularly good protection against billy clubs, but not good in hot weather. Pockets should be zippered. "It's not unusual for the pigs to plant dope on people," SDS warns. (2) Helmets are vital, with motorcycle helmets recommended over football helmets or hard hats. (3) Boots reduce the danger of twisted ankles while running. (4) A wet washcloth carried in a plastic bag will protect against tear gas. (5) "If you wear glasses, have a strap for them, and carry an extra pair." (6) "Women should wear bras, men jock straps or cups." (7) Address books are verboten, says SDS, because "the pigs will record every name in them." But, they advise, "write on your arm some number where a lawyer or a friend can always be reached in case you're busted."

The Great Divide

JUNE 20, 1969. Deep ideological splits break open at a national convention of the Students for a Democratic Society (SDS), as the Progressive Labor Party (PLP) faction makes a strong bid to take over SDS, but is denounced by the Black Panther Party faction as "counter-revolutionary traitors." PLP members reject the Panthers' position that blacks are "the vanguard of the revolution," believing blacks instead to be part of a greater working-class struggle. In two days PLP members will be expelled in a statement read by Bernadine Dohrn, SDS' inter-organizational secretary, who herself will soon become part of another SDS split-off, the ultraradical Weathermen, later the Weather Underground. Meanwhile, anti-PLP members will stage a walkout as PLP delegates chant, "Stay and struggle."

Easy to Be Hard

JUNE 24, 1969. The city of Atlanta begins a war against hippies and homosexuals, an attempt to remove so-called undesirables from the area. Increasingly, young people along Peachtree Street, just north of downtown, are being arrested on such charges as jaywalking, loitering, and obscenity. In Piedmont Park, a gathering place for gays, police have photographed park occupants for intelligence files. One agent photographed customers leaving a theater showing Andy Warhol's *Lonesome Cowboys*. In September a peaceful rock-mu-

Chappaquiddick: Popularity plunge.

sic concert will disintegrate into a small riot after a detective reportedly draws his pistol on jeering hippies.

Water Under the Bridge

JULY 19, 1969. Sen. Edward Kennedy, who became the Senate's assistant majority leader only six months ago, is embroiled in controversy as the Oldsmobile in which he and 28-year-old Mary Jo Kopechne are riding drives off a bridge and into a pond on Chappaquiddick Island near Martha's Vineyard in Massachusetts. Kopechne, described by *Newsweek* as "one of the hard-working, worshipful single girls who seem to gravitate naturally to the Kennedys," had been a secretary in Robert Kennedy's office during his 1968 campaign. Ted Kennedy will claim to have tried to save Kopechne, who drowned in the incident, but questions will linger for years, including what the two were doing in the car and why Kennedy failed to report the accident for nearly 10 hours. As he will tell reporters, "I remember walking around for a period of time and then going back to my hotel room. When I fully realized what had happened this morning, I immediately contacted the police." Critics will question Kennedy's judgment in the incident—and, by extension, his fitness for public office—which will become a key factor in his decisions not to pursue the 1972, 1976, and 1980 presidential races. Kennedy will receive a two-month suspended sentence for the accident.

Red Baiting

SEPTEMBER 19, 1969. Angela Davis, a self-proclaimed member of the Communist Party, is dismissed from her post as acting assistant professor of philosophy at the University of California at Los Angeles. Davis, 25, was hired this past spring to teach a class in dialectical materialism and existentialism. Her dismissal comes in spite of a new UC Regents' policy that "No political test shall ever be considered in the appointment and promotion of any faculty member or employee."

Trying Times

SEPTEMBER 24, 1969. The trial of the "Chicago Eight" opens. The trial pits the Justice Department against an all-star cast of radicals: David Dellinger, a self-described "revolutionary pacifist" who mourns the passing of nonviolent resistance; Tom Hayden, a writer and one of the founders of SDS; Abbie Hoffman and Jerry Rubin, leaders of the Yippie movement; John Froines, an assistant professor of chemistry at the University of Oregon; Lee Weiner, a grad student at Northwestern University; Rennie Davis, radical organizer and son of a White House economist during the Truman administration; and Black Panther Bobby Seale, who had attended the Chicago demonstrations as a fill-in speaker for Eldridge Cleaver, whose parole board had refused to let him leave California. The eight are the first to be tried under the antiriot provision of the 1968 civil rights law that makes criminal the "intent" to incite to riot; each count is punishable by five years in prison and a $10,000 fine. The indictments against the eight charge that they crossed state lines, wrote articles, spoke, and otherwise encouraged others to come and disrupt the Democratic National Convention in Chicago. During the trial—which will be laden with theatrics and star-studded witnesses—the eight defendants will dispute these charges and point to the findings of an investigation of the disruptions, which called the violence "a police riot."

Freaking Fag Revolution

OCTOBER 1, 1969. The Chicago Eight trial, entering its second week, already has created a national debate over the behavior of federal Judge Julius J. Hoffman, 74, who has consistently overruled defense motions and revealed openly biases against the defendants. Hoffman also has ordered the jury sequestered for the remainder of the trial, the result of letters sent to two jurors that read, "We are watching you. The Black Panthers." One assumption is that the Panthers are trying to intimidate jurors because one of their own, Bobby Seale, is on trial. But Seale attributes the notes to "the FBI and/or other lackey foolish pig agents" trying to discredit the defendants. Already Judge Hoffman has issued the first of what will be a string of contempt-of-court judgments against the defendants and their lawyers. Example: Abbie Hoffman's first contempt charge resulted from his blowing a kiss to the jury. Sentence: one day in jail. In all, 175 contempt citations will be issued by the judge before the trial ends, including 38 against defense attorneys William Kuntsler and Leonard Weinglass. The U.S. Court of

Hoffman: Street theater.

Appeals will reverse the contempt charges; upon retrial, only Kunstler, Dellinger, Rubin, and Hoffman will be found in contempt, although no jail sentences will be imposed. In February 1970 the jury will acquit the Chicago Seven—defendant Bobby Seale will have been separated from the others—of conspiracy to incite riots at the 1968 convention. A few days later the chief prosecutor in the case, speaking to a Rotary Club meeting, will call the defendants and their movement a "freaking fag revolution."

...And Throw Away the Key

OCTOBER 10, 1969. *Time* magazine reports that its survey of college freshmen reveals that the Class of '73 is "extremely pessimistic" about the chances of peace in Vietnam within the next year and that almost half the students plan to take an active role in student government. Says *Time*: "Judging from the attitude of these freshmen toward education, college administrators had better lock up the administration building extra-tight...."

'My age is 33. I am a child of the '60s.'

Hoffman: Psychologically, 1960.

December 23, 1969. Week 14 of the Chicago Conspiracy Trial. Defendant Abbie Hoffman is on the stand, being questioned by his own lawyer, Leonard Weinglass:

Q: Will you please identify yourself for the record?

A: My name is Abbie. I am an orphan of America . . . .

Q: Where do you reside?

A: I live in Woodstock Nation.

Q: Will you tell the court and jury where it is?

A: Yes. It is a nation of alienated young people. We carry it around with us as a state of mind in the same way the Sioux Indians carried the Sioux nation around with them. It is a nation dedicated to cooperation versus competition, to the idea that people should have better means of exchange than property or money, that there should be some other basis for human interaction . . . .

Q: Can you tell the court and jury your present age?

A: My age is 33. I am a child of the '60s.

Q: When were you born?

A: Psychologically, 1960.

Q: Can you tell the court and jury what is your present occupation?

A: I am a cultural revolutionary. Well, I am really a defendant—

Q: What do you mean?

A:—full time.

New Mobe

OCTOBER 15, 1969. A candlelight march led by Mrs. Martin Luther King, Jr. past the White House marks the first of two monthly Vietnam moratoriums organized by the New Mobilization Committee to End the War in Vietnam. On November 13 and 14, demonstrations will be held in dozens of other American cities, as well as in Paris, London, Rome, Berlin, and Manila. On the 15th, 100,000 demonstrators will rally in San Francisco and 300,000 will invade Washington for peaceful demonstrations. In Washington local police will surround the White House with buses parked bumper to bumper, while President Nixon watches a football game inside. Meanwhile, the Pentagon will soon announce that the U.S. has lost its 6,000th plane over Vietnam.

Stand By Me

NOVEMBER 3, 1969. Having inherited a war in which more than a half million Americans have fought and 31,000 have died, President Nixon makes a plea for national unity to give him more time to bomb the North Vietnamese to the negotiating table while building a self-sufficient South Vietnamese army. He appeals to "the great silent majority of my fellow Americans" to be "united against defeat." Says Nixon: "North Vietnam cannot defeat or humiliate the United States. Only Americans can do that."

Flashback

Testifiers at the Chicago 7 Trial

Judy Collins
Allen Ginsberg
Arlo Guthrie
Jesse Jackson
Timothy Leary
Country Joe McDonald
Phil Ochs

Massacre

NOVEMBER 16, 1969. The *New York Times* reports that a small U.S. infantry unit massacred more than 500 unarmed men, women, and children suspected of hiding Viet Cong in the South Vietnamese farming village of My Lai in March 1968. News of the incident has been suppressed for years, claim government officials, for fear that it would be used as propaganda by the Viet Cong.

Dear Diary:
Today Congress Wanted the Shirt Off My Back

On Tuesday, October 2, 1968, we appeared before the House Un-American Activities Committee. I went as an Indian with feathers, hunting knife, and a bullwhip. I also carred an electric yoyo and dazzled the Committee with tricks like "Around-the-Capitalist-World," "Split-the-Southern-Cracker," and "Burning-Down-the-Town."

The Committee dragged on with boring testimony trying to link us to Communists (many of whom were active before we were born), and even at one point to Lee Harvey Oswald. The acting chairman of the Committee made repeated warnings against "emotional outburst." By about three o'clock, I was so bored I couldn't take it any longer. I asked permission to make an emotional outburst. They said not in the room, so I retired to the hall and shouted "YOU'RE FULL OF SHIT" so loud it shook the Capitol Building.

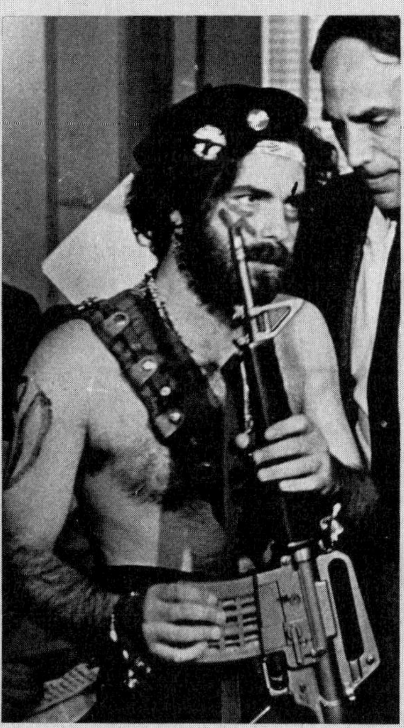

Jerry Rubin meets HUAC: Karl or Groucho?

Wednesday, we broke for Yom Kippur or the World Series . . . .

Thursday, I appeared in a commercially made shirt that has red and white stripes and stars on a blue background. Capitol police arrested me for mutilating the flag and proceeded to rip the shirt off my back. Anita screamed and was arrested for felonious assault on a policeman. Anita's charges were later dropped. I had to spend the night in jail . . . .The other night, I watched Phyllis Diller perform on national television in a miniskirt that looked more like an American Flag than the shirt I wore.

The hearings were adjourned to Thursday and we were ordered to return December 2. I plan to reveal everything, but I must warn the Committee that there will be a continuing language barrier. I requested permission to bring an interpreter to the October hearings, but permission was denied. I brought her anyway, but it was still difficult to understand them. They spoke of Marx and I thought they meant Groucho. My interpreter said, "No, they mean Karl Marx." They spoke of Lenin and I thought they meant John Lennon of the Beatles. My interpreter said, "No, they mean the guy without a first name." It was all getting very confusing, but that's to be expected when *chromosome damage* meets the *dinosaurs*. One thing I will state, however, before I even testify is that "I am not now nor have I ever been a member of the House Un-American Activities Committee."

—Abbie Hoffman, *Revolution for the Hell of It.*

Vietnamese: Women and children first.

After an investigation by the Army's Criminal Investigation Detachment, murder charges will be leveled against 1st Lt. William L. Calley, Jr. and Sgt. David Mitchell, who led the massacre.

Call Out the Cavalry

NOVEMBER 20, 1969. Three boatloads of American Indians land on Alcatraz, site of a former federal prison, claiming that the abandoned island belongs to them.

Pick a Number

DECEMBER 1, 1969. The first draft lottery since 1942 begins, affecting 850,000 men aged 19-26 not already in the military. In a closely watched ceremony, 366 capsules are pulled one at a time from a rotating drum, each containing a day of the year; the order of dates pulled from the drum will determine in what order young men will be drafted. Those born September 14 win the dubious honor of being chosen as number one; June 8 is picked as number 366. But lottery numbers won't affect current deferments for students and others.

Forcing an Issue

FEBRUARY 17, 1970. A group of about 20 women demanding hearings on an Equal Rights Amendment disrupt Senate hearings on the constitutional amendment to grant 18-year-olds the right to vote. The protests will lead to hearings held in May, the first ERA hearings since 1956. In June, Rep. Martha Griffiths will use parliamentary procedure to get ERA out of the House Judiciary Committee and onto the House

Draftees: Lottery winners?

floor, the first time since 1948 that the bill has gotten through a congressional committee. In August, for the first time since its original introduction in 1923, the House will pass the Equal Rights Amendment; the Senate will pass it in 1972, although the act will fall just short of the 38 states needed for ratification as a constitutional amendment.

Happy Earth Day to You

APRIL 22, 1970. The first Earth Day is held, part of a national campaign to promote awareness of environmental problems. For the past six months a wave of publicity has mobilized millions of Americans. One recent poll shows that more people are concerned about the nation's environment than about any other domestic issue. An estimated 20 million people will participate in a broad range of symbolic and substantive activities, including events at 2,000 colleges, 10,000 high schools, and nearly every community in the country. Among the day's activities will be construction at a Washington, D.C.-area high school of a 25-foot-long monument of junk picked up along a nearby highway; burying of a brand new car purchased from a dealer's showroom by students at San Jose State College in California, to symbolize the car's role in creating air pollution; guerrilla theater by blacks in St. Louis to dramatize their special environmental problems, including rats, poisonous lead paint, poor garbage collection, inadequate fire protection, and treeless streets. Meanwhile, the Daughters of the American Revolution, holding its "Continental Congress" in Washington, will pass a resolution calling Earth Day un-American and subversive.

Invasion

APRIL 30, 1970. Even though such activities already had been in progress secretly for more than a year, President Nixon appears on national TV with maps

and charts to announce that U.S. and South Vietnamese troops have invaded Cambodia to rid that country of Viet Cong. The announcement triggers one of the worst outbreaks of violence and protests in American history, including shootings of student protestors on two U.S. college campuses.

Sticks and Stones

MAY 1, 1970. President Nixon declares that all campus radicals who oppose his policies in Vietnam are "bums."

Ohio

MAY 4, 1970. National Guardsmen open fire on a student demonstration at Kent State University in Ohio, killing

Kent State: Slaughter in the grass.

four students and wounding 11. The shootings, in turn, will bring protests at hundreds of colleges and high schools across the country, closing more than 200 campuses; some classes will be cancelled for the remainder of the spring.

All American Boys

MAY 8, 1970. Several hundred New York City hard-hat workers, chanting "All the way, USA" and "Love it or leave it," forcibly break up an antiwar demonstration on Wall Street, injuring 70 demonstrators. The workers then storm City Hall, raising to full-staff the American flag, which has been lowered in honor of the slain Kent State students.

Consciousness Raising

JUNE 15, 1970. The Supreme Court issues a major ruling broadening the definition under which young men can consider themselves "conscientious objectors" to the draft. Previously, their objections have had to be based on their "religious training and belief"—usually the training and belief of a generally recognized major religion. The court's new ruling expands CO status to "all those whose consciences, spurred by deeply held moral, ethical, or religious beliefs, would give them no rest or peace if they allowed themseves to become a part of an instrument of war." But next March the Supreme Court will rule that COs must be opposed to *all* wars and cannot be exempted for objections to the Vietnam or any other war in particular.

Carte Blanche

JUNE 24, 1970. In retaliation for increasing revelations about President Nixon's secret war in Cambodia, the Senate repeals the Tonkin Gulf Resolution, which had granted the President virtually unlimited powers to wage war in Vietnam.

Only the Name is Different

JULY 9, 1970. President Nixon sends Congress a plan to reorganize the executive branch of the government, including creation of an Environmental Protection Agency. The agency, to be established in December, will consolidate 15 federal offices and agencies into a single unit to oversee a wide range of environment and health problems, including air and water pollution and the health hazards associated with solid waste and radiation.

Goofy

AUGUST 12, 1970. The "First International Yippie Pow Wow" is held at Disneyland, but only a few hundred Yippies show up. They are met by 250 police and guards, who watch as the revelers occupy Captain Hook's ship; seize Tom Sawyer Island, where they raise the Viet Cong flag; and knock over stacks of canned goods on Main Street. Disneyland will be closed early this day, and longhairs will be forever banned from the park.

Disney Yippies: Pelting cops with flowers.

Getting Off Easy

NOVEMBER 12, 1970. Lt. William Calley goes on trial at Fort Benning, Ga., for his part in My Lai massacre. In March he will be found guilty of premeditated murder of 22 unarmed civilians and sentenced to life at hard labor but will be paroled after the Supreme Court refuses to review his conviction. Calley will move to Columbus, Ga., where he will become a salesman at his father-in-law's jewelry store.

Calley: Hard labor.

Minor Change

MARCH 23, 1971. With only token opposition, a constitutional amendment lowering the voting age to 18 passes the House after receiving Senate approval two weeks ago. Within minutes after the House approval, Minnesota will become the first state to ratify the bill, with Connecticut, Delaware, Tennessee, and Washington also voting for ratification today. In just over three months, Ohio will become the 38th state to ratify the bill and it will become law on July 5, as President Nixon signs the 26th Amendment to the Constitution.

Mass Appeal

MAY 2, 1971. Police order 30,000 antiwar protesters from their Washington encampment after Nixon administration officials revoke the "May Day Tribe's" demonstration permit for "illegal use of narcotics." The demonstrators, participating in a three-week spring antiwar drive, will refuse to leave and 242 will be arrested. Their anger will result in a massive six-hour riot tomorrow, as demonstrators attempt to disrupt working Washington by barricading major bridges and arteries and by letting air out of car tires. More than 7,000 demonstrators will be arrested and police, including 10,000 federal troops, will use tear gas and nightsticks in an attempt to maintain control.

May Day: Laying down the law.

Temporary detention centers will be set up at RFK Stadium and the Washington Coliseum. Later a three-judge panel of the D.C. Court of Appeals will rule that police violated demonstrators' civil rights when they arrested people in groups and didn't advise them of their rights or charge individuals with specific wrongdoings. In 1975 the American Civil Liberties Union will win a $12 million damage suit against the District of Columbia on behalf of 1,200 arrested demonstrators who were falsely arrested on the Capitol steps. It is the largest civil liberties suit award in U.S. history.

Paper Tiger

JUNE 13, 1971. The *New York Times* publishes the first installment of what will come to be known as "The Pentagon Papers," more than 7,000 pages of sensitive documents taken from the files of the Departments of State and Defense and the Central Intelligence Agency by former Defense Department official Daniel Ellsberg, 39. The documents, which describe military and diplomatic moves in the Vietnam war, result from a secret study commissioned by Johnson Defense Secretary Robert S. McNamara in 1968, covering American involvement in Southeast Asia since World War II. Attorney General John Mitchell will order the *Times* to cease further publication of the papers on the ground that it will cause "irreparable injury to...the United States," but the *Times* will refuse to comply. Soon Ellsberg will surrender to federal authorities in Boston, and in December a grand jury will indict him and Anthony Russo, a coworker at the Rand Institute, with espionage and conspiracy.

Ellsberg, Eleanor Roosevelt: Trying the *Times*.

Pipe Dreams

JULY 17, 1971. John Ehrlichman, President Nixon's chief of staff, organizes the "plumbers," a group of white-collar mercenaries adept at wiretapping and other covert activities, to investigate Daniel Ellsberg, who leaked the Pentagon Papers to the press. Their activities will include breaking into the offices of Ellsberg's psychiatrist and stealing files, an activity for which they—and those who hired them—will be tried and convicted. In April 1973, White House chief of staff John Ehrlichman will tell FBI interviewers that under orders of President Nixon, he hired E. Howard Hunt and G. Gordon Liddy—both convicted in the Watergate break-in—to investigate Ellsberg, which led to the burglary of his psychiatrist's office. Soon after, a U.S. District Court judge will dismiss all charges against Ellsberg and Russo. In his decision, Judge William M. Byrne, Jr. will cite the burglary of files from Ellsberg's psychiatrist and other "improper government conduct shielded so long from public view" that "offended a sense of justice" and "precludes the fair...resolution of these issues by a jury." Ellsberg will tell the press that "This trial is not over until the bombing is over in Cambodia."

Getting to Know You

FEBRUARY 21, 1972. After six months of preparation and negotiation, and following a symbolic but significant era of "ping-pong diplomacy" involving matches between the U.S. and Chinese table-top tennis teams, President Nixon arrives in Peking—accompanied by a throng of international press—at the beginning of an eight-day visit to the

Nixon in China: Breaking down walls.

Wounded G.I.: U.S. needs a lift.

People's Republic of China. His arrival ends a generation of hostility between the two countries, although the U.S. still does not officially recognize China. Tomorrow Nixon and National Security Adviser Henry Kissinger will meet with party leader Mao Tse-tung, in a largely ceremonial visit; the "working" sessions will take place with Premier Chou En-lai. By the end of the visit, which Nixon will call "the week that changed the world," the two leaders will agree to a gradual increase in U.S.-Sino relations and cultural and scientific exchanges. Among the biggest unresolved issues will be U.S. recognition of Taiwan.

Turning Point

MARCH 31, 1972. Communist forces in Vietnam have launched their biggest offensive in four years, with North Vietnamese artillery and rockets attacking nine South Vietnamese bases and towns along the Demilitarized Zone, forcing South Vietnam troops to retreat from two posts. President Nixon responds with massive bombing and, for the first time, mining of key North Vietnam harbors, which will successfully push back the offensive. Military advisers will later argue that the effort was a military turning point for the U.S., and that further military offensives could have broken the North Vietnamese. In June Nixon will announce that "Hanoi is losing," a claim that will later be proven false.

Rallying Back

MAY 15, 1972. Gov. George C. Wallace of Alabama is shot by Arthur H. Bremer at a political rally in Laurel, Md. Bremer, a 27-year-old loner from Milwaukee who has been stalking Wallace for days, will leave Wallace permanently paralyzed from the waist down. Wallace will be forced to drop out of the 1972 presidential race, but he will rally back from his wheelchair, gaining election in 1982 to his fourth nonconsecutive term as Alabama governor.

Third-Rate Burglary

JUNE 17, 1972. Five men are arrested during an early-morning break-in at the Democratic National Committee headquarters in the Watergate office complex in Washington, D.C. The five, wearing surgical gloves to avoid leaving fingerprints, are caught inside the DNC's sixth-floor offices carrying electronic surveillance equipment. They will be charged with attempted burglary and attempted interception of telephone and other communications.

The Laundry Business

AUGUST 26, 1972. The General Accounting Office, the investigative arm of Congress, releases a report citing five "apparent" and four "possible" violations of the Federal Election Campaign Act of 1971 by President Nixon's re-election committee. The report alleges that the committee failed to keep adequate records on thousands of dollars of contributions, including some questionable transactions involving banks in Mexico City. The report will lead to the indictment of the re-election finance committee, which will be fined $8,000 in January after pleading no contest. A more intriguing case will be that of Bernard L. Barker, one of the men arrested during the Watergate break-in, who will be found to have deposited in a Miami bank a $25,000 check intended for Nixon's campaign. Barker will plead guilty in September but will receive only a 60-day suspended sentence on the condition that he surrender his notary license.

Little White Lies

AUGUST 29, 1972. At a White House press conference, President Nixon says that no one then employed in his administration was involved in the Watergate bugging. He announces that an investigation conducted by White House counsel John Dean has turned up no evidence of any connections between the break-in and the Nixon administration.

The Killing Field

SEPTEMBER 6, 1972. Eleven Israeli athletes at the Olympic Games in Munich are killed after eight members of an Arab terrorist group invade Olympic Village. During their 5 AM raid yesterday, the terrorists killed two Israelis, taking nine hostages. Today, as they were being prepared to fly to Cairo with their hostages, a shootout at the airport resulted in the death of the nine hostages as well as one German police officer; five terrorists were killed and three wounded and later captured. After a brief suspension of the festivities and a memorial ceremony at Olympic Stadium, the Games will continue.

Nothing to Sneeze At

SEPTEMBER 10, 1972. The first definitive study of the relationship between air pollution and lung cancer is issued by the National Academy of Sciences. It shows that lung cancer is twice as common among city dwellers as among those who live in rural areas.

Sabotage

OCTOBER 10, 1972. The *Washington Post* reports that President Nixon's re-election committee has been involved in a widespread network of espionage and sabotage against the Democrats, paid for from a secret cash fund. The article charges the Republicans with forging and distributing letters under Democratic candidates' signatures; leaking false information about the Democrats to the press; assembling intelligence files on members of Democratic candidates' families; and planting troublemakers at the Democratic National Convention. A few days later, the *Post* will detail how Maine's Sen. Edmund S. Muskie, once a Democratic presidential hopeful, has been the victim of a "systematic campaign of sabotage," including the theft of campaign files, the mailing of embarrassing material in forged Muskie envelopes, and late-night

The Dean's List, Nixon Style

Among the thousands of documents produced during the Watergate investigations was a memo written by White House counsel John Dean to domestic affairs adviser John Ehrlichman on August 16, 1971. It addressed, as Dean put it, "the matter of how we can . . . use the available federal machinery to screw our political enemies." That "machinery," as would come out in Dean's testimony to a Senate committee, involved Internal Revenue Service tax audits, denial of federal grants, the creation of scandals, and outright prosecution and litigation on a wide range of charges.

Dean: Screwing the enemy.

Here is Dean's list of the Nixon White House's top enemies, along with selected comments made by Dean about them:

Alexander E. Barkan, National Director of the AFL-CIO's Committee on Political Education. "Without a doubt, the most powerful political force programmed against us in 1968."

John Conyers, Congressman from Michigan. "Emerging as a leading black anti-Nixon spokesman. Has known weakness for white females."

Maxwell Dane, partner in the advertising firm Doyle, Dane, and Bernbach, a leading Democratic ad agency. "They destroyed Goldwater in '64. They should be hit hard . . . ."

Sidney Davidoff, New York Mayor John Lindsay's top personal aide. "A first class S.O.B . . . .Positive results would really shake the Lindsay camp and Lindsay's plan to capture the youth vote."

Ronald Dellums, Congressman from California. "Success might help in California next year."

S. Harrison Dogole, president of Globe Security Systems. "Fourth largest private detective agency in U.S. Heavy Humphrey contributor. Could program his agency against us."

Charles Dyson, close business associate of Democratic Party official Lawrence O'Brien. " . . . deeply involved in the Businessmen's Educational Fund which bankrolls a national radio network of 5-minute programs—anti-Nixon in character."

Bernard T. Feld, president, Council for a Livable World. "Heavy far left funding. They will program an 'all court press' against us in '72."

Ed Guthman, managing editor, *L.A. Times*. " . . . former Kennedy aide, was a highly sophisticated hatchetman against us in '68 . . . .It is time to give him the message."

Morton Halperin, leading executive at Common Cause. "A scandal would be most helpful here."

Samuel M. Lambert, president, National Education Association. "Has taken us on vis a vis federal aid to parochial schools—a '72 issue."

Allard Lowenstein, congressman from New York. "Guiding force behind the 18-year-old 'dump Nixon' vote drive."

Mary McGrory, syndicated columnist. "Daily hate Nixon articles."

Stewart R. Mott, philanthropist. "Nothing but big money for radic-lib candidates."

S. Sterling Munro, Jr., Sen. Henry Jackson's (D-Wash.) administrative assistant. "We should give him a try. Positive results would stick a pin in Jackson's white hat."

Paul Newman, actor. "Heavy McCarthy involvement '68. Used effectively in nationwide T.V. commercials. '72 involvement certain."

Arnold M. Picker, United Artists Corporation. "Top Muskie fundraiser. Success here could be both debilitating and very embarrassing to the Muskie machine."

Daniel Schorr, CBS News reporter. "A real media enemy."

Howard Stein, Dreyfus Corporation. "Heaviest contributor to McCarthy in '68. If McCarthy goes, will do the same in '72. If not, Lindsay or McGovern will receive the funds."

Leonard Woodcock, United Auto Workers president. "No comments necessary."

Nixon: Grand Old Politician.

phone calls to voters made by people posing as Muskie canvassers.

The Plot Thickens

OCTOBER 23, 1972. Donald Segretti, a former Treasury Department attorney, has become implicated in the investigations into suspected Nixon campaign committee wrongdoings, according to a report in *Time* magazine. *Time* reports that the FBI began an investigation of Segretti after discovering a record of telephone calls between him and Howard Hunt, one of the Watergate burglers. Other records reveal that Segretti has received more than $35,000 from the President's campaign committee.

Winning Ticket

NOVEMBER 7, 1972. President Nixon and Vice President Agnew handily beat Sen. George McGovern and former Peace Corps director Sargent Shriver in the general presidential election. With the Democrats carrying only Massachusetts and the District of Columbia, Nixon receives 521 electoral votes. Aside from McGovern's too-liberal leanings, part of his defeat may be attributed to the vice-presidential debacle at the Democratic convention, in which McGovern's first choice for running mate, Missouri Sen. Thomas Eagleton, was forced to step aside when it was revealed that he had once received psychiatric treatment for minor depression. Another factor may have been the election eve declaration by Henry Kissinger that "peace is at hand."

"If I'm elected we'll end this war in six months."

Richard Nixon

Tightening the Screws

DECEMBER 18, 1972. Following through on his promise to bomb North Vietnam to the peace table, President Nixon orders bombing of areas around Hanoi and Haiphong. The bombing raids, although vigorously protested at home, will continue for 11 days. This time Nixon's strategy will work. When the bombing stops, the North Vietnamese will agree to resume diplomatic talks, which will begin in early January.

Silent Spring

DECEMBER 31, 1972. A national ban on DDT takes place 11 years after publication of Rachel Carson's *Silent Spring*, a book that warned of the imminent threat such pesticides cause people and the environment. DDT, introduced commercially in 1946 as "the miracle insecticide," became popular during World War II, when it was used to help Allied troops control typhus-carrying fleas in Europe and malarial mosquitoes in the southern U.S. But during the 1960s DDT was found to kill fish and birds as well as insects. Moreover, it remains in the food chain of fish, birds, and humans, and has been connected with death and illness. In recent years about 12 million pounds of DDT have been used annually, mostly in cotton production. The DDT ban—which will eliminate about 98 percent of DDT use—will be credited with increasing substantially the population of such bird species as the bald eagle, the brown pelican, and the peregrine falcon, all of which have faced extinction as a result of eating DDT-contaminated fish.

Scapegoats

JANUARY 10, 1973. The Watergate break-in trial opens in U.S. District Court in Washington, with seven defendants—the five men arrested in the DNC offices (Bernard Barker, Eugenio Martinez, Virgilio Gonzalez, Frank Sturgis, and James McCord) and two others (E. Howard Hunt and G. Gordon Liddy). Within days the number will be reduced to two when Chief Judge John J. Sirica accepts guilty pleas from all but Liddy and McCord. Within three weeks, Liddy and McCord will be found guilty of conspiracy, burglary, and wiretapping. Liddy will receive the heaviest sentence of all seven: a minimum of six years and eight months to a maximum of 20 years in prison, plus a $40,000 fine.

At Last

JANUARY 27, 1973. Cease-fire agreements between the U.S. and North Vietnam are formally signed in Paris. Upon signing, Secretary of Defense Melvin Laird will announce that the draft has ended.

You Talk Too Much

MARCH 27, 1973. Martha Mitchell, wife of former Attorney General John N. Mitchell, calls a *New York Times* reporter and says, "I fear for my husband. I'm really scared....I can't tell you why. But they're not going to pin anything on him...." In another call four days later Mrs. Mitchell will tell a wire service reporter that "I think my husband has become the whipping boy for the whole administration, and they want to hide who is really involved." Administration spokesmen will attempt to discredit Mrs. Mitchell, but on April 19, the *Washington Post* will report that Jeb Stuart Magruder, former deputy director of President Nixon's campaign committee, has accused John Mitchell and White House counsel John Dean of approving and helping plan the Watergate break-in.

Mitchell: Whipping boy?

Slush

APRIL 23, 1973. The *Washington Star-News* reports existence of a half-million-dollar secret fund in California, some of which has been used to pay for Republican sabotage. It is the re-election committee's third secret campaign fund reported so far.

Gray Matter

APRIL 26, 1973. L. Patrick Gray, acting director of the FBI, destroyed documents belonging to convicted Watergate conspirator E. Howard Hunt a few weeks after the break-in, on instructions from White House aides John Ehrlichman and John Dean, according to a story reported in the *New York Daily News*. The revelation will cause Gray to resign, effective tomorrrow.

Shake-Up

APRIL 30, 1973. In an address to the nation, President Nixon announces the resignations of three top aides, H.R. Haldeman, John Ehrlichman, and John Dean, and a cabinet member, Attorney General Richard Kleindienst. Nixon also declares that "I will do everything in my power to ensure that the guilty are brought to justice...."

As the Krogh Flies

MAY 9, 1973. Egil (Bud) Krogh, Jr., the former Nixon White House aide who has admitted organizing efforts to steal files from Daniel Ellsberg's psychiatrist, resigns as Undersecretary of Transportation. Krogh's resignation is the 12th by a former Nixon aide or campaign official.

". . . It is going to require approximately a million dollars to take care of the jackasses who are in jail . . ."

Richard Nixon to John Dean

Haldeman: Capital punishment.

"We have a cancer within close to the presidency, that is growing."

John Dean to President Nixon

Real-Life Soap Opera

MAY 17, 1973. Eleven months to the day after the Watergate break-in, the Senate opens hearings, with North Carolina's Sen. Sam J. Ervin, Jr. presiding; it is the same room that housed the abrasive anti-Communist investigations staged in 1953 by Sen. Joseph McCarthy. The hearings—a kind of real-life soap opera that will attract some of the largest daytime TV audiences since John Kennedy's assassination—open with testimony from Robert C. Odle, Jr., the former administrative director of the Committee for the Re-election of the President. Odle's testimony will begin to fit together a complex network re-

Ervin & Co.: Daytime drama.

vealing direct control over campaign activities by former top Nixon White House aide H.R. Haldeman and Attorney General John Mitchell, and questionable practices organized by top campaign officials. Over the next few days the senators will hear testimony from convicted conspirator James McCord (who will tell how the White House tried to blame the break-in on the CIA) and former White House aide John Caulfield (who will reveal that White House counsel John Dean ordered him to offer McCord executive clemency after the break-in arrest). Within a week of his testimony, Caulfield will resign his post in the Treasury Department. On the hearing's fourth day, President Nixon will issue a 4,000-word statement conceding for the first time that there have been "wide-ranging efforts" in the White House to cover up aspects of the Watergate case, but will deny that they took place with his knowledge or approval.

New Blood

MAY 23, 1973. The Senate Judiciary Committee votes unanimously to approve Elliot Richardson, presently Secretary of Defense, to become the new Attorney General. The committee's vote also endorses Richardson's choice of Harvard law professor Archibald Cox as Watergate special prosecutor. Under guidelines drawn up by Richardson, Cox will have full authority to investigate and prosecute offenses arising out of the Watergate affair, from the President on down.

Running Out of Fools

JUNE 6, 1973. For the third time in five months, there is a major shake-up at the White House. Among the changes, former Defense Secretary Melvin Laird is named counsel to President Nixon for domestic affairs; Gen. Alexander Haig will retire from the Army August 1 to become a Nixon assistant; and Ronald Ziegler, Nixon's press secretary, assumes the duties of former communications director Herbert Klein, who resigned yesterday.

Beauty Contest

JUNE 11, 1973. Vice President Spiro Agnew, addressing the National Association of Attorneys General in St. Louis, criticizes the Senate Watergate hearings as a "beauty contest" with "Perry Masonish impact." Agnew concludes that "There is no question whatever that some men, despite their innocence, will be ruined by all this...."

Telling All

JUNE 16, 1973. Former White House counsel John Dean, in closed testimony before the Senate Watergate committee, alleges that he has documents showing that President Nixon requested tax audits of his friends to be stopped; that Nixon told him to maintain a list of reporters who gave the White House trouble; and that John Mitchell paid convicted conspirator E. Howard Hunt $72,000 to keep him from talking. In nine days Dean will begin a long-awaited public appearance, during which he will tell the committee that he believes Nixon has been aware of

Agnew: President's vice.

the cover-up since September. During his six-hour testimony—the first of four action-packed days of Dean's testimony before the senators—he will reveal that last September 15, the day of the seven indictments for the break-in, he received congratulations from the President that the case had reached no higher than Nixon's former campaign counsel G. Gordon Liddy. Dean, who has been granted partial immunity from prosecution for his testimony, also says that the order to burglarize Daniel Ellsberg's psychiatrist's office came directly from the Oval Office.

Ervin: Trial by committee.

Can't Help Myself

JUNE 20, 1973. In another of her now-infamous phone calls to reporters, Martha Mitchell tells UPI's Helen Thomas that "I don't like Vice President Agnew but, by God, I think he's better than Nixon."

Stonewall

JULY 6, 1973. President Nixon writes to Sen. Sam Ervin, chairman of the Senate Watergate committee, informing him that he will not testify before the committee. Writes Nixon: "No President could function if the private papers of his office, prepared by his personal staff, were open to public scrutiny." The letter begins what will be a year-long battle to force the President to release White House records to congressional investigators.

This Is a Recording

JULY 16, 1973. In what will later be called the bombshell of the entire Watergate affair, former White House aide Alexander P. Butterfield, now administrator of the Federal Aviation Administration, is a surprise witness at the Senate Watergate hearing. He reveals that all of President Nixon's meetings and phone conversations in his White House and Executive Office Building offices have been taped since spring 1971. Butterfield says that the recording equipment is capable of picking up extremely low tones, a matter of great interest to the senators, who have been told by John Dean that Nixon mentioned "in a barely audible tone" that he had discussed executive clemency for one of the Watergate defendants. Later in the day, the White House will confirm existence of the recording equipment and the recordings of Nixon's conversations, taped for posterity for a future Nixon library. Tomorrow Nixon will order the Secret Service to withhold from the senators all information about the tapes.

Service With a Smile

JULY 23, 1973. For the first time in 166 years, when Thomas Jefferson was asked to testify in the trial of Aaron Burr, an American president is subpoenaed, as President Nixon is served with three subpoenas from two sources—two from the Senate Watergate committee and one from Archibald Cox, the govern-

Dean: Making things perfectly clear.

ment's special prosecutor. In three days Nixon will respond to the Cox subpoena by citing the doctrine of the separation of powers among the three branches of government and the idea of executive privilege. "I must decline to obey the command of that subpoena," Nixon will write, noting "the example of a long line of my predecessors...." The Senate Watergate committee will receive a similar refusal and will immediately vote to go to U.S. District Court to seek the recordings.

High Crimes and Misdemeanors

JULY 31, 1973. Rep. Robert F. Drinan (D-Mass.) introduces a resolution calling for the impeachment of President Nixon for "high crimes and misdemeanors," including the secret bombing of Cambodia, Nixon's covert taping of conversations in his office, and the establishment of a "super-secret security force within the White House." The resolution, regarded as premature, will fail.

Expensive Pad

AUGUST 6, 1973. The General Services Administration releases figures showing that American taxpayers spent more than $10 million over four years to ensure the safety and comfort of President Nixon and his family at their homes in San Clemente, Calif., and Key Biscayne, Fla. Included are $730,000 for a helicopter pad and shark net at Key Biscayne.

Pressed Suits

AUGUST 11, 1973. *Congressional Quarterly* reports that the Watergate affair has "triggered eight civil suits, seven congressional inquiries, six grand jury investigations, three trials, and numerous federal agency investigations." And, says *CQ*, several more actions are being planned or threatened.

Cease Fire

AUGUST 15, 1973. U.S. bombing of Cambodia ends, marking the official halt to 12 years of American combat in Southeast Asia.

Tape Delay

AUGUST 29, 1973. Judge John Sirica orders President Nixon to turn over tapes of nine conversations for private judicial review. Sirica says he will decide himself whether the tapes are to be protected by executive privilege. Nixon will immediately reject the order, saying he will take the fight to the U.S. Court of Appeals. On October 12 the appeals court will uphold Sirica's order and Nixon will decide to comply rather than appeal to the Supreme Court.

Holy War

OCTOBER 6, 1973. The fourth and biggest Arab-Israeli war begins when Egyptian and Syrian forces attack Israel while Jews mark Yom Kippur, the holiest day on the Jewish calendar. Tensions had been mounting since January, when Israel downed 13 Syrian MIG jets. As usual, both sides will accuse the other of provoking today's attacks. But this fighting will involve the Soviet Union, which will announce that it will "assist in every way" the Arab effort to retake territory seized by Israel six years ago. The U.S. will counter, supplying military equipment to Israel. By the time a cease-fire is reached on October 24, nearly 20,000 lives will be lost on both sides.

Running On Empty

OCTOBER 17, 1973. In the midst of Arab-Israeli fighting, leaders of OPEC, the oil-producing countries, meeting in Kuwait, announce a 17-percent price increase and a 5-percent monthly reduction in oil exports to the U.S. and other pro-Israeli countries. The move comes as another in a series of oil-related jolts to Western nations. Recently, Libyan leader Col. Muammar el-Qaddafi took over Libyan oil operations, nationalizing millions of dollars in American interests; Iraq similarly nationalized Exxon and Mobil oil operations in that country. Just four days ago, *Oil and Gas Journal*, an industry newsletter, reported that U.S. oil reserves are insufficient to cover the effects of a cutoff by oil-producing countries. The final blow will come tomorrow, as Abu Dhabi becomes the first country to cease all oil exports to the U.S.; Libya, Saudi Arabia, Algeria, Kuwait, Qatar, Bahrain, and other countries will soon follow suit. The announcements will send tremors throughout the Western world. In the U.S., car owners will face long gas lines and many states will restrict how much gas drivers can buy and when they can buy it. President Nixon will urge what environmentalists have been advocating for years: to cut energy use by turning out lights, using less heating and air conditioning, and tuning up cars. Early next year a 55-mile-per-hour speed limit will be imposed nationwide.

Gas pump: Sign of the times.

One Down, One to Go

OCTOBER 10, 1973. Vice President Agnew, one of the few members of the Nixon administration not to be tainted by the Watergate scandal, resigns and pleads no contest in federal court to charges of income tax evasion on $29,500 he received in 1967 while governor of Maryland. Agnew was told he was under investigation in early August and announced at the time that "I am innocent of any wrongdoing." He will be fined $10,000 and put on three years' probation. Replacing him as vice president will be Gerald R. Ford, a little-known but respected congressman from Michigan.

Another Saturday Night

OCTOBER 20, 1973. In what will become known as the "Saturday Night Massacre," Attorney General Elliot Richardson resigns rather than obey President Nixon's order to fire special prosecutor Archibald Cox. Deputy Attorney General William D. Ruckelshaus, also refusing to fire Cox, resigns, too. Solicitor General Robert Bork, next in line at the Justice Department, becomes acting Attorney General and fires Cox. The firing of Cox, whom Nixon previously granted almost unlimited, independent authority to carry out the Watergate investigation, will cause a widespread public outcry for Nixon's resignation or impeachment. Within days House Judiciary Committee chairman Peter Rodino will announce that the committee will "proceed full steam ahead" with the impeachment investigation. On October 23 and 24, when Congress returns from a Veterans Day recess, 46 Watergate-related bills and resolutions will be introduced in Congress, 24 calling for impeachment or an investigation of impeachment procedures. On November 1, Nixon will appoint Leon Jaworski, a well-known Texas trial lawyer, to succeed Cox as Watergate prosecutor.

> *"The trouble with Republicans is that when they get in trouble they start acting like cannibals."*
>
> **Richard Nixon**

Understatement

NOVEMBER 11, 1973. For the first time since hostilities began 25 years ago, Egypt and Israel sign a U.S.-sponsored cease-fire accord. The austere signing ceremony in an open tent at Kilometer 101 on the Cairo-Suez Road—in Israeli-occupied territory—belies the significance of the event.

Silence Is Golden

NOVEMBER 21, 1973. White House special counsel Fred Buzhardt tells Judge John Sirica that an 18 1/2-minute gap has been discovered in one of the subpoenaed White House tapes. The tape involves a conversation between President Nixon and H.R. Haldeman just three days after the Watergate break-in. Later Rose Mary Woods, Nixon's longtime personal secretary, will testify that she accidentally caused the gap while transcribing the tape in October, although she will soon modify her statement, saying that her "accident" could have been responsible for no more than five minutes of the gap. In January, a panel of six technical experts appointed by Sirica will conclude that the gap resulted from five separate deliberate erasures and rerecordings. Sirica will recommend a grand jury investigation into "the possibility of unlawful destruction of evidence and related offenses."

Woods: No accident.

Tania

FEBRUARY 4, 1974. Patricia Hearst, 19-year-old daughter of newspaper publisher Randolph Hearst, is kidnapped at the Berkeley, Calif., apartment she shares with her boyfriend Steven Weed. In three days a tiny radical group calling itself the Symbionese Liberation Army (SLA) will claim responsibility. Through an agonizingly slow release of communiques using local and national media, the SLA will demand that Randolph Hearst set up a $2 million food-giveaway program for the needy as a gesture of good faith to gain his daughter's release. (During the giveaway of the canned goods, Gov. Ronald Reagan will remark that "It's just too bad we can't have an epidemic of botulism.") In early April Patty Hearst will shock the world with the announcement that she has decided to join her captors and has taken a new name, Tania, as part of her commitment to the SLA's revolutionary causes. (One persistent problem, however, is uncertainty over exactly what the group's causes are.) Soon she will participate in the robbery of a San Francisco bank; bank surveillance cameras will show her carrying a sawed-off shotgun. In May six SLA members, including its leader Donald "Cinque" DeFreeze, will die in a shoot-out and subsequent fire in their Los Angeles safe house. Patty Hearst will be feared among the dead but will reveal that she was at a motel 20

Tania: Rebel without a cause.

miles away at the time, watching the incident on TV. By June Hearst will issue her last communique for 17 months before traveling around the country. In September 1975 she will be captured without resistance in San Francisco. Following a trial for the bank robbery, Hearst will be sentenced to seven years in prison; she will have served seven months before her sentence is commuted by President Carter in 1979.

Nixon's the One

FEBRUARY 6, 1974. The House of Representatives votes 410-4 to investigate the conduct of President Nixon to determine whether grounds for impeachment exist. In May, the House Judiciary Committee will formally open impeachment proceedings. The historic hearings will conclude June 30, when the committee will adopt three articles of impeachment charging Nixon with obstruction of justice, failure to uphold laws, and refusal to produce materials subpoenaed by the committee.

Nixon: Final farewell.

Fool Disclosure

APRIL 29, 1974. President Nixon announces he will make public the edited portions of what are now known as the "White House Tapes." The following day, the White House will release a 1,308-page document containing the transcripts, which will become the basis for "instant books" appearing within days from two New York publishers.

That's All, Folks

AUGUST 8, 1974. Finally giving in to pressures from political enemies as well as a growing list of one-time supporters, President Nixon announces on national television that he will resign at noon tomorrow. On August 9, after being sworn in as the 38th President, Gerald Ford will declare, "Our long national nightmare is over."

I Beg Your Pardon

SEPTEMBER 8, 1974. A month after taking office, President Ford grants "full, free, and absolute pardon" to former President Nixon for crimes he "committed or may have committed or taken part in" while in office. Ford claims that the action is being taken to spare both Nixon and the American people further agony in the Watergate affair, but the par-

Ford: Pardon me, Mr. President.

don will cause an immediate uproar. Press Secretary Jerald terHorst, who had been Ford's first appointment, will resign in protest. Some will blame the bitter taste of the pardon for Ford's unsuccessful campaign for reelection against Jimmy Carter.

Hanky Panky

OCTOBER 7, 1974. Rep. Wilbur Mills, the powerful chairman of the House Ways and Means Committee, gets into hot water as the National Park police stop a speeding limousine without lights containing Mills and four others at 2 AM. Anabella Batistella—better known as local stripper Fanne Foxe, the "Argentine Firecracker"—runs from the limo and jumps into the Tidal Basin near the Jefferson Memorial. Mills will deny any relationship with Foxe, but on December 1, after being re-elected to another term, he will appear on stage with her at the Pilgrim Theater in Boston. Two days later Mills will admit himself to Bethesda Naval Hospital for "exhaustion" after House Democrats vote to reduce his powers and begin steps to remove him as Ways and Means chairman.

Mills: Foxe chaser.

Deadly Serious

NOVEMBER 13, 1974. The car and body of Karen Silkwood, an employee at a Kerr-McGee plutonium factory in Oklahoma City, are found in a small stream along Highway 74. Her car has swerved across the highway and careened off an embankment, coming to rest in the muddy stream. Police will rule her death an accident, saying she fell asleep at the wheel, a fact bolstered by levels of Quaalude found in her blood. But there will soon be evidence of foul play when an investigator finds two fresh dents in the rear of her car and other indications of a hit-and-run accident. At the time of the accident, Silkwood had been on her way to a Holiday Inn to meet with a *New York Times* reporter and an official with the Oil, Chemical, and Atomic Workers International. Before the crash she had on the seat next to her an inch-thick folder of documents purported to offer proof of fraud and safety violations at the plutonium plant, violations that, Silkwood has alleged, have exposed dozens of workers to dangerous levels of plutonium, one of the world's most poisonous substances. When police find her car and body, the folder is missing. Silkwood, already diagnosed as having radiation poisoning, had been a leading activist at the plant, fighting for stricter controls over plutonium exposure to workers. In 1979 a federal court will award her estate $10.5 million in damages, holding the nuclear industry "absolutely liable for escape of low-level radiation," but on appeal, all but $5,000 of the award will be dropped. Controversy over Silkwood's death will rage for years, and she will become a symbol for the antinuclear movement. A movie starring Meryl Streep as Silkwood will debut in 1983.

All the President's Men

JANUARY 1, 1975. John Mitchell, H.R. Haldeman, John Ehrlichman, and Robert Mardian are found guilty of obstruction of justice in the Watergate cover-up.

Erlichman: Guilty as charged.

Mitchell, Haldeman, and Ehrlichman will be sentenced next month to 30 months to eight years in jail; Mardian will receive 10 months to three years

Flashback
Vietnam Stats

Year*	Total Troops	Cumulative Killed	Cumulative Wounded
1963	16,300	120	492
1964	23,000	267	1,531
1965	184,300	1,636	7,645
1966	385,300	6,644	37,738
1967	485,600	16,021	99,762
1968	536,100	30,610	192,580
1969	475,200	40,024	262,796
1970	334,600	44,245	293,439
1971	156,800	45,626	302,374
1972	24,200	45,926	303,596
1973	> 250	46,163	303,656
1974	> 250	46,370	303,656

*Statistics are for December 31 of each year. Troop strength figures include only those reported by the Defense Department as assigned to Vietnam and may include troops fighting in other parts of the region. These figures do not include prisoners of war or those missing in action.

Wounded G.I.: More than a statistic.

Bringing It All Back Home

APRIL 29, 1975. As Communist forces drive to within a mile of Saigon city limits, President Ford orders an emergency evacuation of Americans remaining in South Vietnam—about 1,000 members of a force that once numbered half a million. Days earlier, Ford, addressing students at Tulane University, called Vietnam "a war that is finished, as far as America is concerned." Over the past few days U.S. Air Force transports have flown thousands of South Vietnamese out of Saigon. Today, in the desperate final hours, Americans and Vietnamese will be flown by a fleet of 81 U.S. helicopters to a waiting aircraft carrier. Thousands of South Vietnamese will fight to get out, some clinging to departing helicopters up to altitudes of 1,000 feet before falling off; several Vietnamese and Americans will die in the evacuation. The U.S. has been carrying on a "baby lift" for several weeks, flying thousands of Vietnam children out of Vietnam for relocation in the U.S. and other countries. But that, too, hasn't been without tragedy: on April 5 an Air Force C-5A transport carrying 243 Vietnamese orphans to the U.S. crashed and burned shortly after takeoff from Saigon. By tomorrow's unconditional surrender by South Vietnam President Duong Van Minh, some 55,000 Vietnamese will have been evacuated.

Leaving Saigon: Fear of fleeing.

Pirates

MAY 12, 1975. The unarmed American merchant ship *Mayaguez*, carrying 77 containers of unspecified "military goods," is seized by a Cambodian gunboat after it allegedly strays within Cambodia's 12-mile coastal limit, although the U.S. claims the boat was in international waters. In three days, under orders from President Ford—who will call the seizure "an act of piracy"—the *Mayaguez* will be rescued by the U.S. Navy and Marines, 16 of whom will be killed in the effort to rescue the *Mayaguez*' 39 seamen.

Two Misses

SEPTEMBER 5, 1975. President Ford escapes an assassination attempt in Sacramento, Calif., by Lynette "Squeaky" Fromme, a former member of the Charles Manson cult "family." Within 17 days there will be a second attempt on Ford—this one by Sarah Jane Moore, a former volunteer for several leftist groups as well as an FBI informer and former bookkeeper for the Hearst-owned *San Francisco Examiner*, who will fire over the President's head as he gets into his limo outside a San Francisco hotel.

BOOM! CREDITS

Cover

(Sonny and Cher, Monroe, Presley, Nicholson, Beatles and Sullivan) American Film Institute; (Checker) photo by Michael Denning; (Barbie) Mattel Inc.; (astronaut) NASA; (Bruce, Kennedy and Nixon, MacDonald's) copyright *Washington Post*, reprinted by permission of the D.C. Public Library; (Bozo) *Broadcasting* magazine; (Dean) Warner Bros.; (Dylan) Albert Grossman Management; (Ali) AP/Wide World Photos; (soldiers, bomb) Department of Defense; (King) National Archives; (Olympics) UPI/Bettmann Newsphotos.

Introduction

page 11: map © 1985 by Claritas, L.P., Alexandria, Va.; **page 14:** "Name That Boomer"/excerpted from *First Names First*, by Leslie Alan Dunkling (copyright © Leslie Dunkling, 1977; reprinted by permission of Gale Research Company), Gale Research, 1977, pp. 121, 126.

Music

page 20: American Film Institute; **page 21:** American Film Institute; **page 22:** Warner Bros.; **page 23:** American Broadcasting Company; **page 26:** photo by Joel Makower; **page 27:** copyright *Washington Post*, reprinted by permission of the D.C. Public Library; **page 28:** Atlantic Records; **page 29:** American Film Institute; **page 30:** National Archives; **page 31:** American Film Institute; **pages 32-3:** Motown Records; **page 34:** Tamla Records; **page 35:** photo by Michael Denning; **page 36:** (Paul Revere) CBS-TV; (Dylan) Albert Grossman Management; **page 37:** Chess Records; **page 38:** Motown Records; **page 40:** (Peter, Paul, and Mary) National Archives; **page 42:** (Seeger) Harold Leventhal; (Wonder) Tamla Records; **page 46:** (A Hard Day's Night) American Film Institute; (fans) copyright *Washington Post*, reprinted by permission of the D.C. Public Library; **page 47:** (hit parade) courtesy Susan J. Gordon; **page 49:** (Jagger) copyright *Washington Post*, reprinted by permission of the D.C. Public Library; (Sonny and Cher) American Film Institute; **page 51:** (Jefferson Airplane) Grunt Records; (Graham) UPI/Bettmann Newsphotos; **page 52:** (Guthrie) Warner Bros.; **page 53:** Elektra Records; **page 55:** United Artists Records; **page 56:** (Cream) Atco Records; (Beatles) American Film Institute; **page 57:** National Broadcasting Company; **page 58:** Warner Bros.; **page 59:** A&M Records; **pages 60-1:** (Who) Track Records; **page 63:** (Guthrie) Alfred A. Knopf Inc.; (Woodstock) Warner Bros.; **page 64:** Volt Records; **page 65:** (Zappa) Zappa Records; (Ono) Apple Records; **page 69:** Elektra Records; **page 70:** American Film Institute; **page 71:** Asylum Records; **page 73:** Warner Bros.; **pages 74-5:** American Film Institute; **page 77:** "Elvis Preley, Secret Agent" excerpted from article by Washington, D.C., writer Warren Rogers in *Washingtonian* magazine; used by permission of Warren Rogers; **page 78:** M-G-M Records; **page 80:** (Dylan) Albert Grossman Management; (King) Ode Records; **page 81:** (Bee Gees) RSO Records; (Stewart) photo by Betsy Sharp; **page 83:** Warner Bros.; **page 85:** (Flack) Atlantic Records; **page 86:** (Davis) Prestige Records; (John) Universal City Records; **page 89;** ABC/Dunhill Records; **page 91:** American Film Institute.

Media

page 96: Warner Bros.; **page 97:** *Broadcasting* magazine; **page 98:** *Broadcasting* magazine; **page 100:** (Bailey) *Broadcasting* magazine; (Searchers) American Film Institute; (Poitier) American Film Institute; **page 101:** *Broadcasting* magazine; **page 102:** *Broadcasting* magazine; **page 103:** (Bogart) American Film Institute; (Bozo) *Broadcasting* magazine; **page 104:** (Ginsberg) copyright *Washington Post*, reprinted by permission of the D.C. Public Library; (Wallace) *Broadcasting* magazine; **page 105:** (Clark) magazine; *Broadcasting* (Usher) American Film Institute; **page 106:** American Film Institute; **page 107:** (Donna Reed) *Broadcasting* magazine; (Byrnes) American Film Institute; (Gidget) American Film Institute; **page 108:** American Film Institute; **page 109:** (Bonanza) *Broadcasting* magazine; (Untouchables) American Film Institute; **page 110:** *Broadcasting* magazine; **page 111** (Dick and Jane) from *The New Fun With Dick and Jane*, by William S. Gray, et al. Copyright © 1956 by Scott, Foresman and Company. Reprinted by permission; **page 112:** (Lucy) *Broadcasting* magazine; (Birds) American Film Institute; (Twilight Zone) American Film Institute; **page 114:** *Broadcasting* magazine; **page 115:** *Broadcasting* magazine; **page 117:** (Kennedy) AP/Wide World Photos; (Cronkite) *Broadcasting* magazine; (Sales) *Broadcasting* magazine; **page 118:** American Film Institute; **page 119:** American Film Institute; **page 120:** copyright *Washington Post*, reprinted by permission of the D.C. Public Library; **page 121:** American Film Institute; **page: 122** (Kukla, Fran, Ollie) *Broadcasting* magazine; **page 123:** American Film Institute; **page 124:** (Newman) permission *MAD* magazine, © 1985, E.C. Publications, Inc.; (Coppola) American Film Institute; (Blob) American Film Institute; **page 125:** American Film Institute; **page 126:** (Slaughterhouse) American Film Institute; (Beatles) American Film Institute; **page 127:** American Film Institute; **page 128:** (Hullabaloo) *Broadcasting* magazine; (Superman) American Film Institute; **page 129:** *Broadcasting* magazine; **page 131:** American Film Institute; **page 132:** copyright *Washington Post*, reprinted by permission of the D.C. Public Library; **page 133:** *Broadcasting* magazine; **page 134:** *San Francisco Chronicle*; **page 135:** (Mission: Impossible) *Broadcasting* magazine; (Bonnie and Clyde) American Film Institute; **page 136:** American Film Institute; **page 137:** (Wenner) copyright *Washington Post*, reprinted by permission of the D.C. Public Library; (Graduate) American Film Institute; **page 138:** *Broadcasting* magazine; **page 139:** American Film Institute; **page 140:** (Heat of the Night) American Film Institute; (Mod Squad) *Broadcasting* magazine; **page 141:** American Film Institute; **page 142:** (Brand) Random House; (Heidi) American Film Institute; **page 143:** (Hoover) copyright *Washington Post*, reprinted by permission of the D.C. Public Library; (Roth) Random House; **pages 144-6:** (Easy Rider) American Film Institute; **page 147:** copyright *Washington Post*, reprinted by permission of the D.C. Public Library; **page 148:** American Film Institute; **page 149:** (Cossell) *Broadcasting* magazine; (Davis) copyright *Washington Post*, reprinted by permission of the D.C. Public Library; **pages 150-1:** *Broadcasting* magazine; **page 152:** (Sullivan) copyright *Washington Post*, reprinted by permission of the D.C. Public Library; **page 154:** copyright *Washington Post*, reprinted by permission of the D.C. Public Library; **page 155:** (Woodward, Bernstein) UPI/Bettmann Newsphotos; (Steinem) copyright *Washington Post*, reprinted by permission of the D.C. Public Library; **page 156:** (Chambers) American Film Institute; (I Am Curious) American Film Institute; (Ginzburg) courtsey Ralph Ginzburg; **page 158:** American Film Institute; **page 159:** (Grafitti) American Film Institute; **page 160:** copyright *Washington Post*, reprinted by permission of the D.C. Public Library; (Exorcist) American Film Institute; **page 161:** copyright *Washington Post*, reprinted by permission of the D.C. Public Library; **page 162:** American Film Institute; **page 163:** American Film Institute.

Culture

page 166: (Disneyland) Walt Disney Productions; **page 167:** National Library of Medicine; **page 168:** copyright *Washington Post*, reprinted by permission of the D.C. Public Library; **page 170:** Wham-O Inc.; **page 171:** American Film Institute; **page 173:** American Film Institute; **page 174:** (pills) copyright *Washington Post*, reprinted by permission of the D.C. Public Library; (Etch-A-Sketch) Ohio Art Company; **page 175:** (Ham) NASA; **page 176:** Mattel Inc.; **page 177** (Wilkenson) copyright *Washington Post*, reprinted by permission of the D.C. Public Library; (astronauts) NASA; **page 178:** Mattel Inc.; **page 179:** copyright *Washington Post*, reprinted by permission of the D.C. Public Library; **page 180:**

UPI/Bettmann Newsphotos; **page 181:** NASA; **page 182:** copyright *Washington Post*, reprinted by permission of the D.C. Public Library; **page 184:** (Ram Dass and Mr. Zip) copyright *Washington Post*, reprinted by permission of the D.C. Public Library; **page 185:** NASA; **page 187:** copyright *Washington Post*, reprinted by permission of the D.C. Public Library; **page 188:** AP/Wide World Photos; **page 189:** UPI/Bettmann Newsphotos; **pages 192-3:** copyright *Washington Post*, reprinted by permission of the D.C. Public Library; **page 194:** (Warhol) American Film Institute; (Thompson) copyright *Washington Post*, reprinted by permission of the D.C. Public Library; **page 195:** copyright *Washington Post*, reprinted by permission of the D.C. Public Library; **page 197:** copyright *Washington Post*, reprinted by permission of the D.C. Public Library; **page 198:** (cigarettes) copyright *Washington Post*, reprinted by permission of the D.C. Public Library; (Twister) Milton Bradley; **page 199:** Cadaco, Inc.; **page 200:** (Leary) copyright *Washington Post*, reprinted by permission of the D.C. Public Library; (View Master) courtesy View-Master International Group, Inc.; **page 202:** AP/Wide World Photos; **page 204:** (Twiggy) copyright *Washington Post*, reprinted by permission of the D.C. Public Library; (Haight-Ashbury) *San Francisco Chronicle*; courtesy Nicholas Van Hoffman; **pages 207-9:** copyright *Washington Post*, reprinted by permission of the D.C. Public Library; **page 210:** UPI/Bettmann Newsphotos; **page 212:** (Max) copyright *Washington Post*, reprinted by permission of the D.C. Public Library; **pages 212-3** (Armstrong) NASA; **page 214:** (communers) UPI/Bettmann Newsphotos; (Manson) copyright *Washington Post*, reprinted by permission of the D.C. Public Library; **page 216:** (Christo) UPI/Bettmann Newsphotos; **page 217:** courtesy National Council of Teachers of Mathematics; **pages 218-20:** copyright *Washington Post*, reprinted by permission of the D.C. Public Library; **page 221:** photo by Molly Roberts; **pages 222-3:** copyright *Washington Post*, reprinted by permission of the D.C. Public Library.

Politics

page 226: National Archives; **page 227:** (bomb) Department of Defense; **page 228:** (Little Rock) United States Marshals Service; (Castro) copyright *Washington Post*, reprinted by permission of the D.C. Public Library; **page 229:** National Archives; **page 231:** American Film Institute; **pages 232-3:** copyright *Washington Post*, reprinted by permission of the D.C. Public Library; **page 234:** Peace Corps; (King) National Archives; **page 235:** (Kennedy) copyright *Washington Post*, reprinted by permission of the D.C. Public Library; **page 236:** Peace Corps; **pages 236-7:** *New York Times*; **pages 238-9:** Civil Defense Administration; **pages 240-1:** copyright *Washington Post*, reprinted by permission of the D.C. Public Library; **pages 242-4:** National Archives; **page 245:** (LBJ) copyright *Washington Post*, reprinted by permission of the D.C. Public Library; (Vietnam) Department of Defense; **page 246:** copyright *Washington Post*, reprinted by permission of the D.C. Public Library; **page 247:** AP/Wide World Photos; **page 248:** (Johnsons) National Archives; **page 249:** Warner Bros.; **pages 250-1:** National Archives; **page 252:** Department of Defense; **page 253:** National Archives; **page 254:** (Chavez) copyright *Washington Post*, reprinted by permission of the D.C. Public Library; **pages 255-7:** copyright *Washington Post*, reprinted by permission of the D.C. Public Library; **pages 258-9:** copyright *Washington Post*, reprinted by permission of the D.C. Public Library; **page 260** (Wallace) copyright *Washington Post*, reprinted by permission of the D.C. Public Library; **pages 260-1:** photo by Joel Makower; **page 261** (LBJ) copyright *Washington Post*, reprinted by permission of the D.C. Public Library; **page 262:** UPI/Bettmann Newsphotos; **page 263:** (McCarthy dress) National Archives; (RFK) copyright *Washington Post*, reprinted by permission of the D.C. Public Library; **page 264:** Department of Defense; **page 265:** National Archives; **page 267:** UPI/Bettmann Newsphotos; **page 268:** (Hayakawa) copyright *Washington Post*, reprinted by permission of the D.C. Public Library; **page 269:** (feminists) copyright *Washington Post*, reprinted by permission of the D.C. Public Library; (radical) photo by Joel Makower; **pages 270-2:** UPI/Bettmann Newsphotos; **pages 273-5:** copyright *Washington Post*, reprinted by permission of the D.C. Public Library; **page 275:** "Dear Diary" excerpted from pages 209-13 of *Revolution for the Hell of It*, by Abbie Hoffman (New York: Dial Press, 1968), reprinted by permission of Abbie Hoffman; **pages 276-7:** Department of Defense; **page 278:** photo by John Filo, Valley News Dispatch; **page 279:** (Disney) UPI/Bettmann Newsphotos; (Calley and May Day) copyright *Washington Post*, reprinted by permission of the D.C. Public Library; **page 280:** (Ellsberg) copyright *Washington Post*, reprinted by permission of the D.C. Public Library; (Nixon) UPI/Bettmann Newsphotos; **page 281:** Department of Defense; **page 283:** copyright *Washington Post*, reprinted by permission of the D.C. Public Library; **page 284:** National Archives; **pages 285-90:** copyright *Washington Post*, reprinted by permission of the D.C. Public Library; **page 291:** (Woods) copyright *Washington Post*, reprinted by permission of the D.C. Public Library; (Hearst) United States Marshals Service; **pages 292-3:** copyright *Washington Post*, reprinted by permission of the D.C. Public Library; **page 294:** (Erlichman) copyright *Washington Post*, reprinted by permission of the D.C. Public Library; **pages 294-5:** National Archives; **page 295:** (evacuation) Department of Defense.

page 304: author photo by Joan Marcus

...ATLES • ... BEARD...
...NTROL • BLACK POWER • BONDS • JAMES BOND...
...RITISH INVASION • LENNY BRUCE • BA BREEDERS...
...AMBODIA • CAMELOT • CANDY • "CAPTAIN KANGAROO"...
...ARMICHAEL • CARNABY STREET • CASSIUS CLAY • CASTRO...
...ILT CHAMBERLAIN • CHAPPAQUIDDICK • CHICAGO SEVEN...
...OOKS • CHRISTO • THE COLD WAR • COLLEGE MAJORS • COLOR...
...ROCKETT • CULTS • COMPUTERS • CONCERTS FOR BANGLADESH...
...OE • JIM CROCE • DATING • ANGELA DAVIS • MILES DAVIS...
...EAN • DENNIS THE MENACE • DICK AND JANE...
...TRANGELOVE • ...OPS • ...
...ELEPHANT JOKES • ELVIS • ERA • SAM ERVIN...
...ALLOUT SHELTERS • FARM WORKERS • THE FEMININE MYSTIQUE...
...ILM CLASSICS • ROBERTA FLACK • "THE FLINTSTONES"...
...OCK • FOLK MUSIC • THE FREE SPEECH MOVEMENT...
...CANDALS • ALLEN GINSBERG • GIRL GROUPS...
...REASE • THE GREAT SOCIETY • GROUPIES...
...ALLUCINOGENS • TOM HAYDEN • PATTY HEARST...
...ITCHCOCK • ABBIE HOFFMAN • THE HOG FARM...
...OLLY • "THE HONEYMOONERS" • HOW WE INVEST...
...OOPS • THE JACKSON 5 • LBJ • ELTON JOHN • JOHN AND YOKO...
...JUNK FOOD • KENNEDY • KENT STATE • KHRUSHCHEV...
...UTHER KING • KRISHNAS • DON LARSEN • "LAUGH-IN"...
...EVIS • LIZ AND DICK • LUCY AND DESI...
...N.C.L.E." • MANSON • MARIJUANA...
...CDONALD'S • "THE MICKEY MOUSE CLUB"...
...INISKIRTS • JONI MITCHELL...
...ONROE • MOTOWN...
...EW YORK...

BOOM!
INDEX

BOOM! INDEX

BOOM! INDEX

BOOM! INDEX

BOOM! INDEX

BOOM! INDEX

Joel Makower, a writer and editor based in Washington, D.C., was born in 1952 in the San Francisco Bay Area. A rock organist and jazz pianist in high school and college, he is a graduate in journalism from the University of California at Berkeley. His articles on consumer affairs, computers, music, business, politics, and the arts have appeared in numerous magazines and newspapers. This is his fourth book.